Hamas, Jihad and Popular Legitimacy

This book investigates the many faces of Hamas and examines its ongoing evolution as a resistance organisation in the context of the Israel/Palestine conflict.

Specifically, the work interrogates Hamas' interpretation, reinterpretation and application of the twin concepts of muqawama (resistance) and jihad (striving in the name of God). The text frames the movement's capacity to accrue popular legitimacy through its evolving resistance discourses, centred on the notion of jihad and the practical applications thereof. Moving beyond the dominant security-orientated approaches to Hamas, the book investigates the malleable nature of both resistance and jihad including their social, symbolic, political and ideational applications. The diverse interpretations of these concepts allow Hamas to function as a comprehensive social movement. Where possible, this volume attempts to privilege first-order or experiential knowledge emanating from the movement itself, its political representatives and the Palestinian population in general. Many of these accounts were collected by the author during fieldwork in the Middle East. Not only does this work present new primary data, but it also investigates a variety of contemporary empirical events related to Palestine and the Middle East. This book offers an alternative way of viewing the movement's popular legitimacy grounded in theoretical, empirical and ethnographic terms.

This book will be of much interest to students of Hamas, political violence, critical terrorism studies, Middle Eastern politics, security studies and IR in general.

Tristan Dunning is Honorary Research Fellow at the University of Queensland, Australia, and has a PhD in Political Science.

Routledge Critical Terrorism Studies

Series Editor: Richard Jackson
University of Otago, New Zealand

This book series will publish rigorous and innovative studies on all aspects of terrorism, counter-terrorism and state terror. It seeks to advance a new generation of thinking on traditional subjects and investigate topics frequently overlooked in orthodox accounts of terrorism. Books in this series will typically adopt approaches informed by critical-normative theory, post-positivist methodologies and non-Western perspectives, as well as rigorous and reflective orthodox terrorism studies.

Terrorism and the Politics of Response
Edited by Angharad Closs Stephens and Nick Vaughan-Williams

Critical Terrorism Studies
Framing a new research agenda
Edited by Richard Jackson, Marie Breen Smyth and Jeroen Gunning

State Terrorism and Neoliberalism
The north in the south
Ruth Blakeley

Contemporary State Terrorism
Theory and practice
Edited by Richard Jackson, Eamon Murphy and Scott Poynting

State Violence and Genocide in Latin America
The Cold War years
Edited by Marcia Esparza, Henry R. Huttenbach and Daniel Feierstein

Discourses and Practices of Terrorism
Interrogating terror
Edited by Bob Brecher, Mark Devenney and Aaron Winter

An Intellectual History of Terror
War, violence and the state
Mikkel Thorup

Women Suicide Bombers
Narratives of violence
V.G. Julie Rajan

Terrorism, Talking and Transformation
A critical approach
Harmonie Toros

Counter-Terrorism and State Political Violence
The 'War on Terror' as terror
Edited by Scott Poynting and David Whyte

Selling the War on Terror
Foreign policy discourses after 9/11
Jack Holland

The Making of Terrorism in Pakistan
Historical and social roots of extremism
Eamon Murphy

Lessons and Legacies of the War on Terror
From moral panic to permanent war
Edited by Gershon Shafir, Everard Meade and William J. Aceves

Arguing Counterterrorism
New perspectives
Edited by Daniela Pisoiu

States of War since 9/11
Terrorism, sovereignty and the war on terror
Edited by Alex Houen

Counter-Radicalisation
Critical perspectives
Edited by Charlotte Heath-Kelly, Lee Jarvis and Christopher Baker-Beall

Critical Perspectives on Counter-Terrorism
Edited by Lee Jarvis and Michael Lister

Researching Terrorism, Peace and Conflict Studies
Interaction, synthesis, and opposition
Edited by Ioannis Tellidis and Harmonie Toros

Hamas, Jihad and Popular Legitimacy
Reinterpreting resistance in Palestine
Tristan Dunning

Hamas, Jihad and Popular Legitimacy

Reinterpreting resistance in Palestine

Tristan Dunning

LONDON AND NEW YORK

First published 2016
by Routledge
2 Park Square, Milton Park, Abingdon, Oxon OX14 4RN

and by Routledge
711 Third Avenue, New York, NY 10017

First issued in paperback 2017

Routledge is an imprint of the Taylor & Francis Group, an informa business

© 2016 Tristan Dunning

The right of Tristan Dunning to be identified as author of this work has
been asserted by him in accordance with sections 77 and 78 of the
Copyright, Designs and Patents Act 1988.

All rights reserved. No part of this book may be reprinted or reproduced or
utilised in any form or by any electronic, mechanical, or other means, now
known or hereafter invented, including photocopying and recording, or in
any information storage or retrieval system, without permission in writing
from the publishers.

Trademark notice: Product or corporate names may be trademarks or
registered trademarks, and are used only for identification and explanation
without intent to infringe.

British Library Cataloguing-in-Publication Data
A catalogue record for this book is available from the British Library

Library of Congress Cataloging-in-Publication Data
Names: Dunning, Tristan, author.
Title: Hamas, jihad and popular legitimacy : reinterpreting resistance in
Palestine / Tristan Dunning.
Description: New York, NY : Routledge, [2016] | Series: Routledge
critical terrorism studies | Includes bibliographical references and index.
Identifiers: LCCN 2015032544| ISBN 9781138937291 (hardback) |
ISBN 9781315676364 (ebook)
Subjects: LCSH: òHarakat al-Muqåawamah al-Islåamåiyah. | Jihad. | Gaza
Strip–Politics and government. | West Bank–Politics and government. |
Arab-Israeli conflict.
Classification: LCC JQ1830.A98 H37384 2016 | DDC 956.95/3044–dc23
LC record available at http://lccn.loc.gov/2015032544

ISBN 13: 978-1-138-30898-5 (pbk)
ISBN 13: 978-1-138-93729-1 (hbk)

Typeset in Times New Roman
by Wearset Ltd, Boldon, Tyne and Wear

Contents

	Acknowledgements	viii
	List of abbreviations	xi
	Introduction	1
1	Orientalism, Islam and militancy in a post-11 September world	21
2	The 'lesser' jihad: armed resistance	48
3	Sacrifice, steadfastness and symbolism	78
4	From bombs to ballots: political jihad	96
5	Charity, community development and civilian jihad	135
6	Ideational jihad, education and Islamic values	166
	Conclusion: revolution, counter-revolution and war	199
	Index	220

Acknowledgements

I would like to thank the innumerable people who have supported me throughout the course of this project. Unfortunately, I am unable to thank everyone by name: first, because there are simply too many people; second, given the nature of this research, many of these contributions must remain anonymous. Nevertheless, I would like to thank all the gracious people of the Middle East who made me feel welcome throughout my time in the region. The warmth, kindness and hospitality you have shown me have left an indelible imprint on my heart. In particular, I would like to thank everyone who chose to trust me, engage with me and participate in my research, especially those who potentially put themselves in harm's way to do so. Without you this project would not have been possible and I thank you profoundly for all your contributions.

I would also like to thank all the various individuals who provided academic support for this project over the years. In particular, I would like thank Dr Christine Mason whose intrepid ethnographic tales in lectures first inspired me as an undergraduate to pursue postgraduate studies. Later, Christine was to become my first PhD supervisor and provided unconditional support for the ambitious task I had set myself in terms of conducting fieldwork-based research about a semi-clandestine movement of dubious legality. Similarly, I would like to thank Dr Jeroen Gunning for advice and encouragement vis-à-vis conducting fieldwork in the Middle East. Thank you to both the School of Political Science and International Studies, and the Graduate School at the University of Queensland for providing funding to help facilitate my fieldwork.

I would also like to thank my former PhD supervisor Professor Tim Dunne at the University of Queensland for coming on board so late during my candidature, and providing the necessary experience, insight and patience to guide me successfully through the final stages. I would also like to thank Dr Harmonie Toros in this regard during her all-too-brief stay in Australia before returning to the United Kingdom to take up a position at the University of Kent.

Thank you to Professor Richard Jackson for encouraging me to submit a manuscript to Routledge. In a similar vein, I would like to thank the editors at Routledge: first, Andrew Humphrys for guiding me through the submissions process; second, Hannah Ferguson for gently reminding me of deadlines and helping to keep me on track.

In addition, at the University of Queensland, I would like to thank Dr Patrick Jory not only for reading drafts and providing invaluable feedback, but also for his eternal optimism about my prospects in the all-too-uncertain world of an early career researcher in this day and age. I have always enjoyed our extra-curricular after-work chinwags about the state of the world at the local purveyor of malted beverages.

I would also like to thank my fellow travellers in terms of the latter activity, including Dr Owen Powell, Dr Zachari McKenzie, Dr Jessica Paynter, Dr Nick Coxon, Dr Wade Kruger, Dr Tim Aistrope and Ms (soon to be Dr) Lydia McKenzie, among many others, for their empathetic company on such occasions. Needless to say, the trials and tribulations of early career researchers have been discussed at great length. We laughed, we cried; we commiserated and celebrated. Given our manifestly divergent areas of research – indeed, only one of the above mentioned is in a field cognate to my own – our ongoing friendships are a wonderful demonstration of academic inquisitiveness, diversity and solidarity. Thanks for being awesome friends. Ditto for James McDermott and Dr Ian Ball.

I would especially like to thank Dr Roxanne Marcotte at the Université du Québec à Montréal for her constant and unwavering support, always extending well beyond the call of duty. Ultimately, it was your persistent prodding that (eventually) prompted me to develop this manuscript. I owe you a debt of gratitude for the all the help you have provided to me over the years. You are an amazing academic and I can only aspire to what you have achieved.

In Palestine, I would like to thank all my friends who supported me and treated me like one of the family – you know who you are! Among these, I would like to thank Abeer Zaghari and Nejad Kurdi, in particular, for all their help with translations. I would also like to thank an-Najah National University in Nablus, al-Quds University in Abu Dis and Birzeit University for allowing me to conduct surveys with Palestinian university students. A special thanks to the staff who facilitated these endeavours. I would also like to thank Matt Awad for further help with translations back in Australia.

On a more personal note, I would like to thank Nahed for all her companionship, love and support during my time in Palestine and beyond. Your insider perspective and the sometimes delicate negotiations you undertook on my behalf will never be forgotten, nor will the memories of the time that I was fortunate enough to share with you.

Shari, well, thanks for just being you. I know that you don't think your contributions should be acknowledged, but your unfailing ability to make me smile and put everything in perspective – no matter what the circumstance – has helped me more than you will ever know. There's no other way of saying it, my dear: you rock!

Finally, I would like to thank my family, especially my parents Thomas and Kathleen Dunning, and my sister Brittany, for all of their constant support, advice and input over what has been, at times, an arduous journey. The intellectual environment that my parents provided growing up taught me the value of

x *Acknowledgements*

critical analysis and equipped me with the skills to succeed in the academic world.

My father, Dr Thomas Dunning, has always been my most reliable academic supporter, source of feedback and inspiration. The fact that this book is being published at all is testimony to the inspiration that you have always provided me in my life and the respect for intellectual inquiry and justice that you have helped foster within me. I am proud to have followed in your footsteps.

Thank you to everyone who has helped me complete this book and I apologise profusely to the many contributors who I have not mentioned by name. Nevertheless, I hope you all know that, ultimately, my successes are your successes. Any failures or errors contained within, however, are mine, and mine alone.

Tristan Dunning
Brisbane

Abbreviations

AIPAC	American-Israeli Public Affairs Committee
BBC	British Broadcasting Corporation
BDS	Boycott, Divestment and Sanctions Movement
B'tselem	Israeli Centre for Human Rights in the Occupied Territories
EU	European Union
Fatah	*harakat al-tahrir al-watani al-filastini* (the Palestinian National Liberation Movement)
GDP	Gross domestic product
GNI	Gross national income
Hamas	*harakat al-muqawama al-islamiyya* (the Islamic Resistance Movement)
ICG	International Crisis Group
IDF	Israeli Defence Force
ISIS	Islamic State in Iraq and al-Sham
IT	Information technology
ITIC	Intelligence and Terrorism Information Centre
IUG	Islamic University of Gaza
JMCC	Jerusalem Media and Communications Centre
MEMRI	Middle East Media Research Institute
MP	Member of Parliament
NATO	North Atlantic Treaty Organisation
NGO	Non-governmental organisation
OCHA	Office for the Coordination of Humanitarian Affairs
PA	Palestinian Authority
PASF	Palestinian Authority Security Forces
PCSPR	Palestinian Centre for Survey and Policy Research
PFLP	Popular Front for the Liberation of Palestine
PLC	Palestinian Legislative Council
PLO	Palestinian Liberation Organisation
PM	Prime Minister
PSF	Palestinian Security Forces
UK	United Kingdom
UN	United Nations

xii *Abbreviations*

UNDP	United Nations Development Programme
UNESCO	United Nations Economic, Scientific and Cultural Organisation
UNHCR	United Nations High Commissioner for Refugees
UNHRC	United Nations Human Rights Council
UNRWA	United Nations Relief Works Agency for Palestinian Refugees in the Near East
UNSO	United Nations Statistical Organisation
USA	United States of America
USAID	United States Agency for International Development

Introduction

> But those who exerted themselves [perform jihad] in Our Cause – these We shall guide to Our ways. God will assuredly stand with the righteous.
> *The Qur'an* (29:69)

> Palestinians feel that the resistance is the oxygen they breathe. Why? Because without resistance; they couldn't have achieved anything.
> Bashir, Hamas Youth Activities Officer (personal interview, 2010)

Hamas, the Islamic Resistance Movement in Palestine, is somewhat of a paradox. Best known around the world for a multitude of lethal terrorist attacks against Israel, Hamas, however, characterises itself as a moral movement struggling to promote social, political and institutional change. Not only does Hamas engage in armed resistance to the Israeli occupation of the Palestinian Territories, but it also strives to care for the disadvantaged and needy members of Palestinian society. While inspired by the teachings of Islam, widely rejected in the West as inherently antithetical to democracy, Hamas has traditionally espoused a discourse of democracy and electoral accountability. Indeed, Hamas has consistently won extra-parliamentary elections since the early 1990s culminating in its 2006 victory in the Palestinian legislative elections. Hamas eschews secularism and Western discourses pertaining to 'modernity', yet its leadership is replete with technocrats, educated in Europe and the United States, possessing expertise in 'secular' fields such as engineering, medicine and modern approaches to education; that is to say, disciplines that are primarily fixated on the temporal world rather than metaphysical, eschatological or theological concerns. Undoubtedly, Hamas is a socially conservative movement situated within a patriarchal society, yet women are among its most numerous and ardent supporters (Hilal 2005, p. 14). Puzzlingly enough, Hamas is both socially conservative and radical when situated within the prevailing gender orthodoxy of the Arab Middle East, insofar as the movement champions women's rights and promotes a greater role for women in the public sphere (see e.g. Holt 1997; Jad 2005; Amayreh 2010).

How does an organisation beset with such seeming contradictions attract and maintain popular support? Why does an organisation widely conceived of and indeed often legally proscribed as a 'terrorist' organisation command the support

2 Introduction

of such a wide segment of Palestinian society? At the very least, the existence of these apparent contradictions suggests a profoundly flawed understanding of the movement and its place within Palestinian society.

One of the principal reasons for Hamas' popularity are the twin concepts of *muqawama* (resistance) and jihad (to strive or exert oneself in the name of God), the watchwords which inform the multiple discourses of Hamas and its many overlapping and evolving identities. Hamas interprets and reinterprets *muqawama* and jihad in order to remain principally consistent yet practically pragmatic. For Hamas, in essence, the concepts of *muqawama* and jihad are polysemic; that is to say, these concepts are interpreted and reinterpreted according to the prevailing political, historical and societal milieu. Polysemic, in other words, means there are multiple readings, interpretations and understandings of the same text or concept. Hamas views the concepts of *muqawama* and jihad as holistic yet malleable principles, which are framed, reframed and employed to achieve its desired ends: notably the liberation of Palestine and the creation of a virtuous (Islamic) society.

Hamas is a militant socio-political Islamist movement deeply embedded in the Palestinian community (Mishal and Sela 2000, p. vii; Robinson 2004, p. 112). It is a grassroots, counter-hegemonic movement, the leadership of which constitutes a counter-elite to the historically dominant Fatah party.[1] The movement has been governing as a quasi-state entity in the Gaza Strip since 2007, although it is not recognised as sovereign – or 'legitimate' – by large segments of the international community, despite its 2006 victory in the internationally supervised Palestinian legislative elections. Hamas also has a sizeable presence in the Israeli-occupied West Bank, especially with regard to its associated charitable infrastructure, including medical, educational and social organisations, although, since 2007 in particular, these institutions have been subject to constant harassment and closure emanating from both the Palestinian Authority (PA) (*al-Sulta al-Wataniyya al-Filastiniyya*) in the West Bank and the Israeli military (Hroub 2006, p. 19). Nevertheless, it is estimated that 80 to 95 per cent of Hamas' income is dedicated to its social, political and economic programmes (Gunning 2007a, p. 129; Robinson 2004, pp. 127–128). As such, Hamas is recognised among Palestinians as an integral part of the community: politically, socially, culturally and militarily (Abu Amr in Gaess 2002, p. 188). The case of Hamas is especially important as it is the first militant Islamist movement which has acceded to power via legitimate democratic elections.[2]

The prevailing image of Hamas in the West, however, is that of an implacably violent and regressive Islamist 'terrorist' organisation (Le Roy 2006, p. 11). In effect, Hamas has been orientalised to fit the prevalent 'global war on terror' discourse and current political exigencies of Israel and the United States-led West. Hamas, in other words, has been discursively linked to the 'war on terror' (Gunning 2007b, p. 15). In consequence, Hamas is often mentioned in the same sentence as al-Qa'ida, with all the associated connotations of transnational eschatological jihad that accompany such a designation (Khalidi 2005, p. 123; Mearsheimer and Walt 2007, p. 205). Following the 11 September attacks, for

Introduction 3

instance, influential lobby groups in the United States, including the American-Israeli Public Affairs Committee (AIPAC), as well as a number of members of Congress, argued strenuously to have Hamas (and Hizbullah, incidentally) added to Executive Order 13224 specifying a set of measures to be taken against al-Qa'ida, its affiliates and its financial resources (Norton 2007, pp. 75–76). The ensuing amendment to the Executive Order signed in December 2001 designated Hamas as a terrorist organisation of 'global reach' and subjected it to the same measures as al-Qa'ida, despite the fact that Hamas has never perpetrated any attacks beyond the Palestine/Israel arena, nor deliberately attacked US or Western targets.[3]

In a similar vein, then Israeli Prime Minister Ariel Sharon quickly moved to link Israel to the US-led 'war on terror' by declaring that "Arafat is our Bin Laden" with an Israeli spokesman further adding that the former followed the latter's ideology (Whitaker 2001). That Palestinian President Yasser Arafat, long recognised as a legitimate interlocutor for peace, Nobel Peace Prize winner and the leader of the Palestinian cause, was defined by Sharon, and later by the US, as persona non grata, speaks volumes about the esteem in which a proscribed 'terrorist' organisation such as Hamas was held. Indeed, US President George W. Bush had a similar penchant for equating localised resistance groups such as Hamas and Hizbullah with al-Qa'ida's amorphous and ill-defined global franchise (Ettinger 2008). By linking Hamas to al-Qa'ida's transnational eschatological jihad, these distorted hegemonic discourses thus obscure the situation of the community from which Hamas originates. As a result, many Westerners and Israelis have difficulty comprehending how Palestinians could support, and indeed democratically elect, a movement whose ostensible *raison d'être* pertains to violence. The dissonance between Palestinian perceptions of Hamas in contrast to their Western and Israeli counterparts provides the impetus for this study.

Hamas and 'the West'

For the purposes of this project the term 'the West' will be used as shorthand to describe most of North America (the United States and Canada) and most of Europe (the European Union and the Scandinavian states) with the addition of Australia and New Zealand. While there are indeed many variations within these regions and I am wary of the problem of 'Occidentalism' (see Burama and Margalit 2004), there is a general transatlantic consensus, with the addition of various other states outside of this sphere but closely allied to the USA (e.g. Australia, Japan and the Republic of Korea), in terms of actual *practical* application of foreign policy approaches to Hamas and the de facto government in Gaza. The United States, Canada and the European Union list Hamas as a proscribed 'terrorist' organisation in its entirety, whereas Australia and New Zealand have only proscribed Hamas' armed wing, *Kata'ib al-Shahid Izz al-Din al-Qassam* (the Brigades of the Martyr Izz al-Din Qassam, or the Qassam Brigades).[4] In practical terms, all these entities relate to the elected Hamas government as an international pariah; and, over the past decade in particular, have

4 *Introduction*

shown a marked hostility towards Islamist movements in general. Where there are marked divergences in the practical application of foreign policy towards Hamas, this will be duly noted.

The term 'Occidentalism', moreover, suggests a fundamental misreading of the late Edward Said's ([1978] 2003) *Orientalism* thesis. Orientalism is not merely a set of generalisations or stereotyping which homogenised 'Oriental' societies, but rather an intricate system of knowledge production and control that constructed, projected and reified conceptions of reality, both at home and abroad, in order to manage foreign populations and perpetuate Euro-American imperial domination (Said 2003, pp. 3–12). This was accomplished through a gross imbalance of power which allowed the imperial powers to shape how subjected populations perceived themselves in order to control them. To suggest that the stereotypes which foreign populations devise vis-à-vis the United States, Europe, Australia and so forth have, or will have any time in the near future, the effects that European and American imperialism had on the former imperial and neo-imperial domains – that is to say, as an equivalent form of 'Occidentalism' – defies intelligibility. Resistance to a constructed Western 'other' is, however, utilised at local level to demonstrate authenticity, independence and indigenous agency in order to bolster popular legitimacy.

Hamas is often regarded as problematic because it defies Western norms and expectations insofar as it is a religiously inspired organisation which challenges Western conceptions of 'progress' and 'modernity', especially with regard to concepts of secularism, liberalism and democracy. Hamas represents a competing organic (endogenous) narrative which consciously contrasts itself to the prevailing hegemonic Western 'grand narrative' that has placed European Enlightenment values at the core of international institutions such as the United Nations. As a result, Hamas is demonised and isolated for deviating from these accepted (or perhaps expected?) norms. Since Hamas' election in 2006, this international consensus against the movement was extended when the International Quartet for the Middle East Peace Process, consisting of the US, the EU, the United Nations and Russia, announced a boycott of the elected 'Hamas' government until it (1) renounces violence, (2) recognises Israel and (3) abides by the previous agreements signed by the Palestinian Liberation Organisation (PLO) and the Palestinian Authority. Russia, however, has repeatedly diverged from this position by playing host to Hamas leaders and urging for its inclusion in the political process. In 2014 Hamas entered into a reconciliation government with its Fatah rivals, the cabinet of which was devoid of Hamas-aligned politicians, accepting these provisions, but Israel still refused to recognise this government. As such, it is unclear at the time of writing (May 2015) what effect these concessions will have within the broader context of the peace process.

Nevertheless, despite United States and Israeli-led attempts to destroy Hamas or force it into submission, complete with the attendant hardships forced upon the Palestinian population (see Rose 2008; Steele 2007; Morris 2006), Hamas continues to retain the support of a sizeable proportion of the Palestinian populace. The question is: Why? Why is an organisation so maligned by large

Introduction 5

segments of the international community able to retain this support, especially since this support has often led to the deterioration of living standards caused by Western and Israeli boycotts? What do Palestinians find appealing in an entity such as Hamas? How does Hamas adapt to pressures around it to attract and maintain support? And how does Hamas proactively create space for political advancement?

This book introduces antithetical evidence sourced from both the movement itself and the wider indigenous population, which seeks to counter the traditionally hegemonic Israeli and Western narratives pertaining to Hamas. In essence, this project is conceptualised as a subaltern socio-political ethnography. It privileges the largely unheard human voice of the Palestinian community, and in particular Hamas supporters and sympathisers, and thereby foregrounds Palestinian perceptions of their predicament; a predicament which is often much more emotional and subjective than might otherwise be suggested in traditional 'detached' academic transcripts (see Dauphinee 2010).

The voices and circumstances of the community from which Hamas originates are often overlooked in favour of rhetoric and acts of political violence. As such, there is a tendency to homogenise Hamas as a monolithic entity rather than recognise it as part of a heterogeneous conglomeration of Islamic social and political movements operating within the Palestinian Territories. This project moves beyond the dominant security-orientated approaches to the movement in order to investigate its wider formal and informal networks of supporters and sympathisers, as well as its charitable endeavours and community development projects. The intent is to humanise the movement, its supporters, sympathisers and representatives, as well as the Palestinian community in general, with the intent to recognise opportunities for dialogue.

Rather than reiterating facile dichotomies of 'us' and 'them', this work refocuses on the local context of Hamas and explores the possibility of coexistence between the movement, Israel and the West therein. To be precise, the project frames Hamas' activities within its polysemic conceptions of jihad and *muqawama*. Hamas, in effect, interprets and reinterprets the concepts of jihad and resistance according to exigency, practicality and Palestinian popular opinion. These polysemic conceptions of jihad and resistance, and the practical applications thereof, demonstrate Hamas' pragmatic flexibility in temporal, real world terms. By recognising the flexibility of the movement, and its ability to rationalise and diverge from its putative ideological bases, it is possible to discern opportunities for accommodation and ultimately peaceful coexistence with the movement. This is imperative because Hamas' message resonates with a large segment of Palestinian society and, thus, is an integral component to any long-term solution to the Palestine/Israel conflict. The resolution of this conflict is a key element to improving Muslim and non-Muslim relations around the world.

6 *Introduction*

Resistance, jihad and self-determination

Resistance has been one, if not the, central ethos of the Palestinian struggle for self-determination, independence (*istiqlal*) and freedom (*hurriya*). As such, the idea of resistance has long since been an integral component to Palestinian identity.

Armed insurrection with the aim of revolution (*thawra*) is the most commonly identified strategy associated with *muqawama* in the Palestinian Territories. While controversial within the international community, in part due to some of the tactics employed, in part because of the asymmetrical nature of the conflict which grants Israel sovereign legitimacy, armed resistance is overwhelmingly supported by the Palestinian community. Resistance to occupation is viewed by Palestinians as a fundamental right accorded to them, as with all other oppressed peoples, under international law, including UN General Assembly Resolutions 3236 and 3375, as well as the Geneva Conventions, among others (Zuhur 2010, p. 1; Gunning 2008, p. 96). The fundamental aims of Hamas resistance, as with Palestinian resistance in general, are self-determination, independence and sovereignty. The basis of Palestinian self-determination is firmly anchored in international law, not least of all UN General Assembly 181 partitioning British Mandate Palestine into two states which, indeed, provides the basis for Israel's own international legitimacy. Indicatively, not one state recognises the legitimacy of Israel's occupation of the West Bank and Gaza Strip, nor its unilateral annexation of East Jerusalem. In this regard, UN Security Council resolution 242, the basis of a two-state solution, stipulates the "inadmissibility of the acquisition of territory by war" while further demanding the "Withdrawal of Israel armed forces from territories occupied in the recent conflict" and "Termination of all claims or states of belligerency".[5] In 2002, moreover, Security Council Resolution 1397 explicitly "affirmed a vision of a region where two States, Israel and Palestine, lived side by side within secure and recognized borders".

The right to self-determination is one of the underlying tenets of the UN. Article 1.2 of the UN Charter (1945) calls for "friendly relations among nations based on respect for the principle of equal rights and self-determination of peoples". This principle is reaffirmed in the 1960 Declaration on the Granting of Independence to Colonial Countries and Peoples (UN General Assembly Resolution 1514, XV), the 1966 International Covenant on Civil and Political Rights (UN General Assembly Resolution 2200A, XXI), and the 1970 Declaration on Principles of International Law concerning Friendly Relations and Co-operation among States (UN General Assembly Resolution 2625, XXV). Hence there is considerable international consensus that a people have the right to "determine their political status and freely pursue their economic, social and cultural development" (UN General Assembly Resolution 1514, XV) and "this entails both external dimensions of self-determination and internal self-determination" (Burchill 2004, p. 33). By the 1970s international norms explicitly recognised "the legitimacy of the struggle of colonial peoples and peoples under alien

Introduction 7

domination to exercise their right to self-determination and independence by all the necessary means at their disposal" (UN General Assembly Resolution 2708, XXV), in effect legitimising all forms of resistance – including violence – in the struggle for self-determination. International norms mandate the right to self-determination thereby legitimising the struggles of national movements, if not always their methods in practice.

Within the Palestinian context moreover, resistance confers legitimacy. According to Khaled Hroub (2008, p. 60), "Resisting the occupation has become not only the instigator of many political and armed movements, but also the prime measure of popular legitimacy and the identification of their very purpose". Indeed, a 2002 Birzeit University poll (Development Studies Programme) found that 74 per cent of respondents selected the ability to 'confront Israel' as the most important factor when selecting a leader. The same poll revealed that 70 per cent of respondents also chose 'commitment to Islamic values' in this regard. As suggested by its official name, *Harakat al-Muqawama al-Islamiyya* (the Islamic Resistance Movement), both resistance and Islamic values lay at the heart of Hamas' *raison d'être*.

Resistance, however, extends beyond the one-dimensional militant view commonly associated with non-state socio-political movements possessing an armed wing. Resistance is a multi-faceted concept comprising a multitude of differing variations. According to the Deputy Head of the Hamas Political Bureau and US Specially Designated Global Terrorist, Dr Mousa Abu Marzouq (personal interview, 2010),

> The concept of resistance is more comprehensive than the issue of politics, war and peace, and politics and economics. The issue of resistance is a comprehensive story and it also has a culture, which should be devoted and it should include politics, economics, living, and all these issues.

Similarly, Bashir (personal interview, 2010), a 44-year-old Hamas member working in public relations and youth activities, says,

> For the Palestinians nowadays, you may find different levels of understanding the term of resistance. This is either because of political and factional affiliation, or because of the intellectual level. But, in general, some Palestinians look at the resistance as a military action by its elements, while some Palestinians look at the resistance as a preparation for resistance – a resistant act.

Likewise, Dr Aziz Dweik (personal interview, 2010), the American-educated Islamist Speaker of Parliament, contends,

> So if we practice violence, if we throw stones, if we do any kind of action – even my words to you – they are just an expression of the same idea that we got fed up with occupation.

8 Introduction

Resistance, in the eyes of Hamas, not only consists of practical armed resistance to occupation, oppression and injustice, but also incorporates other aspects, including a historical narrative, cultural preservation, psychological imperatives and, indeed, participation in formal politics.

Accordingly, this book examines the historical significance, practical nature and psychological/symbolic importance of resistance to Hamas and its influence on Palestinian society as a whole. Resistance has been framed in such a way that it defines the Palestinian national narrative. Hamas, moreover, has defined resistance as a moral and religious duty (*fard*) predicated on jihad. Indeed, there is a Qur'anic injunction to resist tyranny and oppression (Tamimi 2007, p. 173). *The Qur'an* (42:42–43) stipulates that "Account is demanded of those who oppress people and commit transgressions on earth, unjustly". In essence, the narrative of Hamas is the narrative of resistance, but Islamist resistance is also a battle of ideas and values.

This narrative of resistance also plays into the Palestinian credos of *summud* (steadfastness), *sabr* (patience) and *tadhiyya* (sacrifice), which are so vital to Palestinian identity. According to Kimmerling and Migdal (2003, p. 243), there are three heroic images in Palestinian society the *feda'i* (fighter, literally 'one who sacrifices himself'), the *shahid* (martyr or 'witness to God') and the stoic or survivor (one who exhibits *summud*). To this end, this project explores the significance of these figures and concepts among the Palestinian community and how they relate to Hamas. Specifically, as Hamas emerged as the vanguard of the Palestinian resistance, it also emerged as the personification of these three figures of resistance, especially throughout the course of the second intifada. In effect, Hamas has increasingly become identified as a symbol of Palestinian identity through the exhibition of these traits.

Hamas has successfully "tapped into existing cultural, religious and symbolic frames" to augment its support base (Gunning 2009, p. 171). Central discourses pertaining to self-sacrifice, martyrdom and steadfastness have been instrumental in bolstering Hamas' image. Snow and Benford (1992, pp. 137–138) argue that collective action frames allow a social movement "to articulate and align a vast array of events and experiences so that they hang together in a relatively unified and meaningful fashion". These collective action frames are then, in turn, used for mass mobilisation. Similarly, Maya Rosenfeld (2004, pp. 314–315) argues that resistance is a key factor which facilitates politicisation and enhances identification with the esteemed 'self-sacrificing' organisations.

Defiance, survival and a refusal to submit to Israeli – and by extension Western – subjugation lay at the core of Hamas' appeal, not only within the Palestinian community but also throughout the wider Arab and Muslim world (Crooke 2009, pp. 192–215). Hamas, in essence, eclipsed the resistance credentials of Fatah and the PLO "by transforming the nationalist dynamism of the first generation 'secular' nationalists from a political to a symbolic, cultural force" (Burgat 2003, p. 177).

Hamas infused the narrative of resistance with an Islamic discourse, thereby blending the figure of the *feda'i* with that of the *mujahid* (one who strives in the

Introduction 9

name of Allah, although often translated in the West as 'holy warrior'). According to Talal Asad (2007, p. 48), "Islamic militancy is characterised by a fusion of two elements: the centrality of martyrdom (inspired by the Iranian example) and the individuating process (initiated and promoted by Hamas) centered on the mosque". In light of Hamas' temporal goals of liberation, socio-political reform and the creation of a virtuous Islamic society, jihad, then, is "a form of political action that endows human struggle to remake a common world with existential weight" (Euben 2002, p. 20).

Halim Rane (2009, p. 122), moreover, contends that there are two main streams of jihad dating to the Meccan and Medinan periods of the Prophet Mohammed. The more prevalent of these schools is the popularised 'holy war' interpretation of armed jihad, whereas the Meccan period is characterised by the improvement and consolidation of the community. Despite popular (mis)conceptions however, the 'greater' jihad (*jihad al-akbar*) is the struggle against oneself to lead a virtuous life and contribute to the community, whereas the more popularised 'lesser' jihad refers to the protection of Islam by the sword if need be (Kadayifici-Orellana 2007, p. 87). Hence, by invoking jihad, Hamas imbues its political actions with existential weight and religious legitimacy. In short, Hamas has proven adept at appropriating social and religious traditions to justify and legitimise resistance – violent or otherwise.

Active political resistance, however, was not always the case as Hamas' predecessor, *al-Ikhwan al-Muslimun* (the Muslim Brotherhood), focused on *da'wa* (proselytising or the 'call' to Islam), providing education and social services. According to Article 2 of its charter (*mithaq*), Hamas is the armed wing of the *Ikhwan* in Palestine. Hamas was created as the armed offshoot of the *Ikhwan* to compete for popular support and ensure institutional survival against the backdrop of the first intifada. The idea was to separate the armed wing from the mother movement in order to mitigate Israeli retaliation and repression of its social activities. Hamas, however, would end up eclipsing and subsuming the *Ikhwan*.

As a grassroots "bottom-up" movement rooted in the Palestinian *Ikhwan*, these social endeavours have helped Hamas to build bridges with the Palestinian community, and thereby accumulate social, symbolic and cultural capital. Robert Putnam (1995, p. 67) contends that social capital consists of "features of social organisation such as networks, norms, and social trust that facilitate coordination and cooperation for mutual benefit". Pierre Bourdieu (1991, pp. 14–15), moreover, identifies cultural capital as a set of knowledge, skills, cultural acquisitions and/or technical/educational qualifications, which help to augment the symbolic capital – that is to say, the accumulated prestige and honour – of an individual or organisation. This, in turn, accords the individual or organisation power and a higher status within society. These social endeavours are considered to be an integral part of Hamas' wider programme of resistance, despite the fact that these actions are not necessarily considered to be political per se.

While Hamas was a relative latecomer to active politicised resistance, resistance and jihad are polysemic concepts which may be interpreted and

10 *Introduction*

reinterpreted in a multitude of fashions, namely, for the purposes of this work, the armed, symbolic, political, social and ideational aspects of these concepts. The aim of this work is to privilege Palestinian elucidations explaining these interpretations and reinterpretations dependent on exigency, opportunity and practicality, and to what extent the application of these concepts resonates with the Palestinian population. This, in turn, feeds into a broader question pertaining to the overall reasons why such a large segment of the Palestinian population supports Hamas.

Fieldwork

Fieldwork provides firsthand experience and unique insights into the surrounding cultural, political and social milieu. It also grants the gritty nature of reality the ability to strip away any preconceived, essentialist or romanticist notions of the topic which may be a consequence of primarily document-related research. Reality is much more complicated, subjective and emotional than many social science researchers are prepared to admit in scholarly accounts. The subaltern ethnographic approach attempts to highlight and self-reflexively recognise the human context of knowledge and the influence of lived experience. Accordingly, where possible I have attempted to allow Palestinians to speak for themselves and thereby heighten the prominence of first order knowledge – that is to say, based on experience – which has so often been relegated to an inferior, subordinate or even suspect role within traditional political science literature.

When adopting an ethnographic approach, it is necessary to contextualise the fieldwork and situate the researcher within the surrounding societal milieu. Specifically, it is important to note the highly personalised nature of work and research in the Middle East, which is characterised by a system of patronage dependent on *wasta* (contacts or 'pull'). As a result, it is imperative to highlight the importance of trust and rapport building in a traumatised and repressed society plagued by an acute sense of paranoia. In brief, the amount of assistance or information an individual was willing to provide tended to be dependent upon their initial perceptions of myself. Thus, throughout the course of this book I attempt to self-reflexively recognise how my own background, vocation and demeanour had the capacity to influence the type of data that were able to be obtained. Trust and rapport building are especially important when making contact with and interviewing associates of a semi-clandestine and often legally proscribed organisation such as Hamas. This trust imperative was accentuated by my status as an *ajnabi* (foreigner) and, thus, a potential threat in light of Western antagonism towards Hamas.

Over the course of my fieldwork in 2009 to 2010, I conducted around 50 semi-structured interviews with academics, journalists and politicians in the West Bank, Israel, Syria, Jordan and Lebanon.[6] The semi-structured nature of the interviews allowed greater flexibility to pursue a particular line of thought raised by informants, as well as opportunities to detail their own personal journey and political influences in more depth. The 'dialogic' approach (Euben

Introduction 11

1999, pp. 155–158) adopted over the course of this project seeks to delve deeper into the personal motivations and opinions of my Palestinian interlocutors.

I was also able to administer 131 semi-qualitative anonymous surveys with university students in Nablus, Birzeit and Abu Dis respectively.[7] The anonymous nature of these surveys was designed to circumvent the security concerns of students living in an authoritarian political environment where dissenters, and especially Islamists, have been subject to detention, interrogation and, in some cases, torture by either the Palestinian police or the Israeli army. Palestinian society is rife with Israeli collaborators, whether by financial reward, intimidation or blackmail, as well as Palestinian *mukhabarat* (secret police) and informers. As such, many students, or at least those who were not well acquainted with me on a personal level, were extremely wary of expressing their political opinions in a face-to-face environment. The semi-qualitative nature of the survey was designed to allow students to express rationalisations or motivations for their responses in the absence of widespread face-to-face interviews. Space was left in the appropriate spaces in order to provide students with the opportunity to qualify their responses if they wished to do so.

The results of the surveys provide multiple accounts of student wariness, as well as evidence of repression across the non-Fatah political spectrum. As Maryam (survey 2010), a 20-year-old law student from Nablus, put it, "I don't support any parties because I am afraid that I will be arrested by the PA." Similarly, Daoud (survey 2010), a 23-year-old activist for the Popular Front for the Liberation of Palestine (PFLP), ironically listed the benefits of organisational affiliation as "imprisonment by the Israelis and the PA". Aisha, an 18-year-old IT student, describes life as a Hamas sympathiser entails being "constantly insulted by the pro-Israeli movements" (survey 2010). In short, the suspicion of the West Bank authorities and wariness of voicing dissent is palpable to such an extent that one wag, Zarif (survey 2010), commented, "I haven't been arrested but after this questionnaire I think I will be!"

The upshot of this political repression, however, is that the responses of students who did identify or sympathise with a political movement, especially those not affiliated with Fatah, are likely to be reliable because the potential repercussions of these responses would only have been negative should these have fallen into the hands of either the PA or occupation authorities. In other words, students identifying themselves with an opposition movement had nothing to gain by doing so – quite the opposite – and were therefore likely to be reliable.

In light of PA and Israeli repression, as well as the amount of surveys I was able to collect, I cannot claim that these surveys are statistically representative. Surveys were, moreover, administered on a voluntary basis so a number of students declined to participate. Thus, the quantitative aspects of the surveys are used in a supplementary fashion which are supported, compared or contrasted with official polls where appropriate. Official polls should not be strictly viewed as an accurate representation given the differing methods of data collection and sometimes wildly varying results of different polling stations. Official polls, rather, will be used to track trends rather than illustrate the actual level of support

12 *Introduction*

for any given actor, especially since polling data have proved to be unreliable on these counts in the past.

Nevertheless, these surveys provided students with a forum within which to voice their opinions; opinions that have only rarely been solicited or acknowledged. As a result, the surveys provide hitherto unacknowledged explanations from ordinary Palestinians based on first order or experiential knowledge and, thus, a greater insight into the society as a whole (see Dunning 2013, pp. 43–51 for a more in-depth discussion of the fieldwork undertaken for this project).

Hamas, Islamists, and Change and Reform

Hamas is the main political manifestation of a wider Islamic social movement in the Palestinian Territories. It is a resistance organisation whose official membership would only make up a relatively small percentage of the population. As a political body however, Hamas commands various levels of support including formal membership, ideological alignment, tacit approval of its programme, as well as merely voting for Change and Reform. This accounted for at least 44 per cent of the vote on the party lists of the 2006 PLC elections and some 75 per cent of parliamentary seats elected at a district level. In effect, Hamas is the political manifestation of a number of overlapping socio-political movements.

Thus, when examining the evolution and ascendancy of Hamas as a political movement, it is not only the 'membership' which becomes a legitimate field of analysis, but rather the wider movement of formal and informal affiliations in which exist varying levels of personal, political and ideological affinities (Gunning 2007a, p. 8). These include affiliated charities, women's movements, student associations, as well as youth and sports clubs, among others. According to Gunning (ibid.), therefore, "within this framework, personnel of affiliated charities, student leaders and supporters with no known position within Hamas, but who identify with or expound its theories become relevant 'units of analysis' ".

While it is generally accepted that the Change and Reform list is supported by and represents the interests of Hamas – directly or indirectly – Change and Reform parliamentarians are not necessarily Hamas members per se. Indeed, those individuals who actually were Hamas members were required to resign from any leadership positions within the movement before entering government in an attempt to ensure the separation of the political party and the resistance organisation (Brown 2012, p. 15). These individuals are political representatives. None of the West Bank parliamentarians whom I interviewed indicated to me that they were official members of Hamas and several made it explicitly clear that they were not, despite, for example, such characterisations in the international press.

Any individual, moreover, possesses multiple overlapping identities, whereby one may be an Islamist representative, but also a university professor, engineer and member of a local *zakat* (alms) committee, so it is neither fair nor accurate to reduce an individual's identity to one appellation. In a similar vein, the presence of a Hamas member or sympathiser on the board of a charity, for example, does not mean that this charity necessarily *belongs* to Hamas, even if it is orientated around Islam and ideologically sympathetic to the movement.

Dr Nasser ed-Din al-Shaer (personal interview 2010), the former Deputy Prime Minister and Minister of Education of the tenth "Hamas" administration, for example, wanted it to be explicitly clear that he is an independent Islamist and neither a spokesman nor representative for either Hamas or the PLO, citing the need to be non-partisan in the field of education. Dr al-Shaer argued that he was not a member of the PLC and was approached as a result of his technical expertise and the fact that he may have been perceived as ideologically consistent or 'kindred' by Hamas in light of his position and expertise as a professor of *sharia* law.

Dr Sameer Abu Aisha (personal interview 2010), a professor in engineering at an-Najah and the former Minister of Planning, similarly indicated to me that he was neither a member of the PLC nor of Hamas but was rather approached by the tenth administration according to his technical expertise. There is, however, at the very least an ideological kinship, as Dr al-Shaer implied. Dr Abu Aisha (personal interview 2010) was previously elected as President of the Teachers' Union in the Palestinian Territories, rationalising, "that was because I am sort of independent but I was, again, supported by the Islamic list ... in that election at the university."

Moreover, the fact that these individuals served in the tenth administration – colloquially designated as the 'Hamas' government – as prominent members of the cabinet suggests that they had, at the very least, considerable influence over the administration's – and by extension, Hamas' – public policy initiatives. Dr Hafez Shaheen (personal interview 2010), former Islamist Deputy Mayor for Planning and Technical Affairs in Nablus, explains that during the 2004/2005 municipal elections, for instance,

> They [Hamas] did approach people, professors from the universities ... [and] businessmen. Okay, they are pro-Islam, not Hamas members but pro-Islam and can support or can, let's say, achieve the interests or work for the interests of the ideas that Hamas is supporting.

Hence, while it is not within my remit to categorise who is and who is not Hamas, an understanding exists where Hamas, as the main manifestation of political Islam in the Palestinian Territories, endorses trusted candidates who, in turn, become legitimate areas of analysis whether they are, or at some time were, official members of Hamas. In other words, these individuals, as the public representatives of political Islam in the Palestinian Territories, have the capacity to influence Hamas' policy and/or work to further some of Hamas' political goals.

Book summary

This book consists of six chapters. The first chapter conceptualises and outlines the research project, whereas the following chapters investigate Hamas'

14 *Introduction*

polysemic conceptions of resistance and jihad, including their armed, symbolic, political, social and ideational aspects. Each chapter presents and analyses certain common conceptions and misconceptions associated with Hamas' interpretation and application of jihad. Each chapter endeavours to provide the historical, social, cultural, political and/or economic contexts relevant to each interpretation, framing and application of the twin concepts of resistance and jihad. The combination of these diverse interpretations of resistance and jihad allow Hamas to function on multiple levels as a comprehensive social movement.

Chapter 1 outlines the research project by first examining and analysing some of the prevalent discourses surrounding Hamas, Islamism and armed sub-state activism in general, especially within the context of the 'war on terror'. Specifically, the chapter begins with a critique of Orientalist and security orientated approaches to Hamas, Islamism and terrorism before presenting some alternative discourses based on post-colonial studies and critical theory. The methodology utilised for this project is largely derived from a critical approach to terrorism studies; however, it also incorporates key aspects of post-structuralism, post-colonial theory, history, religious studies and anthropology. As a result, this interdisciplinary approach is not strictly based on a recognisable canon but, rather, different authors, disciplines and approaches surface at various points throughout the project in order to provide a synthesis of the various understandings of sub-state militancy, Hamas and Islamism in general. This chapter also examines the utility of the secular/religious divide in the Muslim Middle East. To this end, it interrogates whether Hamas is predominantly a religious or political movement in order to frame the movement's actions that are discussed in the following chapters.

Chapter 2 analyses the most obvious and recognisable form of Hamas jihad and resistance: political violence. First, it situates Palestinian violence and support thereof within the context of Israeli occupation. In this regard, it explores how exposure to violence can lead to the radicalisation of society and increase support for armed resistance. Second, it tracks the establishment of Hamas within the context of the first intifada and its increasingly deadly militancy dating from the early 1990s. Third, this chapter examines the practical nature of political violence and how this has the capacity to accumulate popular support. Specifically, it explores the instrumental nature of political violence, its role as armed propaganda, the influence of inter-factional competition, as well as the impact of Israeli violence, in determining Hamas' conception and application of armed resistance. Rather than being driven by religious imperatives, Hamas engages in 'controlled violence' dictated by temporal exigencies (see Mishal and Sela 2000, pp. 19–82). The perceived efficacy of armed resistance will be investigated vis-à-vis the Israeli withdrawal from the Gaza Strip in 2005.

Chapter 3 examines the role of central symbolic discourses centred on self-sacrifice, martyrdom and steadfastness in bolstering Hamas' image. To be precise, it discusses how frame amplification in relation to heroic figures such as

Introduction 15

the *feda'i*, the martyr, the stoic and the prisoner has increased identification with and augmented popular support for the movement. In addition, this chapter will investigate the culture of death which emerged amid an increasingly deadly second intifada; the resilience, *summud* and survival of the de facto government in Gaza during Israel's 2008/2009 attack code-named 'Operation Cast Lead'; and the role of prisoners in Palestinian society. Opinion polls are utilised throughout the course of Chapters 2 and 3 in order to track the impact of key events upon Hamas' popular support.

Chapter 4 explores Hamas' conceptions of, and participation in, politics, both in an extra-parliamentary sense as well as formal institutional settings. This chapter traces Hamas' evolution from an extra-parliamentary actor, expressing itself primarily through professional associations and unions, to an eventual participant in municipal and legislative elections since 2004. The chapter then explores Hamas' conceptions of politics, including the dialectic between resistance and politics, and the movement's views on democracy. To be precise, it investigates the notion that Hamas sees politics as a form of jihad. Political participation, in essence, is conceived of as a legitimate alternative, or indeed complementary route to achieve the movement's goals.

The chapter then examines the impact of Hamas' participation in institutionalised politics through an examination of its successes in the 2004/2005 municipal elections and its subsequent victory in the 2006 elections for the Palestinian Legislative Council. It investigates how Hamas was able to attract a wider political base to vote for it beyond its traditional 'core' constituency. In particular, it examines how Hamas' unity, superior organisation and ability to field better candidates allowed it to frame the terms of debate during election campaigns. The ability to field better quality candidates is especially important given the personalisation of politics in the Palestinian Territories. In brief, Hamas candidates often possessed more social, symbolic and moral capital than their Fatah counterparts. This, in turn, translated into political capital at the polls, especially at a local level where Palestinians voted for an individual rather than for a party. Finally, this chapter examines the aftermath of Hamas' surprise election to government in 2006, including the impact of international sanctions against the movement, Fatah duplicity and the eventual split between the West Bank and Gaza in June 2007.

The final two chapters, Chapters 5 and 6, focus on civilian conceptions of jihad and resistance as embodied by Hamas' work in charity, community development, *da'wa* and education. Chapter 5 examines Hamas' work in charity and community development, whereas Chapter 6 engages with Hamas' ideational jihad aimed at Islamisation. These social endeavours are deeply intertwined with Islamic values and have allowed Hamas to build trust within the Palestinian community. According to assassinated founding member of Hamas, Ismail Abu Shanab (cited in Roy 2011, p. 162), "We teach Islam by example, through our actions."

Chapter 5 begins by examining the oft-cited premise that Hamas charity functions as a 'womb to tomb' operation aimed at indoctrination and terrorist

16 *Introduction*

recruitment. To this end, this section will investigate to what extent Islamic social institutions in the Palestinian Territories are actually linked to or controlled by Hamas.

This chapter, in addition, contextualises the Islamic social work within the Palestinian Territories, including the historical antecedents and prevailing socio-economic and socio-political circumstances which gave rise to, and perhaps necessitate, the existence of Islamic social institutions. It is important to recall that social and community work were the focus of Hamas' predecessor, the *Ikhwan*. It also examines the Islamic reference point for these endeavours insofar as it ties back to the notion of *zakat* (literally 'purity') or alms. Charity and volunteerism are central components of Islamic philosophy.

Islamic social work and charity is further divided between traditional charity entailing the provision of goods and services and a more broad-based strategy focused on institution building, community development and vocational education. Over the course of the militarised second intifada, however, social work was more fixated on crisis management in the absence of security than on institution building. Accordingly, this chapter will detail some of the previous and current activities conducted by Islamic social institutions, especially key and novel organisations, as well as the role of charity throughout the second intifada.

Chapter 6 returns to Hamas' conceptions of Islam: the reference point and basis which ties together the movement's multi-faceted activities. Islamisation and the creation of a virtuous society based on Islam are perhaps Hamas' highest putative goals. According to Hamas, *da'wa* is one of the highest forms of jihad. Hamas believes that societal renewal begins with the individual and this commences with an Islamic education. Accordingly, this chapter explores Hamas' focus on education, both in terms of its moral and practical applications. Education, whether it be in the mosque or in the classroom, is utilised to disseminate values and encourage good behaviour.

It is necessary, however, to specify what exactly Hamas means by 'Islam' because there is no one Islam or Islamism but, rather, a variety of different 'Islams' interpreted according to time, circumstance and location. As such, this chapter examines some of the historical antecedents influencing Hamas' ostensibly ideological agenda. The notion of Islamic exceptionalism, espoused by Islamists and Orientalists alike (albeit to different ends), positing that Islam is unique due to its holistic nature is analysed and challenged. In particular, two of Hamas' more controversial ideological platforms – its interpretation and application of *sharia* law and dedication to its charter – are explored, thereby revealing that the movement's ideological tenets, like jihad and resistance, are fluid and evolving concepts subject to change.

Finally, this book contextualises the political rise and reinventions of Hamas by consistent reference to the changing nature of the occupation and the failures of the hitherto dominant Fatah movement. In essence, an increasingly repressive and violent occupation has led to the radicalisation of the Palestinian electorate resulting in a concomitant rise in support for Hamas, whereas the failure of the peace process has led to Palestinian disillusionment with Fatah (Shamir and

Introduction 17

Shikaki 2010, pp. 76–77). Fatah is seen as elitist, corrupt and dependent on external forces to the point of collusion, whereas political Islam is often seen as more grassroots, egalitarian and independent (Tuastad 2009, p. 263). Thus, not only has Fatah been tarnished by its governing record, but it has also been systematically discredited and humiliated by Israel and the international community. In addition, the policies of the occupation have undoubtedly influenced Hamas' conceptions of resistance and jihad, as well as when these differing interpretations are employed.

This study does not purport to offer a final definitive evaluation of Hamas' continued reinvention of itself through the reinterpretation and application of resistance and jihad – indeed, this is an impossibility given that Hamas is a fluid, evolving actor – but rather subscribes to the view that research within the social sciences and humanities is part of an ongoing discussion which ebbs and flows in line with political, economic and social realities. The conclusion, however, will draw together and examine the implications of the reinvention and evolution of Hamas and its consequent effects on the Palestinian political arena. It also explores the implications of Hamas' ongoing evolution within the context of the 'Arab Spring', particularly with regard to the rise and fall of the Muslim Brotherhood in Egypt; periodic conflict in Gaza, notably in 2012 and 2014; and the resurgence of eschatological jihadism as embodied by the dramatic rise of the Islamic State in Iraq and al-Sham (ISIS) and its putative regional affiliates.

The success, survival and endurance of the Hamas phenomenon, within the context of Palestine/Israel, is one of the most important political developments of the twenty-first century and, in many ways, a reflection of the wider society and its experiences. As a result, this is not only a study on Hamas but an exploration which helps to better understand the Palestinian condition within the Occupied Territories.

Notes

1 Fatah is an inverted acronym for *Harakat al-Tahrir al-Watani al-Filastini* (the Palestinian National Liberation Movement) literally meaning 'open', but often translated as 'victory' or 'conquest' as it refers to the historical 'opening', that is to say conquest, of Egypt by Islam. Fatah is the party founded by the late Yasser Arafat and currently headed by Palestinian President Mahmoud Abbas. Al-Fatah is also the opening chapter of *The Qur'an*.

2 In 1992, however, *le Front Islamique du Salut* (the Islamic Salvation Front) swept the polls in Algeria precipitating a military coup (with Western support), resulting in the cancellation of the election. The end result was over a decade of civil war entailing well over 100,000 deaths. The Hizbullah has also had a parliamentary presence in Lebanon since the 1990s.

3 Western citizens have been killed in various attacks within Israel and the Palestinian Territories, however.

4 In 2014, a court order removed Hamas from the European Union's list of proscribed terrorist organisations on procedural grounds but the EU is appealing against the decision, so Hamas has remained on the list with its assets frozen pending judgment by the Court of Justice.

18 *Introduction*

5 Supporters of the Israeli occupation argue that the absence of the definitive article 'the' in front of the word 'territories' means that Israel does not have to withdraw from *all* the territories captured in the 1967 war. The equally valid and authentic French version, however, does contain the definitive article. The argument in favour of the Israelis retaining some of the territories, moreover, does not acknowledge the preamble to the resolution stipulating the "inadmissibility of the acquisition of territory by war".

6 Unfortunately, I was unable to conduct any fieldwork in the Gaza Strip, not through an inability to make contact there, but rather through an inability to obtain permission from outside authorities to enter. Repeated enquiries to Israeli authorities in this regard tended to lead to one of three reactions when the word 'Gaza' was mentioned: (1) broken promises to call me back; (2) redirection to a Hebrew message bank or incorrect number; or (3) the person on the other end of the phone simply hanging up. Egyptian authorities were of little more use. As a result, I have been forced to utilise the material gathered by other authors when discussing the situation in the Gaza Strip.

7 While the number of surveys administered was relatively small, utilising university students ensured a decent geographical spread across the West Bank. Students in Nablus generally came from Nablus, Jenin and their surrounding villages. Birzeit students predominantly came from Ramallah/al-Bireh, Jerusalem and their environs. Respondents in Abu Dis were more heterogeneous, coming from Abu Dis, Jerusalem, Bethlehem, Hebron and Jericho, among others.

References

Amayreh, K. 2010. *Islamist Women's Activism in the Occupied Territories: Interviews with Palestinian Islamist Women's Leaders on Women's Activism in Hamas*. Beirut: Conflicts Forum.

Asad, T. 2007. *On Suicide Bombing*. New York: Columbia University Press.

Bourdieu, P. 1991. *Language and Symbolic Power*. Cambridge: Polity Press with Blackwell.

Brown, N. 2012. *Gaza Five Years On: Hamas Settles In*. Washington, DC: Carnegie Endowment for International Peace.

Burama, I. and Margalit, A. 2004. *Occidentalism: A short history of anti-Westernism*. New York: Penguin Books.

Burchill, R. 2004. 'Self-determination'. In *Defining Civil and Political Rights: The Jurisprudence of the United Nations Human Rights Committee*, edited by Scott Davidson, Alex Conte and Richard Burchill. Aldershot: Ashgate.

Burgat, F. 2003. *Face to Face with Political Islam*. London: I.B. Tauris.

Crooke, A. 2009. *Resistance: The essence of Islamist revolution*. New York: Pluto Press.

Dauphinee, E. 2010. 'The Ethics of Autoethnography'. *Review of International Studies* 36(3): 799–818.

Development Studies Programme. 2002. Poll no. 8. Birzeit: Birzeit University.

Dunning, T. 2013. 'Reinterpreting Resistance: Hamas' Polysemic Conceptions of Jihad and the Search for Popular Legitimacy'. PhD thesis. Brisbane: University of Queensland.

Ettinger, Y. 2008. 'Bush: Hezbollah, Hamas and al-Qa'ida Are All the Same'. *Ha'aretz* (Israel), 15 May.

Euben, R. 1999. *Enemy in the Mirror: Islamic Fundamentalism and the Limits of Modern Rationalism*. Princeton, NJ: Princeton University Press.

Euben, R. 2002. 'Killing (for) Politics: Jihad, Martyrdom, and Political Action'. *Political Theory* 30(1): 4–35.

Introduction 19

Gaess, R. 2002. 'Interviews from Gaza: Palestinian Options under Siege (Ziad Abu Amr; Haider Abdel Shafi)'. *Middle East Policy* 9(4): 115–121.

Gunning, J. 2007a. 'Hamas: Socialization and the Logic of Compromise'. In *Terror, Insurgency and the State: Ending protracted conflicts*, edited by M. Heiberg, B. O'Leary and J. Tirman. Philadelphia: University of Pennsylvania Press.

Gunning, J. 2007b. *Hamas in Politics: Democracy, Religion, Violence*. London: Hurst & Company.

Gunning, J. 2008. 'Terrorism, Charity and Diasporas: Contrasting the Fundraising Practices of Hamas and al Qaeda among Muslims in Europe'. In *Countering the Financing of Terrorism*, edited by T.J. Biersteker and S.E. Eckert. London: Routledge.

Gunning, J. 2009. 'Social Movement Theory and the Study of Terrorism'. In *Critical Terrorism Studies: A new research agenda*, edited by M.B. Smyth, R. Jackson and J. Gunning. New York: Routledge.

Hilal, J. 2005. 'Hamas's Rise as Charted in the Polls 1994–2005'. *Journal of Palestine Studies* 35(3): 6–19.

Holt, M. 1997. 'Palestinian Women and the Contemporary Islamist Movement'. *Encounters* 3(1): 64–75.

Hroub, K. 2006. *Hamas: A beginner's guide*. London: Pluto Press.

Hroub, K. 2008. 'Palestinian Islamism: Conflating National Liberation and Socio-political Change'. *International Spectator* 43(4): 59–72.

Jad, I. 2005. 'Between Religion and Secularism: Islamist Women of Hamas'. In *On Shifting Ground: Muslim Women in the Global Era*, edited by F. Nouraie-Simone. New York: Feminist Press at the City University of New York.

Kadayifici-Orellana, S.A. 2007. *Standing on an Isthmus: Islamic narratives of war and peace in Palestinian Territories*. New York: Lexington Books.

Kimmerling, B. and Migdal, J. 2003. *The Palestinian People: A History*. Cambridge, MA: Harvard University Press.

Le Roy, T. 2006. 'Le vote Hamas: quoi de neuf?' *Revue d'etudes palestiniennes* 99.

Mishal, S. and Sela, A. 2000. *The Palestinian Hamas: Vision, violence and coexistence*. New York: Columbia University Press.

Morris, H. 2006. 'Quartet Gathers amid Mounting Pressure on Hamas'. *Financial Times*, 30 January.

Norton, R. 2007. *Hezbollah: A short history*. Princeton, NJ: Princeton University Press.

Putnam, R. 1995. 'Bowling Alone: America's Declining Social Capital'. *Journal of Democracy* 6(1): 65–78.

Qur'an, The. 2008. Translated and edited by T. Khalidi. London: Penguin Books.

Rane, H. 2009. *Reconstructing Jihad amid Competing International Norms*. New York: Palgrave Macmillan.

Robinson, G. 2004. 'Hamas as Social Movement'. In *Islamic Activism: A social movement theory approach*, edited by Q. Wiktorowicz. Indianapolis: Indiana University Press.

Rose, D. 2008. 'The Gaza Bombshell'. *Vanity Fair*, April.

Rosenfeld, M. 2004. *Confronting the Occupation: Work, education, and political activism of Palestinian families in a refugee camp*. Stanford, CA: Stanford University Press.

Roy, S. 2011. *Hamas and Civil Society in Gaza: Engaging the Islamic social sector*. Princeton, NJ: Princeton University Press.

Said, E. [1978] 2003. *Orientalism*. New York: Vintage Books.

Shamir, J. and Shikaki, K. 2010. *Palestinian and Israeli Public Opinion: The public imperative in the second intifada*. Bloomington: Indiana University Press.

20 *Introduction*

Snow, D. and Benford, R. 1992. 'Master Frames and Cycles of Protest'. In *Frontiers of Social Movement Theory*, edited by A. Morris and C. Mueller. New Haven, CT: Yale University Press.

Steele, J. 2007. 'Hamas Acted on a Very Real Fear of a US-sponsored Coup'. *Guardian* (United Kingdom), 22 June.

Tamimi, A. 2007. *Hamas: A history from within*. Northampton, MA: Olive Branch Press.

Tuastad, D. 2009. *Primary Solidarity: A Comparative Study on the Role of Kinship in Palestinian Local Politics*. PhD thesis. Oslo: University of Oslo.

United Nations Charter. 1945.

United Nations General Assembly. 1960. Resolution 1514, XV.

United Nations General Assembly. 1966. Resolution 2200A, XXI.

United Nations General Assembly. 1970. Resolution 2625, XXV.

United Nations General Assembly. 1970. Resolution 2708, XXV.

United Nations General Assembly. 1967. Resolution 242.

United Nations Security Council. 2002. Resolution 1397.

Whitaker, B. 2001. 'Sharon Likens Arafat to Bin Laden'. *Guardian* (United Kingdom), 14 September.

Zuhur, S. 2010. *Hamas and Israel: Conflicting strategies of group-based politics*. Carlisle, PA: Strategic Studies Institute.

Interviews and surveys

Abu Marzouq, M., Deputy Head of the Hamas Political Bureau, US Specially Designated Global Terrorist and Doctor of Engineering, Damascus, May 2010.

Aisha, an 18-year-old Hamas sympathiser studying information technology, anonymous survey, an-Najah National University, Nablus, March 2010.

al-Shaer, N., Former Deputy Prime Minister and Minister of Education for the Tenth 'Hamas' Administration, Professor of *Sharia* Law at an-Najah National University, Nablus, February 2010.

Bashir, a 44-year-old Hamas member and youth activities officer, Damascus, May 2010.

Daoud, a 23-year-old activist for the Popular Front for the Liberation of Palestine, anonymous survey, an-Najah National University, Nablus, March 2010.

Dweik, Islamist Speaker of Parliament, elected PLC Deputy and Professor of Urban Geography, Hebron, May 2010.

Maryam, unaffiliated 20-year-old studying law, anonymous survey, Birzeit University, April 2010.

Zarif, a 22-year-old former Fatah supporter studying political science and media, anonymous survey, al-Quds University, Abu Dis, May 2010.

1 Orientalism, Islam and militancy in a post-11 September world

> The sword of Muhammad and the Ko'ran are the most stubborn enemies of Civilization, Liberty and Truth which the world has yet known.
>
> William Muir, 1861 (Muir and Weir 1912 [1861], p. 522)

> They hate our freedoms: our freedom of religion, our freedom of speech, our freedom to vote and assemble and disagree with each other.... Every nation in every region now has a decision to make: Either you are with us or you are with the terrorists.
>
> US President George W. Bush, 21 September 2001

Following the 11 September attacks on the World Trade Center and the Pentagon, it is unsurprising that there has been a renewed focus on Islam, and militant Islam in particular. What followed – the response of a wounded superpower, the invasions of Afghanistan and Iraq and the widespread Islamophobia which has afflicted much of West – has seen Muslims largely demonised, categorised as a threat and homogenised under the rubric of the US-led 'war on terror' (see e.g. Powell 2012; Greenwald 2012; Bayoumi 2012; Grenier 2012; Jones 2012). Non-state actors, especially those of an Islamic hue, frequently continue to be packaged under this all-encompassing rubric and conflated with al-Qa'ida's transnational militant jihad. In Palestine/Israel, amidst an increasingly deadly second intifada, the Israeli government endeavoured to tie Palestinian militancy confronting foreign domination to the US-led global 'war on terror'. More than a decade after 11 September, real world grievances and local processes on the ground are often systematically elided in favour of dichotomous 'us' and 'them' discourses imbued with Orientalist tendencies.

This chapter situates the project within existing discourses pertaining to Islam, terrorism and Hamas. It critiques the resurgence of Orientalist meta-discourses and highlights some of the flaws of traditional scholarship, especially with regard to terrorism, before refocusing on some alternative approaches based on post-colonial studies and critical theory. The chapter also investigates whether Hamas is predominantly a religious or political organisation with the intent of framing the movement's actions discussed in the following chapters. The project seeks to refocus on the local dynamics of the Palestinian condition in the West

22 *Orientalism, Islam and militancy post 9/11*

Bank and Gaza Strip, especially with regard to the actions, motivations and rationales of the Islamic Resistance Movement, Hamas.

Orientalism and the 'war on terror'

Since the end of the Cold War, and post-11 September in particular, there has been a renewed flourishing of Orientalist positions among mainstream liberals and conservatives alike, especially with regard to the Muslim world. Mainstream discourses, both academic and popular, pertaining to political Islam are often of an essentialist nature depicting Islam as possessing certain innate characteristics. In effect, Islamist movements, including Hamas, are often homogenised and portrayed as an interconnected and largely monolithic ideological entity. This is what the late Edward Said (2003, p. 40) described as Orientalism, whereby the West ascribes characteristics to the Arab and Muslim Middle East to fit certain political, economic or hegemonic exigencies, regardless of their relation to reality. Specifically, commentators posit Islam's incompatibility with democracy and modernity (see Huntington 1998; Fukuyama 2006; Nusse 1998, p. 180; Black 2001, p. 351).

Influential Orientalist Bernard Lewis (1990), for instance, believed that the rejection of 'modernity' is at the 'roots of Muslim rage'. A later post-11 September work, *What Went Wrong? The clash between Islam and modernity in the Middle East*, similarly investigates the Islamic world's putative rejection of modernity (Lewis 2002). Asserting a 'wrong', as Alam (2002, p. 56) points out, suggests a Muslim deviation from 'what is just and good' or, in other words, a (Westernised) 'right'. According to Alain Gresh (2005), moreover, the common theme of Lewis' work is "the idea that the Muslim world is fossilised in fundamental opposition to the West". Edward Said (2003, p. 315) concurs insofar as: "The core of Lewis's ideology about Islam is that it never changes ... any political, historical and scholarly account of Muslims must begin and end with the fact that Muslims are Muslims."

George W. Bush, Dick Cheney, Donald Rumsfeld, Paul Wolfowitz and other high-ranking officials of the Bush Administration are admirers of Lewis and, as such, his views on the Muslim world are reputed to have "provided the intellectual ammunition for the Iraq war" (Berman 2011; see also Hirsh 2004; Miles 2004; Weisberg 2007; Gresh 2005). In essence, Lewis argued to various White House heavyweights for the forced democratisation and (Western) modernisation of the Middle East. According to Richard Perle (cited in Waldman 2004), Head of the US Defence Policy Board in September 2001 and close adviser to then Defence Secretary Donald Rumsfeld, "Bernard Lewis has been the single most important intellectual influence countering the conventional wisdom on managing the conflict between radical Islam and the West." Peter Waldman (2004), writing for the *Wall Street Journal* in 2004, argued that under the Bush Administration, "The Lewis Doctrine, in effect, had become U.S. policy".

In a similar vein, amidst the triumphalism of the post-Cold War-era West, Francis Fukuyama (2006) famously (and naively) proclaimed 'the end of history' and the victory of liberal democracy, while concomitantly deriding the backwardness of Islamic societies. Fukuyama (p. 83) believes that Islamism is the "deliberate rejection of technology and a rationalized society". Fukuyama (2001) later refers to "retrograde areas [of the world] that resisted that process [of modernisation]" and specifies Muslim societies as "particularly resistant to modernity". The utilisation of modern technology by al-Qa'ida and then the far more adept campaign by ISIS, driven by social media tools such as Twitter, Facebook, YouTube and so forth, to disseminate propaganda are just two examples that disprove Islamists' rejection of technology.

Samuel Huntington (1998) likewise bemoans the lack of democracy in the Muslim world, but whereas as Fukuyama envisages the triumph of liberal democracy, Huntington foresees civilisational clashes among putative meta-cultures which include such generalisations as 'Islamic', 'Asian' and 'African'. Notwithstanding the problems with classifying such diverse groupings under a single label, Huntington (1988, pp. 256–258) takes it a step further by arguing that Muslims are inherently more violent than other meta-cultures which he purportedly identifies. In defence of this argument, Huntington cites the higher instances of political violence among Muslim majority countries, yet fails to take into account the residual effects of European imperialism and ongoing American hegemony in large swathes of the Muslim world, especially the Middle East. Robert Kaplan (2000, p. 42) echoes these sentiments when he describes the Muslim world as the "vast and volatile realm of Islam".

Orientalist literature, in this regard, depicts a unified, fundamentalist and regressive Islam in a 'clash of civilisations' with the progressive, liberal and 'rational' West. As Said (2001) points out, however,

> Huntington is an ideologist, someone who wants to make 'civilizations' and 'identities' into what they are not, shut down, sealed off entities that have been purged of the myriad currents and counter-currents that animate human history and that over the centuries have made it possible for that history to contain not only wars of religion and imperial conquest but also exchange, cross-fertilization, and sharing.

Nevertheless, rejection of (Western) modernity is frequently attributed to backwardness, tribalism and religious fundamentalism. Bruce Hoffman (2006, p. 161), for instance, asserts that Islamic suicide bombers are driven by a "medieval Assassins' doctrine, invoking the paradise that awaits the holy terrorists ... including the pleasures of alcohol – which all Muslims are forbidden in their lives – and sex". Here Hoffman exhibits the Orientalist tendency to situate contemporary phenomena affecting non-Western subjects in antiquity.

Walter Lacquer (2003, p. 105) similarly plays to gender stereotypes, asserting that "Even Muslim women had the right to engage in jihad, without the permission of their husbands if need be, just as slaves had the right to go on jihad without asking their masters". Here, Lacquer seems to infer that Muslim women possess approximately the same rights as slaves vis-à-vis their husbands.

24 *Orientalism, Islam and militancy post 9/11*

Hoffman and Lacquer infantalise suicide bombers, contending that they are motivated by an egotistical desire for rewards in the afterlife, especially desires such as promiscuous sex and alcohol, which are considered *haram* (forbidden) in the temporal world. Hoffman (2006, p. 163), in addition, argues that "the families [of suicide bombers] ... are co-opted into supporting – if not encouraging – their relations' homicidal self-destruction by the promise of an assured place in heaven as well", citing a belief that the martyr can intercede with God on behalf of 70 of their relatives. Juergensmeyer (2001, p. 201) takes it a step further, arguing that "the young bachelor self-martyrs in the Hamas movement ... expect that the blasts that kill them will propel them to a bed in heaven where the most delicious acts of sexual consummation will be theirs for the taking". As such, the suicide bomber is perceived to be driven by metaphysical rewards of the intoxicating and carnal variety – forbidden to Muslims on Earth – rather than temporal concerns pertaining to the often arduous nature of their current existence (for instance, the continuing occupation of the Palestinian Territories). The *Qur'an* itself, however, explicitly denies carnal pleasures and alcohol in Paradise (Khalidi 2008, p. xvii). The *Qur'an*'s (52:23) description of Paradise, "Wherein there is no drunken uproar, nor any wrongdoing", for instance, would seem to preclude the possibility of drunken orgies.

These charges of egotistical rewards are also strenuously denied by Hamas. Indeed, Sheikh Ahmed Yassin (cited in Milton-Edwards and Farrell 2010, p. 141), the assassinated founder and spiritual leader of Hamas, explains:

> This is a society raised on war and it wears the clothes of occupation. We have the right to retaliate if they kill our civilians and target them. And they have killed many more of our women and children than we have done.... A sacrifice in this way is for the nation and brings our people step closer to liberation.

Thus, Yassin points to the reality of a decades-long military occupation and the struggle for self-determination as the catalysts for Hamas violence, not egotistical rewards in the afterlife (Milton-Edwards 2011, p. 191).

The Hamas movement itself, conversely, is portrayed as being driven by cold, tactical considerations ruthlessly brainwashing simple-minded youth to their doom. Consider the following by Lacquer (2003, p. 87):

> According to a survey by the Israeli security services in 2002, details of which have not been published, a significant percentage of Palestinian suicide bombers suffered from an advanced form of serious diseases, organic or mental. Because this report was not scheduled to be published, propagandistic intentions were unlikely to be involved.

Notwithstanding the motives of the Israeli security services and their methods of data collection – not to mention the difficulty of assessing the emotional, mental and physical state of successful suicide bombers – that Lacquer would insinuate that a document prepared by a hostile security service, during a time of war no less, is valid precisely *because* it is unpublished, borders on preposterous. If propagandistic intent was unlikely, as Lacquer claims, it seems rather convenient that the putative results of the study would make it into the Israeli daily newspapers, albeit safe from further scrutiny.

Lacquer (2003, p. 90) also seems confused and appears to contradict himself when he goes on to cite Ariel Merari three pages later:

> a Tel Aviv University psychologist who has studied the phenomenon of Palestinian suicide terrorism probably more closely than anyone else, noted on the basis of many interviews that he did not find a single psychotic among the candidates for terrorism suicide.

A later study by Bader Araj and Robert Brym (2010) found that, in reality, suicide bombers during the second intifada tended to be more highly educated than the society at large.

Hoffman also seems to contradict himself. Thus while, for instance, Hoffman (2006, pp. 145–165) asserts that suicide bombers are driven by the promise of rewards in the afterlife, he also believes that no suicide bombers were driven by desperation; and he later concedes that Hamas suicide operations were rational attacks driven by tactical, temporal considerations, namely inter-factional competition (as opposed to, say, the actual target of such attacks, the Israeli occupation). Audrey Cronin (2009, p. 56) goes further by reducing Palestinian suicide attacks during the second intifada to being primarily fixated on inter-factional competition. By reducing Palestinian attacks primarily to inter-factional competition, Cronin implicates Palestinian society as tribal – or pre-modern – while casting Israel as a convenient scapegoat rather than as an occupying power. While there is indeed intense inter-factional competition among the Palestinian movements, little mention is made of Israeli and American efforts to foment that divide, especially following the election of Hamas to the legislature in 2006.

Orientalist thinking has gained much popular traction and informs Western popular consciousness and unconsciousness, especially in the wake of the 11 September attacks. Media 'experts', academics, politicians and other institutional forces reinforce and propagate this view ascribing institutional credibility to such claims (Bourdieu 1998, p. 106; Said 1997, p. 7; Herman and Chomsky 2002, p. 23). Pulitzer Prize-winning journalist Thomas Friedman, writing for the *New York Times* (cited in Fernandez 2011, pp. 70–71), regarded by many as the most influential journalist in the world, maintains "that Arabs and Muslims are 'backwards' and intent on maintaining a situation in which 'the past buries the future'". During a visit to Iraq a month after the 2003 invasion, for instance, Friedman (2003) opines, "It would be idiotic to even ask Iraqis here how they felt about politics. They are in a pre-political state of nature"; and thereby reduces Iraqi political consciousness to what it was before the seventeenth century. Friedman (2002, p. 266) then plausibly depicts the 'war on terror' as a

26 *Orientalism, Islam and militancy post 9/11*

'war of ideas'. Upon expansion of this notion, however, Friedman resorts to facile dichotomies between Islamic backwardness and Western enlightenment. According to Friedman (ibid.),

> It is a war between the future and the past, between development and under-development, between authors of crazy conspiracy theories versus those espousing rationality, between advocates of suicide bombing and those who know that you can't build a society out of gravestones.

Here, Friedman exhibits his Orientalist tendencies by juxtaposing Western 'modernity' and 'rationalism' to the perceived deficiencies of the Muslim world.

Mainstream academia is similarly complicit and, moreover, frequently alarmist in nature. Following 11 September, for instance, 60 prominent academics as divergent as Samuel Huntington, Theda Skocpol, Michael Walzer, Francis Fukuyama and Amitai Etzioni signed a 10-page petition endorsing the "'war on terrorism' on the grounds that it defended 'American values', 'our way of life' and 'the achievements of civilization'" (Abrahamian 2003, p. 533). In a similar vein, Cronin (2009, p. 6) believes that "In the twenty-first century, terrorism has become a threat to the fabric of the Western liberal state" (see Mueller 2005, p. 495 for further examples). But just how much of a threat is terrorism to the Western liberal state? John Mueller (2005, p. 498) soberly asks the question:

> How many airliners would have to crash before flying becomes as dangerous as driving the same distance in an automobile?... The conclusion is that there would have to be one set of 9/11 crashes a month for the risks to balance out. More generally, they calculate that an American's chance of being killed in one non-stop airline flight is about one in 13 million (even taking the September 11 crashes into account), while to reach that same level of risk when driving on America's safest roads, rural interstate highways, one would have to travel a mere 11.2 miles.

It would appear, moreover, that Orientalist thinking has penetrated to the highest political echelons of the most powerful Western states. Writing for *Foreign Affairs*, then UK Prime Minister, Tony Blair (2007), evidently believes that:

> The struggle against terrorism in Madrid, or London, or Paris is the same as the struggle against the terrorist acts of Hezbollah in Lebanon, or Palestinian Islamic Jihad in the Palestinian Territories, or rejectionist groups in Iraq. The murder of the innocent in Beslan is part of the same ideology that takes innocent lives in Libya, Saudi Arabia, or Yemen. And when Iran gives support to such terrorism, it becomes part of the same battle, with the same ideology at its heart.[1]

Gold (2007) similarly collects groups as diverse as a Shi'ite Iranian theocracy, Wahabbi Salafi jihadists and Sunni national liberation movements under the

Orientalism, Islam and militancy post 9/11   27

same rubric, notwithstanding the ideological, cultural and political cleavages among such groupings.

Walter Lacquer (2003, p. 107) likewise asserts that Iran is the main supporter of Hamas, thereby inferring that Hamas is an Iranian proxy or puppet rather than a localised, grassroots component of the Palestinian national movement. Yet Lacquer (p. 109), seemingly in contradiction with himself, later claims that, for Hamas, "the Shi'ite religion was considered a deviation from true Islam, and to collaborate with it was considered almost as bad as a Protestant fundamentalist accepting the authority of the pope". If Hamas is driven purely by religious imperatives, as Lacquer claims, then how is this to be explained apart from references to strategic, tactical or temporal concerns? Here, Lacquer also reveals a realist mindset which tends to dismiss the agency and importance of non-state actors (even if these actors are striving for a state themselves).

Lacquer (2003, p. 100), moreover, seems to believe that the question of Palestine embroils Israel in "a religious confrontation with the whole Muslim world". This is despite Hamas' repeated and public insistence on a grievance-based conflict centred on occupation and the usurpation of land in British Mandatory Palestine (see Yousef 2007; Mishal 2006; Abu Marzouq 2006; Haniyeh in Weymouth 2006). In short, the discourses surrounding political Islam, the 'war on terror' and Hamas are often characterised by a set of reductive generalisations based on institutionalised stereotypes.

This dominant 'static' approach anchored in Orientalist tendencies suggests that Hamas cannot and will not change (see e.g. Ross 2006, pp. x–xi). Orientalist and terrorism studies frequently fall back on tired clichés pertaining to 72 virgins in paradise, masked men hiding behind women and children, and repeated recourse to Hamas' putative (and long-abandoned) desire for a "pan-Islamic empire" (Lacquer 2003, p. 113; Hoffman 2006, p. 161; Cronin 2009, p. 41). Lacquer (2003, p. 112) points to the "intensity of hate and fanaticism in the motivation of the radical Islamic groups" in the Palestinian Territories. Michael Walzer (2009) similarly ascribes to this Orientalist view, asserting a primordial hatred which prevents Hamas' ability to even negotiate with Israel because of "its rabid anti-Semitism: the Hamas Charter reiterates an ancient hatred that long predates the Zionist project and the wars of 1948 and 1967". That an author as respected and influential as Walzer would resort to such essentialist discourses is especially problematic because these static, alarmist and Orientalist representations are thereby ascribed immense institutional credibility.

Lacquer then proceeds to invoke the spectre of Nazism and the Holocaust when referring to Hamas. According to Lacquer (2003, p. 106), "Hamas followed the doctrine of the extreme right in Europe and of Nazism; there was no fashionable nonsense about anti-imperialism or anti colonialism, let alone postmodernism." Here, Lacquer and Walzer demonstrate the continued inability of mainstream authors to move beyond Hamas' charter which calls for the complete liberation of historical Palestine, including what is today recognised as the State of Israel. As such, Lacquer and Walzer either elide or are unaware of Hamas' shifting discourses, in particular its focus on foreign occupation and

28 *Orientalism, Islam and militancy post 9/11*

international law (for instance, UN resolutions in both the Security Council and General Assembly) as the point of reference for self-determination. Instead, Lacquer and Walzer cling to the static Orientalist approach which defines the movement by a document which: (1) was written over two decades ago; (2) never went through the consultative decision-making and approval processes which would come to characterise the movement; and (3) was never adopted as a policy document, even after Hamas took power in 2006.

In a similar vein, terrorism scholar Audrey Cronin (2009, p. 31) dismisses, a priori, the possibility of negotiating with Hamas thus:

> The election of a Hamas government and degeneration of the political and economic situation in the Palestinian Territories means that there is no credible negotiation partner to settle the struggle over this small area that holds both peoples, and little hope of the emergence of politically effective, moderate Palestinian forces in the near future.

Here, Walzer, Cronin and Lacquer appear to omit or are unaware of the repeated public statements of Hamas implicitly accepting a two-state solution, as well as a commitment to any political solution reached by Palestinian President Mahmoud Abbas provided it is endorsed by popular referendum (see e.g. McCarthy 2008; Ravid 2008; Yousef 2007).

There also seems to be a double standard applied to Hamas and the 'secular' and 'moderate' Fatah. Cronin (2009, p. 51), for instance, cites Arafat's injunction of the Treaty of Khudabiyya between the Prophet Mohammed and the polytheists of Mecca as an indication of Arafat's desire for a negotiated settlement, yet fails to mention that Hamas has also proposed a negotiated solution based on the same precedent since the 1990s.

The 'static' Orientalist tendencies are flawed moreover, since they do not account for the evolution of Hamas' political thought and practice. Orientalist thinking is also unable to account for the manifest differences (political and practical) of Islamist movements. Islam is interpreted depending on the political, socio-economic and cultural contexts of each specific movement (Burgat 2004, p. 78).

Statism, 'terrorism' and Israeli exceptionalism

Since Hamas is considered a terrorist organisation in much of the West, Jeroen Gunning (2007, p. 152) contends that the movement is often approached from a 'terrorism' paradigm preventing dialogue and understanding. As a result, terrorism studies are, for the most part, an extension of the above reductive essentialism. Tellingly, terrorism studies are written almost entirely from a Western and Israeli perspective (Illardi 2004, p. 225). As such, there is often an ethnocentric ignorance of local political processes and conditions on the ground. In particular, there is undue focus on violence and vitriolic rhetoric which obscures the complexity of socio-political insurgent movements. Matthew Levitt (2006)

Orientalism, Islam and militancy post 9/11   29

and the Intelligence and Terrorism Information Centre (2005) in Israel argue, for instance, that Hamas' many aspects are merely a façade for terror and effecting violence.

This focus on political violence often means that writings on terrorism are of a prescriptive nature which treats the insurgent movement as an adversary to be defeated rather than a socio-political phenomenon to be understood (Brannan *et al.* 2001, p. 4; Horgan 2004, p. 30). Cronin (2009, p. 1), for instance, states that the aim of her research on terrorism is to help the United States and its allies "to win" by outlining "how best to construct a counterthrust" to non-state militancy. When coupled to the demonisation of Islam, the socio-economic and political context of the Palestinian community is systematically circumvented. In other words, it is easier to condemn a movement than attempt to understand its motives and the circumstances from which it springs (Silke 2004, p. 19).

Another critique of traditional approaches to research on terrorism is that it too often entails a replication of secondary sources with an over-reliance on the media, government and security sources (Schmidt and Jongman 1998, p. 138; Hroub 2000, p. 4; Silke 2004, p. 60; Saad-Ghrorayeb 2002, p. 96; Harb and Leenders 2005, pp. 176–177). The over-reliance on the media and journalistic accounts is problematic on several accounts. First is the symbiotic relationship between acts of terrorism and the media, whereby violence is given undue prominence due to its media appeal. Violence is then used as 'proof' of fanaticism (Burgat 2003, p. 167). In other words, there is a tendency by the media to simplify, dramatise and sensationalise so that Islamists with the 'bombs not ballot papers' are made more visible (Said 1992, p. 143; Herman and Chomsky 2002, p. xiv; Burgat 2003, p. 167). Security sources are similarly problematic given that intelligence agencies are prone to deception and their sources are often, by their very nature, unverifiable.

Relying on government and security sources can also be overly state-centric. State-centric approaches to terrorism understate the role of the state in creating and sustaining resistance and take the legitimacy of the status quo for granted (O'Leary and Tirman 2007, p. 12; Gunning 2007b, p. 15; Illardi 2004, p. 223). Lacquer (2003, p. 112), for instance, infers that Palestinian existence is characterised by "the gentlest of occupation". Perhaps state-centric views are not altogether surprising given that almost all of the funding for terrorism studies comes from governments (Silke 2004, p. 18). As a result, the material tends to be tailored to fit a certain policy demand and falls within relatively prescribed parameters of 'accepted' thought (Bourdieu 1998, p. 106; O'Leary and Silke 2007, pp. 392–393). In other words, these works may have a specific political agenda. In the case of Hamas and the question of Palestine in general, it is surprisingly necessary to point out that it is the West Bank under occupation and Gaza an open air prison, not Israel. As Sara Roy (2007, p. 1) points out, "More often than not power politics produces the 'scholarship' it needs to legitimize itself." In short, there are potential problems relating to academic integrity.

The problem of academic independence is most acute and concerning in the United States – by far and away the largest producer of academic scholarship in

30 *Orientalism, Islam and militancy post 9/11*

the world – where academics, politicians and journalists are routinely targeted for alleged anti-Israeli or anti-American bias, especially with regard to the question of Palestine (and, indeed, policy in the Middle East region in general). Martin Kramer (2001), for instance, advocates unashamedly that the US government withhold funding from Middle Eastern research projects which do not explicitly further the national interest. A pro-Israeli organisation, Campus Watch, publicly lists, targets and intimidates academics who it deems to be of an anti-Israeli bias. In a similar vein, a 2012 advertisement in the *New York Times* sponsored by David Horowitz's Freedom Centre publicly listed the names and contact details of professors supporting the Palestinian Boycott, Divestment and Sanctions (BDS) Movement against Israel, while comparing it to the beginning of the Holocaust and accusing those named of inciting the murder of Jewish children (Abunimah 2012). Daniel Pipes (2008, p. xv) likewise charges that "few academics have a genuine interest in the Palestinians. Rather, they devote outsized attention to this otherwise small and obscure population because it represents a convenient and potent tool with which to malign Israel." Here, Pipes seems to insinuate that criticism of Israel has little to do with its policies but rather because the critics themselves are anti-Semites. In short, there is a sustained campaign of public intimidation branding academics critical of Israeli policy in the Palestinian Territories as anti-Semites and apologists for terrorism in an attempt to silence these views.

In 2002, no less than then president of Harvard University Laurence Summers took it a step further when he declared that criticism of Israel and measures taken against the state, such as European boycotts, BDS petitions among US universities (including the Massachusetts Institute of Technology and Harvard) and anti-globalisation rallies during which Israel was criticised "are anti-Semitic in their effect if not their intent", thereby setting a new distinction between *intentional* as opposed to *effective* anti-Semitism (Butler 2003). As Judith Butler (ibid.) points out,

> If the president of Harvard is letting the public know that he will take any criticism of Israel to be effectively anti-semitic, then he is saying that public discourse itself ought to be so constrained that such statements are not uttered, and that those who utter them will be understood as engaging in anti-semitic speech, even hate speech.

How, then, is one to voice criticism or disagreement of Israeli policy if this is then retroactively defined as 'effective' if not 'intentional' anti-Semitism? Indeed, Butler (ibid.) continues: "If we say that every time the world 'Israel' is spoken, the speaker really means 'Jews', then we have foreclosed in advance the possibility that the speaker really means 'Israel'."

This campaign of intimidation is not only limited to scholars and journalists but also extends to politicians. Pro-Israeli organisations such as the AIPAC, for instance, wield enormous influence in Congress, so much so that senior officials, including the President himself, periodically speak at their conferences. AIPAC and other pro-Israeli organisations frequently fund campaigns against politicians who are publicly critical of Israeli policy in the Palestinian Territories (Mearsheimer and Walt 2007). These accusations of anti-Semitism clearly constitute an attempt to intimidate and silence outspoken critics of Israeli policy in the Occupied Territories.

Israel also benefits from statist interpretations of international relations which accord it sovereign legitimacy. Lacquer (2003, p. 113), for instance, resorts to clichés portraying Palestinian resistance fighters as cowardly murderers "hiding behind women, children and elderly people" while extolling the virtues of the state. Lacquer's (ibid., pp. 113–114) considered opinion asserts that "the weak have privileges which the other side does not have: they are entitled to kill civilians, women and children, whereas the security forces of a state according to existing norms must not execute anyone without due process." Lacquer is either deliberately opaque or unaware that Israel has assassinated hundreds of Palestinian political leaders without due process, not only in Gaza and the West Bank, but also breaching the sovereignty of a multitude of states in order do so. This not only includes friendly states in Europe, as well as Jordan and Malta, but also others such as Tunisia and Dubai.

While Cronin (2009, p. 3) admits that "States also employ force for political ends, many of which a perfidious and much worse than terrorism" and "a comparison that in terms of body counts was undeniable", she (ibid., p. 7) rationalises that "state use of force is subject to international norms and conventions" without analysing the legitimacy of the state itself or, more to the point, the legitimacy of state policy (in this case embodied by the occupation of the West Bank and Gaza). This is especially the case in post-colonial states whereby imperial cartographers created these entities without consultation with, or appreciation of, the population on the ground. Indicatively, not one state recognises the legitimacy of Israel's occupation of the West Bank and Gaza or its annexation of East Jerusalem.

Israel, in addition, is in breach of the Fourth Geneva Convention, Article 7 of the Rome Statute of the International Criminal Court, as well as numerous Security Council and General Assembly resolutions, all of which highlight the illegitimacy of the occupation and its ongoing settlement enterprise throughout the West Bank. Article 49 of the Fourth Geneva Convention, for instance, states, "The Occupying Power shall not deport or transfer parts of its own civilian population into the territory it occupies", a commitment which Israel has clearly breached since 1967 given that there are now over 500,000 Israeli settlers living in East Jerusalem and the West Bank (B'tselem 2010). Nevertheless, on a political level, Israeli infringements of international law are routinely explained away with, at best, a verbal show of consternation by the United States and its allies with little recourse to genuine sanctions.[2] The US, moreover, has exercised its power of veto dozens of times in defence of Israel in the UN Security Council.

Cronin's (2009, p. 52) assertion that Israel pulled out of "most of the Gaza Strip" following the 1993 Oslo Accords is also open to contestation. What Cronin fails to explain is that up until 2005, around 10,000 Israeli settlers possessed approximately one-third of Gaza's territory, the rest of which housed

32 *Orientalism, Islam and militancy post 9/11*

over 1,000,000 Palestinians cut into several non-contiguous segments separated by Israeli bypass roads (see Map 1.1).

Cronin also fails to note that Israel continues to control most of Gaza's borders including its sea and air space which, in collusion with US ally Egypt, makes it extremely difficult for Palestinians and goods to leave or enter the Gaza Strip. Israel also enforces a buffer zone extending 500 metres into the Gaza Strip depriving Gazans of much of their prime agricultural land (see Map 1.2).

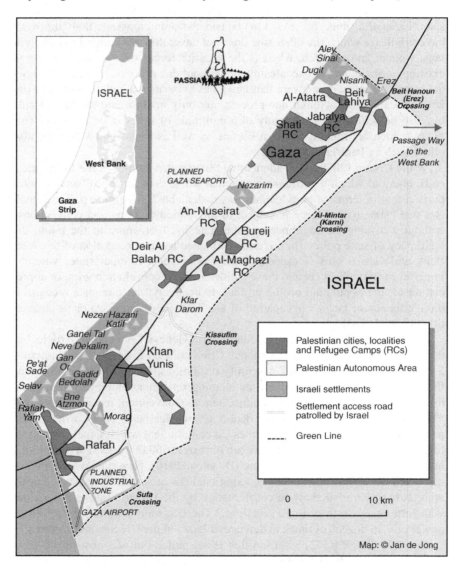

Map 1.1 The Gaza Strip, 2000 (source: Reproduced with permission of the Palestinian Academic Society for the Study of International Affairs (PASSIA) and Jan de Jong).

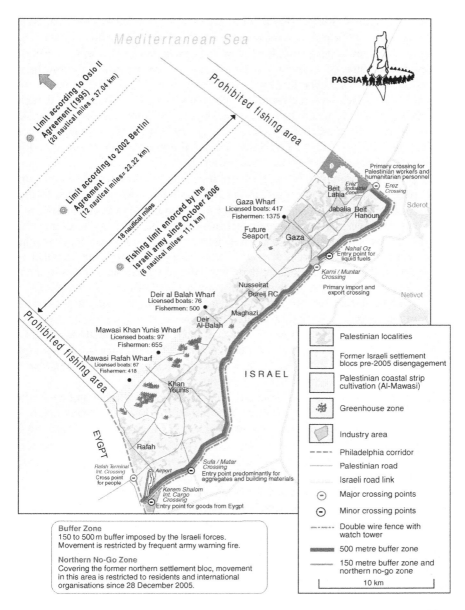

Map 1.2 The Gaza Strip, 2007 (source: Reproduced with permission of the Palestinian Academic Society for the Study of International Affairs (PASSIA)).

34 *Orientalism, Islam and militancy post 9/11*

Cronin also has a tendency to blur the historical timeline, thus muddying cause and effect. Writing about the deportation of Hamas leaders to Lebanon in 1992, Cronin (2009, p. 51) subsequently asserts that "Meanwhile, Hamas and Islamic Jihad, newly powerful after the intifada, mounted a series of increasingly deadly suicide attacks" before referring to a (largely unsuccessful) Islamic Jihad attack on Israeli soldiers in September 1993. Notwithstanding whether the Islamic Jihad attack on Israeli soldiers constitutes 'terrorism' (generally defined in relation to targeting civilians), Cronin appears to infer that suicide attacks were occurring in abundance between 1992 and 1993 when this was not the case (there was one in April 1993 targeting an Israeli army bus which succeeded in killing the perpetrator and a Palestinian bystander).

Importantly, Cronin (2009, p. 52) does mention Jewish terrorism in the form of Baruch Goldstein's 1994 massacre of 29 Palestinians and wounding a further 150 worshipping at the *Ibrahimi* mosque/Cave of the Patriarchs in Hebron. She does not, however, interrogate the consequences of this attack. The timing and circumstances convinced many Palestinians that the Israeli military was in collusion. Not only was Goldstein dressed in IDF reservist fatigues and brandishing an IDF-issued assault rifle, but the Israeli military on guard duty failed to intervene, despite being just outside the door. Another 19 Palestinians were killed by Israeli forces during the ensuing riots. Hamas, moreover, explicitly cites the Hebron massacre as the catalyst for its decision to start suicide attacks targeting Israeli civilians (Zuhur 2010, p. 55). Indeed, the first suicide bombings deliberately targeting civilians did not occur until 6 April 1994; in other words, 40 days, or the period of mourning in Islamic tradition, following the Hebron massacre (Milton-Edwards and Farrell 2010, pp. 78–80).

Furthering essentialist and Orientalist tendencies of traditional approaches to both Islam and terrorism is the idea of 'new terrorism' driven by existential, millenarian objectives rather than concrete real world concerns (Hoffman 2006, p. 94; Rapoport 2004; Lacquer 2003, p. 9). These movements are supposedly separated from the political sphere, unconcerned with popular support or governance, and thus their violence is more indiscriminate and deadly (Hoffman 2006, p. 39). This label has been applied to Hamas due to its Islamic orientation and promotes facile ahistorical generalisations which obscure real world grievances. The practical application of such labelling has clear policy implications.

By casting Hamas as a 'total spoiler' (Stedman 1997; Knudsen and Ezbidi 2007, p. 198) or "'zealots' ideologically incapable of compromise and intent on wrecking the peace process through violence" (Darby 2001, p. 48), the policy maker has little option but force. Indeed, Benjamin Barber's (2002, p. 242) assessment of Islamist groups, regardless of the difference between global jihadi franchises such as al-Qa'ida and localised national liberation movements such as Hamas, is that "their deeds are unspeakable, and their purposes can neither be rationalized nor negotiated.... The terrorists offer no terms and can be given none in exchange … bringing it to justice can only take the form of extirpation – root, trunk and branch." Hamas' participation in the 2005 municipal and 2006 legislative elections (not to mention prior participation in student and professional union elections) clearly contradicts these claims that Hamas is detached from temporal concerns, as does its social and charitable work within the community. Exaggerating the threat posed by terrorism for political purposes is by no means a new development, however; indeed, in 1977, John Bowyer-Bell (1977, pp. 476–477) commented: "The academic response to terrorism has been ahistorical, exaggerated and closely associated with congenial political postures."

Political violence emanating from Muslim socio-political movements is similarly framed within Orientalist notions pertaining to millenarianism, backwardness and religious fanaticism. In a dichotomy characteristic of Orientalist literature condemning religion and state-centric studies pertaining to 'new' terrorism, Hoffman (2006, p. 83) argues:

> terrorism motivated either in whole or in part by a religious imperative, where violence is regarded by its practitioners as a divine duty or sacramental act, embraces markedly different means of legitimation and justification than committed by secular terrorists, and these distinguishing features lead, in turn, to yet greater bloodshed and destruction.

Notwithstanding what exactly "in part" constitutes, Hoffman (2006, p. 83), and Lacquer (2003, p. 9) for that matter, neatly divide the world into 'secular' and 'religious' terrorists without discussing the utility or meaning of either label. The authors, in essence, establish secularism, and in particular the putative divide between religion and politics, as the normative approach to politics without investigating what this term might mean, if anything, when situated within divergent historical, cultural, political or economic environments.

Modernity and rationality

Orientalist tendencies and security-orientated approaches firmly entrench the notion that 'modernity' is synonymous with liberal democracy, market capitalism and, ultimately, Westernisation. As such, Orientalist literature tends to juxtapose an ostensibly unified, fundamentalist and regressive Islam with the progressive, liberal and 'rational' values of the West (Ayoob 2004; Tuastad 2003). By reducing Islamist actions to perverted religion or irrationality, defence of such thought becomes almost unthinkable, since, as Pierre Bourdieu (cited in Burgat 2003, p. xiii) points out,

> Who could possibly declare their support for butchers, rapists and murderers? Especially when those murderers are 'Islamic crazies', a description which brooks no consideration of history? Cloaked by the term 'Islamic extremism', they are hidden beneath this atavistic symbol of oriental fanaticisms. It is a term well suited for providing racist prejudice with an inscrutable alibi of legitimacy founded on ethical and secularist grounds.

Orientalism, 'modernity' and rationality, therefore, become the intellectual justification for Western policy, domination and interventions in the Middle East,

36 *Orientalism, Islam and militancy post 9/11*

including current policies towards the Hamas government and the siege of Gaza (Moaddel 2002, p. 362; Said 2003, p. 3).

European imperialism and American hegemony, however, have hardly provided liberalism or Westernised modernity with a glowing reputation among the everyday populaces of the Muslim Middle East, nor did they make any meaningful attempts at democratisation. Following decolonisation, in addition, European and American interests resulted in strategic agreements with a variety of highly unpopular dictatorial regimes which helped perpetuate the longevity of their rule (Khalidi 2005; Esposito 2012). The United States, for instance, provided Hosni Mubarak's kleptocracy in Egypt with political support and military aid for over 30 years until the Tahrir Square uprising became irrepressible in 2011. Similarly, Zine El Abidine Ben Ali's Tunisia enjoyed the patronage of France right up until he fled to Saudi Arabia during the 2011 Jasmine Revolution.

Conversely, the monarchies of Saudi Arabia and Bahrain, the largest oil producer in the world and home to the US Fifth Fleet respectively, managed to retain the support of the US in 2011 to 2012 despite their own violent crackdowns on anti-government demonstrations. Thus, in practice, the West has been largely complicit (although not to say strictly responsible) in stymieing democratic development in the Middle East and North Africa for decades, in spite of its rhetoric advocating democratisation. The populaces of the Middle East are well aware of the gap between Western rhetoric and the practical effects of Western foreign policy. The boycott of the elected Hamas government since 2006 has only served to highlight the hypocrisy of the West's selective endorsement of democracy. The speed with which the West normalised relations with Abdul-Fatah al-Sisi's regime in Egypt following the military coup against the elected Islamist president Mohammed Morsi in 2013, despite the massacre and imprisonment of thousands of Muslim Brotherhood supporters, is similarly reflective of the West's contingent commitment to democracy within the region.

The more nuanced approaches to Islamism centred on post-structuralism and post-colonial studies contend that it is a rearticulation of modernity within an endogenous framework (Esposito and Piscatori 1991; Burgat 2003, p. 50; Irving Jensen 1998, p. 212). This is a result of the failure of Western imported ideas which have come to be associated with de-culturalisation, colonialism and exploitation, as well as autocratic, corrupt and unpopular regimes (Said 1994, p. 224; Nusse 1998, p. 15; Juergensmeyer 2008, pp. 31–33). As such, Islamist thought is a conscious differentiation from the West that may be viewed as a reassertion of local identity or the redressing of local nationalism in an Islamic idiom (Pasha 2005, p. 544; Thurfjell 2008, p. 158; Burgat 2003, p. xiv). According to Ernest Gellner (1981, p. 5), "In Islam, purification/modernisation on the one hand, and the re-affirmation of a putative old *local* identity on the other, can be done in one and the same language and set of symbols." In this light, Islam acts as a set of guidelines or parameters interpreted according to the specific social, historical and political contexts of each movement.

A critical approach to 'terrorism'

With this in mind, this project largely adopts a critical approach to terrorism studies incorporating key components of post-structuralism, post-colonial studies, history, religion, anthropology and a critical approach to sub-state militancy (see Gunning 2009; Jackson *et al.* 2009). According to Robert Cox (1986, p. 208), engaging in critical scholarship means "to stand apart from the prevailing order of the world and ask how that came about", whereas " 'traditional' studies entail taking the world as it finds it, with the prevailing social and power relationships and the institutions into which they are organized, as the given framework for action". Jeroen Gunning and Harmonie Toros (2009) argue that the application of this critical approach to terrorism studies will lead to two key shifts in the field. The first entails:

> a process of *deepening*, of uncovering the ontological and ideological assumptions and interests behind terrorism studies, leading to a radical shift in how terrorism is to be conceived, as contextually constituted, rather than a timeless, objective category, and with humanity, not the state, as the central unit to be preserved.
>
> (Gunning and Toros 2009, p. 89)

The second involves the broadening of the field of inquiry to move beyond non-state political violence to incorporate the historical context, the impact of state violence, as well as the prevailing social, political and cultural milieux which may influence the movement in question (ibid., p. 89). To this end, this project seeks consciously to contextualise the actions, motivations and rationales of Hamas and the Islamic movement in the Palestinian Territories by incorporating historical, religious and anthropological sources to build upon post-colonial critiques of traditional scholarship.

This critical approach to terrorism studies was chosen because much of the existing literature pertaining to armed socio-political movements, political Islam and Islam itself, as demonstrated in the previous discussion, is of an essentialist nature lacking adequate context and, indeed, is often perceived as such by the supposed subjects under study. Over the course of my own fieldwork, multiple participants complained that interviews and studies conducted by foreign researchers were often less of a dialogue than a series of accusations which required defensive answers.[3] As a result, I have endeavoured to adopt what Roxanne Euben (1999, pp. 155–158) calls a "dialogic approach" whereby the researcher takes the comments and discourses of the cultural 'other' or interviewee as serious before analysing and potentially criticising their content. This entails accepting Islamism as a legitimate alternative space and discourse within which a wide segment of the Palestinian community centres and articulates itself, thereby 'provincialising' dominant Western discourses (Thurfjell 2008, p. 159).

My research is conceptualised as a subaltern socio-political ethnography which attempts to (critically) privilege endogenous Palestinian, and in particular

38 *Orientalism, Islam and militancy post 9/11*

Islamist, voices. First, this is to counter the traditional privileging of the Western and Israeli narratives regarding the question of Palestine (Pappé 2006, p. 6). Second is the fact that rhetoric and policy documents do not necessarily reflect the personal views of Hamas' constituents, supporters or even political representatives. Grandiose rhetoric, official policy documents and structural accounts do not necessarily relate to the quotidian experiences of the individual (Irving Jensen 1998, p. 199; Frenea in Burgat 1993, p. 3). As such, much of the original data for this project were acquired over the course of two periods of fieldwork in the Middle East, the bulk of which was spent in the Israeli-occupied West Bank, but also featured time in Jordan, Syria, Lebanon, Israel and Egypt respectively.

My aim is to refocus on the unique context of Hamas supporters, sympathisers and representatives at a local community level, away from the hyperbolic and essentialist discourses of the 'war on terror'. To this end, Hamas is a localised movement sensitive to the needs and welfare of its constituents with very specific localised goals, not an intangible, detached and abstract global phenomenon like al-Qa'ida (Gunning 2004, p. 244). To be precise, the focus of my research is the dialectic between Hamas and its constituents rather than the movement per se, because I would argue that the two are, in a sense, practically inseparable.

It is also important to note the predominantly verbal nature of Palestinian society and the currency – for better or worse – of rumours, conspiracy theories and popular wisdom, even among highly educated members of society. Clearly, in a society historically characterised by occupation, repression and frequent incarceration, the documentation of dissenting political opinions is not necessarily the norm in light of the potential negative repercussions which may result from such exposure. Indeed, James Scott (1990) argues that dominated societies produce 'hidden transcripts' which, in themselves, serve as a form of everyday resistance to oppression. As a result, the popular wisdom of the street is not necessarily verifiable through 'reliable' or 'scientific', documented, academic, governmental or journalistic sources. Nevertheless, popular wisdom and experiential knowledge do possess the capacity to influence political opinions (Shamir and Shikaki 2010, p. 37). Mansoor (survey 2010), for instance, an unaffiliated 20-year-old studying media at al-Quds University, cited 'daily life' as a primary source of his political information. Where possible I have endeavoured to include independent verification of accepted popular wisdom.

Religious or political?

Through Hamas, and political Islam in general, it is possible to discern the intertwining of politics and religion, deemed to be so problematic in the West because there has been an ostensible separation between religion and the state since the Peace of Westphalia in 1648, thereby resulting in secular governance. Thus, the melange of religion and politics, as espoused by Islamists, is often deemed 'illegitimate' in secular eyes and incompatible with democracy (Keane 2000, p. 29; Esposito 1999, pp. 257–258). Religion, therefore, is frequently used as a weapon by Hamas' enemies – including Fatah, certain members of the

Orientalism, Islam and militancy post 9/11   39

secular elite, Israel and the US – to internationally delegitimise Hamas and brand it as an al-Qa'ida-inspired entity allegedly concerned with eschatological jihad (see Said 1997; Mearsheimer and Walt 2007, p. 305).

In contrast, defenders of Hamas depict it as a political movement inspired by Islamic thought in a manner akin to Christian Democrat parties in Europe (albeit, of course, possessing an affiliated armed militia). Islamists, moreover, believe that Islam is a holistic, practical religion which regulates all of life, including politics (Irving Jensen 2009, p. 5). In addition, according to Palestinian journalist Khalid Amayreh (personal interview 2010), 'secularism' is often interpreted in the Middle East as a direct attack on Allah or inherently anti-theistic rather than the promotion of political plurality and the separation of religion and politics. Mariam Salah (personal interview 2010), the former Minister for Women's Affairs for the short-lived 'Hamas' government of 2006 to 2007 and Professor of *Sharia* Law at al-Quds University, likewise asserts that "The West wants to secularise our culture because, going back, they don't want anything called Islam". To this end, Salah (ibid.) continues, Western policies of 'secularisation' are seeking "the obliteration of the Islamic identity and the banishment of people from their religion".

Indicatively, there is no word for secularism in Arabic (Keane 2000, p. 35).[4] Hence, the term 'secular' is problematic in itself within the context of the Muslim Middle East, especially as it is often associated with unpopular, autocratic and corrupt regimes propped up by a variety of major Western powers (Tamimi 2000, p. 28; Burgat 2003, p. 127). In effect,

> secularity has won a reputation for humiliating Muslims – humiliating them through the exercise of Western double standards in Kuwait, Algeria and Palestine, through the corrupt despotism of comprador governments, and through the permanent threat of being crushed by the economic, technological, political, cultural and military might of the American-led West.
>
> (Keane 2000, p. 36)

In contrast to secular movements, Islamists derive much of their political thought from Islamic texts, especially the *Qur'an*, the *sunnah* and *hadith* (the sayings and actions of the Prophet Mohammed). For Islamists, the holy texts provide a framework to interpret, legitimate and guide their actions in the temporal world. Indeed, while it is clear that many of its supporters and sympathisers are inspired by its religious foundation, Hamas' primary goals are 'secular' or temporal in nature. According to Hafez Shaheen (personal interview 2010), then Deputy Mayor of Nablus for Planning and Technical Affairs representing the Hamas-backed Change and Reform party list, and Professor of Engineering at an-Najah National University,

> The Palestinian has two motivations. He has ... the political motivation which is the Palestinian case that he should care of and, of course, in Islam, you are asked to take care of the political interests of the Muslims.

40 *Orientalism, Islam and militancy post 9/11*

Notwithstanding the definitional problems with secularism in Arabic described above, surveys (respondents n=96) conducted with university students at an-Najah, Birzeit and al-Quds universities from March to May 2010 suggest that perceptions of Hamas as a religious movement are split among the Palestinian youth. Critics, especially those indicating a preference for Fatah, allege that Hamas utilises religion as a mask or a symbolic façade with which to pursue its own interests. Nevertheless, a slim majority of 50.5 per cent believe that Hamas is a religious movement, whereas 37.9 per cent assert the opposite. The remaining 11.6 per cent professed ambivalence.

Undoubtedly, however, Hamas utilises religious rhetoric to buttress, popularise and legitimise its political positions. Indeed, one of Hamas' more controversial strategies has been to utilise *fatwas* (religious edicts) disseminated through its *da'wa* arm and the mosques to legitimise its actions and mobilise the masses (Barghouti 2007, p. 52). Thus, according to Nuh (survey 2010), a 21-year-old history student, Hamas "uses religion, employs it, embodies it, and customises it in order to achieve what it seeks".

It is, however, important to distinguish between official ideologies and political programmes. This is variously described as the "tension between fundamental and operative ideologies", the difference between material and symbolic lenses, and the divergence between intellectual structure and political programmes (Seliger 1970; Harb and Leenders 2005; Klein 2007, p. 443). The distinction is necessary because, often, dogmatic ideologies are not applicable to political realities. Hence, while, ideologically, Hamas advocates a variety of Islamist reforms, such as the implementation of an Islamic state based on *sharia* law, its political programme is focused on policies of social justice, anti-corruption and efficient governance (Hroub 2006, pp. 10–11; Klein 2007, p. 441). In essence, Hamas juxtaposes the intellectual with the political which concomitantly allows the preservation of principles and the ability to deal with quotidian exigencies relating to institutional survival (Mishal and Sela 2000, p. 13). In other words, Hamas' political platforms, and indeed other political documents published since its inception, differ markedly from its 1988 charter (Klein 2009, p. 891). To this end, Khaled Hroub (2006) contends that Hamas' charter should be viewed as a historical rather than a political document.

It is also important to recognise that both ideologies and political programmes are dynamic rather than static (Snow and Byrd 2007, p. 121). As US Specially Designated Global Terrorist and Deputy Head of the Political Bureau, Mousa Abu Marzouq (personal interview 2010), points out: "ideological thoughts must not collide with reality. So, when you think about them, you must think logically. Hence, pragmatism exists even in the ideology of the movement." Indeed, Hamas leaders and affiliates depict it as a fundamentally political movement consisting of religious people with sometimes divergent ideological and political aims. Ibrahim (survey 2010), a 22-year-old student politician and part of *al-Qutla al-Islamiyya* (the Islamic Bloc) at Birzeit University near Ramallah, likewise asserts that:

From a theocratic point of view, Hamas is not a religious party. But it is an organisation that includes religious members. Hamas believes in the Islamic reference in life, and this is important in the situation, time and location.

To this end, most of Hamas' leaders are not religious authorities as such, but pious individuals often educated in highly specialised temporal fields including engineering, medicine and education. In other words, Hamas leaders are lay preachers with little formal religious training. As Beverley Milton-Edwards (1996, p. 127) explains, Hamas' "religiosity and spirituality is realised through a path that is political rather than metaphysical".

Conclusions

This chapter has explored and offered critiques of Orientalist meta-discourses and security-orientated approaches to Islam, Hamas and sub-state political violence in general, especially within the context of the 'war on terror'. These approaches are often of an essentialist nature and have a tendency to demonise and homogenise a diverse array of actors possessing differing ideologies, methods and goals. The combined application of Orientalist and terrorist labels to Hamas is not merely an abstract concern but also engenders practical, temporal ramifications. The term 'terrorist', for instance, is a notoriously pejorative term; one of its primary purposes being to identify and designate actors as 'illegitimate' because 'We don't negotiate with terrorists'. Indeed, according to Mark Juergensmeyer (2001, p. 9), "The designation of terrorism is a subjective judgement about the legitimacy of certain violent acts as much as it is a descriptive statement about them."

The spectre of terrorism has also been invoked to justify myriad political and military responses, not only motivating full-fledged wars abroad but also justifying the curtailment of civil liberties at home, among others. As Robert Fisk (2005, p. 378) points out, "'Terrorism' is a word that has become a plague on our vocabulary, the excuse and reason and moral permit for state sponsored violence." The 'terrorist' label, in addition, belies the complexity of multi-faceted socio-political movements such as Hamas, which not only comprise an armed wing, but also a political organisation, wider community-orientated social projects and, indeed, a de facto government in the Gaza Strip.

Orientalist tendencies anchoring contemporary phenomena in antiquity, and which have flourished since the 11 September attacks, have only served to compound the putative problems associated with studies on terrorism. The combination of Orientalist tendencies depicting static ideologue movements and terrorism-orientated approaches has the propensity to engender self-fulfilling prophecies. According to many mainstream authors, Islamist 'terrorists' are driven by millenarian concerns rejecting 'modernity' which render them inherently unmalleable to negotiations and compromise. Faced with such an entity, the policy maker is left with little option but force. Thus, a tautology ensues: the movement is defined in advance as being unamenable to negotiation or

42 *Orientalism, Islam and militancy post 9/11*

compromise, so there is no attempt to negotiate, therefore resulting in violence. As such, the application of Orientalist and terrorist labels is deeply limiting in terms of constructive engagement between competing adversaries.

This project, in contrast, adopts a critical approach to Islamism which situates Hamas at a local level within its historical, cultural and socio-political contexts. Any analysis of ideology and socio-political activism should be contextualised and situated within its historical, temporal and cultural environment. Indeed, the *Qur'an* itself is considered to be *hammalu awjuhin*, that is to say, "a bearer of diverse interpretations" (Khalidi 2008, pp. x–xi). As such, Hamas is a product of its circumstances. Hamas is a localised, popularly driven grassroots movement primarily concerned with temporal goals seeking to improve the living conditions of Palestinian society. It is heterogeneous in nature and supported by large and varying segments of the Palestinian community. To this end, Hamas should not be homogenised, essentialised and conflated with al-Qa'ida-inspired transnational militarism. Specifically, there is no one Hamas as such. Hamas is a political movement. Yet Hamas is also a social movement. There is Hamas the militant actor, and Hamas the ideology. This project investigates, contextualises and analyses these multi-variant aspects of the movement framed within the concepts of resistance and jihad. In brief, this work seeks to critically highlight the human aspect of knowledge and Islamic socio-political activism in the Palestinian Territories.

Notes

1 If we consider NATO's air campaign in Libya in 2011, ironically, Blair must be referring to anti-Gaddafi forces in light of the fact that Libya's relations with the West, and the UK in particular, were well and truly normalised at the time this was written.
2 While, however, Israel has repeatedly been the target of various UN bodies, this had produced very few tangible effects on the ground.
3 It was clear, on occasion, that certain lines of questioning (for example, how literally *sharia* law should be interpreted and the role of armed resistance in inter-factional rivalry) had the capacity to perturb some respondents as evidenced by marked changes in tone of voice, facial expression and/or body language. I attributed these changes as a reaction to what may have been perceived as Western accusations of backwardness, tribalism and barbarity.
4 There is a neologism *'alamaniyah* which derives its roots from the Arabic word for world (*'alam*), developed by a Christian Lebanese scholar, Boutrus al-Bustani, at the end of the nineteenth century. The literal translation *la diniyah* or non-religious is not considered applicable to Islam because Islam does not strictly differentiate between the temporal and spiritual planes.

References

Abrahamian, E. 2003. 'The US Media, Huntington and September 11'. *Third World Quarterly* 24(3): 529–544.

Abu Marzouq, M. 2006. 'What Hamas is Seeking'. *Washington Post*, 31 January.

Abunimah, A. 2012. 'New York Times Ad Accuses BDS Movement, College Professors of Inciting Murder of Jewish Children'. *Electronic Intifada*, 24 April.

Alam, M.S. 2002. 'Bernard Lewis and the New Orientalism: Scholarship or Sophistry?' *Studies in Contemporary Islam* 4: 51–78.

Araj, B. and Brym, R. 2010. 'Opportunity, Culture and Agency: Influence on Fatah and Hamas Strategic Action during the Second Intifada'. *International Sociology* 25(6): 842–868.

Ayoob, M. 2004. 'Political Islam: Image and Reality'. *World Policy Journal* 1–14.

Barber, B. 2002. 'On Globalization'. In *The Democracy Reader*, edited by S. Meyers. New York: IDEA.

Barghouti, I. 2007. *Religion and State in Palestine*. Ramallah: Ramallah Centre for Human Rights.

Bayoumi, M. 2012. 'Fear and Loathing of Islam'. *The Nation* (USA), 2–9 July.

Berman, D. 2011. 'The Revered and Reviled Bernard Lewis: A Retrospective of the Scholar Who Provided the Intellectual Ammunition for the Iraq War'. *Moment*, September/October.

Black, A. 2001. *The History of Islamic Political Thought: From the Prophet to the Present*. Edinburgh: Edinburgh University Press.

Blair, T. 2007. 'A Battle for Global Values'. *Foreign Affairs*, January/February.

Bourdieu, P. 1998. *Contre-feux: Propos pour servir à la résistance contre l'invasion néo-libérale*. Paris: Liber – Raisons d'Agir.

Bowyer-Bell, John. 1977. 'Trends of Terror: The Analysis of Political Violence'. *World Politics*, 29 April.

Brannan, D.W., Elser, P.F. and Anders Stringberg, N.T. 2001. 'Talking to "Terrorists": Towards an Independent Analytical Framework for the Study of Violent Substate Activism'. *Research on Terrorism* 24(3): 3–24.

B'tselem. 2010. *By Hook and by Crook: Israel's Settlement Policy in the West Bank*. Jerusalem: Israeli Information Centre for Human Rights in the Occupied Territories.

Burgat, F. 1993. *The Islamic Movement in North Africa*. Austin: University of Texas Press.

Burgat, F. 2003. *Face to Face with Political Islam*. London: I.B. Tauris.

Burgat, F. 2004. 'Les courants Islamistes contemporains entre «dénominateur commun identitaire» et internationalisation de la résistance à un ordre mondialise'. *Revue Mouvements* 36: 77–88.

Bush, G.W. 2001. War on Terror Speech. 20 September.

Butler, J. 2003. 'No, It's Not Anti-Semitic'. *London Review of Books* 25(16).

Cox, R. 1986. 'Social Forces, States and World Order: Beyond International Relations Theory'. In *Neorealism and its Critics* edited by R. Keohane. New York: Columbia University Press.

Cronin, A. 2009. *How Terrorism Ends: Understanding the Decline and Demise of Terrorist Campaigns*. Princeton, NJ: Princeton University Press.

Darby, J. 2001. *The Effects of Violence on Peace Processes*. Washington, DC: US Institute of Peace Press.

Esposito, J. 1999. *The Islamic Threat: Myth or Reality?* New York: Oxford University Press.

Esposito, J. 2012. 'Romney's Approach to Foreign Policy: "Deja vu All Over Again?"' *al-Jazeera*, 10 October.

Esposito, J. and Piscatori, J. 1991. 'Democratization and Islam'. *Middle East Journal* 45(3): 427–440.

Euben, R. 1999. *Enemy in the Mirror: Islamic Fundamentalism and the Limits of Modern Rationalism*. Princeton, NJ: Princeton University Press.

Fernandez, B. 2011. *Thomas Friedman: The Imperial Messenger*. New York: Verso.

44 *Orientalism, Islam and militancy post 9/11*

Fisk, R. 2005. *The Great War for Civilization: The Conquest of the Middle East*. New York: Alfred A. Knopf.

Friedman, T. 2002. *Longitudes and Attitudes: Exploring the World after September 11*. New York: Farrar, Strauss, Giroux.

Friedman, T. 2003. 'Hold Your Applause'. *New York Times*, 3 April.

Fukuyama, F. 2001. 'The West Has Won'. *Guardian* (United Kingdom), 11 October.

Fukuyama, F. 2006. *The End of History and the Last Man*. New York: Free Press.

Gellner, E. 1981. *Muslim Society*. Cambridge: Cambridge University Press.

Gold, D. (ed.). 2007. *Iran, Hizbullah, Hamas and the Global Jihad*. Jerusalem: Jerusalem Centre for Public Affairs.

Greenwald, G. 2012. 'NYPD Spying Program Aimed at Muslims'. *Salon*, 22 February.

Grenier, R. 2012. 'Islamophobia and the Republican Party'. *al-Jazeera*, 25 July.

Gresh, A. 2005. 'Malevolent Fantasy of Islam'. *Le Monde Diplomatique*, August.

Gunning, J. 2004. 'Peace with Hamas? The Transforming Potential of Political Participation'. *International Affairs* 80(2): 233–255.

Gunning, J. 2007a. 'Hamas: Socialization and the Logic of Compromise'. In *Terror, Insurgency and the State: Ending Protracted Conflicts*, edited by B. O'Leary, J. Tirman and M. Heiberg. Philadelphia: University of Pennsylvania Press.

Gunning, J. 2007b. *Hamas in Politics: Democracy, Religion, Violence*. London: Hurst & Company.

Gunning, J. 2009. 'A Case for Critical Terrorism Studies?' *Government and Opposition* 42(3): 363–393.

Gunning, J. and Toros, H. 2009. 'Exploring a Critical Theory Approach to Terrorism Studies'. In *Critical Terrorism Studies: A New Research Agenda*, edited by R. Jackson, M. Smyth and J. Gunning. London: Routledge.

Harb, M. and Leenders, R. 2005. 'Know Thy Enemy: Hizbullah, Terrorism and the Politics of Perception'. *Third World Quarterly* 26(1): 173–197.

Herman, E. and Chomsky, N. 2002. *Manufacturing Consent/Content: The Political Economy of the Mass Media*. New York: Pantheon Books.

Hirsh, M. 2004. 'Bernard Lewis Revisited'. *The Washington Monthly*, November.

Hoffman, B. 2006. *Inside Terrorism*. New York: Columbia University Press.

Horgan, J. 2004. 'The Case for Firsthand Research'. In *Research in Terrorism: Trends, Achievements and Failures*, edited by A. Silke. London: Frank Cass.

Hroub, K. 2000. *Hamas: Political Thought and Practice*. Washington, DC: Institute of Palestine Studies.

Hroub, K. 2006. 'A "New Hamas" Through its New Documents'. *Journal of Palestine Studies* 35(4): 6–27.

Huntington, S. 1998. *The Clash of Civilizations and the Remaking of World Order*. New York: Simon & Schuster.

Illardi, J.G. 2004. 'The Future of Terrorism Research and the Search for Empathy'. In *Research in Terrorism: Trends, Achievements and Failures*, edited by A. Silke. London: Frank Cass.

Irving Jensen, M. 1998. 'Islamism and Civil Society in the Gaza Strip'. In *Islamic Fundamentalism: Myths and Realities*, edited by A.S. Moussalli. Ithaca, NY: Ithaca Press.

Irving Jensen, M. 2009. *The Political Ideology of Hamas: A Grassroots Perspective*. London: I.B. Tauris.

ITIC. 2005. *'Charity' and Palestinian Terrorism – Spotlight on Hamas-run al-Tadahmun Charitable Society in Nablus, Special Information Bulletin*. Israel: Intelligence and Terrorism Information Centre.

Jackson, R., Smyth, M.B. and Gunning, J. (eds). 2009. *Critical Terrorism Studies: A New Research Agenda*. London: Routledge.

Jones, O. 2012. 'Islamophobia – for Muslims, Read Jews, and Be Shocked'. *Independent* (United Kingdom), 13 July.

Juergensmeyer, M. 2001. *Terror in the Mind of God: The Global Rise of Religious Violence*. Berkeley: University of California Press.

Juergensmeyer, M. 2008. *Global Rebellion: Religious Challenges to the Secular State from Christian Militias to al Qaeda*. Berkeley: University of California Press.

Kaplan, R. 2000. *The Coming Anarchy*. New York: Random House.

Keane, J. 2000. 'The Limits of Secularism'. In *Islam and Secularism in the Middle East*, edited by J. Esposito and A. Tamimi. London: Hurst & Company.

Khalidi, R. 2005. *Resurrecting Empire: Western Footprints and America's Perilous Path in the Middle East*. Boston, MA: Beacon Press.

Khalidi, R. 2008. 'Introduction'. In *The Qur'an*, translated and edited by T. Khalidi. London: Penguin Books.

Klein, M. 2007. 'Hamas in Power'. *The Middle East Journal* 61(3): 442–459.

Klein, M. 2009. 'Against the Consensus: Oppositionist Voices in Hamas'. *Middle Eastern Studies* 45(6): 881–892.

Knudsen, A. and Ezbidi, B. 2007. 'Hamas and Palestinian Statehood'. In *Where Now for Palestine? The Demise of the Two-state Solution*, edited by J. Hilal. London: Zed Books.

Kramer, M. 2001. *Ivory Towers on Sand: The Failure of Middle Eastern Studies in America*. Washington, DC: Washington Institute for Near East Studies.

Lacquer, W. 2003. *No End to War: Terrorism in the Twenty-first Century*. New York: Continuum.

Levitt, M. 2006. *Hamas: Politics, Charity and Terrorism in the Service of Jihad*. New Haven, CT: Yale University Press.

Lewis, B. 1990. 'The Roots of Muslim Rage'. *The Atlantic Monthly*, September.

Lewis, B. 2002. *What Went Wrong? The Clash between Islam and Modernity in the Middle East*. London: Weidenfeld & Nicolson.

McCarthy, R. 2008. 'We Can Accept Israel as Neighbour, Says Hamas'. *Guardian* (United Kingdom), 21 April.

Mearsheimer, J. and Walt, S. 2007. *The Israel Lobby and U.S. Foreign Policy*. New York: Farrer, Strauss, Giroux.

Miles, O. 2004. 'Lewis Gun'. *Guardian* (United Kingdom), 17 July.

Milton-Edwards, B. 1996. *Islamic Politics in Palestine*. London: I.B. Tauris.

Milton-Edwards, B. 2011. 'Islam and Violence'. In *The Blackwell Companion to Religion and Violence*, edited by A. Murphy. Chichester: Wiley-Blackwell.

Milton-Edwards, B. and Farrell, S. 2010. *Hamas: The Islamic Resistance Movement*. Cambridge: Polity Press.

Mishal, K. 2006. 'We Will Not Sell Our People and Principles for Foreign Aid'. *Guardian* (United Kingdom), 31 January.

Mishal, S. and Sela, A. 2000. *The Palestinian Hamas: Vision, Violence and Coexistence*. New York: Columbia University Press.

Moaddel, M. 2002. 'The Study of Islamic Culture and Politics: An Overview and Assessment'. *Annual Review of Sociology* 28: 359–386.

Mueller, J. 2005. 'Six Rather Unusual Propositions About Terrorism'. *Terrorism and Political Violence* 17(4): 487–505.

Muir, W. and Weir, T.H. 1912 [1861]. *The Life of Mohammed from Original Sources*. Edinburgh: John Grant.

46 *Orientalism, Islam and militancy post 9/11*

Nusse, A. 1998. *Muslim Palestine: The Ideology of Hamas.* Amsterdam: Harwood Academic Publishers.

O'Leary, B. and Silke, A. 2007. 'Bridging Research and Policy'. In *Terror, Insurgency and the State: Ending Protracted Conflicts,* edited by M. Heiberg, B. O'Leary and J. Tirman. Philadelphia: University of Pennsylvania Press.

O'Leary, B. and Tirman, J. 2007. 'Thinking about Durable Political Violence'. In *Terror, Insurgency and the State: Ending Protracted Conflicts,* edited by M. Heiberg, B. O'Leary and J. Tirman. Philadelphia: University of Pennsylvania Press.

Pappé, I. 2006. *A History of Modern Palestine: One Land, Two Peoples.* Cambridge: Cambridge University Press.

Pasha, M.K. 2005. 'Islam, "Soft" Orientalism and Hegemony: A Gramscian Rereading'. *Critical Review of International Social and Political Philosophy* 8(4): 543–558.

Pipes, D. 2008. 'Foreword'. In *Hamas vs. Fatah: The Struggle for Palestine,* by J. Schanzer. New York: Palgrave Macmillan.

Powell, M. 2012. 'Police Monitoring and a Climate of Fear'. *New York Times,* 27 February.

Rapoport, D. 2004. 'The Four Waves of Modern Terrorism'. In *Attacking Terrorism: Elements of Grand Strategy,* edited by A. Cronin and J.M. Ludes. Washington, DC: Georgetown University Press.

Ravid, B. 2008. 'In 2006 Letter to Bush, Haniyeh Offered Compromise with Israel'. *Ha'aretz* (Israel), 14 November.

Ross, D. 2006. 'Foreword'. In *Hamas: Politics, Charity and Terrorism in the Service of Jihad,* by M. Levitt. New Haven, CT: Yale University Press.

Roy, S. 2007. *Failing Peace: Gaza and the Palestinian–Israeli Conflict.* London: Pluto Press.

Saad-Ghrorayeb, A. 2002. *Hizb'ullah: Politics and Religion.* London: Pluto Press.

Said, E. 1992. *The Question of Palestine.* New York: Vintage Books.

Said, E. 1994. *Culture and Imperialism.* New York: Vintage Books.

Said, E. 1997. *Covering Islam: How the Media and the Experts Determine How we See the Rest of the World.* New York: Vintage Books.

Said, E. 2001. 'The Clash of Ignorance'. *The Nation* (USA), 4 October.

Said, E. [1978] 2003. *Orientalism.* New York: Vintage Books.

Schmidt, A. and Jongman, A. 1988. *Political Terrorism: A New Guide to Actors, Authors, Concepts, Databases, Theories and Literature.* New York: Transaction Books.

Scott, J. 1990. *Domination and the Arts of Resistance: Hidden Transcripts.* London: Yale University Press.

Seliger, M. 1970. 'Fundamental and Operative Ideology: The Two Principal Dimensions of Political Argumentation'. *Policy Sciences* 1(1): 325–338.

Shamir, J. and Shikaki, K. 2010. *Palestinian and Israeli Public Opinion: The Public Imperative in the Second Intifada.* Bloomington: Indiana University Press.

Silke, A. 2004. 'An Introduction to Terrorism Research'. In *Research on Terrorism: Trends, Achievements, and Failures,* edited by A. Silke. London: Frank Cass.

Snow, D. and Byrd, S. 2007. 'Ideology, Framing Processes, and Islamic Terrorist Movements'. *Mobilization: An International Quarterly* 12(2): 199–136.

Stedman, S. 1997. 'Spoiler Problems in Peace Processes'. *International Security* 22(2): 5–53.

Tamimi, A. 2000. 'The Origins of Arab Secularism'. In *Islam and Secularism in the Middle East,* edited by J. Esposito and A. Tamimi. London: Hurst & Company.

Thurfjell, D. 2008. 'Is the Islamist Voice Subaltern?' In *Neither East nor West: Post-colonial Essays on Literature, Culture and Religion*, edited by K. Shands. Elanders, Sweden: Sodertorns Hogskola.

Tuastad, D. 2003. 'Neo-Orientalism and the New Barbarism Thesis: Aspects of Symbolic Violence in the Middle East Conflict(s)'. *Third World Quarterly* 24(4): 591–599.

Waldman, P. 2004. 'A Historian's Take on Islam Steers US in Terrorism Fight'. *Wall Street Journal* (New York), 3 February.

Walzer, M. 2009. 'Is the Two State Solution Viable after Gaza?' *Dissent*, 3 March.

Weisberg, J. 2007. 'AEI's Weird Celebration'. *Slate Magazine*, 14 March.

Weymouth, L. 2006. 'We Do Not Wish to Throw Them into the Sea' (Interview with Ismail Haniyeh). *Washington Post*, 26 February.

Yousef, A. 2007. 'Open Letter to the Secretary of State'. *New York Times*, 10 December.

Zuhur, S. 2010. *Hamas and Israel: Conflicting Strategies of Group-based Politics*. Carlisle, PA: Strategic Studies Institute.

Interviews and surveys

Abu Marzouq, M., Deputy Head of the Hamas Political Bureau, US Specially Designated Global Terrorist and Doctor of Engineering. Damascus, May 2010.

Amayreh, K., Palestinian Freelance Journalist, Dura, January 2010.

Ibrahim, a 22-year-old student politician involved with *al-Qutla al-Islamiyya* (the Islamic Bloc) at Birzeit University, anonymous survey, Birzeit University, Birzeit, April 2010.

Mansoor, an unaffiliated 20-year-old studying media, anonymous survey, al-Quds University, Abu Dis, May 2010.

Nuh, a 21-year-old studying history at Birzeit University, anonymous survey, Birzeit, April 2010.

Salah, M., former Islamist Minister for Women's Affairs, elected PLC Deputy, and Professor of *Sharia* Law at al-Quds University, Ramallah, May 2010.

Shaheen, H., then Deputy Mayor of Nablus for Planning and Technical Affairs, local councillor for Change and Reform, and Professor of Engineering at an-Najah National University. Nablus, March/April 2010.

2 The 'lesser' jihad

Armed resistance

> Fight in the cause of God those who fight you, but do not commit aggression:
> God loves not the aggressors.... Whoever commits aggression against you, retaliate against him in the same measure as he committed against you.
>
> *The Qur'an* (2:190–194)

> Armed resistance must stem from Islamic guidance.... We should go back to our Islamic values to fight the occupation. – Yasmin, a 20-year-old Hamas supporter studying IT.
>
> (survey 2010)

Hamas and political violence are often treated as synonymous in mainstream Western discourses. Hamas, however, prefers to depict its violence as a defensive jihad or resistance against a foreign occupier. As such, it is necessary to situate Hamas' use of political violence within the context of occupation. Indeed, political violence perpetrated by Hamas does not occur in a vacuum and is primarily, although not exclusively, a result of a long history of foreign occupation, violent repression and the continued expropriation of Palestinian land. Thus, it is important to investigate the reasons why Hamas chooses to employ political violence rather than the all-too-often resort to facile ahistorical generalisations or Orientalist characterisations of pathological religious hatred. Political violence is usually motivated by practical, symbolic and psychological imperatives.

First, this chapter seeks to situate Hamas' use of political violence within the context of foreign domination. In short, how do Palestinians perceive the occupation? And how does this affect Palestinian support for armed resistance?

The second section details the creation of Hamas by the Palestinian branch of the Muslim Brotherhood (*al-Ikhwan al-Muslimun*) and its subsequent turn to violence during the first intifada. In essence, why did a hitherto predominantly non-violent movement turn to militant activism? What catalysts prompted this change?

Moreover, why does Hamas engage in armed resistance against an enemy that it has no chance of defeating militarily? What purposes does it serve? What are the practical effects of armed resistance? To this end, this chapter explores the

The 'lesser' jihad: armed resistance   49

instrumental value of armed resistance, its use as armed propaganda and its role in inter-factional competition. The perceived efficacy of armed resistance is investigated in relation to Israel's unilateral withdrawal from the Gaza Strip in 2005.

This chapter should not be construed as condoning political violence but, rather, as an attempt to understand, analyse and explain the motivation, intent and causes behind Hamas militancy. It will then extrapolate from this to examine the extent to which such actions have the capacity to elicit popular support and legitimacy.

The occupation

Violence and the threat of violence are omnipresent in the Palestinian Territories. From the highly visible and humiliating checkpoints to the arsonist settler 'price tag' campaign, the presence of Israelis on the ground in the West Bank is constantly in evidence.[1] From time to time, one will encounter the acrid scent of burning tyres from behind which Palestinian youths hurl rocks, while slightly older Israeli soldiers target them with tear gas and rubber-coated steel bullets. Even in the comfort of one's home, the supersonic passages of fighter jets roaring overhead, unseen, periodically cause the windows to rattle and jump around in their frames. In isolated Gaza, this unseen threat frequently materialises in more concrete and destructive forms on the ground. The pervasiveness of the occupation is perpetually present whether it is seen, felt, heard or smelt. As such, a constant reminder of violence and power manifests itself continually within the quotidian lives of the Palestinian population, a depressing reminder of their own powerlessness. Violence is not an aberration in the Palestinian Territories but is interwoven into the fabric of everyday life (Makdisi 2010; Allen 2008; Swedenburg 1995, p. 34). And yet life goes on, young couples get married, babies are born and children grow up and go to school; all small acts of resistance to foreign domination (see e.g. Junka 2006).

Indeed, as Michel Foucault ([1976] 1990, p. 95) points out, "Where there is power, there is resistance, and yet, or rather consequently, this resistance is never in a position of exteriority in relation to power." In the Palestinian case, resistance is primarily a reaction to Israeli power exercised in the form of occupation, domination and repression. According to Hamas, moreover, armed jihad is conceived as a purely defensive measure. Khalid Mishal (cited in Crooke 2009, p. 204), Head of the Hamas Political Bureau, explains,

> We engage in struggle, jihad, resistance against the enemy who steals our land and destroys our houses, commits sacrilegious acts against our holy places, assaults children and woman and kills people. It is our normal, natural right to resist, to struggle against them. All the laws given by God, and international law, give us this right. So, jihad is a response to aggression; it does not initiate aggression.... It should not be directed against peaceful peoples – such aggression is not permitted in Islam.

50 *The 'lesser' jihad: armed resistance*

In order to analyse Palestinian public support for armed resistance and its capacity to attract popular support, it is necessary to understand the way in which Palestinians perceive the occupation and the underlying tenets of the Palestinian condition. The overwhelming dynamics of the Palestinian condition are feelings of frustration, humiliation and disillusionment. Much of this sentiment stems from the Israeli occupation and a history of dispossession. Laila, a 31-year-old American-educated businesswoman (personal communication 2010), describes the occupation within the context of the first intifada as follows:

> As a child, you can't comprehend the occupation. It was just a monster waiting to take your father, shoot your brother, imprison your uncle ... I literally can't think of any family I knew at the time that hasn't had a 'real' taste of the occupation one way or another.

Dr Eyad Sarraj (2002, p. 72), a leading Palestinian psychiatrist, civil society proponent and founder of the Gaza Community Mental Health Programme, likewise cites studies showing that "55% of [Palestinian] children had witnessed their fathers being humiliated or beaten by Israeli soldiers" during the first intifada. In a more contemporary setting, Palestinian journalist Khalid Amayreh (personal interview 2010) asserts that:

> the Israeli occupation of late is designed to limit Palestinian horizons and make Palestinians contemplate reality, or at least to cause in the hearts of the Palestinian people that they are a defeated people and they have no other choice but succumbing to the Israeli whim. This is why resistance is going to continue to be inevitable and inescapable, because of the Israeli action.... It is almost an instinctive desire.

While the occupation is often used as a scapegoat or excuse for other problems, it is undoubtedly pervasive and regulates much of Palestinian existence, including fundamental human rights such as freedom of movement and association but also more basic needs, including (limiting) access to water and electricity (Hass 2012; Randles and Alqasis 2012). As such, Palestinian resistance must be placed within the context of resistance to occupation and repression, as well as an acute sense of dislocation, dispossession, honour and humiliation (Said 1992; Schulz and Hammer 2003, p. 106). Often analyses of non-state resistance – and armed non-state resistance in particular – elide the role of governmental or military authorities in fomenting this resistance (Gunning 2007, p. 15). In the case of the Palestinian Territories, the overarching power is the Israeli military apparatus, since it exclusively controls some 60 per cent of the West Bank, including its airspace, borders and water supplies, routinely violates the 'sovereignty' of PA administered areas (approximately 17 per cent of the West Bank; see Map 2.1), and essentially wields a veto on PA decisions, especially those pertaining to security (Morris 2001, p. 628). As a result, Palestinians perceive Israel to be the main source of their misery. According to Palestinian Professor of Political

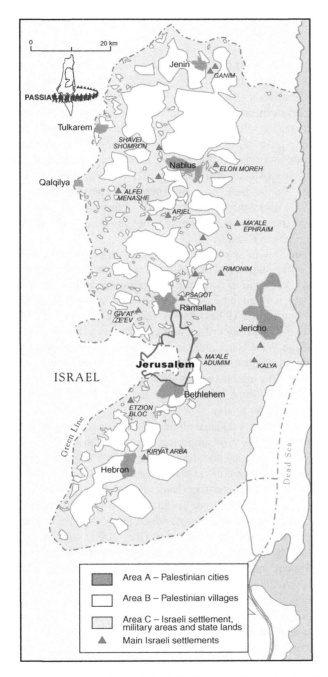

Map 2.1 West Bank and Oslo II, 1995 (source: Reproduced with permission of the Palestinian Academic Society for the Study of International Affairs (PASSIA)).

52 *The 'lesser' jihad: armed resistance*

Science Sameer Hammoudeh (personal interview 2009), there is a view among Palestinians that one cannot separate the occupation from other matters such as societal and institutional malaise.

Increasingly, however, the traditional post-1967/1968 Palestinian leadership, as embodied by the PA and the PLO, has been identified as a co-culprit for the stagnation of Palestinian society and its failure to realise Palestinian national and economic aspirations. There is a growing disconnect – both ideational and financially – between the Western-backed Palestinian leadership and their putative constituents on the street (Roy 2007, pp. 71–72; Haddad 2007). This phenomenon pre-dates the first intifada, manifested itself in opposition to the Oslo Accords, continued throughout the Arafat-era and culminated in Hamas' victory in the 2006 PLC elections (McGeough 2009, p. 62; Farsoun and Aruri 2006, p. 208; Shikaki 2006). In the past, as Laila (personal communication 2010) explains, "they [the PLO] spoke the unified language of the struggle and occupation. Now, even the way they address the people is not something that an average person comprehends or gets touched by."

For many Palestinians, Fatah abandoned the fundamental principle of resistance and the PA was either duped by, or complicit with, the Israeli occupation. There is, in a sense, a perception of a double occupation, whereby the PA, and by association Fatah, is perceived to be Israel's policeman in the Palestinian Territories (Bryne 2009). During the 1990s, the PA cracked down on both Islamist and leftist opposition to the Oslo Accords, a process that has only intensified following the division of the West Bank and Gaza in 2007. These crackdowns are deeply unpopular among the Palestinian community which prizes the concept of Palestinian unity (*itihad*). Mu'minah (survey 2010), for instance, a 20-year-old Hamas supporter, explains: "Some events make me hate Fatah because they threw almost all of my family in prison."

Israeli intransigence and Fatah's reliance on the United States to secure Palestinian national rights are arguably the most important factors which led to the start of the second intifada, thereby sidelining and discrediting Fatah's 'narrative of negotiation' and pushing Hamas' 'narrative of resistance' back to the forefront of Palestinian politics. The outbreak of this second uprising may be interpreted as a product of 'relative deprivation' (see Gurr 1978, pp. 22–58) and thwarted expectations following the optimism of the Oslo peace process, which many Palestinians believed would lead to an independent state within five years (Roy 2002; Khan 2008, p. 36; Salah 2009; Sayre 2010). By March 2004 – that is to say, three and a half years into the second intifada – Hamas' resistance credentials placed it ahead of Fatah in the polls for the first time: 31 to 28 per cent (Brym and Araj 2006, p. 855).

An embrace by Israel and the United States is often a liability in the Palestinian polity, as it is throughout the wider Middle East and North Africa region. Indeed, Zogby polling in 2002 and 2004 found that hostility towards the US had increased during this period. In 2002,

> 76 percent of Egyptians had a negative attitude toward the United States, compared with 98 percent [in 2004]. In Morocco, 61 percent viewed the

country unfavorably in 2002, but in two years, that number has jumped to 88 percent. In Saudi Arabia, such responses rose from 87 percent in 2002 to 94 percent in June.

(Linzer 2004)[2]

Aligning oneself with such an unpopular entity as the US is thus more likely to be a liability than an asset for Middle Eastern regimes in terms of popular opinion.

In contrast, defiance, independence and self-sufficiency are deemed honourable (Crooke 2009). As Nathan Brown (2010, p. 2) points out: "There is [one] actor that urges Palestinians to worry far less about currying favour with foreigners and instead take matters into their own hands – Hamas." Indeed, Hamas utilises its pariah status among the international community as a mobilising tool by symbolising its defiance and refusal to submit to Israel and the West, especially when juxtaposed against its Fatah rival (Farrell 2006).

Halim Rane (2009, p. 35) posits that concepts of dignity, honour and justice are of primary importance throughout Arab cultures. Pertinently, Dominique Moisi (2010, p. 56) argues that the occupation is characterised by a 'culture of humiliation' with which Palestinians must contend on a day-to-day basis. In this light, according to Gazan analyst Wasseem el-Sarraj (2011),

Hamas represents an organic, though troubling, response to the Palestinian struggle for a legitimate and dignified existence. U.S.-backed Fatah leaders lived in villas; Hamas Ministers choose to live in the dwellings of the poor. Hamas speaks the language of resistance. Fatah speaks the defunct language of Oslo.

The changing nature of the occupation and Israeli domination are thus highly influential in determining the course of Palestinian resistance and, to an extent, the political fortunes of Palestinian political movements (Rosenfeld 2004). In essence, the higher the optimism for a negotiated settlement resulting in a Palestinian state and the greater the ability for Palestinians to lead something resembling a normal life, the less support there is for armed resistance (Shamir and Shikaki 2010, pp. 70–79).

Repression, despair and disillusionment, on the other hand, lead to an increase in armed resistance. Exposure to violence, in turn, generates more support for counter-violence and an increase in militancy (Sarraj 2002; Hayes and McAllister 2001). Indeed, according to Hroub (2008, p. 223, my translation), "the popularity and force of Hamas are narrowly linked to the brutalities and continued humiliations that Palestinians endure because of the Israeli occupation, as well as Israel's refusal to recognise Palestinian rights".

During times of heightened threat perception and insecurity, moreover, populations have a tendency to turn towards more uncompromising actors to ensure security and the preservation of national principles, especially if the conflict is perceived to be of an existential nature (Barzilai 1996, p. 64; Lieberfeld 1999).

54   *The 'lesser' jihad: armed resistance*

Unsurprisingly, many Palestinians (and indeed Israelis) view the conflict as existential; a perception that was only enhanced by the increased militancy, violence and consequent reciprocity of the second intifada. As Daoud (survey 2010), a 23-year-old PFLP activist, explains, "Our struggle is that of existence, not borders."

Where during the first intifada (1987–1993) Palestinians protested with rocks, Molotov cocktails and civil disobedience, the second uprising (2000–c.2004/2005) consisted of attacks with firearms and suicide bombs, including attacks on Israeli population centres. Indicatively, over the course of the first intifada from 1987 to 1993, over 1100 Palestinians and 100 Israelis lost their lives.[3] In contrast, the death-toll of the first four years of the al-Aqsa intifada clearly illustrates this shift towards armed insurrection with over 3500 Palestinians and some 950 Israelis killed with thousands more injured on each side. This increase in violence further manifested itself in 'Operation Summer Rains' (July 2006), 'Operation Cast Lead' (2008/2009) and 'Protective Edge' (2014), during which Palestinian fatalities increased to an unprecedented level in Gaza with around 400 Palestinians killed in 2006, 1400 in 2008/2009 and some 2200 in 2014, all within a population of some 1.5 million people.

But the damage inflicted on Palestinian society is far greater than the death-toll alone would suggest. Seasoned Middle East commentator Donald McIntyre (2010) describes Israeli policy towards the Gaza Strip as less of an attack on Hamas than "the gradual but systematic dismantling of a vital, historically well-educated, and in many respects self-reliant civilisation". Baruch Kimmerling (2003) goes so far as to characterise Israeli policy, and particularly the policies of former Prime Minister Ariel Sharon, as the attempted 'politicide' of the Palestinian people. This perception of existential survival generates a variety of psychological, practical and retaliatory reactions among the threatened populace.

When a group's identity or survival is perceived to be at stake, in essence a perceived zero-sum conflict, "fear about an uncertain future increase[s] the frequency of war, especially for non-State societies" (Druckman 2006, p. 13). Thus, when peaceful paths to change are blocked, combined with the limited efficacy of appealing to the dominant group's sense of morality in a repressive and politically exclusivist system such as the Israeli occupation of the Palestinian Territories, violence becomes a tool used to obtain leverage against the status quo power, attract international attention and mobilise the populace.

Political violence also has the capacity to trigger an over-reaction by the dominant power, which can serve to delegitimise it or lead to international condemnation. Examples of this include the US-led invasions of Afghanistan and Iraq which squandered international sympathy and goodwill in the aftermath of 11 September and, more pertinently for this study, the 2008/2009 Israeli attack on the Gaza Strip, which led to the Goldstone Report accusing Israel, and to a lesser extent Hamas, of war crimes.[4] Following Israel's attack on the Gaza Strip in July to August 2014, the Palestinian Authority joined the International Criminal Court in 2015. As a result of the PA's recognition of the Rome Statute, the

The 'lesser' jihad: armed resistance 55

prosecutor of the International Criminal Court opened preliminary investigations into possible war crimes committed in the Palestinian Territories dating from before the 2014 conflict in Gaza (Lis 2015).

There are, of course, risks involved in perpetuating violence against an enemy with vastly superior military capabilities, including the destruction of the movement at the hands of state repression. The Liberation Tigers of Tamil Elam in Sri Lanka are a recent example of a movement which met this fate in 2009.

Consequently, political violence tends to be a weapon of last resort when alternative means to political advancement have been curtailed. In a remarkably prescient comment made during the post-Oslo euphoria of 1994, one resident of the Aida refugee camp near Bethlehem stated, "Fatah are here to help us share the peace and the good time. When we need Islam is that point when our suffering returns to us from Israel's hands and to our hearts and heads" (cited in Milton-Edwards and Farrell 2010, p. 74). Indeed, according to Palestinian pollster Khalil Shikaki (personal interview 2009), the outbreak of the second intifada led to an upsurge in Palestinian religiosity. Thus, the certainty of religion – in this case Islam – provides shelter in times of difficulty, disillusionment and desperation; attributes that were so characteristic of the al-Aqsa intifada. Indicatively, Lori Allen (2008, p. 467) reveals that over the course of the second intifada there was a consistent refrain among Palestinians that 'We are living an ongoing *nakba*'. As a result, Palestinians increasingly gravitated towards Hamas, a movement which: (1) refuses to compromise on fundamental Palestinian principles centred on resistance to occupation and national liberation, and (2) articulates itself within a familiar normative (Islamic) discourse. In effect, these two key components of Hamas' message dovetailed throughout the course of the second intifada and led to an increase in its popular support.

Accordingly, throughout the course of the second intifada, the popularity of Hamas increased concomitant with its resistance actions, a lack of central authority and heightened threat perception, as well as a general disillusionment with the efficacy of negotiations. Similarly, within the context of the 2008/2009 attack on Gaza, Milton-Edwards and Farrell (2010, p. 101) posit that Hamas operated on the premise that "when Palestine burns, its support grows". While this is undoubtedly a contributing factor to Hamas' popularity, this statement exhibits a reductionist view of Hamas' interpretation of resistance and dehumanises the political leadership. Hamas' wider programme of action includes a variety of reformist, positive and constructive non-violent agendas aimed at ameliorating the living conditions of the Palestinian population rather than provoking Israel's wrath and consequent suffering of the wider population. The Islamist Speaker of Parliament Dr Aziz Dweik (personal interview 2010) contends that:

> All the violence which comes … from the Palestinian side is just a message to the world. Maybe it is the wrong [message] sometimes okay, but it was a message to the world saying that we got fed up with occupation. Enough is enough. We would like to live as free as any other nation in the world.

56 The 'lesser' jihad: armed resistance

The idea of being 'fed up' (*zahqan*) with foreign occupation, alongside its accompanying frustration and an omnipresent threat of violence, is a common sentiment which may push individuals to turn to armed resistance or retaliatory violence (Allen 2008, pp. 473–474).

Exposure to violence

Eyad Sarraj (2002), a leading Palestinian psychiatrist, attributes the rise in militancy to the younger generation's exposure to violence during the first intifada and a general sentiment of despair. Fifty-five per cent of Palestinian children during the first intifada witnessed their father being beaten or humiliated at the hands of Israeli soldiers, thereby causing the deterioration of the father figure. In other words, the child is witness to the fact that his or her parents cannot even protect themselves, let alone the lives of the children; that is to say, they are unable to fulfil one of their primary roles as parents, and this thus leads to the devaluation of traditional figures of authority (ibid.). Indeed, by 1993 Sara Roy (2007, pp. 71–72) noted that "Children in the Gaza Strip are increasingly incapable of conceptualizing authority in traditional terms since parents and teachers, unable to protect the young from constant abuse and threat, have ceased to exist as authority figures." As a result, the child becomes more militant or turns to alternative bodies in the hope of finding security and/or redress. In short, the children of the first intifada became the much more violent militants of the second intifada which came to be dominated by Hamas. Further exposure to violence during this second uprising, moreover, caused the radicalisation of the electorate which generated more support for militant actors, the primary beneficiary in this case being Hamas (Gunning 2007, p. 219).

In a similar vein, a study on Northern Ireland by Hayes and McAllister (2001) concludes that exposure to violence often increases popular support for political violence emanating from one's own side. Hayes and McAllister posit that there are three types of exposure to violence: direct exposure, indirect exposure and collective exposure (ibid., p. 908). Similar to Northern Ireland, Palestinian society is characterised by close-knit communities centred on large extended families and/or clans (singular, *hamula*). As a result of these networks, an individual's exposure to violence engenders much wider social repercussions. In the case of the Palestinian Territories, almost the entire community has been exposed to or affected by violence. Indeed, according to Shamir and Shikaki (2010, p. 39), "Periods of conflict intensify individuals' security needs and enhance identification and attachment with the collective." In brief, the higher the perceived threat, the more support there is for violent measures (ibid., p. 70).

The leadership, cadres and sympathisers of Hamas are no strangers to violent repression and retaliation whether this emanates from Israel or the Palestinian Authority. Abd al-Aziz al-Rantisi, an assassinated former leader of Hamas in the Gaza Strip and successor to Sheikh Ahmed Yassin, cites the death of his uncle, grandfather and three cousins as major catalysts which convinced him of the necessity of armed struggle against the Israeli occupation (Juergensmeyer 2001, p. 74).

Accordingly, Palestinian-Israeli professor Shaul Mishal (personal interview 2009) contends that the third generation of the Palestinian–Israeli conflict, on both sides, is more 'zealot' and violent than the preceding generations. This is the generation whose formative years comprised the highly militarised al-Aqsa intifada. As Menachem Klein (2011) points out, "The second intifada and Israel's iron fist shaped the teen years of today's 20-somethings, and constituted their first contact with politics.... Soldiers, settlements, checkpoints and restrictions have long been part of their daily life." Tellingly, 76 per cent of university students surveyed by myself from March to May 2010 supported armed resistance ($n = 110$) with 66 per cent rejecting the idea of a two-state solution ($n = 108$).[5] The ascendancy of Hamas is the major political development of this generation. In contrast, a March 2010 poll (PCSPR, poll no. 35) found that only 47 per cent of Palestinians supported a resumption of armed resistance, whereas 57 per cent supported a two-state solution based on 1967 borders. Whether this discrepancy is a result of youthful impulsiveness/conviction which will become more pragmatic in the future or indicative of a potential long-term shift remains to be seen.[6] By June 2012 however, PCSPR poll no. 44 found that opposition to a two-state solution had risen to 49 per cent among the wider population, while 55 per cent believed it was no longer viable in practical terms due to the continued expansion of Israeli settlements.

The first intifada and the Islamists' turn to violence

Hamas' predecessor, the *Ikhwan*, focused initially on the provision of social services and *da'wa*. In the early 1980s however, there was a split within the Palestinian Islamists with a more militant section, unhappy with the *Ikhwan's* passivity towards the Israeli occupation, leaving the mother movement and creating Palestinian Islamic Jihad (Abu Amr 1993, p. 90). Indeed, prior to Hamas' creation in 1987, Israel provided at least tacit support and tolerance for the *Ikhwan's* activities (Filui 2012; McGeough 2009, p. 41). Ironically, in light of the present situation, Israel hoped that the *Ikhwan*'s focus on social change through Islam would undermine the militant, nationalist PLO headed by Yasser Arafat's Fatah movement.

During the 1980s, Islamic Jihad engaged in a series of daring attacks which captured the imagination of the Palestinian population. These included an unprecedented jail break, as well as the kidnap and murder of the head of the Israeli military authorities in Gaza, all of which set off a chain of events leading to the first intifada ('a shaking off' or civil uprising) in December 1987 (Tamimi 2007, p. 50).

In effect, Islamic Jihad inverted the *Ikhwan's* ideological approach pertaining to "the centrality of the Palestinian issue and proper time for liberating the country" (Abu Amr 1993, p. 9). The *Ikhwan* contended that only after a virtuous (Islamised) Palestinian society was created would it be strong enough to throw off the Israeli occupation. In contrast, Jihad advocated liberation first and Islamisation later. Islamic Jihad's operations against the occupation forced the *Ikhwan*

58 The 'lesser' jihad: armed resistance

to create a separate armed wing, Hamas, in order to ensure institutional survival and successfully compete for popular support.[7] Hamas combines social and political agendas with armed struggle and Islam. Islamic Jihad, conversely, does not have a current social or political agenda beyond armed resistance. Hamas pursues a dual strategy combining the *Ikhwan's* traditional focus on *da'wa* with the concept of armed jihad against the occupation (Tamimi 2007, p. 36).

The first intifada was a pivotal event which resituated political activity and resistance back within the Occupied Territories. Hitherto, the main political organ, the PLO, operated predominantly in exile, variously shifting its base of operations from Jordan to Beirut before being exiled to far-off Tunisia. Hamas as a grassroots movement, in contrast to the exiled PLO leadership, was in a primary position to capitalise.

The intifada marked a mass awakening of the Palestinian national consciousness within the Occupied Territories which, henceforth, Israel would be unable to subdue (Nusseibeh 1990, p. 134). The first intifada was a broad-based series of predominantly civil and non-violent actions in which the entire community participated. The emblematic image of the first intifada was that of stone-throwing children facing down heavily armed Israeli soldiers (Zuhur 2010, p. 25). While throwing rocks is not strictly non-violent, these images highlighted the grossly asymmetrical nature of the conflict and thereby inverted the hitherto dominant image of the conflict whereby Israel was cast as an innocent victim of Palestinian terrorism.

The driving force of the intifada was focused on a "contested space tied to Palestinian conceptions of self-determination, cultural integrity and personal dignity" (Farsoun and Aruri 2006, p. 209). It is important to note that for a significant proportion of Palestinians, the intifada was a protest against *both* the Israeli occupation *and* the PLO leadership (ibid., p. 208; McGeough 2009, p. 62). In this light, part of Hamas' appeal lies less in its ideology than in *being seen* as a counter-hegemonic movement believed to be substantially less corrupt than the PLO (Roy 2007, p. 72). It was also during this period that Hamas established its resistance credentials and set itself up as an Islamic alternative to the PLO. Hamas, for example, began to rival the PLO by issuing rival communiqués (*bayanat*), strikes and mass demonstrations. Violence was employed by Hamas from the beginning but this mainly involved targeting Palestinian collaborators and informants.

Hamas was initially ignored or tacitly encouraged by the Israelis who saw it as a potential counterbalance to the more threatening PLO. The turning point occurred on 8 October 1990, when Israeli troops stormed *al-Haram al-Sharif* (the Noble Sanctuary), massacring 22 Palestinians in the process and injuring another 200.[8] On the same day, a Palestinian man, reputedly close to Hamas, stabbed three Israeli soldiers to death in Jerusalem and injured a fourth in retaliation, thus commencing the 'war of the knives' (Tamimi 2007, p. 61). Following a series of knife attacks, the final provocation for Israel was another knife attack in Jaffa on 14 December 1990, with a note dedicating the attack to Hamas in commemoration of the second anniversary of its founding. This attack precipitated an Israeli campaign against Hamas which entailed the arrest of over 1700 supporters. In 1992, over 400 Hamas and Islamic Jihad supporters were rounded up and deported to no-man's land between Israel and Lebanon in contravention of international law. Here, in a place called Marj al-Zuhur (the Meadow of Flowers), the Islamists set up camp in the snow-capped mountains, attracting international attention and Palestinian sympathy (Kepel 2002, p. 327). According to Tamimi (2007, p. 61), during the first intifada "the Israelis were oblivious to the fact that whenever they hit Hamas, and no matter how hard they hit, they only earned it further popular sympathy and support". Palestinian valorisation of sacrifice and resistance in the face of Israeli oppression continued throughout the course of the second intifada, as well as four full-scale Israeli attacks on Gaza in 2006, 2008/2009, 2012 and 2014.

The upshot for Hamas entailed the development of intimate contacts with the Lebanese Hizbullah (the Party of God) which provided aid and assistance during these difficult times. Robert Pape (2005, pp. 73–74) contends that Hamas learnt the tactic of suicide bombings – or martyrdom operations (*al-amaliyyat al-istishhadiyya*) as the Palestinians call them – from Hizbullah during this period. These would be employed against civilians for the first time in the aftermath of the 1994 Hebron massacre by Israeli settler Baruch Goldstein.

Hamas' dedicated armed wing, *Kata'ib al-Shahid Izz al-Din al-Qassam* (the Brigades of the Martyr Izz al-Din al-Qassam or Qassam Brigades), was founded in 1992 in response to the increasingly harsh repression of the first intifada, which had hitherto consisted of relatively non-violent actions, such as civil disobedience, but also symbolised by the "children of the stone" (Tamimi 2007, pp. 62–63). By October 1993, it was evident that Hamas' resistance actions had begun to reap dividends with its support increasing to over 60 per cent in the Gaza Strip (PCSPR poll no. 2, 1993). In contrast, by February 1994, amidst the post-Oslo optimism, Hamas' popularity dropped dramatically to 17.1 per cent (PCSPR poll no. 6, 1994). This again demonstrates the influence of optimism for the future, which leads to greater support for Fatah and its narrative of negotiations, whereas pessimism for a negotiated solution and despair leads to greater support for principled, uncompromising and steadfast actors of which the main embodiment in the Palestinian Territories is Hamas.

Armed resistance, moreover, is a path to empowerment and political legitimacy. As Shaul Mishal (personal interview 2009) points out, "Both intifadas raised the status of the younger generation and weakened traditional structures … this has happened after every major event since 1948." This elevation of the 'younger' generation is clearly evident in the ranks of Hamas' political leadership. Similarly, a more militant generation of Fatah activists who rose to prominence during the first intifada – the so-called 'Young Guard' (themselves in their forties and fifties) symbolised by figures such as the popular but imprisoned Marwan Barghouti – are seeking to challenge the dominance of the 'Old Guard' Fatah apparatchiks from the days of Yasser Arafat. Indeed, Hamas and this younger generation of Fatah activists coordinated military operations throughout the course of the second intifada.

60 *The 'lesser' jihad: armed resistance*

The practical nature of militant jihad

For Palestinians, the classical image of the *feda'i* (literally, 'one who sacrifices himself') is the romanticised figure of a *kuffiyeh*-clad, Kalashnikov-wielding guerrilla fighter epitomised in the leadership of the late Yasser Arafat. The figure of the *feda'i* represents sacrifice, resilience and defiance among the Palestinian community. Since Fatah seized control of the PLO in 1968, the popularised figure of the *feda'i* is most commonly associated with the notion of 'armed struggle' to bring about revolution.

From indiscriminate home-made *qassam* rockets fired from the Gaza Strip to buses ripped apart by suicide operations, Hamas has undeniably been responsible for a multitude of exceptionally violent attacks against Israel, many of which have deliberately targeted the civilian population. Despite the media fixation on self-immolation attacks however, these types of attacks have been vastly outstripped by conventional attacks against IDF installations and heavily armed settlements (Benmelech and Berrebi 2007, p. 225). Over the course of the second intifada, while there were over 25,000 attacks against Israelis, only 151 of these were suicide operations (ibid.).

Armed resistance and political violence serve a variety of purposes, including propaganda and deterrence, but are also driven by more emotional motives, such as revenge, despair and empowerment. Violent resistance, then, is: (1) driven by a widespread belief among Palestinians of its efficacy; (2) an effective tool of propaganda, revenge, redress and deterrence; (3) an extra-parliamentary means of political advancement in the absence of institutional opportunity; and (4) a result of inter-factional rivalry and competition for popular support. Thus, political violence can serve to bolster domestic credibility, while simultaneously undermining the legitimacy of the status quo power and its policies. Political violence against Israel, for example, highlights Palestinian dissatisfaction with, and the illegitimacy of, the Israeli occupation. Again, it is important to highlight that Hamas conceives of armed jihad as a defensive measure against the Israeli occupation (Juergensmeyer 2001, p. 74; Crooke 2009, p. 209).

Despite characterisations of a fourth wave of indiscriminate religious terrorism (Hoffman 2006, p. 92; Rapoport 2004), political violence is a means to an end for most armed socio-political movements, not an end in itself. Fundamentally, violence is an expression of power, instrumental in nature, a means to political ends (Hassan 1997, p. 239). To paraphrase Clausewitz ([1832] 1997), violence, war and, by extension, armed resistance may be interpreted as a continuation of politics by other means.

For Hamas more precisely, there is a dialectic between politics and armed resistance whereby the two complement and condition each other. For Hamas, there is no contradiction between the simultaneous application of force and the pursuit of a political solution. Hamas argues that Israel only makes concessions when it is forced to do so, especially concessions of the territorial kind. Indeed, there is a widespread belief among Palestinians in the efficacy of violent resistance and that it produces gains which could not have been achieved through

The 'lesser' jihad: armed resistance   61

negotiations. PCPSR Public Opinion Polls no. 1 (July 2000), no. 3 (December 2001), no. 8 (June 2003) and no. 11 (March 2004), for example, found, respectively, that 57 per cent, 61 per cent, 65 per cent and 67 per cent of respondents believed this to be true. Following Israel's disengagement from the Gaza Strip in September 2005, this sentiment was held by 73 per cent of respondents (Shamir and Shikaki 2010, p. 73). Thus, violence is viewed as a source of leverage for Hamas whether it be in terms of prestige, accumulation of popular support and/ or pressuring the Israeli occupation into concessions. The above poll results also indicate a growing belief in the efficacy of political violence over the course of the second intifada, thereby correlating with the exposure to violence hypothesis articulated earlier in this chapter.

According to Mishal and Sela (2000, p. 19), Hamas violence is not indiscriminate like the violence ascribed to *salafi* jihadist groups akin to al-Qa'ida.[9] As Mark Juergensmeyer (2001, p. 5) points out, "'Terrorism' has more frequently been associated with violence committed by disenfranchised groups desperately attempting to gain a shred of power or influence." Hence, Hamas engages in 'controlled violence' which is usually driven by political considerations and cost–benefit analyses (Mishal and Sela 2000, pp. 19–82). Indeed, Hamas, and especially its internal leadership, are subject to the same pressures attendant on the occupation as the rest of society. As such, Hamas is highly attuned to public opinion and reacts accordingly, often tempering its application of violence in line with the prevailing public sentiment. In other words, for Hamas, political violence is a tactical means to a strategic end. Violence is not an article of faith but rather a tactic driven by political opportunity, exigency and practicality. As Mahmoud (survey 2010), a 27-year-old Hamas member, explains, "[armed] resistance is for freeing Palestine, and not just resistance in itself". Similarly, Khalid Mishal argues that "armed resistance is not an end in itself, it is a means of reaching an end" (cited in Hroub 2008, p. 214, my translation).

Accordingly, Hamas limits its theatre of military operations to the territories of former British Mandate Palestine in contrast to the transnational eschatological jihad attributed to al-Qa'ida-inspired entities (and, indeed, the previous international scope of PLO militancy). In addition, Hamas has repeatedly offered a quid pro quo moratorium on attacks against civilians; Israel has never responded to this proposition (Gunning 2004, p. 241). Finally, Hamas has engaged in several official and unofficial *tadi'a'* ('periods of calm') as well as offered a long-term *hudna* (ceasefire) based on pre-1967 borders recognising the *reality* but not the *legitimacy* of Israel's existence (Wagemakers 2010, pp. 357–358). Sheikh Yassin, the assassinated founder and spiritual leader of Hamas, indicated that a *hudna* would be automatically renewed at the end of 10 years (Klein 2007, p. 455). Hence, Hamas is not an implacably violent organisation with a penchant for existential violence as its critics allege, but rather one which predominantly utilises violence for its instrumental value, including propaganda and a means of leverage against its internal and external enemies.

The upshot for Hamas is that its violence, and consequent Israeli retaliation, has often served the additional purpose of delegitimising Fatah, not only within

62   The 'lesser' jihad: armed resistance

Palestinian society but also with its Israeli interlocutors. During the second intifada, for example, Israel believed that Fatah, and particularly Yasser Arafat, was tacitly turning a blind eye to, or even encouraging, Hamas attacks as a source of leverage at the negotiating table (Milton-Edwards and Farrell 2010, pp. 95–96). Violence also served the purpose of helping derail the Oslo peace process to which Hamas was so resolutely opposed. Violence, in addition, has the capacity to alter Israeli policy and internal politics. Khaled Hroub (2000, p. 244) argues that it was Hamas' suicide bombing campaign against Israel in conjunction with Israel's failed 'Grapes of Wrath' campaign against Hizbullah in Lebanon which led to the fall of Shimon Peres' Labour government and the election of right-winger Binyamin Netanyahu in 1996 (who also, incidentally, was against the peace process).

For the Palestinian public, however, violence and resistance is also a psychological and emotional response. Khalid Amayreh (personal interview 2010) contends that:

> In the past, resistance was a pro-active value obviously, but today, increasingly, it is becoming a psychological value ... or a reaction to Israeli hegemony, which is more and more felt by ordinary Palestinians. So resistance cannot be divorced from the Israeli action.

Israeli actions have fostered a 'culture of humiliation' through the continued expansion of its settlement enterprise as well as forcing Palestinians to submit to the daily travails of the occupation's extensive checkpoint regime (Moisi 2010, p. 65). Humiliation, moreover, is a sign of impotence (ibid., p. 56) and, as Hannah Arendt (1972, p. 153) points out, "Impotence breeds violence". Thus, armed resistance is a sign of agency, empowerment and defiance. In this light, according to assassinated Palestinian-Lebanese journalist Samir Kassir (2006, p. 80), the attraction of Islamist armed jihad lies in the fact that it is "the only ideology that seems to offer relief from the victim status the Arabs delight in claiming".

There is also a sort of visceral appeal to violence against one's enemies, especially when there is gross disparity among military capabilities. This appeal is most vividly illustrated by popular support for suicide or self-immolation attacks which produced mass Israeli casualties. Hamas claims that such attacks are retaliation – one might say revenge – for the assassination of its leaders or mass deaths of Palestinian civilians (Mishal and Sela 2000, p. 69; Juergensmeyer 2001, pp. 73–74). As Ishaq (survey 2010), a 20-year-old English student, points out, "Violence creates violence. When Israel kills innocent children, women, and the elderly, naturally, the other side will react the same." There is an eye-for-an-eye mentality which pervades the political culture of the Middle East and finds legitimisation within differing interpretations of Islam and Judaism.

Political violence as armed propaganda

Traditionally, acts of political violence are armed propaganda. The primary aims of political violence are to attract media attention, disseminate fear among the target audience and attract popular support, either by inspiring a sense of empowerment among the repressed population or triggering a violent (over)-reaction by the state which then, in turn, vindicates armed resistance. This is especially the case for broad-based national liberation or self-determination movements, such as Hamas, which rely on a widespread constituency in contrast to single-issue terrorism which only seeks to rectify a problem within the system rather than completely replace it. Political violence is also designed to attract new recruits. In the Palestinian Territories, the accruement of popular support and the ability to recruit new supporters is facilitated by a historical narrative of armed resistance, as well as a social environment which holds fighters and martyrs in the highest esteem (Rosenfeld 2004, pp. 314–315).

In the aftermath of the 1947/1948 *nakba* ('catastrophe') which led to the exile of some 750,000 Palestinians from what is now Israel, the Palestinian national movement petitioned futilely against their 'non-existence' before the UN for decades before the PLO emerged as an autonomous actor, headed by Fatah calling for an 'armed struggle' to liberate the Palestinian people in 1968 (Khalidi 1989, p. 6). Until UN General Assembly Resolution 2535 B XXIV in 1969, UN documents simply referred to the Palestinian people as 'Arab Refugees' from the first Arab–Israeli War of 1948/1949 (Kirkpatrick 1989, p. 25). Successive Israeli leaders, moreover, vehemently denied the existence of a Palestinian people. According to assassinated co-founder of Fatah Abu Jihad (Khalil al-Wazir) (cited in Sayigh 1997, p. 25), what the Palestinians faced after 1948 was "the elimination of Palestine, suppression of Palestinian identity, eradication of the Palestinian character, and the merging and dissolving of the Palestinian decision and Palestinian will". Faced with this existential crisis, Palestinian resistance organisations needed to attract the attention of the international community and redefine the issue as a struggle for national self-determination.

A series of high-profile plane hijackings by the leftist PFLP from 1968 to 1970 catapulted the Palestinian problem back on to the international agenda, which had hitherto been relegated to an issue of refugees rather than one of national self-determination. The PFLP also forced Israel to negotiate with a 'terrorist' organisation for the first time in order to secure the release of its hostages (Morris 2001, p. 376). The attacks on the Israeli team at the 1972 Munich Olympics had a similar effect in eliciting media coverage. Thus, terrorism propelled the issue of Palestine back into the spotlight within the context of an international community which had largely forgotten about the problem. This logic of 'armed propaganda' continues to pervade the thinking of Hamas which, unsurprisingly, concludes that if international attention is only forthcoming against the backdrop of Israeli fatalities, then the path is clear (Milton-Edwards and Farrell 2010, p. 145). Political violence, therefore, is a tactic utilised when it is deemed to be effective in generating media coverage and eliciting popular

64 *The 'lesser' jihad: armed resistance*

support. Hamas also utilises political violence to deflect attention from domestic problems associated with the difficult governing situation in the Gaza Strip (ICG 2011). The audience is thus is not only external but also internal. Indeed, Buhjah (survey 2010), an unaffiliated 19-year-old law student, believes that armed resistance "can be useful because it shows that there are people willing to fight for their rights and their country to prove that they still exist". Likewise, Munawwar (survey 2010), a 23-year-old Fatah activist studying political science, supports armed resistance because it "makes the enemy aware of Palestinian existence". Yousef (survey 2010) supports armed resistance "so the enemy won't step on our necks". Armed resistance is thus both a symbolic demonstration of survival and a form of domestic and international propaganda.

Inter-factional competition

Coercive power, ultimately, is buttressed by the threat of sanction and armed force. According to Hannah Arendt (1972, p. 137), "violence is the most flagrant manifestation of power". Political power, through a social contract, also rests on the ability to enforce sanctions and protect constituents. Max Weber ([1919] 1978, p. 221) thus defined the state as "a human community that (successfully) claims the monopoly of the legitimate use of physical force within a given territory". Mao Zedong (1938, p. 221) put it much more crudely: "Political power grows from the barrel of a gun." While not an ideal measure of political legitimacy by any stretch of the imagination, such is the case of a population whose history is characterised by resistance to oppression, foreign occupation and a lack of effective centralised government; all of which has engendered a chronic sense of insecurity. Thus, the ability to exercise force in such circumstances not only has the capacity to empower, liberate and protect erstwhile constituents, but also to undercut competing adversaries unable or unwilling to provide a similar service.

Although usually met with short shrift, visible annoyance and a marked change in tone when suggested during interviews, it would be naïve to discount the argument that political violence against Israel is not, at least in part, driven by Palestinian inter- (and indeed, intra-) factional competition. Indicatively, as one layperson (Laila, personal communication 2010) opined on the 2008/2009 Israeli attack on the Gaza Strip,

> Hamas benefited from the world showing empathy – to support their case – while civilians paid the price. And so will the case be if a 'third' intifada should break out as some people suspect. It's like a switch that gets turned on and off to achieve political scores.

Indeed, it was only following the increasingly brutal nature of the Israeli occupation, and the emergence of an Islamic competitor, Palestinian Islamic Jihad, that the *Ikhwan* included armed struggle in its programme of action (Tamimi 2007, p. 43).

The 'lesser' jihad: armed resistance   65

Maya Rosenfeld (2004, pp. 314–315) similarly identifies Palestinian resistance as a primary factor contributing to the politicisation of an individual, which engenders further identification with resistance organisations. This correlates with surveys administered by myself which found that support for armed actions was more prevalent among individuals identifying with a political movement than those who did not; 82.9 per cent of respondents who nominated a preferred party supported armed resistance, in contrast to 62.5 per cent support from those who did not (n = 110).[10]

Despite characterisations of implacable religious 'terrorism', even Hoffman (2006, pp. 145–165) concedes, in apparent contradiction of himself, that Hamas' political violence is a tactical, temporal consideration, often linked to inter-factional rivalry over popular support. The International Crisis Group, for example, attributed a March 2011 escalation in violence against Israel to Hamas' need to fend off criticism from Islamic Jihad and other *salafi* jihadist organisations charging that Hamas had abandoned the principle of armed resistance (ICG 2011).

The use of violence against Israel as a tool to facilitate political mobilisation, attract popular support and bequeath legitimacy was especially pertinent prior to the 2004/2005 municipal and 2006 PLC elections due to the absence of any meaningful democratic governance. As a result, few instruments existed for political advancement by institutional means, that is, if one discounts nepotism, corruption and cronyism. Throughout the course of the second intifada, in particular, there was a marked absence of almost any centralised government and concomitant sense of security.

With the outbreak of the second intifada, the IDF's subsequent reoccupation of the PA-administered areas of West Bank, and the almost total breakdown of central authority, the rule of the gun became even more pronounced. According to Jeremy Pressman (2006, p. 126), "In the absence of democratic governance for Palestinians, being armed was the major currency of political power. One's ability to defend one's political strength turned, in part, on one's ability to show or use force." Similarly, Bashir (personal interview 2010), then a Damascus-based Hamas member, contends that "having weapons, in any way, is a form of resistance. Having weapons in any way is resistance."

Thus, in the absence of a central authority and a heightened state of insecurity, Palestinians turned to other actors, such as Hamas, to provide security, support and sustenance in a sort of de facto social contract. In effect, Hamas was/is viewed as a security provider operating within an environment characterised by uncertainty (Gunning 2007, p. 175). During the second intifada in 2002/2003, for instance, Hamas set up localised neighbourhood militias (*jaysh al-murabitoun* or Army of Holy Defenders) in order to provide security in the absence of effective government security (Sayigh 2011a, p. 46). Since Hamas seized sole control of the Gaza Strip in June 2007, moreover, the de facto government has provided security for the enclave's 1.5 million inhabitants. In this regard, Hamas has been successful in instituting the rule of law and order which eluded the previous Fatah-led administrations, despite possessing only a fraction

66   *The 'lesser' jihad: armed resistance*

of the resources (Sayigh 2011b). Specifically, Hamas has managed to reorganise the security forces in Gaza so that their numbers have been reduced from 56,887 prior to its takeover to around 15,000 (Sayigh 2011a, p. 58).

The years of the second intifada were characterised by chaos and factionalism, dominated by clan, warlord and gang affiliations. Most of these gangs and warlords were attributed to Fatah, especially following the death of Yasser Arafat. These incessant intra-factional clashes within Fatah were often occulted in favour of the reductionist Islamist (Hamas and Jihad) and Nationalist (Fatah) divide (Pressman 2006, p. 126). In contrast, the mosque, predominantly associated with Hamas sympathisers or supporters at the time, was perceived to be a source of stability and calm within an otherwise chaotic environment (Tuastad 2009, p. 238).

The overwhelming use of lethal force by Israel, especially at the beginning of the second intifada when Palestinians had yet to turn to arms, prompted retaliatory measures in kind, not only against Israeli forces but also targeting civilians. Israel, in addition, resorted to collective punishments of the entire population, including closures, indefinite curfews and the cut-off of electricity and water, causing immense hardship to the general population. This unprecedented level of repression led to calls for redress and revenge. Thus, increasingly,

> in the contest for the support of the Palestinian public, the commitment to the use of force was the default position. If a faction rejected this approach, they risked looking like an American-Israeli accomplice and thereby losing support.
>
> (Pressman 2006, p. 126)

Political violence, moreover, is a source of recruitment in the form of 'armed propaganda'. On the one hand, it is 'armed propaganda' insofar as it attracts media coverage. On the other hand, it is a form of 'auto-propaganda' designed to inspire, fortify and recruit members for the movement (Hoffman 2006, p. 199).

In the Palestinian Territories, *fedayeen* and their families enjoy an elevated social status (Rosenfeld 2004, p. 221). Fighting and sacrificing oneself for the Palestinian cause is a source of prestige among a community whose history consists of occupation, repression and dispossession. Indeed, Menachem Klein (2002, pp. 37–38) observes that for some aspiring leaders, "their prestige, status, and popularity, relies on their image as fighters for freedom and against corruption", an image that Hamas was able to successfully project. The prestige, status and popularity accorded to fighters, in turn, provide a model to be emulated and thus a source of recruitment, popular support and political legitimacy. The idolisation of fighters and martyrs also stems from a psychological need for empowerment and agency, especially in light of the fact that most Palestinian fatalities are civilian, and often of a passive nature.

It is clear from my own survey research that the idea of armed resistance and jihad is a draw card for Hamas among the youth. Hamas sympathisers, without fail, note and prioritise the notions of liberation, armed resistance and jihad, as well as opposition to Israel. When asked to explain the allure of Hamas, Qismah (survey 2010), a 20-year-old student studying finance, recalls, "Since I was little

The 'lesser' jihad: armed resistance   67

I was attracted to the fact that this party supports armed resistance". In a similar vein, Huda (survey 2010), an American-born engineering student, cites the fact that Hamas "encourages armed resistance to liberate Palestine". A third, Fatima (survey 2010), describes Hamas as "A movement that resists the Israeli enemy and has no allegiance to it". Other respondents cite martyrdom and sacrifice as underlying principles. Mona (survey 2010), for example, a 21-year-old former Hamas sympathiser from Jerusalem, believes that "the situation was better with martyrdom operations".

The idea that Hamas has 'no allegiance' to Israel is indicative of the fact that the Palestinian Authority, and by extension Fatah, is often perceived to be Israel's policeman in the West Bank (and Gaza before 2007). As such, violent repression of the Palestinian populace has not been the exclusive domain of the Israeli occupation but the Palestinian Authority as well (and, indeed, to a lesser extent, Hamas since its armed seizure of Gaza in 2007) (Sayigh 2011a, pp. 33–36). Indeed, the PA has routinely been accused of torture and Hamas members have been known to die in PA custody. These measures have historically been deeply unpopular since the 1994 establishment of the PA and are often perceived by Palestinians to be a betrayal of the principle of resistance.

Hamas, in contrast, tapped into Palestinian historical principles during the second intifada by depicting itself through the prism of sacrifice, armed resistance and martyrdom. Following Israel's harsh targeting of Fatah and the PA at the beginning of the second intifada, Hamas emerged as the vanguard of Palestinian resistance operating clandestinely from the relative safety of densely populated urban centres and refugee camps. Thus, Fatah was rendered doubly impotent and redundant given the complete collapse of the peace process.

More cynically, military participation, whether as part of an 'unofficial' militia or member of an official security apparatus, can also be a source of income within the context of a society plagued by high unemployment and limited opportunity. The family of 'martyrs', for example, received financial assistance derived from either local or foreign sources. The lure of financial reward, disparagingly touted as a key motivator in mainstream Western discourses, for the martyr's family is probably overstated. On the one hand, it is true that foreign sources such as Saddam Hussein gave money to those who lost family members to the occupation, and extra to those of self-immolating *shuhada* (martyrs) (Milton-Edwards and Farrell 2010, pp. 140–141). On the other hand, Israel has a policy of demolishing the family homes of suicide bombers so any financial reward or convenience would seem negligible. In this light, the community looks after the family of the *shahid* so they do not starve or endure unnecessary hardship (Sarraj 2002, p. 75). As Abu Ashraf (cited in Milton-Edwards 2011, p. 191), a Hamas military leader, points out:

> We struggle for freedom, not money. Money won't buy a place in paradise for the martyr or his family.... Do you see the families of the martyrs living in luxury in the wake of their son's death? Or do you see them sitting in the shattered ruins of their homes as Israel's punishment?

68   *The 'lesser' jihad: armed resistance*

When asked directly whether payments to the families of suicide bombers might encourage such attacks, Mahmoud Misleh (cited in ICG 2003, p. 24), director of the Islamic Charitable Society of al-Bireh, responded, "Does our sponsoring collaborators' children encourage people to collaborate with Israel?" As such, the financial incentives for deliberate suicide operations are probably overstated in Western discourses and more likely a manifestation of neo-Orientalist thought depicting Arabs as inherently 'backward' or 'barbaric' because these types of operations are by no means limited to either Arabs or Muslims in general (Tuastad 2003).

Nevertheless, it is probable that at least some fighters were motivated by economic considerations given the trying circumstances. The abstention of many members of the Fatah-dominated security forces during the brief but bloody civil war in the Gaza Strip in 2007, and the rapid Hamas victory therein, for example, suggest that many of those in the security forces were motivated by financial considerations rather than by the conviction of their principles.

The efficacy of violence and the liberation of the Gaza Strip

Within the context of the Palestinian–Israeli conflict, there is a mutual belief among both Israelis and Palestinians that the enemy only understands the language of force. Fatima (survey 2010), an 18-year-old Hamas supporter, for instance, believes that armed resistance "leads to the occupation's psychological defeat". If anything, the idea of violent resistance seems to resonate even more strongly with the younger generation whose formative years consisted of the exponentially more violent al-Aqsa intifada. Among university students who support armed resistance there is a recurring theme that "what was taken by force can only be restored by force" (Qismah, survey 2010, Hamas) because "resistance is our right, and what was stolen must be retrieved" (Shahd, survey 2010, no party) among almost all Palestinian political factions.

The unilateral Israeli withdrawal from southern Lebanon in 2000 after 18 years of occupation reinforced this view insofar as it was perceived to be a victory for the Hizbullah model of sustained armed resistance (Hroub 2006, p. 46). Against a backdrop of Palestinian disillusionment and a faltering peace process, the Israeli withdrawal convinced many Palestinians that emulating Hizbullah would pay concrete dividends and, as such, contributed to the militarisation of the second intifada. Fadwa (survey 2010), an unaffiliated 20-year-old student studying education, believes that "Armed resistance must be planned and undermine the occupation. Hizbullah has proven success here." Indeed, prior to the outbreak of the second intifada, PCSPR Opinion Poll no. 1 (27–29 July 2000) found that "63 per cent of all respondents agreed that the Palestinians should emulate Hizbullah methods".

Accordingly, throughout the course of the al-Aqsa intifada, Hamas guerrillas mounted persistent attacks against IDF units and 'settlements', especially within the Gaza Strip, and is credited with forcing Israel to withdraw its settlements and forces from the coastal enclave in 2005 (Hroub 2006, p. 45). Despite the

The 'lesser' jihad: armed resistance   69

devastating impact on Palestinian society over the course of the second intifada, the unilateral withdrawal of the IDF from the Gaza Strip in 2005 seemed to vindicate the notion that Israel only makes concession under duress and reinforced the view that violence reaps rewards. The unilateral nature of the withdrawal allowed Hamas to claim that Israel retreated under force of arms rather than any coordinated agreement with the Fatah-dominated Palestinian Authority. Thus, the 2005 withdrawal is widely interpreted among Palestinians as a victory for armed resistance and, in particular, Hamas. According to PCSPR poll no. 17 taken on the eve of the Gaza withdrawal in September 2005, 84 per cent of those polled interpreted the Israeli withdrawal as a victory for armed resistance, with 40 per cent attributing the withdrawal to Hamas, whereas only 21 per cent gave credit to the PA and 11 per cent to Fatah.

Hamas thus came to be seen as the principal force capable of taking on the Israeli occupation. In essence, the Gaza Strip was perceived to be the first piece of Palestinian Territory 'liberated' by force of arms and, therefore, evidence of the efficacy of armed resistance. The idea that Israel was driven from the Gaza Strip by force of arms has since been internalised, not only by Hamas, its supporters and its political representatives, but this notion also resonates with the wider population as a whole (Hass 2010).[11] Yousef (survey 2010), an unaffiliated university student, for example, who does not support any party and "never will", said he "likes the way they [Hamas] faced the enemy's terror and forced them to withdraw from Gaza".

In contrast to the 'liberation' of the Gaza Strip, Fatah presides over the West Bank where the Israeli occupation and colonisation continues apace. Undoubtedly, Hamas' 'victory' in Gaza contributed to its rising popularity, since it was seen as the only institutional force able to resist Israeli occupation, especially given the saliency of resistance to Palestinian identity. According to Abdul Sattar Qassam (personal interview 2010), a former presidential candidate and Professor of Political Science at an-Najah National University in Nablus, in Palestinian politics, legitimacy traditionally derives itself from the gun.

In many ways, the comparison is quite stark: in 2005 Israel withdrew 8000 settlers occupying one-third of the Gaza Strip – Hamas' stronghold. In contrast, settlement activity in the West Bank and Palestinian East Jerusalem has continued unabated, where the settlers now number over 500,000 and control 48 per cent of the land (B'tselem 2010). The question of whether or not Israel actually withdrew from Gaza under duress is irrelevant because Palestinian popular wisdom believes this to be the case. Thus the unilateral withdrawals of the IDF from Gaza and Lebanon strengthened the pre-existing belief among Palestinians that Israel only understands the language of force. This is reflected in the fact that a majority of Palestinians consistently believe that armed resistance helps to further national goals in a way that negotiations cannot.

Yet a contradictory consciousness does exist pertaining to the role of armed resistance. When sceptically questioned about the actual efficacy of armed resistance, Jibril (personal interview 2010), a senior Parliamentary Deputy and former member of the planning committee during the intifada, conceded that "Military

70 *The 'lesser' jihad: armed resistance*

resistance will not put an end to the occupation, this is true. But the resistance shows that there is a problem that all the world will have to resolve." Despite their ineffectual nature, the rockets fired from Gaza are viewed in a similar light because these are "a gesture that Palestinians would not lie down and accept Israel's forty-year military rule over them, even if it cost their lives" (Milton-Edwards and Farrell 2010, p. 156). Thus, armed resistance may be interpreted as a symbolic act demonstrating defiance and a refusal to submit to Israeli domination.

Conclusions

Armed resistance committed by Hamas must be placed within the context of occupation. Hamas violence is not a pathological, irrational or religious given but a response to a political problem. Moreover, it needs to be recognised that the actual and implied violence of the occupation far outstrips that perpetrated by Palestinian factions, Hamas included. Not only is this evident through the relative death-tolls of major outbreaks, but the ongoing increase in Palestinian fatalities is often not deemed newsworthy by the international media. Between 1965 and 1988 Israeli violence caused 30 times more Palestinian civilian deaths than Israeli civilian deaths caused by Palestinian violence (Khalidi 1989, p. 15), not to mention the disproportionately high number of civilian deaths attendant on both intifadas and subsequent attacks on the Gaza Strip in 2008/2009 and 2014. In this light, armed resistance and militant jihad are responses to far more excessive violence committed by the state, whether these actions are rationalised in practical, symbolic or emotional terms.

Militant jihad and armed resistance are a means to a political end for Hamas, namely the establishment of a Palestinian state. Peaceful initiatives have routinely been shot down, both literally and figuratively, so violence becomes a tool used to obtain leverage, attract media attention and accrue popular support. To this end, Hamas has repeatedly ceased violent operations for prolonged periods of time, especially when provided with the institutional or non-violent means to accrue political gains. Despite several major escalations in 2006, 2008, 2012 and 2014 respectively, this is demonstrably the case with regard to Hamas' formal participation in the political system since 2006 during which violence against Israelis has been comparatively minor, especially when contrasted to the preceding years of the second intifada. The impact of the home-made *qassam* rockets and mortars fired from the Gaza Strip has been routinely overstated when one considers that these weapons have accounted for 19 Israeli fatalities between June 2004 and the end of Operation Cast Lead on 17 January 2009.[12] Violence against Palestinians, in contrast, has continued to increase, demonstrably so during the 2008/2009 and 2014 attacks on the Gaza Strip.

Mahmoud al-Ramahi (personal interview 2010), the Islamist Secretary General of Parliament and medical doctor by trade, sums it up:

> There is a big difference between the forces, between us and the Israelis. But resistance in some places, they make the Israelis withdraw from, as in

Lebanon and Gaza. But the resistance, at the same time, they show the world that there is a problem that must be resolved, and they [the resistance] harm the Israelis as [the Israelis] harm us.

While ultimately acknowledging Palestinian military weakness vis-à-vis Israel, al-Ramahi succinctly demonstrates the Palestinian belief that political violence is an effective tool in terms of redress for Israeli violence, precipitating the withdrawal of Israeli troops and disseminating propaganda, which serves the dual purpose of attracting international attention and, more cynically as argued – but it would be naïve to assume otherwise – inter-factional jostling for popular support and political legitimacy. But what psychological and symbolic purposes might armed jihad serve if senior Islamist planners admit that "military resistance will not put an end to the occupation"?

Notes

1 The Israeli settler 'price tag' campaign stipulates that any measures taken to curb the expansion of Israeli settlements in the West Bank entail a 'price' to be paid by the Palestinian population. Examples of the 'price tag' campaign include the immolation and desecration of mosques, the mass destruction or theft of olive trees, the poisoning of water sources, crop burning and so forth.

2 It would seem likely that the deteriorating image of the US – not that the initial polls in 2002 showed it to be held in high esteem – was a result of the US-led invasion of Iraq in 2003.

3 Most of the Israeli fatalities, moreover, occurred in the last two years of the intifada when some Palestinians were beginning to lose faith in the efficacy of popular resistance. The number of deaths resulting from both intifadas is contested by various Israeli and Palestinian government sources, as well as by a variety of humans rights NGOs. The actual end of the second intifada is also contested so that fatalities resulting from this are, again, in dispute. This project places the de facto end of the intifada in late 2004 to early 2005 and utilises statistics from independent NGOs, namely B'tselem and the Palestinian Centre for Human Rights.

4 While a discussion of the Goldstone Report is beyond the scope of this project, there is quite a discrepancy between the gravity of the alleged crimes committed by each side. The Goldstone Report accused Palestinian militants of directly firing *qassam* rockets at residential areas inside Israel, resulting in the death of three Israeli civilians. Ten Israeli soldiers also died during the conflict, four as a result of 'friendly fire'. According to the B'tselem, Israeli armed forces killed 1397 Palestinians, including 764 non-combatants and 345 minors. A further 248 civilian police officers were killed inside police stations. The Goldstone Report concluded that these police officers were predominantly for civilian law enforcement in the Gaza Strip, not military confrontation. Israel was also accused of a variety of crimes, including the illegal use of white phosphorous in built-up areas and wilful destruction of civilian infrastructure, among others. In general, the Goldstone Report concluded that Israel engaged in disproportionate force and did not employ adequate measures to minimise the damage to civilians and civilian infrastructure. According to the media summary,

> The Israeli operations were carefully planned in all their phases as a deliberately disproportionate attack designed to punish, humiliate and terrorize a civilian population, radically diminish its local economic capacity both to work and to provide for itself, and to force upon it an ever increasing sense of dependency and vulnerability.

72 The 'lesser' jihad: armed resistance

The Israeli government refused to cooperate with the fact-finding mission. See Human Rights in Palestine and Other Occupied Arab Territories: Report of the United Nations Fact-Finding Mission on the Gaza Conflict (UN Human Rights Council, 25 September 2009). Available at www2.ohchr.org/english/bodies/hrcouncil/docs/12session/A-HRC-12-48.pdf.

5 Anonymous surveys conducted at an-Najah National University (Nablus), Birzeit University (Birzeit) and al-Quds University (Abu Dis) from March to May 2010 (n = 110 and n = 108, respectively).

6 Interestingly, there is no meaningful distinction between students who nominated a faction and neutral students, with each rejecting the proposition by 65 per cent and 67 per cent, respectively. Anecdotally, personal acquaintances within this age group, who were generally of a secularised/Westernised nature, overwhelmingly rejected the possibility of a two-state solution.

7 The intention was to separate Hamas from the mother organisation in order to mitigate any Israeli retaliation for resistance activities. Hamas, however, would end up eclipsing the *Ikhwan*, thus highlighting the importance of resistance in terms of accruing popular legitimacy. It is also important to note that Islamisation from below is still a primary concern of Hamas.

8 This is the compound which houses the Al-Aqsa Mosque and the golden Dome of the Rock. Jerusalem, or al-Quds as it is known in Arabic, is considered to be one of three holy cities in Islam alongside Mecca and Medina. According to Muslim tradition, Jerusalem was the first *qibla* – the direction in which Muslims pray – prior to the Prophet Mohammed's conquest of Mecca. It is more commonly known in English as the Temple Mount and it is also the site of the Wailing or Western Wall, the most holy site in Judaism.

9 Whether al-Qa'ida is truly as nihilistic or millenarian as it is often portrayed in mainstream Western media and academia, of course, is also open to debate.

10 Anonymous surveys, an-Najah National, Birzeit and al-Quds Universities, March to May 2010. Total number of respondents n = 110. Of these, 70 nominated a preferred movement and 40 did not.

11 Personal interviews conducted with senior Hamas and Change and Reform representatives from January to May throughout the West Bank and in Damascus, Syria.

12 See B'tselem at www.btselem.org/english/israeli_civilians/qassam_missiles.asp.

References

Abu Amr, Z. 1993. 'Hamas: A Historical and Political Background'. *Journal of Palestine Studies* 22(4): 5–19.

Allen, L. 2008. 'Getting By the Occupation: How Violence Became Normal during the Second Intifada'. *Cultural Anthropology* 22(3): 453–487.

Arendt, H. 1972. *Crises of the Republic*. New York: Harcourt Brace Jovanovich.

Barzilai, G. 1996. *Wars, Internal Conflicts and Political Order: A Jewish Democracy in the Middle East*. New York: State University of New York Press.

Benmelech, E. and Berribi, C. 2007. 'Human Capital and the Productivity of Suicide Bombers'. *Journal of Economic Perspectives* 21(3): 223–238.

Brown, N. 2010. *Are Palestinians Building a State?* Washington, DC: Carnegie Endowment for Peace.

Brym, R. and Araj, B. 2006. 'Suicide Bombing as Strategy and Interaction: The Case of the Second Intifada'. *Social Forces* 84(4): 1969–1986.

Bryne, A. 2009. *'Businessmen Posing as Revolutionaries': General Dayton and the 'New Palestinian Breed'*. Beirut: Conflicts Forum.

B'tselem. 2010. *By Hook and by Crook: Israel's Settlement Policy in the West Bank*. Jerusalem: Israeli Information Centre for Human Rights in the Occupied Territories.

Clausewitz, C. [1832] 1997. *On War*. Ware: Wordsworth.

Crooke, A. 2009. *Resistance: The Essence of Islamist Revolution*. New York: Pluto Press.

Druckman, D. 2006. 'Explaining National Identity: From Group Attachment to Group Action'. Occasional Paper. Brisbane: University of Queensland.

El-Sarraj, W. 2011. 'Gazans Are No Fools'. *The Huffington Post* (USA), 5 January.

Farrell, S. 2006. 'Hamas Tries to Exploit its Pariah Status at the Ballot Box'. *The Times* (London), 24 January.

Farsoun, S. and Aruri, N. 2006. *Palestine and Palestinians: A Social and Political History*. Boulder, CO: Westview Press.

Filui, J-P. 2012. 'The Origins of Hamas: Militant Legacy or Israeli Tool?' *Journal of Palestine Studies* 41(2): 74–70.

Foucault, M. [1976] 1990. *The Will to Knowledge: The History of Sexuality*. London: Penguin Books.

Gunning, J. 2004. 'Peace with Hamas? The Transforming Potential of Political Participation'. *International Affairs* 80(2): 233–255.

Gunning, J. 2007. *Hamas in Politics: Democracy, Religion, Violence*. London: Hurst & Co.

Gurr, T. 1978. *Why Men Rebel*. Princeton, NJ: Centre of International Studies, Princeton University Press.

Haddad, T. 2007. 'Whose Intifada – Theirs or Ours? On the Growing Popular Alienation from the Palestinian Leadership: An Interview with Husam Khader'. In *Between the Lines: Israel, the Palestinians and the U.S. War on Terror*, edited by T. Honig-Parnass. New York: Haymark Books.

Hass, A. 2010. 'How Will the Next Palestinian Uprising Look?' *Ha'aretz* (Israel), 3 March.

Hass, A. 2012. 'Two Pipes for Two Peoples: The Politics of Water in the West Bank'. *Ha'aretz* (Israel), 23 September.

Hassan, B. 1997. 'On the Politics of Pure Means: Benjamin, Arendt, Foucault'. In *Violence, Identity and Self-Determination*, edited by H. De Vries and S. Weber. Stanford, CA: Stanford University Press.

Hayes, B. and McAllister, I. 2001. 'Sowing Dragon's Teeth: Public Support for Political Violence and Paramilitarianism in Northern Ireland'. *Political Studies* 49(5): 901–922.

Hoffman, B. 2006. *Inside Terrorism*. New York: Columbia University Press.

Hroub, K. 2000. *Hamas: Political Thought and Practice*. Washington, DC: Institute of Palestine Studies.

Hroub, K. 2006. *Hamas: A Beginner's Guide*. London: Pluto Press.

Hroub, K. 2008. *Le Hamas*. Paris: Demipolis.

ICG. 2003. *Islamic Social Welfare Activism in the Occupied Palestinian Territories: A Legitimate Target?* Brussels: ICG.

ICG. 2011. *Radical Islam in Gaza*. Brussels: ICG.

Juergensmeyer, M. 2001. *Terror in the Mind of God: The Global Rise of Religious Violence*. Berkeley: University of California Press.

Junka, L. 2006. 'Camping in the Third Space: Agency, Representation and the Politics of Gaza Beach'. *Public Culture* 18(2): 348–359.

Kassir, S. 2006. *Being Arab*. New York: Verso.

Kepel, G. 2002. *Jihad: The Trail of Political Islam*. London: I.B. Tauris.

74 *The 'lesser' jihad: armed resistance*

Khalidi, W. 1989. 'At a Critical Juncture: The United States and the Palestinian People'. Occasional Paper. Washington, DC: Georgetown University.

Khan, C. 2008. *States, Scarcity and Civil Strife in the Developing World.* Princeton, NJ: Princeton University Press.

Kimmerling, B. 2003. *Politicide: Ariel Sharon's War Against the Palestinians.* New York: Verso.

Kirkpatrick, J. 1989. 'How the PLO was Legitimized'. *Commentary Magazine* 88(1): 21–28.

Klein, M. 2002. 'The Origins of Intifada II and Rescuing the Peace for Israelis and Palestinians'. Washington, DC: Foundation for Middle East Peace, 2 October.

Klein, M. 2007. 'Hamas in Power'. *The Middle East Journal* 61(3): 442–459.

Klein, M. 2011. 'Israel Cannot Use Force Against the Next Palestinian Uprising'. *Ha'aretz* (Israel), 3 August.

Lieberfeld, D. 1999. *Talking with the Enemy: Negotiation and Threat Perception in South Africa and Israel/Palestine.* West Port, CT: Praeger.

Linzer, D. 2004. 'Poll Shows Growing Arab Rancor at U.S.'. *Washington Post*, 23 July.

Lis, J. 2015. 'ICC Opens Initial Probe into Possible War Crimes in Palestinian Territories'. *Ha'aretz* (Israel), 16 January.

Makdisi, S. 2010. *Palestine Inside Out: An Everyday Occupation.* New York: W.W. Norton.

McGeough, P. 2009. *Kill Khalid ... Mossad's Failed Hit and the Rise of Hamas.* Crow's Nest, NSW: Allen & Unwin.

McIntyre, D. 2010. 'It's Up to Us to Live the Siege'.'' *Independent* (UK), 2 June.

Milton-Edwards, B. 2011. 'Islam and Violence'. In *The Blackwell Companion to Religion and Violence*, edited by A. Murphy. Chichester: Wiley-Blackwell.

Milton-Edwards, B. and Farrell, S. 2010. *Hamas: The Islamic Resistance Movement.* Cambridge: Polity Press.

Mishal, S. and Sela, A. 2000. *The Palestinian Hamas: Vision, Violence and Coexistence.* New York: Columbia University Press.

Moisi, D. 2010. *The Geopolitics of Emotion: How Cultures of Fear, Humiliation and Hope Are Reshaping the World.* New York: Doubleday.

Morris, B. 2001. *Righteous Victims: A History of the Zionist–Arab Conflict, 1881–2001.* New York: Vintage Books.

Nusseibeh, S. 1990. 'A Palestinian View of the Occupied Territories'. In *The Elusive Search for Peace: South Africa, Israel and Northern Ireland*, edited by H. Giliomee and. J. Gaiano. Capetown: Oxford University Press.

Pape, R. 2005. *Dying to Win: The Strategic Logic of Suicide Terrorism.* New York: Random House.

PCPSR. 1993. *Poll no. 2, October 5–10.* Ramallah: PCSPR.

PCPSR. 1994. *Poll no. 6, February 19.* Ramallah: PCSPR.

PCPSR. 2000. *Public Opinion Poll no. 1, July 27–29.* Ramallah: PCSPR.

PCPSR. 2001. *Public Opinion Poll no. 3, December 19–24.* Ramallah: PCSPR.

PCPSR. 2003. *Public Opinion Poll no. 8, June 19–22.* Ramallah: PCSPR.

PCPSR. 2004. *Public Opinion Poll no. 11, March 14–17.* Ramallah: PCSPR.

PCPSR. 2005. *Public Opinion Poll no. 17, September 27–29.* Ramallah: PCSPR.

PCPSR. 2010. *Public Opinion Poll no. 35, March 4–6.* Ramallah: PCSPR.

PCPSR. 2012. *Public Opinion Poll no. 44, June 21–23.* Ramallah: PCPSR.

Pressman, J. 2006. 'The Second Intifada: Background and Causes of the Israeli–Palestinian Conflict'. *The Conflict Journal* 23(2): 114–141.

Qur'an, The. 2008. Translated and edited by T. Khalidi. London: Penguin Books.

Randles, S. and Alqasis. A. 2012. 'Seam Zones Turn 50,000 Palestinians into "Internally Stuck Persons" '. *Jadaliyya*, 22 August.

Rane, H. 2009. *Reconstructing Jihad amid Competing International Norms*. New York: Palgrave Macmillan.

Rapoport, D. 2004. 'The Four Waves of Modern Terrorism'. In *Attacking Terrorism: Elements of Grand Strategy*, edited by A.K. Cronin and J.M. Ludes. Washington, DC: Georgetown University Press.

Rosenfeld, M. 2004. *Confronting the Occupation: Work, Education, and Political Activism of Palestinian Families in a Refugee Camp*. Stanford, CA: Stanford University Press.

Roy, S. 2002. 'Why Peace Failed: An Oslo Autopsy'. *Current History* 101: 8–16.

Roy, S. 2007. *Failing Peace: Gaza and the Palestinian–Israeli Conflict*. London: Pluto Press.

Said, E. 1992. *The Question of Palestine*. New York: Vintage Books.

Salah, B. 2009. 'An Econometric Analysis of Palestinian Attacks: An Examination of Deprivation Theory and Choice of Attacks'. *European Journal of Social Sciences* 7(4): 17–29.

Sarraj, E. 2002. 'Suicide Bombers: Dignity, Despair, and the Need for Hope: An Interview with Eyad El Sarraj'. *Journal of Palestine Studies* 31(4): 71–76.

Sayigh, Y. 1997. 'The Armed Struggle and Palestinian Nationalism'. In *The PLO and Israel: From Armed Conflict to Political Solution, 1964–1994*, edited by A. Sela and M. Ma'oz. New York: St Martin's Press.

Sayigh, Y. 2011a. *'We Serve the People': Hamas Policing in Gaza*. Brandeis University: Crown Centre for Middle East Studies.

Sayigh, Y. 2011b. *Policing the People, Building the State; Authoritarian Transformation in the West Bank and Gaza*. Washington, DC: Carnegie Endowment for Peace.

Sayre, E. 2010. 'Relative Deprivation and Palestinian Suicide Bombings'. *Asian Journal of Social Sciences* 38(3): 442–461.

Schulz, H. and Hammer, J. 2003. *The Palestinian Diaspora: Formation of Identities and Politics of Homeland*. New York: Routledge.

Shamir, J. and Shikaki, K. 2010. *Palestinian and Israeli Public Opinion: The Public Imperative in the Second Intifada*. Bloomington: Indiana University Press.

Shikaki, K. 2006. 'Sweeping Victory, Uncertain Mandate'. *Journal of Democracy* 17(3): 116–130.

Swedenburg, T. 1995. 'With Genet in the Palestinian Field'. *Fieldwork under Fire: Contemporary Studies of Violence and Survival*, edited by C. Nordstrom and A. Robben. Berkeley: University of California Press.

Tamimi, A. 2007. *Hamas: A History from Within*. Northampton, MA: Olive Branch Press.

Tuastad, D. 2003. 'Neo-Orientalism and the New Barbarism Thesis: Aspects of Symbolic Violence in the Middle East Conflict(s)'. *Third World Quarterly* 24(4): 591–599.

Tuastad, D. 2009. *Primary Solidarity: A Comparative Study on the Role of Kinship in Palestinian Local Politics*. PhD thesis. Oslo: University of Oslo.

Wagemakers, J. 2010. 'Legitimizing Pragmatism: Hamas' Framing Efforts from Militancy to Moderation and Back?' *Terrorism and Political Violence* 22(3): 357–377.

Weber, M. [1919] 1978. 'Politics as Vocation'. In *Max Weber: Selections in Translation*, edited by W. Ruciman. Cambridge: Cambridge University Press.

76 The 'lesser' jihad: armed resistance

Zedong, M. 1938. *Selected Works*, Vol. II. Peking: Foreign Languages Press.
Zuhur, S. 2010. *Hamas and Israel: Conflicting Strategies of Group-based Politics*. Carlisle, PA: Strategic Studies Institute.

Interviews and surveys

al-Ramahi, M., Islamist Secretary General of Parliament, elected PLC Deputy and anaesthetist, Ramallah, January 2010.

Amayreh, K., Palestinian freelance journalist, Dura, January 2010.

Bashir, a 44-year-old Hamas member and youth activities officer, Damascus, May 2010.

Buhjah, an unaffiliated 19-year-old student studying law, anonymous survey, Birzeit University, Birzeit, April 2010.

Daoud, a 23-year-old activist for the Popular Front for the Liberation of Palestine, anonymous survey, an-Najah National University, Nablus, March 2010.

Dweik, A., Islamist Speaker of Parliament, elected PLC Deputy and Professor of Urban Geography, Hebron, May 2010.

Fadwa, an unaffiliated 20-year-old student studying education, anonymous survey, an-Najah National University, March 2010.

Fatima, an 18-year-old Hamas supporter, anonymous survey, an-Najah National University, Nablus, March 2010.

Hammoudeh, S., Professor of Political Science at Birzeit University, Birzeit, November 2009.

Huda, a Hamas sympathiser and American-born engineering student, anonymous survey, Birzeit University, Birzeit, April 2010.

Ishaq, a 20-year-old studying English, anonymous survey, an-Najah National University, Nablus, March 2010.

Jibril, PLC Deputy and former member of the Hamas Planning Committee for the second intifada, the West Bank, February 2010.

Laila, a 31-year-old American-educated NGO project director, Ramallah, 2010.

Mahmoud, a 27-year-old Hamas member, anonymous survey, an-Najah National University, Nablus, March 2010.

Mishal, S., Palestinian-Israeli Professor of Political Science at Tel Aviv University, Tel Aviv, November 2009.

Mona, a 21-year-old former Hamas sympathiser from Jerusalem, anonymous survey, an-Najah National University, Nablus, March 2010.

Mu'minah, a 20-year-old Hamas supporter, anonymous survey, Birzeit University, Birzeit, April 2010.

Munawwar, a 23-year-old Fatah activist studying political science, anonymous survey, al-Quds University, Abu Dis, May 2010.

Qassam, A-S., former presidential candidate and Professor of Political Science at an-Najah National University, Nablus, January 2010.

Qismah, a 20-year-old Hamas supporter studying finance, anonymous survey, Birzeit University, Birzeit, April 2010.

Shahd, an unaffiliated university student, anonymous survey, an-Najah National University, Nablus, March 2010.

Shikaki, K., Director of the Palestinian Centre for Policy and Survey Research, Ramallah, November 2009.

Yasmin, a 20-year-old Hamas supporter studying information technology at Birzeit University, anonymous survey, Birzeit, April 2010.

Yousef, an unaffiliated university student, anonymous survey, an-Najah National University, Nablus, May 2010.

Websites

B'tselem (The Israeli Information Centre for Human Rights in the Occupied Territories), www.btselem.org/.
Palestinian Centre for Human Rights, www.pchrgaza.org/portal/en/.

3 Sacrifice, steadfastness and symbolism

> Today the martyr is glorified. The martyr for them is the power of the people, the power to take revenge on behalf of the victims.
>
> Palestinian psychiatrist Eyad Sarraj (2002, p. 72)

Wandering the empty streets of Nablus, encircled by Israeli checkpoints and cut off from the rest of the West Bank in late 2007, the walls are plastered with photos of the dead. In one, a skinny, uninspiring young man brandishes an automated weapon. He is little more than a child. In another, a heavily bearded, serious-looking man with spectacles is dressed in khaki. And in a third, the smiling face of a small child. Such is the culture of death which permeated Palestinian society throughout the second intifada and, indeed, continues in its aftermath. Similar phenomena are in evidence throughout the West Bank from the refugee camps (*mukhyamat al-laja'een*) to Ramallah.

In 2010, five years after what is generally considered to be the end of the second intifada, life returned to the streets of a relatively accessible Nablus. The faded remnants of these posters, however, continue to adorn the walls of the Old City – albeit in lesser numbers – gradually eroded by the sun, the rain and the passage of time. Periodically, new faces appear, staring down at passers-by, hauntingly depicting the latest of those deemed to have been sacrificed on the altar of Palestinian freedom. Memorials, streets and squares dedicated to martyrs litter the landscape from the white sarcophagus of Yasser Arafat in Ramallah to *shuhada* Street in Hebron, now abandoned to Israeli settlers and their IDF guardians. Indeed, the saliency of sacrifice and martyrdom is not difficult to discern, even to the most casual observer of Palestinian society. Accordingly, this chapter examines the centrality of sacrifice, steadfastness and martyrdom to Palestinian society, and to Hamas in particular.

This chapter also explores the social, political, psychological and symbolic ramifications of the notion of sacrifice and martyrdom attendant upon notions of armed jihad. Sacrificial acts, demonstrative of Hamas' commitment to resistance, helped elevate the movement's status among large segments of the Palestinian public, especially over the course of the second intifada. Specifically, this chapter examine how the concepts of self-sacrifice, *sabr* (patience) and *summud* (steadfastness) helped accrue popular support and institutional legitimacy for the movement.

Martyrdom

The *shahid*, or martyr, is perhaps the most revered figure among Palestinians. While a special status is accorded to those who died actively fighting the occupation, it is important to note that many Palestinians consider all those who died directly or indirectly as a result of the occupation as martyrs. The importance of sacrifice and martyrdom – or the ethos of 'death or glory' – has become such, suggest Milton-Edwards and Farrell (2010, p. 139), that the act of dying may have become more important than the ostensible tactical advantage of such an action, citing IDF accounts which describe Palestinian fighters recklessly throwing their lives away (in contrast, for example, to Hizbullah fighters in Lebanon). Nevertheless, there is a consistent discourse present in Palestinian society vaunting the sacrifice of martyrs, especially among Hamas supporters and sympathisers. Gunning (2007a, p. 49) argues that, throughout the course of the second intifada, suicide bombings became a measure of political influence (see also Bloom 2005, pp. 19–44).

Although the number of conventional armed attacks against the IDF and settlers far outstripped such attacks, suicide bombings, self-immolation attacks or martyrdom operations as the Palestinians call them, became one of the most emblematic images of the second intifada. Images of buses torn apart like tin cans were seared into the consciousness of Israel and the West; an image that became all the more salient in the wake of the 11 September attacks and ensuing 'war on terror'. Hamas is believed to be the first Sunni Muslim group to resort to suicide attacks (Tamimi 2007, p. 171).

For the most part, the perpetrators of suicide bombings are vilified, demonised and denigrated in mainstream Western discourses. Characterisations of sexual repression, mental disability, cowardice and psychological pathology seek to delineate or construct an irrational, deviant and nihilist 'type' in opposition to Western conceptions of modernity, rationality and civilisation (see Feldner 2001; Burama 2006; Gupta and Mundra 2005, p. 574; Barnidge 2009, pp. 265–268). According to this view, militant Islamists are driven by "bestial wild instincts aroused in them by religious teaching, which incite to rejection of the other, to the killing of the other, and to the denial of the other" (MEMRI 2005). The discourses pertaining to Islam within the context of the 'war on terror' in particular offer a facile stereotype whereby the perpetrators of suicide attacks are driven by a carnal desire for 72 virgins (or, to be more precise, *houris* or 'maidens of paradise') as a reward for one's deeds (Hoffman 2006, p. 161; Juergensmeyer 2001, p. 201).

These notions, so prevalent within mainstream Western discourses, systematically elide the historical, political and economic contexts of the individuals involved. In contrast, Robert Pape (2005) argues that the common denominator for suicide bombing campaigns is the presence of and resistance to foreign occupation. According to Pape (cited in Fernandez 2011, p. 70),

80   Sacrifice, steadfastness and symbolism

The central fact is that overwhelmingly suicide-terrorist attacks are not driven by religion as much as they are by a clear strategic objective: to compel modern democracies to withdraw military forces from the territory that the terrorists view as their homeland. From Lebanon to Sri Lanka to Chechnya to Kashmir to the West Bank, every major suicide-terrorist campaign – over 95 per cent of all the incidents – has had as its central objective to compel a democratic state to withdraw.

Indicatively, there is no 'type' and Palestinian suicide bombers represent varying aspects of society incorporating not only disillusioned young men but also highly educated men and women, including mothers and fathers. A study by Araj and Brym (2010), in addition, shows that suicide bombers during the second intifada were more highly educated than the society at large and the more high profile the target the more educated the individual. It was this lack of 'type' that made these attacks so difficult to pre-empt, anticipate and intercept. Indeed, as Israeli expert Ariel Merari (cited in Jones 2002) explains, "There was no psychopathology to speak of. These were normal guys, just a cross-section of society" (see also Allen 2002).

The notion that suicide operations are exclusive to Islamist political violence is also spurious and does not stand up to scrutiny. The modern pioneers of suicide operations, the Liberation Tigers of Tamil Elam, were an ostensibly secular organisation with Marxist tendencies (Weiss 2011, pp. 67–77; Pape 2005, p. 4). Similarly, Japanese Kamikaze pilots adopted suicide tactics towards the end of the Second World War. More to the point, all of the major Palestinian factions, including the secular leftist organisations, employed suicide bombings throughout the course of the second intifada, although none could match the numbers and deadliness of Hamas.

At the core of martyrdom is the notion of sacrifice. Sacrifice in the name of a cause is demonstrative of conviction, dedication and devotion. According to Talal Asad (2007, p. 42), "Sacrifice is a profoundly social action". Martyrdom is perhaps the ultimate sacrifice or demonstration of resistance insofar as the individual is willing to die for the cause. Hence, the act of martyrdom is considered to be an altruistic act demonstrative of concern for the greater good of the community (Pape 2005, p. 183). Thus, martyrdom is a social act (Alshech 2008, p. 48). Accordingly, a martyr's "death transcends the individual and endows the community with purity and grace, as well as making their family the object of admiration and support" (Euben 2002, p. 20). In the Palestinian Territories, the 'felicitations' of the community are visited upon the family in the form of sustained visits expressing congratulations, admiration and bestowing prestige. The martyr's actions, therefore, are seen as heroic and the martyr's family enjoys an elevated social status. According to Palestinian psychiatrist Eyad Sarraj (2002, p. 72),

People, including young people, need to feel respected. They want status within their society.... They have all these romantic notions. They see the

Sacrifice, steadfastness and symbolism 81

martyr as courageously sacrificing himself or herself for the sake of everyone, as a symbol of freedom.

Sarraj (ibid., pp. 72–73) then goes on to describe how his mental health clinic needed to treat an individual for depression when he was passed over for a self-immolation operation because he could not be located at the requisite time.

The funerals of martyrs, moreover, are communal events which routinely turn into political demonstrations against the occupation. Indeed, given the militarised nature of the second intifada which sidelined the majority of the Palestinian population, funerals became "an outlet through which people could show some sign of resistance, or simply show solidarity with the families who had lost a relative to the occupation" (Allen 2006, p. 112).

A number of suicide bombings, undoubtedly, were emotional rather than intellectual responses motivated by revenge, desperation and despair for the future. Indicatively, the first waves of Hamas suicide bombings deliberately targeting civilians were in retaliation to the 1994 massacre of some 29 civilians worshipping at the *Ibrahimi* mosque in Hebron by Israeli settler Baruch Goldstein. As noted by Milton-Edwards and Farrell (2010, p. 78),

> In a communiqué entitled 'The settlers will pay for the massacre with the blood of their hearts', it said that, if Israel was indiscriminate in distinguishing between "fighters and unarmed civilians", then Hamas would be "forced … to treat the Zionists in the same manner. Treating like with like is a universal principle."

Revenge is a common justification for Hamas suicide operations. At least until the outbreak of the second intifada in 2000, suicide bombings tended to follow the assassination of Hamas notables, such as bomb maker Yahiya 'the Engineer' Ayyash in 1996, or the mass killings of Palestinian civilians (Mishal and Sela 2000, p. 75).

The spiralling escalation of violence on both sides following the outbreak of the al-Aqsa intifada in 2000 makes the cause-and-effect correlation a little more difficult to ascertain but these were often justified by Hamas as retaliation to Israeli assassinations or massacres, and the desire for further deterrence thereof (Roy 2004, p. 265; Juergensmeyer 2008, pp. 71–72). Political analyst and former Palestinian Authority Cabinet Minister Ghassan Khatib (cited in Milton-Edwards and Farrell 2010, p. 142) ruminates thus on the phenomena of violent self-immolation:

> You are trying to treat the Palestinian activities as politicized in a rational way. They are not rational. They are instinctive reactions. It is just wanting to take revenge and fight back. All the criticism is correct, but it will continue. It is like somebody is trying to stab you, and instinctively you find a nail and stab him back. It's not rational, it is how human nature works.

82 *Sacrifice, steadfastness and symbolism*

It would seem evident, however, that suicide bombings also serve a variety of practical and political purposes. Pape (2005, pp. 28–29), for instance, argues that suicide campaigns, quite simply, are more effective than conventional insurgent or terrorist actions. Specifically, Pape (ibid., p. 71) credits two Hamas suicide bombing campaigns in 1994 and 1995 as accelerating the IDF's withdrawal from West Bank towns; a withdrawal which, hitherto, had been indefinitely delayed beyond the agreed-upon deadlines.

During the second intifada from 2000 to 2005, moreover, 151 suicide operations killed 515 Israelis and injured a further 3500, whereas the total number of Palestinian attacks against Israeli citizens numbered around 25,000 and killed some 1000 Israelis (Benmelech and Berribi 2007, p. 225). Thus, it is evident that despite accounting for only 0.6 per cent of the total number of attacks, suicide bombings succeeded in engineering over half of Israeli fatalities during that period (ibid.).

Throughout the course of my own interviews and surveys, there were also consistent mentions of 'preventative measures' – that is to say, deterrence – retaliation and the psychological impact that such attacks have upon Israelis. Suicide operations are consistently referred to as a weapon of last resort in the face of such an overwhelmingly asymmetrical military situation. The ostensible deterrence created by suicide attacks acted as a 'balance of terror' intended to limit the lopsided balance of power (survey, Abdul-Karim, 2010; Kepel 2004, p. 22). Abd al-Aziz al-Rantisi, the assassinated successor to Sheikh Ahmed Yassin, justified suicide operations as the Palestinian equivalent of an Israeli F-16 or attack helicopter (Human Rights Watch 2002, pp. 56–57; Gill 2007, p. 148).

Palestinian popular support for suicide bombings is not a pathological given but is dependent upon the prevailing socio-political and socio-economic circumstances. There are two periods in which Palestinians supported suicide bombings. The first of these was in 1996 following a prolonged closure of the Palestinian Territories and curfews (Gunning 2007b, p. 171). The second period occurred post-2000 in light of the collapsed peace process, the outbreak of the second intifada and unprecedented Israeli repression, whereby 50 Palestinians were killed and over 1000 wounded during the first five days of the intifada, which, hitherto, had primarily consisted of civil actions (Pressman 2006, p. 131). By the IDF's own admission, Israeli armed forces discharged over a million rounds during the first three weeks of the intifada, or, as one IDF officer admitted to Israel's most widely circulated daily, *Yediot Aharonot*, "a bullet for every child" (cited in Pressman 2006, p. 131). In response to this unprecedented use of Israeli force, Hamas began suicide operations against Israeli targets, including civilians. At the time, suicide bombings were popular among a Palestinian population eager to see their enemies experience the same pain and suffering as themselves.

Suicide bombings are simultaneously a sign of despair and empowerment. During the second intifada many Palestinians were killed as passive bystanders caught in the wrong place at the wrong time. Fighting, thus, is a sign of agency taken by an individual to die for the cause actively resisting rather than as an innocent victim killed in one's own home. According to Sarraj (2002, p. 72),

> Today, the symbol of power is the martyr. If you ask a child in Gaza today what he wants to be when he grows up, he doesn't say that he wants to be a doctor or a soldier or an engineer. He says he wants to be a martyr.

Hence, many Palestinians, and especially among the youth of Gaza, see no hope for the future, whether it be for peace or prosperity, thus leading to despair. Gazan psychologist Fadl Abu Hein (cited in Levitt 2006, p. 110) echoes this sentiment insofar as "Martyrdom has become an ambition for our children. If they had a proper education in a normal environment, they won't have looked for a value in death."

Thus, there exists a romantic ideal that the Palestinian *shahid* snatches back responsibility for his life and death from the Israeli occupier by immolating himor herself in the name of a greater cause (Asad 2007, p. 49). In other words, such acts may be conceived as a final gesture of "despair, revenge or an attempt to burst out of a lifetime of powerlessness" (Milton Edwards and Farrell 2010, p. 137). Talal Asad (2007, p. 75) furthermore contends that suicide bombings may be interpreted as the "aesthetic performance of an idea" which stretches all the way back to the biblical story of Samson and the temple.

Martyrdom operations are perceived to be empowering because, despite the vast asymmetry in power between the warring parties, Israel was unable to stop these attacks. The impacts of such attacks on Israeli society were clear to all, be it in terms of deaths, casualties or the psychological effects on the wider population suddenly situated at the front line of a war.

Following the almost complete reoccupation of the West Bank in 2002, Hamas took the lead in resistance operations, which included suicide bombings against civilian targets. While all the major Palestinian factions employed suicide bombings, none could compete with Hamas in terms of sheer numbers and deadliness (Alshech 2008, p. 44). Indeed, Hamas' Qassam Brigades were responsible for around 40 per cent of Palestinian self-immolation operations (Benmelech and Berribi 2007, p. 22).

For the Hamas leadership, self-immolation attacks were driven by political consideration and practical utility. This is reflected in the cessation of such operations in the immediate aftermath of the 11 September attacks on the World Trade Center and the Pentagon. Although this was only a temporary measure which was dropped in the face of Israeli assassinations and collective punishment, this, along with several other *tadi'a'* ('periods of calm'), demonstrates that Hamas' violence – or at least that dictated by the upper echelons of the movement – is employed according to circumstance. Hamas eventually declared a moratorium on suicide bombings in 2005 which it held until claiming a single attack in 2010. By 2005, support for these operations had dropped in light of the negative impact of such attacks on international opinion, which markedly detracted support and sympathy for the Palestinian cause (McGeough 2009, p. 404).

84 *Sacrifice, steadfastness and symbolism*

Nevertheless, Eli Alshech (2008) contends that these suicide bombings contributed to the success of Hamas in the 2004/2005 municipal elections and, by extension, the 2006 legislative elections. Pre-recorded posthumous tapes of self-immolation martyrs helped to facilitate and disseminate ideals of sacrifice and martyrdom. These videos are available for hire at local stores throughout the Palestinian Territories. Alshech (ibid., p. 31) argues that the creation of a 'martyr' figure through the ritualisation of these videos is a deliberately cynical ploy by Hamas:

> By carefully structuring its texts as a martyrology, Hamas was able to *reconstruct*, rather than simply *describe*, the martyrs' life and death experiences, thereby casting an archetype of piety and martyrdom that Hamas wished others to emulate. Moreover, through 'Islamization' of the texts Hamas successfully produced a message that resonated with pious commoners.

These recordings thus provide a platform to frame the act within a familiar (Islamic) normative framework of morality, selflessness and sacrifice for the greater good.

This view is somewhat vindicated, although in this case from a position of pride, by the Deputy Head of the Political Bureau, Mousa Abu Marzouq (personal interview 2010) who, likewise, attributes the dramatic rise of Hamas' popularity to the movement's "martyrdom operations" which were "used to form a model for hundreds of youth who came to Hamas and joined Hamas". Thus, through frame amplification, the ritualisation of the act conveys meaning with the intent of creating a hero figure and attracting support, legitimacy and prestige for the organisation. In this light, "self-chosen martyrs", as Abd al-Aziz al-Rantisi liked to call them, "were trying not to avoid life but to fulfil it in what they considered to be an act of both personal and social redemption" (Juergensmeyer 2001, p. 171).

In a similar vein, Lori Allen (2006) and Dag Tuastad (2009, p. 218) argue that martyrs associated with particular movements have the capacity to attract symbolic capital which may then be translated into political support. Allen (ibid., p. 108) further argues that "personal sacrifice is, for many, a sign of one's faith in God, and for most, a manifestation of profound personal commitment to the goal of national independence".

A controversial example of this cult of martyrdom is the dubious nature of the children's programming on Hamas' *Al-Aqsa TV*. One of the more egregious examples of this was a Mickey Mouse look-alike, Farfour, who preached martyrdom and jihad against the occupation. Upon widespread international criticism pertaining to indoctrination Hamas chose to kill off the character, literally, at the hands of an actor dressed as an IDF soldier (BBC 2007). One can only imagine the impact that the murder of a favourite children's character by an all-too-real enemy would have upon the mentality of a child.

Hamas suicide bombings elicited severe Israeli reprisals, including collective punishment and a campaign of targeted assassinations against political notables.

Israeli attacks took a heavy toll on Hamas' political leadership with the assassination of spiritual leader and founder Sheikh Ahmed Yassin – a wheelchair-bound quadriplegic – his successor Abd Al-Aziz Rantisi and several other founding members such as the 'moderate' Ismail Abu Shanab. But the effects of these assassinations were not exactly what Israel intended, since each attack afforded Hamas much sympathy, support and solidarity (Gunning 2007a, p. 225). Following the assassinations of Yassin and Rantisi, Hamas' support jumped 4 per cent overall to 24 per cent in June 2004, whereas in the Gaza Strip Hamas polled 29 per cent compared to 27 per cent for Fatah (PCSPR *Poll no. 12*, 2004). The combined strength of the Islamists (Hamas, Islamic Jihad and independent Islamists), moreover, increased from 29 per cent in the previous poll in March to 35 percent (38 per cent in the Gaza Strip) in this poll. At the time, this was the highest level of support for the Islamists since 1995 (ibid.). In effect, the assassination of high-profile leaders and the mass funerals which followed in their wake increased the visibility of Hamas and resulted in a consequent rise in popular support (Gunning 2007a, p. 50).

Hence, in an attempt to decapitate the leadership of Hamas, Israel inadvertently created martyrs, paradoxically strengthening Hamas by expanding its support base. In essence, Hamas supporters were simultaneously seen not only as heroic resistance fighters who caused the Israeli withdrawal from Gaza, but also as victims of Israeli aggression and disproportionality. Hamas, moreover, emphasises that individual leaders are not important in themselves, but only because their suffering reflects that of all Palestinians (Milton-Edwards and Farrell 2010, p. 97). Indeed, "at the heart of Islamic law lies the notion of communal salvation; personal salvation is neither valued nor encouraged" (Alshech 2008, p. 37). This, in turn, helps facilitate identification with the movement among the wider population.

Thus, the high price paid by Hamas and its leadership in the face of Israeli aggression is again interpreted as a sign of its conviction, steadfastness and dedication to resistance. Similarly, the general consensus and immediate polls afterwards suggest that Hamas' credibility and popularity actually increased from its prior level as a result of the Israeli attack on the Gaza Strip in 2008/2009 (PCPSR *Poll no. 31*, 2009; JMCC *Poll no. 67*, 2009). Polls following Israel's attack on Gaza in 2014 recorded a similar trend showing that Hamas would have won both parliamentary and presidential elections if elections had been held at the time (PCPSR 2014). The polls also showed for the first time that Ismail Haniyeh would have even beaten imprisoned national hero Marwan Barghouti. Hence, it would appear that Hamas derives much of its strength from the sacrifices of its supporters, sympathisers and members. And, as Kassir (2006, p. 83) points out, "Sacrifice has been at the root of all human conflict since the dawn of history ... and this is the meaning of jihad in the martial sense."

86 *Sacrifice, steadfastness and symbolism*

Summud under fire: 'Operation Cast Lead'

The 2008/2009 war in Gaza provides an exemplary example of the melange between steadfastness and resistance. At first glance this is somewhat paradoxical, given the lacklustre performance put up by Hamas, in a confrontation during which some 1397 (mostly civilian) Palestinians were killed in contrast to 13 Israelis (several of whom died as a result of 'friendly' fire). Nevertheless, the popularity of Hamas increased as a result of 'Operation Cast Lead' as did its political legitimacy, especially in the West Bank. The Gaza war also served to delegitimise the Abbas/Fayyad PA in the West Bank. Throughout the course of the war the PA in the West Bank remained mute in its condemnation of the Israeli attack, as well as violently suppressing demonstrations in the West Bank expressing solidarity with the people of Gaza. *Summud*, "particularly during attack ... [is] to publicly, and defiantly, display steadfastness and therefore [is] an action that further[s] the national cause" (Peteet 1991, p. 183). *The Qur'an* (8:46–47), in addition, exhorts Muslims to "Remain steadfast: God stands with the steadfast."

A January 2009 poll for the Jerusalem Media and Communications Centre (*Poll no. 67*) in the immediate aftermath of the war found that Hamas' support had risen from 19.3 per cent in April 2008 to 28.6 per cent in January 2009, whereas Fatah fell from 34 per cent to 27.9 per cent over the same period. In the West Bank, Hamas' popularity increased from 12.8 per cent to 26.5 per cent during this period. In a similar vein, trust in de facto Prime Minister of the Gaza Strip Ismail Haniyeh increased from 12.8 per cent to 21.1 per cent, whereas trust in President Abbas fell from 15.5 per cent to 13.4 per cent (ibid.). In addition, 40.7 per cent of respondents believed that the Haniyeh government in Gaza was doing better, up from 29.6 per cent in the previous poll, whereas Fayyad's West Bank Authority fell from 36 per cent to 26.9 per cent. Crucially for Hamas' ethos of armed resistance, 50.8 per cent of Palestinians said that rockets launched from Gaza helped "achieve the Palestinian national goals", an increase from 39.3 per cent in the previous poll, thus somewhat vindicating these actions (ibid.).

In a similar vein, PCSPR *Opinion Poll no. 31* taken in March 2009 – that is to say, after nationalist sentiment and raw emotions had somewhat calmed down in comparison to the JMCC poll – found that the popularity of Hamas increased by five points in the aftermath of the Gaza operation from 28 per cent to 33 per cent. During the same period the positive evaluation of the Haniyeh government's performance increased significantly from 36 per cent to 43 per cent, as did its legitimacy. According to the polls, 35 per cent nominated Haniyeh's government in the Gaza Strip as the legitimate administration, whereas only 24 per cent legitimated Fayyad's West Bank Authority. Three months prior to that, Fayyad's government narrowly led Haniyeh's in the legitimacy stakes: 30 per cent to 28 per cent. Haniyeh's personal popularity rose to 47 per cent in order to eclipse the 45 per cent attributed to President Abbas (see PCPSR *Poll no. 31* 2009). Commentators for the liberal Israeli daily *Ha'aretz* opined that "the major damage Cast Lead did [to Israel] was in legitimizing Hamas as the ruler of the

Sacrifice, steadfastness and symbolism 87

Gaza Strip, with increasing calls for 'reconciliation talks' that will return the organization to the Palestinian leadership" (Harel *et al.* 2009). Indeed, the 2014 attack on Gaza later prompted Hamas and Fatah to move from a reconciliation government to a unity government (Hass 2014).

The poll also revealed an increase in support for armed attacks against Israeli civilians (54 per cent, up from 48 per cent before Cast Lead) and an increased sense of pessimism vis-à-vis the peace process. Indeed, 73 per cent of respondents believed that the creation of an independent Palestinian state in the next five years was "slim to non-existent" (PCPSR *Poll no. 31* 2009).

The attack on Gaza even fell flat among many Fatah supporters. According to Fadi (survey 2010), a 21-year-old Fatah supporter studying political science, the war in Gaza "made me more aware of the situation because the war is not against Hamas but against all Palestinians". Milton-Edwards and Farrell, likewise, report that many Palestinians accepted "Hamas' argument that Israel was simply using Hamas as a pretext to destroy Palestinian life and society, as it had with Yasser Arafat and the PLO before" (Milton-Edwards and Farrell 2010, p. 303). Thus, if the attack on Gaza was meant to pummel Palestinians into submission or delegitimise Hamas, it would appear that it was a demonstrable failure.

A similar occurrence of PA popular delegitimisation transpired in October 2009 following its decision to postpone the UN vote vis-à-vis the Goldstone Report condemning Israel, and to a lesser extent Hamas, of war crimes committed during the 2008/2009 conflict in the Gaza Strip. In a similar vein, secret US embassy cables leaked by WikiLeaks, as well as classified negotiation documents obtained by *al-Jazeera* and the *Guardian* in 2011, 'The Palestine Papers', seemed to indicate that the Palestinian Authority in the West Bank was informed of the 2008/2009 attack on Gaza in advance; an attack, it seems clear, that completely took Hamas by surprise. Accordingly, the Palestinian Centre for Survey and Policy Research (*Poll no. 34* 2009) concluded,

> It is likely that the popularity of Fatah and Abbas has deteriorated considerably right after the eruption of the crisis over the Goldstone Report when a vote on the report was postponed by Abbas.

In short, the postponement of this vote was interpreted as the PA kowtowing to Israeli and US pressure, in opposition to Palestinian principles of steadfastness, resistance and struggle.

Despite Hamas' lacklustre military performance and criticism that it shied away from battle during the 2008/2009 conflict in Gaza, the asymmetrical nature of the conflict and the vast power disparities between the conflicting parties meant that Hamas was able to claim victory insofar as Israel was unable to achieve its objectives which were, officially, deterrence, stopping the rockets and freeing abducted IDF soldier Gilad Shalit. In other words, Hamas defined the parameters of the conflict in such a way that it was able to claim victory by default. As a result, Hamas was transformed into a symbol of resistance not only to Palestinians, but also to the wider Arab world accustomed to humiliating

88 *Sacrifice, steadfastness and symbolism*

military routes at the hands of the IDF. This, in turn, strengthened the conviction of Hamas supporters. According to Mahmoud (survey 2010), a 27-year-old Hamas member, "The war's purpose was to eliminate Hamas, and Israel did not achieve that goal, this only increased my belief in Hamas." Similarly, Nuh (survey 2010), a 21-year-old student of history, stipulates, "Undoubtedly, the war affected my [political] standpoint as the resistance in Gaza has proved its steadfastness and challenged the Israeli blockade."

Summud in this light "represents staying put despite continuous assault" (Schulz and Hammer 2003, p. 106). Thus, for Palestinians, survival against the odds and the exhibition of *summud* are interpreted as victories in themselves, especially in light of the vastly asymmetric military capabilities of the warring parties. The notion of *summud*, especially in the face of assault and adversity, is particularly salient for Palestinians because "the act of flight is equated with surrender, and the loss of Palestine in 1948" (Peteet 1991, p. 183). Within the context of asymmetrical conflicts, in contrast, the mere act of survival is often equated with victory.

As a result, the 2008/2009 Gaza war elevated the status of Hamas in the wider Arab world, especially among Sunni Muslims. Prior to this, Sunni Muslims were forced to look to the 'victories' of the non-Arab and Shi'a Iranian Revolution in 1979, where a predominantly non-violent people's uprising swept away a militarily powerful, Western-backed and entrenched dictatorship, and the Arab, but Shi'a, fortitude of Hizbullah and its resistance, defiance and perceived victories against Israel. According to former presidential candidate and Professor of Political Science at an-Najah National University Abdul Sattar Qassam (personal interview 2010), the Shi'a examples were simultaneously an inspiration for Arabs and Sunni Muslims alike, but also a source of consternation insofar as Sunni Muslims were perceived to be 'falling behind' their Shi'a brethren. Thus, Hamas' steadfastness under fire helped facilitate its elevated status among Sunni Muslims in particular.

The roles of Iran and Hizbullah as symbols of Islamic resistance are contentious, and can, at times, be problematic for Hamas as a Sunni organisation. On the one hand, Palestinians welcome resistance to what is perceived to be Western imperialism but, on the other, they are suspicious of (alleged) non-Arab and/or Shi'a expansionism. This concern is demonstrably evident among the West Bank Authority and wider Arab leadership, as revealed by Wikileaks and *al-Jazeera*'s 'Palestine Papers'. Thus, Iran is simultaneously seen as a symbol and a threat. Hence, according to Omar (personal survey 2010), a 23-year-old Hamas supporter, "the best thing is the armed resistance and Islamic factions. All Arabs should turn to Tehran because it is the symbol of the revolution." Others hold to a more conspiratorial line that Hamas is a vehicle for Iranian – and by extension Shi'a – interests. Abdullah (personal survey May 2010), a 30-year-old Fatah member, for example, contends that Hamas' "political decision is always connected to other countries such as Iran and Syria".

Indeed, Hamas does have regional sponsors and receives diplomatic and/or economic support from Turkey, Qatar and Iran respectively, but Hamas is first

Sacrifice, steadfastness and symbolism   89

and foremost part of the Palestinian national movement. Sunni Hamas' alliance with Shi'a Iran does make for strange bedfellows, but it is a tactical rather than ideological affinity given their manifest disparities. The pragmatism of these relationships may be underscored by the deterioration of Hamas' relationship with the Syrian government – Iran's principal strategic ally. Until 2012, the Hamas Political Bureau was located in Damascus and considered part of a regional 'axis of rejection' (as it is branded by the US), which included Syria and Hizbullah; the grouping, in contrast, preferred to style itself as an 'axis of resistance' against Western and Israeli imperialism. However, Hamas' refusal to publicly support the Syrian government following popular and then armed uprisings against the regime of Bashar al-Assad led to the surreptitious relocation of its Political Bureau to Qatar. According to the International Crisis Group (2012, p. 6), Hamas offered to mediate between the government and the rebels in an attempt to balance the movement's gratitude towards its long-time patron and commitment to grassroots political activism, but was rebuffed by the government. This distancing from the Assad regime, in turn, caused tensions with Iran. Nevertheless, pragmatic political concerns appear to have won out once more as ties between Hamas and Iran have been restored (Reuters 2011; ICG 2012a, p. 10; Berti 2014), once again demonstrating that Hamas, and Iran for that matter, act as conventional political actors despite their Islamic proclivities.

The case of Palestinian prisoners

At the crux of these narratives of sacrifice, stoicism and *sabr*, lay the figure of the Palestinian prisoner. While Israel considers Palestinian prisoners as criminals or 'terrorists', Palestinians perceive prisoners as patriots, heroes and prisoners of war worthy of emulation. Prisoners and their families enjoy an exalted social status within Palestinian society (Rosenfeld 2004, p. 221). In essence, Palestinians view "political imprisonment as a productive and honourable deed – a procreative act in relation to the national community" (Jean-Klein 2011, p. 98). Thus, prisoners are perceived to be embodiments of resistance serving the greater cause of Palestinian self-determination. As such, prisoners are a model for recruitment and the collective prestige of an organisation. The fact that both contending Palestinian governments in the West Bank and Gaza Strip possessed a Ministry for Prisoners' Affairs highlights the centrality of political prisoners to Palestinian society.[1] Since 1967 more than 700,000 Palestinians – or one-fifth of the population – have been held in Israeli prisons, mostly, in the eyes of Palestinians, as political prisoners (Zuhur 2010, p. 2).

Bashir (personal interview 2010), a Hamas public relations and youth activities officer then based in Damascus, traces his political inspiration to an imprisoned uncle, recounting:

> One of my uncles was arrested in an Israeli jail until 1985. Throughout the whole time he had spent in jail, I was sending him letters and he used to

90 *Sacrifice, steadfastness and symbolism*

> send me letters as well. So, I had some national emotions ... I think this is important. Not only important but very important because when I was a child, I had a picture of my uncle and I knew my uncle was a hero.

The experience of prisoners, thus, is an important factor in politicising younger generations by providing models worthy of emulation (Rosenfeld 2004, p. 231). For Hamas, furthermore, prisoners are one of its main pillars of decision making. The reason why the 2006 National Reconciliation Document – colloquially known as the Prisoner's Document – was taken so seriously is a result of the high esteem in which prisoners are viewed within Palestinian society.

Imprisonment is also perceived to be a sign of conviction and a badge of honour worn with pride. According to Jibril (personal interview 2010), a high-ranking Parliamentary Deputy and former member of the planning committee during the intifada,

> I pass[ed] six years in prison because I am a supporter of Hamas. It is not a benefit, not a material benefit, but we understand that we are sacrificing for our society and for that we found it is something that we [are willing to] lose our life.

According to supporters and activists, time spent in jail often reinforces their convictions of proper conduct and evidence that they are pursuing the right course of action to serve society better. Indeed, Mahmoud al-Ramahi (personal interview 2010), the Islamist Secretary of Parliament, contends that:

> Whenever the Israelis didn't like a Palestinian, it means that this Palestinian is going the straightway. Whenever they have a good relationship with Israel – for example, with Fatah – that means that Fatah has started to go outside from the way of the liberation and resistance.

Similarly, Mahmoud (survey 2010), a 27-year-old Hamas member, recounts: "I was imprisoned for four years, but the experience did not change my orientation; on the contrary it increased my belief in my party."

The release of prisoners is an emotional affair among the Palestinian population. In October 2009, Hamas obtained the release of 20 Palestinian women in exchange for a video showing that abducted Israeli corporal Gilad Shalit was still alive (Khoury *et al.* 2009). In short, Hamas is an activist movement which is perceived, by and large, to keep its promises. Negotiations over Shalit's fate entailed the release of hundreds of high-profile Palestinian prisoners and elicited widespread support for Hamas. Despite claiming to be the President of all Palestinians, including Islamists in prison, Mahmoud Abbas was so worried about such an eventuality that he threatened to dismantle the PA in such an event. According to Uri Blau (2008), moreover, "publication of Abbas' threat to dismantle the PA if Israel releases the Hamas parliamentarians is liable to discredit him massively in the eyes of many Palestinians."

The negotiations over Shalit, and the subsequent consequences, are similarly portrayed as exhibitions of steadfastness and sacrifice. Hamas largely refused to budge on its negotiating principles despite the immense amount of Israeli and international pressure which had been brought to bear as a result. In the immediate aftermath of Shalit's abduction in 2006, Israel rounded up and imprisoned almost all of the elected deputies for the Change and Reform list in the West Bank and launched a massive attack on the Gaza Strip code-named 'Operation Summer Rains', killing some 400 people, mostly civilians. Many of these deputies were sentenced to hefty terms in prison, thereby paralysing the Palestinian Legislative Council. Despite the devastation in the Gaza Strip and the paralysis of Parliament, Hamas refused to release Shalit or compromise on its negotiating principles. As Bashir (personal interview 2010) observes, many Palestinians and Hamas "look at resistance as rejection of concessions and pressure – pressure from the International Quartet or from the Arab countries. They have rejected the pressure and decided to stick to Palestinian national attitudes." The eventual denouement of the Shalit affair in October 2011 seemed to result in an overwhelming victory for Hamas, entailing the release of over 1000 Palestinian prisoners in exchange for the Israeli corporal. Those released included around 280 prisoners serving life sentences for orchestrating or assisting deadly attacks against Israeli targets.

In consequence, a JMCC *Poll no. 75* in November 2011 and a later PCPSR poll conducted in December indicated an increased level of trust and goodwill towards Hamas among the wider populace. According to JMCC (2011), "The prisoner exchange positively affected the position of the majority of respondents (58.1%) towards Hamas while it negatively impacted the position of a limited number of respondents (3.8%)." Similarly, PCPSR *Poll no. 42* (2011) reported that 37 per cent of respondents indicated that their support for Hamas has increased as a result of the exchange. The exchange was so overwhelmingly one-sided that even Palestinian President Mahmoud Abbas, Hamas' principal rival, reportedly described the deal as a "national achievement" (*The Australian* 2011). The timing of the deal also suggests a tactical decision, as the release of prisoners overshadowed Abbas' attempt to win recognition for the State of Palestine at the UN. Hamas, in other words, produced concrete results consequent to armed resistance in contrast to the largely symbolic actions taken by the Palestinian President.

This image of steadfastness in negotiations, and the ability of Hamas to back up their words with actions (for example, in the form of prisoner releases, resistance and 'liberating' the Gaza Strip) is in direct contrast to the perceptions of Fatah, the Palestinian Authority and their relations with Israel. As Abdul Sattar Qassam (personal interview 2010) derisively points out, "If Fatah now recognises Israel, they were telling us they wanted to liberate Palestine, and now they are just asking for a freeze of the settlements!" Hence, there are matters of principle, pride and honour at stake, which Hamas is perceived to have held to even in the face of adversity, whereas Fatah is perceived to have 'sold out' Palestinian rights as recognised under international law.

Conclusions

There is also consistent discourse among Palestinians that if Israel and the United States strike at an individual or organisation they are more likely to become popular because this is a sign of resistance, dedication and sacrifice in the name of the Palestinian cause. According to Jibril (personal interview 2010),

> Until now, they [Israel and the United States] didn't understand the mentality of our people. Whenever the United States says I am against you, the people will support you.... The boycotting and punishment of Hamas increases our popularity because our people [are] clear [sighted]; the US is supporting Israel so the USA is our enemy now. For that whenever they punish any Palestinian, the popularity of this Palestinian will increase.

Indeed, Australian journalist Paul McGeough (2009) argues in his book *Kill Khalid: Mossad's Failed Hit ... and the Rise of Hamas* that it was the failed assassination attempt of the Head of the Political Bureau Khalid Mishal, in Amman in 1997, which directly facilitated Hamas' emergence as an actor on the world stage. The consequent fall-out of the botched operation, on friendly Jordanian soil and thus tantamount to a declaration of war in the eyes of King Hussein, required no less than the personal intervention of then US President Bill Clinton. In order to salvage the 1994 Jordanian–Israeli peace treaty, which King Hussein had signed at great personal risk to himself in the face of popular opposition from a population consisting predominantly of Palestinian refugees,[2] the (first) Netanyahu government was forced to provide the antidote required to save Mishal's life in exchange for several captured Mossad agents. Sheikh Ahmed Yassin, the spiritual leader and founder of Hamas, was released from prison in recompense for violating Jordanian sovereignty and, more importantly in the eyes of King Hussein, the trust he had placed in Israel at great risk to himself and his monarchy (ibid., p. 193). Yassin subsequently conducted a 'victory' tour of the Middle East, accruing both symbolic and monetary capital before returning to the Gaza Strip.

As Friedrich Nietzsche ([1913] 2003, p. 54) points out, "Speaking generally, punishment hardens and numbs, it produces concentration, it sharpens the consciousness of alienation, it strengthens the power of resistance." Indeed, this is the essence of *summud*, as well as the *feda'i*, the *shahid* and the prisoner, all of whom are deemed to have sacrificed themselves in the name of Palestinian freedom.

Notes

1 According to B'tselem, at the end of April 2011, Israel held more than 5300 Palestinians in jail, including over 200 under 'administrative detention' – that is to say, indefinitely held without charge – and some 180 minors under the age of 18. See www.btselem.org/Statistics/Detainees_and_Prisoners for up-to-date details.

2 King Hussein personally witnessed his own father, King Abdullah, being gunned down by a Palestinian in front of the al-Aqsa mosque in Jerusalem because of the (correct) perception that Abdullah had colluded with Israel in order to seize the West Bank during the first Arab–Israeli war of 1948/1949. Indeed, Hussein only survived because the assassin's bullet ricocheted off a medal pinned to his military uniform.

References

Allen, L. 2002. 'There Are Many Reasons Why: Suicide Bombers and Martyrs in Palestine'. *Middle East Report* 223: 34–37.

Allen, L. 2006. 'The Polyvalent Politics of Martyr Commemoration in the Palestinian Intifada'. *History and Memory* 8(2): 107–138.

Alshech, E. 2008. 'Egoistic Martyrdom and Hamas' Success in the 2005 Municipal Elections: A Study of Hamās Martyrs' Ethical Wills, Biographies, and Eulogies'. *Die Welt des Islams* 48(1): 23–49.

Araj, B. and Brym, R. 2010. 'Opportunity, Culture and Agency: Influence on Fatah and Hamas Strategic Action during the Second Intifada'. *International Sociology* 25(6): 842–868.

Asad, T. 2007. *On Suicide Bombing*. New York: Columbia University Press.

Australian, The. 2011. 'Hamas Agrees to Free Captive Israeli Soldier Gilad Shalit in Palestinian Prisoner Exchange'. *The Australian*, 12 October.

Barnidge Jr., R. 2009. 'War and Peace: Negotiating Meaning in Islam'. *Critical Studies on Terrorism* 1(2): 263–278.

BBC. 2007. 'Hamas "Mickey Mouse" killed off'. BBC, 30 June.

Benmelech, E. and Berribi, C. 2007. 'Human Capital and the Productivity of Suicide Bombers'. *Journal of Economic Perspectives* 21(3): 223–238.

Blau, U. 2008. 'Abbas Vows to Dismantle PA if Israel Free Hamas Prisoners for Shalit'. *Ha'aretz* (Israel), 30 July.

Bloom, M. 2005. *Dying to Kill: The Allure of Suicide Terrorism*. New York: Columbia University Press.

Burama, I. 2006. 'Extremism: The Loser's Revenge'. *Guardian* (UK), 25 February.

Euben, R. 2002. 'Killing (for) Politics: Jihad, Martyrdom, and Political Action'. *Political Theory* 30(1): 4–35.

Feldner, Y. 2001. '72 Black-eyed Virgins'. MEMRI, 30 October.

Fernandez, B. 2011. *Thomas Friedman: The Imperial Messenger*. New York: Verso.

Gill, P. 2007. 'A Multi-dimensional Approach to Suicide Bombing'. *International Journal of Conflict and Violence* 1(2): 142–159.

Gunning, J. 2007a. *Hamas in Politics: Democracy, Religion, Violence*. London: Hurst & Co.

Gunning, J. 2007b. 'Hamas: Socialization and the Logic of Compromise'. In *Terror, Insurgency and the State: Ending Protracted Conflicts*, edited by M. Heiberg, B. O'Leary and J. Tirman. Philadelphia: University of Pennsylvania Press.

Gupta, D. and Mundra, K.M. 2005. 'Suicide Bombing as a Strategic Weapon: An Empirical Investigation of Hamas and Islamic Jihad'. *Terrorism and Political Violence* 17(4): 573–598.

Harel, A., Issacharoff, A. and Benn, A. 2009. '40 Days After the War, Hamas Rule of Gaza Gaining Legitimacy'. *Ha'aretz* (Israel), 27 February.

Hass, A. 2014. 'Real Gaza Rehabilitation Requires More Than Israeli "Lifting Restrictions"'. *Ha'aretz* (Israel), 12 October.

94 *Sacrifice, steadfastness and symbolism*

Hoffman, B. 2006. *Inside Terrorism*. New York: Columbia University Press.

Human Rights Watch. 2002. *Erased in a Moment: Suicide Bomber Attacks against Israeli Civilians*. New York: Human Rights Watch.

Jean-Klein, I. 2011. 'Nationalism and Resistance: The Two Faces of Everyday Activism in Palestine During the Intifada'. *Cultural Anthropology* 16(1): 83–126.

Juergensmeyer, M. 2001. *Terror in the Mind of God: The Global Rise of Religious Violence*. Berkeley: University of California Press.

Juergensmeyer, M. 2008. *Global Rebellion: Religious Challenges to the Secular State from Christian Militias to al Qaeda*. Berkeley: University of California Press.

JMCC. 2009. *Poll no. 67, January*. Jerusalem: JMCC.

JMCC. 2011. *Poll no. 75, November*. Jerusalem: JMCC.

Jones, C.P. 2002. 'Speaker Says Terrorists Are Normal People'. *Michigan Daily* (USA), 2 December.

Kassir, S. 2006. *Being Arab*. New York: Verso.

Kepel, G. 2004. *The War for Muslim Minds: Islam and the West*. Cambridge, MA: Belknap Press/Harvard University Press.

Khoury, J., Lis, J., Issacharoff, A. and Ravid, B. 2009. 'Gilad Shalit in Video: I've Been Longing for my Freedom for a Long Time'. *Ha'aretz* (Israel), 2 October.

Levitt, M. 2006. *Hamas: Politics, Charity and Terrorism in the Service of Jihad*. New Haven, CT: Yale University Press.

McGeough, P. 2009. *Kill Khalid ... Mossad's Failed Hit and the Rise of Hamas*. Crow's Nest, NSW: Allen & Unwin.

MEMRI. 2005. 'LA Psychologist Wafa Sultan Clashes With Algerian Islamist Ahmad Bin Muhammad Over Islamic Teachings and Terrorism'. MEMRI, 26 July.

Milton-Edwards, B. and Farrell, S. 2010. *Hamas: The Islamic Resistance Movement*. Cambridge: Polity Press.

Mishal, S. and Sela, A. 2000. *The Palestinian Hamas: Vision, Violence and Coexistence*. New York: Columbia University Press.

Nietzsche, F. [1913] 2003. *The Genealogy of Morals*. New York: Dover Publications.

Pape, R. 2005. *Dying to Win: The Strategic Logic of Suicide Terrorism*. New York: Random House.

PCPSR. 2004. *Public Opinion Poll no. 12, June 24–27*. Ramallah: PCPSR.

PCPSR. 2009a. *Public Opinion Poll no. 31, March 5–7*. Ramallah: PCPSR.

PCPSR. 2009b. *Public Opinion Poll no. 34, December 10–12*. Ramallah: PCSPR.

PCPSR. 2011. *Public Opinion Poll no. 42, December 15–17*. Ramallah: PCPSR.

PCPSR. 2014. *Special Gaza War Poll, September 2*. Ramallah: PCPSR.

Peteet, J. 1991. *Gender in Crisis: Women and the Palestinian Resistance Movement*. New York: Columbia University Press.

Pressman, J. 2006. 'The Second Intifada: Background and Causes of the Israeli–Palestinian Conflict'. *The Conflict Journal* 23(2): 114–141.

Qur'an, The. 2008. Translated and edited by Tarif Khalidi. London: Penguin Books.

Reuters. 2011. 'Iran Cuts Hamas Funding for Failing to Show Support for Assad'. *Ha'aretz* (Israel), 21 August.

Rosenfeld, M. 2004. *Confronting the Occupation: Work, Education, and Political Activism of Palestinian Families in a Refugee Camp*. Stanford, CA: Stanford University Press.

Roy, S. 2004. 'Religious Nationalism and the Palestinian–Israeli Conflict: Examining Hamas and the Possibility of Reform'. *Chicago Journal of International Law* 5(1): 251–270.

Sarraj, E. 2002. 'Suicide Bombers: Dignity, Despair, and the Need for Hope: An Interview with Eyad El Sarraj'. *Journal of Palestine Studies* 31(4): 71–76.

Schulz, H. and Hammer, J. 2003. *The Palestinian Diaspora: Formation of Identities and Politics of Homeland*. New York: Routledge.

Tamimi, A. 2007. *Hamas: A History from Within*. Northampton, MA: Olive Branch Press.

Tuastad, D. 2009. *Primary Solidarity: A Comparative Study on the Role of Kinship in Palestinian Local Politics*. PhD thesis. Oslo: University of Oslo.

Weiss, G. 2011. *The Cage: The Fight for Sri Lanka and the Last Days of the Tamil Tigers*. London: The Bodley Head.

Zuhur, S. 2010. *Hamas and Israel: Conflicting Strategies of Group-based Politics*. Carlisle, PA: Strategic Studies Institute.

Interviews and surveys

Abdul-Karim, an unaffiliated 21-year-old student studying political science, anonymous survey, Birzeit University, Birzeit, April 2010.

Abdullah, a 30-year-old Fatah member, anonymous survey, al-Quds University, Abu Dis, May 2010.

Abu Marzouq, M., Deputy Head of the Hamas Political Bureau, US Specially Designated Global Terrorist and Doctor of Engineering, Damascus, May 2010.

al-Ramahi, M., Islamist Secretary General of Parliament, elected PLC Deputy and anaesthetist, Ramallah, January 2010.

Bashir, A 44-year-old Hamas member and youth activities officer, Damascus, May 2010.

Fadi, a 21-year-old Fatah supporter studying political science, anonymous survey, Birzeit University, Birzeit, April 2010.

Jibril, PLC Deputy and former member of the Hamas Planning Committee for the second intifada, the West Bank, February 2010.

Mahmoud, a 27-year-old Hamas member, anonymous survey, an-Najah National University, Nablus, March 2010.

Nuh, a 21-year-old student studying history at Birzeit University, anonymous survey, Birzeit, April 2010.

Omar, a 23-year-old Hamas supporter, anonymous survey, al-Quds University, Abu Dis, May 2010.

Qassam, A.S., former presidential candidate and Professor of Political Science at an-Najah National University, Nablus, January 2010.

Websites

Al-Jazeera, 'The Palestine Papers', www.aljazeera.com/palestinepapers/.

B'tselem, Detainees and Prisoners, www.btselem.org/Statistics/Detainees_and_Prisoners.

4 From bombs to ballots
Political jihad

al-Islam din wa dawlah – Islam is religion and state.

We, as Palestinians, suckle politics with the milk of our mothers.
Islamist Speaker of Parliament, Dr Aziz Dweik (personal interview 2010)

Although the most visible aspect of Hamas in the mainstream media is its application of armed resistance, the primary motivation of this violence is fundamentally political in nature. Political violence is just one of many strategies employed by Hamas in order to achieve the liberation of Palestine. More to the point, the shortcomings and failures of political violence in forcing an Israeli withdrawal from the West Bank are manifestly clear in light of Israel's continued occupation and concomitant settlement expansion. Thus, in spite of the romanticised popularity of armed struggle, Palestinian aspirations are inherently socio-political. To this end, Hamas pursues a political track based on electoral participation to complement its programme of armed resistance. This is unsurprising in itself given that many paramilitary organisations have contemporaneously pursued a political track in conjunction with armed activities; for instance, the Irish Republican Army and its political wing Sinn Fein (see Weinburg and Pedahzur 2003).

Armed struggle within a demonstrably asymmetrical situation, moreover, is necessarily restricted to a very small percentage of the population. Hence, as a semi-clandestine paramilitary organisation, Hamas' military wing and official membership would only constitute a very small percentage of the total population. Clearly, this is not conducive to facilitating a mass social movement concerned not only with self-determination from a foreign occupier but also with the socio-political reform of society in general. For this, Hamas must appeal to a wider civilian base. Political participation is one such way which simultaneously allows Hamas to appeal to the broader public based on social and political issues, as well as garner domestic and, to a lesser extent, international legitimacy. Thus, as a political body, Hamas' constituency comprises supporters existing on multiple levels of identification, including formal members, ideological alignment, approval of its political programme or simply voting against the pre-2006 Fatah-dominated status quo.

Hamas, however, is often portrayed in mainstream discourses as a rigid religious organisation more concerned with eschatological, theocratic and even genocidal ends rather than with the political advancement of the Palestinian national cause (see e.g. Levitt 2006; Rubin 2006). The policies of many major Western governments, such as the United States and most EU countries, tend to reflect and reify this common conception. Dennis Ross (2006, pp. ix–xi), for example, a Middle East envoy for both the Clinton and Obama Administrations, argues that Hamas is a radical, ideologically rigid, religious organisation which cannot and will not change into a legitimate political actor. This view is reflected in US and EU policy boycotting the Hamas government – or indeed any actor perceived to be Hamas affiliates – despite its 2006 election victory. The ensuing boycott immediately after the 2006 election is indicative of the fact that Hamas clearly caught the major Western powers off guard, especially given their acquiescence to Hamas participation.

Hamas and its political affiliates, in contrast, depict Hamas as a mainstream Islamist organisation dedicated to pursuing what former Finance Minister, Parliamentary Deputy and Professor of economics Dr Omar Abdul-Razeq (personal interview 2010) describes as *wasatiya* or 'the middle way'. Indeed, the more nuanced scholarship contends that Hamas is a pragmatic, activist, sociopolitical movement with religious ideological grounding rather than a movement driven by theocratic ends (Hroub 2000; Mishal and Sela 2000; Tamimi 2007; Gunning 2007; Roy 2011). In this regard, Hamas' political (as opposed to ideological) support accounted for 44.5 per cent of the party list votes and some 70 per cent of seats elected by local constituencies during the 2006 Palestinian Legislative Council elections.

This chapter examines the role of electoral politics, its utility to Hamas, and more specifically the political strategies Hamas employs to attract popular support and augment its power base. First, the chapter explores the political evolution of Hamas since its inception in 1987. Why did Hamas boycott the general elections in 1996? How did it engage in politics following the initial PLO–Israeli reconciliation embodied by the Oslo Accords? Beyond 'spoiler' attacks against Israel, what mechanisms did Hamas utilise to influence internal politics during the Oslo years if not formal electoral participation?

The second section details Hamas' conceptions of politics and democracy. How does Hamas conceive of politics? What are its views on democracy? What is it trying to achieve? What purposes does political participation serve? Specifically, this section will investigate the dialectic between resistance and politics, as well as the idea that democratic participation is a form of resistance and, indeed, a type of jihad in itself.

The third section investigates Hamas' decision to participate in the 2004/2005 municipal and 2006 elections. Why did Hamas choose to participate in the 2004/2005 municipal elections? What electoral strategies did it employ? Why did Hamas participate in the 2006 legislative elections when it had previously boycotted the 1996 elections resulting from the Oslo Accords? In essence, an unfavourable military position vis-à-vis Israel combined with a change in the

98 *Bombs to ballots: political jihad*

political opportunity structure facilitated Hamas' shift from armed to political resistance.

The fourth section interrogates the reasons why Hamas emerged triumphant in 2006. Why did Hamas win such a comprehensive victory in these elections? What electoral strategies did Hamas employ to win over the more 'moderate' base of Palestinian society?

The final section explores some of the repercussions of Hamas' victory upon internal Palestinian dynamics, as well as Palestinian relations with Israel and the major Western powers. What impact, for instance, did the ensuing Western and Israeli boycott have upon the actions of the newly elected government? To what extent did external actions push Palestinians to outright civil conflict resulting in the political separation of the West Bank and Gaza Strip? How did the Israeli siege of Gaza affect the actions of the de facto Hamas government in the coastal territory? How did all of these factors affect the Palestinian population? These are some of the questions this chapter will endeavour to answer.

The political evolution of Hamas: extra-parliamentary participation in a one-party system

At its inception in December 1987, within the context of the first intifada, Hamas existed as a revolutionary, anti-establishment movement, seeking to establish itself as an Islamic alternative to the PLO (Roy 2007, pp. 167–168). Hamas' goal was to radically reform the Palestinian polity with the ultimate aim of establishing an Islamic state (although the specifics of this state, and what it would look like, have always been vague at best) (for further discussion see Gunning 2007, pp. 57–93). In the absence of any formal political process within the context of Israeli occupation, Hamas competed with the PLO on the level of the street by setting up rival demonstrations, issuing rival communiqués, and engaging in both civic and, occasionally, armed resistance actions against the occupation during the first intifada.

The 1993 Oslo Accords, and subsequent other protocols providing for limited Palestinian autonomy in urbanised areas, radically changed the dynamics of the conflict by shifting it (at least temporarily) to the political arena predicated on negotiations between Israel and the PLO. As a result, Hamas' street-level resistance vis-à-vis the occupation was sidelined amid the post-Oslo euphoria which many Palestinians assumed would lead to an independent Palestinian state (Hilal 2005, p. 7). Caught between its own principled rejections of the Oslo Accords as illegitimate, the 'triumphant' return of resistance icon Yasser Arafat and Fatah militants reconstituted as Palestinian police, as well as its own dwindling political popularity in an era of negotiations, Hamas wrangled internally over whether to participate in the nascent institutions embodied by the 1994 creation of the Palestinian National Authority and the subsequent parliamentary elections in 1996.

Despite founder and spiritual leader Sheikh Ahmed Yassin, as well as present luminaries such as Gazan PM Ismail Haniyeh, advocating for electoral participation in order to prevent PA capitulation to Israeli pressure, Hamas boycotted the

Bombs to ballots: political jihad 99

1996 general elections for fear it would legitimise the Oslo Accords (Milton-Edwards and Farrell 2010, pp. 82–83). There also existed a conviction that the elections would not be fair (although this perhaps elides the marginal support for the Islamists at the time).

Nevertheless, an abortive affiliate party, *Hizb al-Khalas al-Watini al-Islami* (the National Islamic Salvation Party), was set up, suggesting that, even in 1995, Hamas was not as dogmatic as portrayed (Klein 2009, p. 887). In this instance however, Hamas chose to maintain ideological and political 'purity' for fear of being co-opted. Hamas argued that the Oslo Accords would merely entrench and normalise the occupation in another form. Thus, according to senior Hamas leader Dr Mahmoud Zahar (cited in Milton-Edwards and Farrell 2010, p. 70), "we need a peace process not a security arrangement.... [The Israelis] are still controlling the crossings, preventing pilgrimage. Every day they harass people who search for work.... This is not a peace process, this is still occupation." Ultimately, over 20 years later, amid a burgeoning number of Israeli settlers continuing to colonise the West Bank and the absence of any comprehensive peace agreement, Hamas appears to have been correct in its initial assessment.

While boycotting institutions related to the Oslo process, Hamas did continue to operate in an extra-parliamentary sense, especially in terms of its social agenda. Hamas also participated in a variety of extra-parliamentary political forums, including professional associations as well as teacher and student unions, which soon came to represent the few contested political forums under an increasingly autocratic Arafat regime based on neo-patronage and 'divide and rule'. In 1992, for instance, Palestinian Islamists founded the Islamic Workers' Union (Zuhur 2010, p. 7). The unions and professional associations, in effect, were used as political proxies in the absence of meaningful democratic governance during a time of relative peace (Barghouti 2007, p. 47). Participation in these forums allowed Hamas to wield influence and pressure the PA without appearing to validate the Oslo Accords or its associated institutions.

In 1993, for example, a coalition between *al-Qutla al-Islamiyya* (the Islamic Bloc) and leftist forces managed to pull off victory at Birzeit University near Ramallah – a traditional secular bastion – running on a platform of opposition to the Oslo Accords. In the same year, Hamas also claimed victory in the traditionally Christian-dominated Ramallah Chamber of Commerce, indicating an increasing level of trust for the Islamist movement, even among other denominations (Gunning 2007, p. 160). Hamas would also unofficially back specific candidates which it deemed ideologically acceptable in order to wield purchase in various public forums.

During this period, in essence, Hamas evolved from a revolutionary anti-establishment actor into an extra-parliamentary socio-political actor seeking reform within the context of an autocratic one-party political system (Roy 2011, pp. 85–88). Thus, Hamas was able to retain its ideological and political purity, while the Fatah-led administration would ultimately be held accountable for any failures which may occur, both in terms of governing and the progression of the peace process.

100 *Bombs to ballots: political jihad*

Student political movements operating from abroad, most notably in Kuwait and Egypt, provided sources of recruitment, funding and ideological inspiration. Indeed, student unions proved a fertile training ground for future leaders. Khalid Mishal, the present Head of the Political Bureau, contemporaneously pursued his education, became involved in founding the Islamic Association of Palestinian Students, which subsequently spread throughout the Palestinian Diaspora, and ran a fundraising organisation from Kuwait until the Iraqi invasion of 1990/1991 (see Zuhur 2010, p. 29; McGeough 2009, pp. 37, 52–53; Tamimi 2007, pp. 71–73). Hamas affiliates, including former – now Deputy – Head of the Political Bureau, Mousa Abu Marzouq (personal interview 2010), also cut their teeth as student union leaders and allegedly ran fundraising operations in Europe and the United States until his prolonged detainment in the US in 1995 and subsequent deportation to Jordan in 1997.

The entry of Arafat and the establishment of the PA in the Palestinian Territories in 1994 also prompted a scramble for political positions, authority and competition for funding. A government based on neo-patronage and centralised power ensued, eventually coming to resemble the other Arab autocracies in spite of the PLO's ostensible desire for a plural secular democracy. The signing of the Oslo Accords led to a dearth of political ideology in the Palestinian Territories as Arafat effectively centralised power in his own office (Roy 2007, p. 172). Indeed, such was the power vested in Arafat that "One Deputy sarcastically suggested in the midst of a parliamentary debate in 1998 that Arafat simply be declared to be God" (Brown 2007, p. 5). Arafat, moreover, ensured that the majority of US and EU donations were routed through the PA. As a result, leftist NGOs and political parties became dependent on PA patronage to operate.

Hamas, in contrast, possessed alternate, non-Western flows of funding derived from internal and external *zakat* (alms) donations, as well as select foreign governments, including Saudi Arabia, various members of the United Arab Emirates and Iran (Pascovich 2012, p. 131; Gunning 2007, p. 45; Van Natta and O'Brien 2003). As a result, only Hamas and several large international NGOs remained functionally autonomous despite Arafat's attempts to rein them in. According to Sara Roy (2007, p. 194), Hamas, a party of religious principle and conviction, benefited from this ideational void during the Oslo years because it offered a clear vision for the future based on traditional Palestinian notions buttressed by Islamic thought. Conversely, Fatah has never really possessed a clear ideology beyond national liberation, instead attempting to attract additional supporters, primarily through its historical legacy and patronage stemming from control of the nascent Palestinian Authority and security forces.

Nevertheless, by the end of the 1990s, PA and Israeli repression had almost completely emasculated the armed wing of Hamas, whereas Arafat's autocratic rule had rendered formal politics almost meaningless as a forum for political advancement. In this light, Hamas chose to refocus on its social agenda – a form of non-violent civic resistance – until the outbreak of the second intifada in 2000, whereupon it emerged as the vanguard of Palestinian armed resistance. Following the death of Arafat in 2004, Mahmoud Abbas (nom de guerre Abu

Bombs to ballots: political jihad 101

Mazen) was elected to the Palestinian Presidency and four rounds of municipal elections were held over 2004/2005. It was at this point, buoyed up by its elevated resistance credentials derived from the second intifada, that Hamas chose to engage in electoral politics.

Resistance and politics

At a base level, politics is about power. As such, according to Foucault ([1976] 1990, pp. 87–89), traditional juridico–political discourses identify politics, and the consequent ability to make legislative decisions, as one of the principal manifestations of power in society. Pierre Bourdieu (1991, p. 181) characterises political parties as "combative organisations specially adapted so as to engage in this sublimated form of civil war by mobilizing in an enduring way" (although, within the context of the Palestinian polity, this civil war took a more literal form in June 2007). In the context of the twenty-first century, political legitimacy, in Western eyes, is supposedly derived from putative international norms based on democratic elections. Within the Muslim Middle East, domestic legitimacy is often predicated on Islamic values. With its victory in the 2006 legislative elections, Hamas appeared to successfully fuse Islam, resistance and democracy. Accordingly, this section details Hamas' conception of politics as a form of resistance or jihad, as well as its views on democracy. In brief, Hamas utilises electoral politics to augment its power, enhance its legitimacy, resist the occupation and help engineer social change.

Hamas is first and foremost a resistance movement but, as with any sociopolitical movement, it is a resistance movement with political motives. Within the context of occupation, Hamas' resistance is primarily concerned with confronting Israeli power. As such, the dialectic between resistance and politics profoundly influences the actions of Hamas. Omar Abdul-Razeq (personal interview 2010) asserts that one of the key reasons the Islamists entered formal national politics was

> to prevent the criminalisation ... of resistance because we thought the direction of the so-called 'peace process' ... is that one of the conditions of the Israelis is to have any resistance activities be a criminal activity.

Indeed, Article 2.11 of the Change and Reform electoral manifesto stipulates "Protecting the resistance, vitalizing its role in resisting the occupation and accomplishing the mission of liberation" (Appendix VI in Tamimi 2007, p. 295).

Hamas, moreover, views politics as a vehicle of resistance. As Mousa Abu Marzouq (personal interview 2010) explains, "we are a resistance movement but politics couldn't be kept away of it. Politics is part of the resistance." This is again reflected in the Change and Reform electoral platform which states that electoral "participation is intended to be an act of support for the program of resistance and intifada to which our people have happily resorted as a strategic option to end the occupation" (Appendix VI in Tamimi 2007, pp. 292–293).

102   *Bombs to ballots: political jihad*

Mariam Salah (personal interview 2010), a Change and Reform Deputy, former Minister for Women's Affairs and Professor of *Sharia* Law at al-Quds University, expands upon these statements, asserting that:

> We, as Muslims, call politics al-jihad. Politics is a kind of jihad as we are supposed to explain to other people what our religion is and to defend our land, homeland, properties and everything that relates to us or belongs to us.

These statements suggest a reconstruction or reinterpretation of the concepts of resistance and jihad beyond armed resistance, which allows Hamas to be more pragmatic and thus able to incorporate a variety of strategies in terms of political practicalities and achieving the liberation of Palestine. Thus, in light of an overwhelmingly asymmetrical military situation and a war-weary populace following the deadly years of the second intifada, Hamas was presented with an opportunity for political advancement by institutional means in the form of elections and chose, at least temporarily, to reinterpret resistance and jihad so as to align these concepts with political change and reform.

Views on democracy

Throughout the course of my own interviews and surveys, Hamas and its political affiliates espoused remarkably consistent discourses pertaining to democracy, political opportunity, intellectual persuasion and a desire to 'serve' the Palestinian people. Yezid Sayigh (2011a) reports a similar mantra of 'serving' the people in the Gaza Strip.

Internally, Hamas is characterised by a culture of collective leadership based on regular elections. This internal democracy consists of *shura* (consultation) councils which operate at local, regional and national levels (Hroub 2006, pp. 117–120; Gunning 2007, p. 59). Decision making, in Hamas' view, should be predicated on the concepts of *shura* and *ijma'* (consensus). In essence, Hamas believes that the legitimacy of the leadership is derived from consultations with the populace: a *"shura* democracy" (Gunning 2007, p. 59). Indeed, Khalid (survey 2010), a 22-year-old Hamas member, describes Hamas' political thought as being based on 'collective action'. This collective leadership structure is not only more democratic than Fatah's Leninist-inspired 'centralised democracy' (in reality, a dictatorship based around Arafat and his select coterie for decades, more or less perpetuated by Mahmoud Abbas, albeit with important discrepancies), but also pragmatic given the intense nature of Israeli and PA repression (Pappé 2006, p. 190). In this light, perhaps, it is somewhat unsurprising that Hamas, as the main opposition party within an autocratic political system, was one of the principal advocates for democratic reform prior to 2004/2005 given that it had the most to gain from such reforms. Repression is such that, even during the free and fair legislative elections of 2006, PCSPR exit polls suggested a Fatah victory with Fatah receiving 42 per cent of the vote to Hamas' 35 per cent (PCPSR 2006). The actual results, however, found that Hamas received

Bombs to ballots: political jihad 103

44.5 per cent of the vote to Fatah's 41 per cent, all of which seems to indicate that Hamas voters were wary of Fatah reprisals (ibid.).

Hamas' democratic thought, in part, derives from the election of the first four *rashidun* or rightly guided Caliphs who were chosen to lead the *umma* (community of believers) following the death of the Prophet Mohammed. Hamas emphasises the inclusive, egalitarian aspects of Islam and equates legitimate leadership with consultation (Gunning 2004, p. 244). Accordingly, Hamas is *au courant* to public opinion through its everyday contact with the general population courtesy of its social networks spread throughout the community. Indeed, Hamas has repeatedly shown itself sensitive to public opinion and reacts accordingly. Following criticism of its sometimes heavy-handed approach to dissent in Gaza, for instance, Hamas has instituted educational courses for overzealous policeman and cadres attempting to enforce Islamic norms at street level (ICG 2011, p. 20; Sayigh 2011a, pp. 28–29).

One may also ascertain some of the international dimensions influencing Hamas' turn to electoral politics. Putative international norms in the twenty-first century regard democratic elections as the basis for political legitimacy. Hence, Hamas' advocacy of democratic values attempted to align itself with US foreign policy in the region ostensibly promoting democracy. According to Iyad Barghouti (2007, p. 48), Hamas "found in democracy a weapon against its local persecutors, as well as against its international enemies, notably the USA, Israel and many European countries". For Hamas, Barghouti (ibid.) continues, democracy was "the best means for confronting Western democracy; democracy should be confronted in the name of democracy". Hamas therefore sees democratic participation as a legitimate form of resistance because it accrues the movement's legitimacy and undercuts Western objections to the movement by conforming to democratic norms.

The emergence of al-Qa'ida and, in particular, the 11 September attacks in Washington and New York, ironically prompted Hamas (and indeed a variety of other Islamist actors) to develop more coherent, pragmatic and reformist programmes of action (Gunning 2007, pp. 226–227). In practice, this entailed greater willingness to participate in formal democratic elections, all of which culminated in the movement's participation in the 2004/2005 municipal and 2006 legislative elections. In doing so, Hamas attempted to disassociate itself from al-Qa'ida's revolutionary, transnational and eschatological agenda (with varying degrees of success). Hamas continues to explicitly distance itself from both the actions and ideology of al-Qa'ida-inspired entities. In fact, according to Yezid Sayigh (2011a, pp. 12–18) and the International Crisis Group (ICG 2011), the main source of unrest, competition and criticism in the Gaza Strip is no longer conflict between Hamas and Fatah. Rather it is between Hamas and more hardline *salafi* elements challenging Hamas' Islamic credentials. The result has been a number of bloody confrontations between Hamas security forces and al-Qa'ida-inspired militants.

The Western education of many contemporary luminaries within Hamas and its political proxies also exposed them to forms of Western governance predicated on free elections and democratic rule. Interestingly, given the movement's

104 *Bombs to ballots: political jihad*

antipathy towards US policy vis-à-vis the question of Palestine, Omar Abdul-Razeq (personal interview 2010) credits his time spent pursuing a PhD in the United States as a catalyst for becoming politically involved:

> It started in the States where you learn and live the values of democracy.... We did not have the chance, the right to vote, as residents in the States, but we felt it, we learnt that culture, we learnt those values ... I got to really like that atmosphere and, in some ways, I wanted to pass it on or to bring it home.... So I used to talk about it all the time to my students.... You cannot apply the whole model, but this concept of elections, this concept of accepting the other, this concept of partnership in taking responsibility for the society ... that you have to make some contribution to this, build up together with others, accept the others, I guess this is the main idea that attracted me to the values. You cannot take the whole American system and apply it to Palestinian society with Islamic [values], with the Muslim religion, and with those traditions which we live in and so on, but you can take a portion that preserves your rights and calls upon you to mutually respect each other.

Sameer Abu Aisha (personal interview 2010), the former Minister for Planning, reports a similar phenomenon citing his time spent studying in the US as an inspiration for promoting democratic reforms at home.

Although Islamists are often criticised for their putative lack of commitment to political pluralism, Hamas has engaged in pragmatic alliances and cooperation with leftist forces, politically and most poignantly, perhaps, in the area of women's rights, specifically with regard to honour killings and underage marriage (Gunning 2004, p. 257). Moreover, Hamas offered to form a unity government with the other Palestinian factions following its 2006 victory in the legislative elections, signalling, at the very least, its intent, if not necessarily its actual ability, to work in conjunction with its political rivals.

Critics, however, charge that Islamist political participation and alleged acceptance of plurality and democracy is merely a tactic which they will abandon in favour of an Islamic state once in power (Burgat 2003, p. 137). Indeed, Hamas' violent takeover of Gaza in June 2007 appears to indicate that the movement is willing to exercise force in order to acquire power and prompted a wave of condemnation, both within the international community and, more damagingly, the domestic arena. This analysis, however, strips the actions of their context. These condemnations, of course, forget that Hamas was overwhelmingly elected in January 2006 and Fatah refused to hand over control of the security forces to the interior ministry. In addition, Fatah actively worked to undermine the Hamas administration. Most pertinently, perhaps, Fatah forces were being armed and trained by the US (see Rose 2008; Steele 2007; Zuhur 2010, p. 19). In this light, and despite its brutality, the armed takeover of Gaza by Hamas was less the 'coup' disparaged by large sections of the Western media, than a legally and democratically elected government enforcing its writ within its territory.

Bombs to ballots: political jihad   105

Since Hamas' takeover of Gaza, moreover, there have been few overt signs of official Islamisation on the part of the government, although individual officials have sometimes privately attempted to push this agenda. With regard to courts and schools, for example, neither the PA curriculum nor its constitution have been modified (ICG 2008, p. 15). There have, however, been increasing levels of public self-censorship propelled by Gaza's isolation and increased hardship, but these do not appear to be instigated by official government policy (although it is likely that the government tacitly accepts street-level Islamisation in order to placate its ideological base frustrated at the slow pace of Islamic reform) (ICG 2011, pp. 26–31; Sayigh 2011a, pp. 12–18). It is also possible that the government finds it useful to utilise individual officials or affiliates as 'weather balloons' to ascertain the limits of Islamisation policies (ICG 2011, pp. 26–31). According to Yezid Sayigh (2011a, p. 12), however, there has been an overall increase in public Islamisation since 2010.

The boycott of the democratically elected Hamas government by the US and most European governments has, unsurprisingly, been perceived in a hypocritical light by many Palestinians and Arabs given Western – and particularly the Bush Administration's – putative advocacy of democracy throughout the Middle East. Consequently, there exists much disillusionment and apathy regarding democracy because the concept of free elections appears to be null and void should the population vote for the 'wrong' party. Ali, a 22-year-old Fatah member (survey 2010) from Jerusalem, for instance, dismissed a survey question on voting preference as "incorrect because liberal and impartial elections took place before". In a similar vein, Nabihah (survey 2010), an unaffiliated 21-year-old studying political science, elucidates: "No, I will not vote because the elections took place before and they were impartial but no one recognised them, so why should I vote?"

The subsequent actions of Fatah, at first refusing to accept the result, then passing legislation ascribing additional powers to the (Fatah) Presidency, namely control of the security forces, were viewed as duplicitous by the victorious Islamists and eventually led to civil war in the Gaza Strip. These events have, in turn, strengthened hardliners at the expense of Hamas' pragmatic wing, who argued for advancement through political integration. Despite these occurrences, however, Palestinians still seem to retain enthusiasm for the idea of democratic governance. My own surveys at Birzeit, an-Najah and al-Quds Universities reveal that 74.4 per cent of respondents (n = 125) would vote in free and fair elections, increasing to 89 per cent among students who nominated a factional inclination.[1] Similarly, a June 2012 poll showed that 69 per cent of respondents would participate in new legislative elections involving all factions (PCSPR *Poll no. 44* 2012).

In short, Hamas has attempted to reconcile tensions between the absolutist, ideological view that only Allah is sovereign (*hakimiyya*), and the necessity for pragmatic laws formulated by human beings in order to regulate affairs which are not legislated in the *Qur'an* due to historical, technological and other extenuating circumstances that did not exist at the time of the Prophet Mohammed.

106 *Bombs to ballots: political jihad*

Menachem Klein (2007, p. 444) contends that for Hamas, "the voice of the masses ... is the expression of God's will". Thus, when the opportunity to participate in free elections presented itself, Hamas embraced the chance to institutionally safeguard the resistance, as well as sell its social and political message to the Palestinian people via formal electoral participation.

Electoral participation, 2004 to 2006

Until the 2004/2005 municipal elections, there existed few opportunities, and thus little incentive, for Hamas to advance itself through institutionalised politics. Under Arafat, subsequent elections to 1996 were either indefinitely postponed or cancelled at both a municipal and legislative level. Arafat personally appointed local government in the municipalities, meaning that there was no opportunity for Hamas to advance itself through formal institutionalised politics during this period; hence, Hamas limited itself to social work and extra parliamentary politics in the form of professional associations and union elections.

From 2004, the death of Yasser Arafat and subsequent reformation of the political system presented Hamas with the opportunity to make political gains by institutional means. First, Arafat's death allowed for municipal elections to be held throughout 2004/2005. Arafat's death also led to the election of the ostensibly democratic Mahmoud Abbas to the Palestinian Presidency in January 2005. Hamas did not contest the presidential elections because "Part of the President's role was to negotiate with Israel, and the position would therefore have placed Hamas in an impossible situation" (Milton-Edwards and Farrell 2010, p. 241). Hamas also believed that the prevailing circumstances were not conducive to free and fair elections (Tamimi 2007, p. 211).

Abbas' election, however, led to the reformation of the political system, as stipulated by the March 2005 Cairo Agreement among 13 Palestinian factions, calling for legislative elections in 2006 based on a mixed electoral system: half proportional representation, half elected individuals at a local district level. The liberalisation of the political system gave opposition parties, most notably Hamas, the incentive to participate in the political system rather than operating as an extra-parliamentary force (Gunning 2007, p. 241). The new system also granted the legislature additional power vis-à-vis the Presidency which had been absent during Arafat's reign. In short, elections allowed Hamas to make political gains through recognised institutional means and thereby safeguard its resistance agenda in all of its forms. Electoral participation may thus be seen as a shift towards political resistance following the failure of the second intifada to end the Israeli occupation (Reinhart 2006, p. 105). Until the reformation of the political system and the exit of Yasser Arafat from the political scene, this was deemed as unfeasible.

With the reformation of the Palestinian political system, Hamas seized the opportunity to participate in municipal and legislative elections, declaring a ceasefire and moratorium on suicide attacks in accordance with the 2005 Cairo Agreement (which also, incidentally, implies the acceptance of a two-state

Bombs to ballots: political jihad 107

solution based on pre-1967 borders). Although Hamas boycotted legislative elections in 1996 because it did not want to legitimise the Oslo Accords, the movement's electoral platform justified its decision to participate in 2006 thus:

> The blessed al-Aqsa Intifada has created new facts on the ground that have rendered the Oslo program a thing of the past, and different parties, including the Zionist occupation, have already spoken about 'burying Oslo'.
> (Appendix VI in Tamimi 2007, p. 315)

In other words, as far as Hamas was concerned, the Oslo process was dead, so the movement would not be ideologically compromised by electoral participation. Hamas, thus, reinterpreted and expanded its resistance agenda to include participation in the democratic process.

Notwithstanding his failings, Arafat is seen by Palestinians as the father and symbol of the Palestinian national movement. Arafat was an iconic, charismatic leader who elicited much popular support (Jarbawi and Pearlman 2007; Pradhan 2008, p. 300). However, power was centralised with Arafat and he ruled Fatah and the PA with an iron hand. Palestinian-Israeli professor Shaul Mishal (personal interview 2009) contends that, consequently, Fatah suffers from a "routinisation of charisma". In contrast, even after years of exclusive Hamas rule in the Gaza Strip,

> Hamas has shown few signs of the personalization and backbiting that grew to dysfunctional proportions in Fatah under Arafat. When Fatah lost its lifelong leader, the movement disintegrated, but Hamas has already lost most of its founders and has soldiered on nonetheless. It still has a viable collective leadership.
> (Brown 2012, p. 16)

In essence, Arafat's death triggered a leadership crisis within Fatah, a crisis which continues today. While the initial transition to Mahmoud Abbas was generally quite smooth, Abbas lacks the charisma, authority and legacy of his iconic predecessor. A power struggle within Fatah has since ensued, predominantly between the Old Guard or 'outsiders' (the older generation of Arafat-era PLO activists, most of whom spent the pre-Oslo years in exile) and Young Guard or 'insiders' (the younger generation of leaders who grew up under occupation and rose to prominence during the first intifada) (Pradhan 2008, pp. 313–317).

In practical terms, Arafat's death exposed divisions within Fatah, causing it to lose popular legitimacy and prompting some former Fatah supporters to turn to a comparatively united, motivated and disciplined Hamas (ibid.). According to Jamal (survey 2010), a 21-year-old Fatah member studying political science, Fatah has "changed since the death of Yasser Arafat, because the party has abandoned its basic principles". In a similar vein, Hussein (survey 2010), a 22-year-old former student representative of Fatah at an-Najah National University in

108 *Bombs to ballots: political jihad*

Nablus, supported Fatah "in the time of Yasser Arafat. [But] I stopped because the movement is not taking any action towards the current situation in Palestine and Jerusalem." Hatim (survey 2010), a 20-year-old Fatah member from Ramallah, believes furthermore that Fatah's "actions are weak and the party needs a new leadership". Following the death of Yasser Arafat, these splits within Fatah would manifest themselves during the 2006 elections when slighted Fatah electoral candidates ran as independents, thereby splitting Fatah's vote at a district level (Shikaki 2006).

Municipal elections, 2004/2005

Hamas had long since indicated that it would participate in municipal elections because, unlike the 1996 general elections for the PLC, these were not viewed as part of the Oslo process and thus legitimate arenas for electoral participation. Indeed, the occupation authorities held several abortive attempts at municipal elections in the 1970s which were then cancelled when Palestinians voted in pro-PLO leaders. The occupation then attempted to appoint pliable collaborators to do its bidding through its Village Leagues initiative but such individuals held little credibility among the general populace (Younis 2000, p. 152; Litvak 1997, p. 187). Despite promising municipal elections, Arafat continued this practice of appointment and, thus, an autocratic and neo-patrimonial-based rule ensued. In fact, the willingness of Hamas to participate in municipal elections led Fatah to postpone such endeavours repeatedly (Brown and Hamzawy 2010, p. 167). Unsurprisingly, this engendered corrupt practices among political appointees within the context of local governance.

Following Arafat's death, democratic elections for the municipals were scheduled over five rounds and Hamas announced its intention to participate. It is debatable, however, whether local governance is perceived to be political in nature, as the municipals are principally charged with delivering services rather than political policy per se, so putative Islamist ideological convictions were backgrounded in favour of practical realities requiring interaction with the occupation authorities (Gunning 2007, p. 158). Indeed, Dag Tuastad (2009, p. 259) argues that local politics are a distinct autonomous sphere from nationalist politics. Nevertheless, Hamas viewed municipal elections as a testing ground to gauge its grassroots popular support, campaigning under a banner of Change and Reform (Caridi 2010, p. 170). Palestinians, moreover, enthusiastically embraced their first elections since 1996.

Hamas won approximately one-third of the seats during four rounds of municipal elections held between December 2004 and December 2005.[2] A fifth round was cancelled following the election of Hamas to the legislature in January 2006. Overall, Fatah won 121 municipalities to Hamas' 81. These results, however, are misleading because even though Hamas won fewer municipalities, it tended to be victorious in the more populous areas, including the important cities, towns and refugee camps (Gunning 2007, p. 148). Thus, by December 2005, "over 1,000,000 Palestinians now live[d] in municipalities governed by Hamas,

Bombs to ballots: political jihad 109

compared with about 700,000 in municipalities controlled by the hitherto dominant Palestinian movement, Fatah" (Litvak 2005). This included areas such as Ramallah's sister city al-Bireh where the Islamists took control. The success of Hamas in these elections – especially in urban areas where traditional authority structures are less evident and voters are therefore less susceptible to familial or clan-based based pressures – showed that it was a disciplined, efficient and organised movement where, in contrast, Fatah demonstrated that it was disorganised, divided and often driven by parochial interests.

Corruption topped the agenda of municipal elections during which many voters decided to send Fatah a message of discontent, especially in the highly populated urban areas where this corruption was most visible (Milton-Edwards and Farrell 2010, p. 243). This perception of Fatah as a corrupt political party was markedly contrasted to the voluntary social services which Hamas offers to society (Alshech 2008, p. 46). Hamas' social and charitable networks, with their reputation for transparency, accountability and efficiency, are credited with eliciting support for the movement (Denoeux 2002, p. 78; Farhat 2006; Abu Amr 2007, pp. 169–170). This reputation contributed to the successes of Hamas in the 2004/2005 municipal elections.

Indicatively, an exit poll for the fourth round of municipal elections held in the major West Bank cities of Nablus, Ramallah, al-Bireh and Jenin found that a majority of respondents (56%) believed that their former municipal councils were corrupt, whereas 93 per cent believed that the newly elected municipal councils would fight corruption (PCSPR 2005). In total, Hamas won 59 per cent of the vote in these elections (71% in Nablus, 31% in Ramallah, 57% in al-Bireh and 39% in Jenin), in comparison to 26 per cent for Fatah. According to PCSPR (ibid.), 99 per cent of respondents nominated the integrity and incorruptibility of candidates as the most important factor accounting for their vote. Gunning (2007, p. 121), moreover, contends that Islam is synonymous with integrity for many Palestinians. Fighting against corruption and excess may thus also be viewed as key components of the greater jihad aimed at personal improvement and community well-being.

Hamas also demonstrated a willingness to compromise on core messages when necessary and, accordingly, put forward respected candidates who were non-partisan, or not specifically affiliated with the movement, in order to attract swinging voters and disillusioned Fatah supporters (ibid., pp. 157–158). The elected Mayor of Nablus, Adly Ya'ish, a respected businessman, for example, helped attract the Christian and Samaritan vote in Nablus, where the Hamas-backed list won 13 of 15 council seats in what had previously been a Fatah stronghold. Ya'ish, well known for his charitable work, added not only his own local popularity but also a reputation for efficiency, honesty and, in light of his cordial relationships with the Israelis, the confidence that a Hamas-backed council would cooperate with the occupation authorities on relevant matters, including water, electricity and sewerage (ibid., p. 158). In Bethlehem, a Christian Marxist from the PFLP likewise made a winning alliance with Hamas based on anti-corruption and Christian votes, in exchange for a reassurance that

110 *Bombs to ballots: political jihad*

Hamas' Islamist agenda would not impact upon Christian/Muslim coexistence in the city (Legget 2005).

Indicatively, while Hamas received 59 per cent of the total votes in the fourth round of elections held in Nablus, Ramallah, al-Bireh and Jenin, only 42 per cent of respondents indicated that they supported Hamas (PCSPR 2005). In comparison, while 28 per cent of respondents indicated that they supported Fatah, only 26 per cent actually voted for Fatah lists. Hence, as PCPSR (ibid.) points out, "about one quarter of the votes received by Hamas' lists came from voters who do not support Hamas, including voters who in fact support Fatah". Thus, Hamas demonstrated its ability to strike pragmatic alliances with other denominations and factions – a cornerstone of any democratic process – as well as attract non-partisan voters throughout the wider populace. This, in turn, implicitly legitimised the movement's wider programme of resistance beyond the scope of its supporters and sympathisers.

Gunning (2007, pp. 162–166) contends, moreover, that perceptions of public piety, individual competency and community service worked in favour of Hamas-backed candidates. In short, much of Palestinian politics is based on social capital (Tuastad 2009, p. 194). Dr Nihad Masri (personal interview 2010), then Deputy Mayor of Nablus, physician and a former Marxist turned Islamist, thus elucidates on the role of social capital and public profile in explaining the municipal elections in Nablus:

> I am a well-known doctor here. I have good respect from people in Nablus and villages around and, if mentioned, the name of Adly Ya'ish, the Mayor, or me or [Deputy Mayor for Planning and Technical Affairs] Hafez Shaheen, I mean, it should be known to the people.

In addition, Masri continues, "Islam is [a] more respectable ... belief than Marxism". Accordingly, during municipal elections in January 2005, an exit poll found that a majority of voters in Gaza (58%), where Hamas won 68 per cent of the vote (in contrast to 20 per cent for Fatah), considered religiosity an important factor when choosing a candidate. In the West Bank, where 38 per cent of voters selected a Hamas candidate (in comparison to 35 per cent for Fatah), 46 per cent of respondents indicated the importance of a candidate's perceived religiosity (Alshech 2008, p. 46).

The aforementioned themes of corruption, piety and community service are evident in a case study on the local elections in the Bureig refugee camp in Gaza, where Dag Tuastad (2009, p. 238) identifies the unity, organisation and local orientation of the Hamas-backed list as leading to their electoral victory. Hamas-backed candidates were chosen amid local consultations, for example, whereas Fatah-backed candidates were initially nominated by the central Executive Committee and then appointed by the *mukhabarat* (secret police) despite local objections (ibid., p. 237). Confronted by a superior Hamas-backed list chosen according to local conditions, Fatah was forced to reorganise its list in a more democratic fashion. Rather than attempting to define the election on its own terms, however, Fatah attempted to imitate the Hamas-backed list, with little success. As a result, Hamas defined the main electoral issues as corruption, sacrifice, security and safety (ibid., p. 238). The first of these issues pertains to a personal jihad through which an individual in a position of influence does not abuse their power, whereas the latter three are clearly tied to Hamas' resistance themes discussed in the previous chapters (for instance, acting as a de facto security provider throughout the second intifada and fighting the occupation).

Personal reputation and religious orientation also played a significant role. Indicatively, Hamas controlled seven out of eight mosques in Bureig, which issued *fatwas* (religious edicts) in support of the Hamas-backed list. Following the carnage of the second intifada and the inability of the PA to impose law and order, "the mosques represented control and purity rather than violence and anarchy" (ibid., p. 238). In contrast, Fatah candidates were perceived as corrupt and beholden to parochial interests. Hamas, on the other hand, had accrued moral capital, which was then translated into political capital, through resistance, sacrifice and engagement with daily affairs among the community (Gunning 2007, pp. 152–153). Alshech (2008) contends that conceptions of self-sacrifice, as embodied by self-immolation attacks during the second intifada, contributed to Hamas' electoral success in the municipal elections.

Hamas capitalised on its community engagement by mapping out the district via its extensive social networks. Hamas candidates visited every home and possessed offices in every block, highlighting the personalisation of politics in the Palestinian Territories, especially at a local level. The existence of these networks, or lists of beneficiaries, also meant that Hamas was cognisant of the needs of everyday people and the hardships they faced on a quotidian basis. According to one resident, Hamas would "drive the people who are in wheelchairs; they have gone through the registration lists and found what the special needs of the people are, who needs driving and such things. Fatah have no such system" (cited in Tuastad 2009, p. 240).

In a similar vein, in Gaza, Hamas

> not only organized squads of volunteers to clean up Gaza's streets prior to local elections – showcasing what it would do when in power as well as building rapport by encouraging locals to join in – but [also] ... filmed the cleaning operations for use as promotional material during its election campaign.
>
> (Gunning 2007, p. 153; see also Gutman 2005)

These actions, moreover, while not only practical, tapped into latent values concerning the importance of community, charity and volunteerism in Islam. Tellingly, as Salma Abu Gazar (cited in the *Daily Star*), a 51-year-old resident of the Rafah refugee camp in Gaza, explains, she voted for Hamas because "We want clean streets and new projects, like sewage treatment, and our destroyed homes to be rebuilt. I believe that Fatah will monopolise everything like they have done before."

112 *Bombs to ballots: political jihad*

When Hamas emerged victorious in Bureig, Fatah accused Hamas of rigging the vote and its armed militia occupied the electoral offices. Hamas blithely responded that "It is the first time that the party in power organizing the election accuses the opposition of winning through cheating" (cited in Tuastad 2009, p. 244). In fact, it was Fatah which reputedly attempted to buy votes. In the end, the elections were cancelled due to pressure from the PA and Fatah, which, in turn, led to more frequent confrontations between Hamas and Fatah resulting in increasing *fawda* (anarchy) (ibid., pp. 248–250). Nevertheless, the results of the municipal elections demonstrated Hamas' democratic acumen in terms of strategic voting, while providing a harbinger of Fatah duplicity which would manifest itself following the parliamentary elections in 2006 (Gunning 2007, p. 148).

Legislative elections, 2006

In contrast to 1996, Hamas rationalised that the second intifada had killed the Oslo process and thus it was permissible to participate in the 2006 legislative elections (Barghouti 2007, p. 52). No doubt it also sought to capitalise on its new-found popularity stemming from the second intifada. Public opinion, moreover, pointed towards a cessation of hostilities with Israel. While Hamas would most likely never admit this on the record, it seems likely that the weakening of its military wing and the assassination of many of its top leaders helped push the movement towards the political track.

Fatah and the PA had also been drastically weakened by Israeli policy which seemed to target its erstwhile interlocutors for peace, especially Arafat, as much if not more than ostensibly rejectionist movements such as Hamas and Islamic Jihad (Milton-Edwards and Farrell 2010, p. 103). Arafat's death dovetailed with the United States' putative agenda advocating democratisation of the region. Prior to his death, Arafat had been declared persona non grata by both Israel and the United States but he continued to retain substantial popular support among the Palestinian public – indeed, his 'defiance' of both the US and Israel meant he was the most popular he had been in years. Prior to his death in November 2004, in June 2004 PCSPR *Poll no. 12* found in an open question that 54 per cent of respondents would nominate Arafat for the Presidency, whereas no other figure received more than 2 per cent. Thus, the US and Israel had no desire to legitimise Arafat through democratic elections.

Following Arafat's death, the PA convinced the US to allow Hamas to participate in legislative elections in order to restore the crumbling legitimacy of the PA, despite Israeli objections and consternation among segments of Fatah. Newly elected President Mahmoud Abbas was perceived as pro-democratic, especially given his previous advocacy of democratic reform which had been perpetually stymied by his iconic predecessor. Consequently, Hamas believed that the election would be fair, especially given that the US and Israel had allowed Hamas to participate. Omar Abdul-Razeq (personal interview 2010) thus explains his decision to participate in the legislative elections:

Bombs to ballots: political jihad 113

I guess it's the chance. I mean, ever since before the Authority was established, there was no way that you can be involved in a political activity with the occupation.... Now, the political process – you can start it with the establishment of the Authority – however, the Authority started as a one-party Authority like any other Arab country and actually as a police system ... prior to the legislative elections in 2006, I felt there was some will on the part of the world, on the part of the Authority, or some leaders of the Authority, especially probably [PA President] Abu Mazen, to arrange a free election. And so I thought this is a chance: you can prove yourself, prove your programme, and try to sell this to the society, the cause that you have. Had the situation been the same as it was, for example, under Arafat in 1996, I would not have thought to have run for elections because I knew that the elections were arranged – prearranged – at the time.

Thus, a change in the political opportunity structure facilitated Hamas' reframing of resistance and jihad to equate these concepts to political participation.

This demonstrates, moreover, that given the incentive to advance itself through institutional means, Hamas chose to sideline armed resistance in favour of political participation. According to Khalid (survey 2010), a 22-year-old member of Hamas studying media and political science, Hamas' political programme was "The attempt to make a combination between the authority and the resistance but this programme failed because of historical and objective circumstances". By pursuing the acquisition of authority through the frame of resistance, Hamas again illustrated its political pragmatism and the malleability of its conceptions of resistance.

Explaining Hamas' victory in 2006

In 2006, parliamentary seats were allocated 50/50 according to two distinct electoral lists. At a national level, an individual voted for a party list and seats were allocated by proportional representation. At a district level, voters endorsed individual candidates listed by name, whereby each district was awarded seats according to the size of its population. Nablus, for example, possessed six district-level seats, Hebron possessed nine, Gaza City possessed eight and so on. Each voter was allocated a number of votes according to how many seats existed in each area. Thus, in Nablus, voters could number up to six candidates, nine in Hebron and eight in Gaza City.[3] These seats were then awarded according to the total number of votes an individual candidate received. It was at the district level where Hamas trounced Fatah, winning 45 seats to 17.[4]

One factor accounting for Hamas' victory and this discrepancy at a district level was the superior organisation and unified nature of the Hamas-backed list. Hamas appointed the number of candidates it believed could win seats in each district so as not to split the vote, and then instructed constituents to vote for each of their candidates (Gunning 2007, p. 154). These numbers were calculated according to sophisticated pre-poll surveys conducted by the movement

114 *Bombs to ballots: political jihad*

(personal interview with Abdul-Razeq 2010; Gunning 2007, p. 154). In contrast, Fatah initially fielded two lists reflecting Fatah's division between the 'Old Guard', as characterised by the old Arafat coterie, and the 'New Guard's' *al-Mustaqbal* ('the Future') party led by the popular but imprisoned Marwan Barghouti.[5] Eventually, Fatah managed to unify its list prior to the 2006 election but slighted Fatah candidates ran as independents, thereby splitting the nationalist vote at a district level (Shikaki 2006). According to former Arafat security adviser and long-time PLO official William Nasser (personal interview 2010), moreover, internal jostling, poor planning and personal animosity/ambition among Fatah candidates and slighted 'independents' meant that Fatah voters were not necessarily instructed to nominate additional Fatah candidates commensurate with a given district. One exemplary example of Fatah's suicidal division of the vote is the case of Hebron, where Hamas attracted 51.1 per cent of the vote in comparison to Fatah's 35 per cent, yet won all nine seats because Hamas fielded only nine candidates, whereas Fatah split its vote between nine official candidates and other 'independents' (FairVote 2006, p. 4).

Perhaps even more striking is the case of Nablus where Hamas won five out of six seats with 38.2 per cent of the vote because the movement fielded only five candidates, whereas Fatah won only one seat despite obtaining 36.5 per cent because it ran six candidates and it was unable to prevent its 'independents' from siphoning off votes (ibid.). Similarly, in Ramallah, Hamas ran four candidates who polled 38.4 per cent of the vote whereas Fatah ran five candidates polling 36.2 per cent of the vote, yet Hamas won four seats out of five and Fatah won only one (ibid.). In Jerusalem, Hamas fielded four candidates to win four out of six seats whereas Fatah and 'Fatah' independents managed to field a staggering 30 candidates between them (Kalman 2006a) – the two seats that Hamas did not win were reserved for Christians. In total only 11 of Hamas' field of 56 district candidates were *not* elected, whereas only 17 of Fatah's 66 candidates succeeded. In brief, Fatah's inability to control its affiliated independents in conjunction with the leadership's overconfidence and failure to adequately ascertain the movement's electoral strength prior to the elections resulted in Hamas' dominance at a district level (Gunning 2007, pp. 154–155).

Thus, despite winning a plurality of the vote (44.5%) at a proportional level (compared to 41.4 per cent for Fatah), Hamas won a comfortable victory overall based on better/more trusted candidates and superior organisation at a district level. The election results present somewhat of a conundrum with Hamas winning 44.5 per cent of votes as a party list, while simultaneously winning some 70 per cent of seats at a district level based on individual candidates, despite winning only 41 per cent of the total votes in comparison to Fatah's 36 per cent (FairVote 2006, p. 2). Hence, seats allocated by proportional representation tended to be decided by brand name, whereas the district lists reflected Hamas' superior organisation, as well as the personalisation of politics and the importance of personal reputation within the Palestinian Territories.

Political programmes and election issues at a national level

During the election campaign there was a noticeable absence of Hamas' absolutist ideological discourse vis-à-vis Israel in its political programme (Hroub 2006b). Instead, the movement's electoral manifesto called for "a free and independent Palestinian state with sovereignty over the whole of the West Bank, Gaza Strip and Jerusalem, without concession of any span of the historic land of Palestine" which, in effect, implicitly endorses a two-state solution while remaining ideologically consistent (ICG 2006, p. 22).

Furthermore, the electoral and political programmes of Hamas omitted or backgrounded Islamist agendas in favour of social policies and governmental reform. Hamas, for example, does not mention its putative ideological goal of an Islamic state in its political programme. Similarly, the charter/covenant of Hamas is not cited or mentioned in any of its political texts (Klein 2007, p. 450). Hamas' focus on 'Change and Reform', for instance, rather than its ostensible ideology vis-à-vis confronting Israel and an Islamic state allowed swing voters to vote for Hamas even if they were in favour of the peace process and secular governance (Gunning 2007, p. 142). Indeed, the Change and Reform electoral manifesto mentions 'armed resistance' only once under Article 1.4 (although armed resistance is implicitly acknowledged under Article 3.6 which "Consider[s] occupation to be the ugliest form of terrorism and resisting with all means is a right" guaranteed by divine and international law) (Appendix VI in Tamimi 2007, pp. 294, 297). Thus, throughout the electoral campaign, Hamas sought to change its image from a militant organisation to a responsible political actor (Zweiri 2006, p. 677).

This is not to say that the religious aspect of Hamas was absent. Religion certainly did play a part in Hamas' mobilisation strategies. Qur'anic verses and *hadith*, for instance, are frequently found throughout the movement's slogans and electoral platform. Indeed, the phrase 'Change and Reform' "combines a political message with a reference to two passages from the Quran that encourage personal development in order to deepen faith" (Kalman 2006b).

While Hamas initially used mosques to spread its message, the movement eventually signed a pact banning electioneering in mosques and churches (Regular 2006). According to Iyad Barghouti (2007, p. 52), however, Hamas issued a *fatwa* in 2004 encouraging its supporters to register for elections through its

> Ifta Committee ensuring that combined evidence from the Quran and Tradition render elections legal in Islamic jurisprudence. It maintained that scholars perceive elections as a form of testimony and trust. It is an imperative religious duty for the Muslim to give testimony if it is seen as crucial to reform corruption or to establish justice or returning the right to its people.

Indicatively, the main issues of the 2006 elections focused on corruption and (an absence of) law and order.

116   *Bombs to ballots: political jihad*

This was particularly salient in the mostly urban Area A – the 17 per cent of the West Bank, and Gaza, supposedly under PA control – where PA corruption and its inability to maintain law and order were most visible. Change and Reform performed especially well among the major urban centres, as evidenced by its domination of Fatah in these areas. Indeed, a JMCC poll (*no. 57*) in February 2006 found that 43 per cent of respondents nominated corruption as the primary reason they voted for Hamas, in contrast to a combined 30 per cent for political or socio-economic reasons – that is to say, 10.7 per cent to improve living standards, 11.8 per cent for Hamas' political agenda and 7.5 per cent to curb Fatah control – with 19 per cent citing religious rationales. Through the transparency of its charities and its administration of various municipalities, Hamas acquired a reputation for honest and efficient governance, in turn contributing to its victory in the 2006 legislative elections (Turner 2006, p. 748; Reinhart 2006, p. 146).

The failure of the peace process was a lesser concern throughout the course of the election. The real damage of the failure of the peace process was the outbreak of the second intifada that led to the weakening of Fatah and the destruction of PA infrastructure at the hands of the IDF. Consequently, Fatah's ability to operate as a *fida'i* (self-sacrificing) resistance organisation and the PA's ability to provide goods and services were drastically curtailed, thus leaving the field open to Hamas on both of these counts (Gordon and Filc 2005, p. 553; Alshech 2008, p. 44). Moreover, the failure of the peace process invalidated Fatah's strategy of negotiations and pushed Hamas' narrative of resistance back to the forefront of Palestinian political discourse. Indicatively, Hamas' popularity doubled throughout the course of the second intifada.

Hamas also advocated reform of the many varied and competing Palestinian security forces (personal interview, Abdul-Razeq 2010), many of which possessed reputations little better than self-serving bandits. Indeed, one Fatah official describes PA forces operating in the West Bank as "security mafia" with "vested interests" (ICG 2011b, p. 17). Article 2.9 of the movement's electoral manifesto calls for:

> Correcting and rationalizing the role of the security agencies in protecting the security of the citizen, ending erroneous and arbitrary practice, guaranteeing the liberties of citizens, protecting public properties, and making these agencies accountable to the Palestinian Legislative Council.
>
> (Appendix VI in Tamimi 2007, p. 295)

The last clause pertaining to the accountability of security forces is especially telling because Palestinian security agencies were perceived to be Fatah partisans – a perception which continues in the West Bank today (Milton-Edwards 2008, p. 663). During the reign of Arafat, the different apparatuses were played off against each other so that none could accrue sufficient power to challenge Arafat's rule. In effect, the security agencies were directly answerable to Arafat alone. These agencies, in addition, had conspicuously failed to institute the rule

Bombs to ballots: political jihad 117

of law and order, especially following the outbreak of the second intifada. The security agencies in the West Bank continue to be implicated in a variety of egregious excesses both in terms of corruption and human rights' abuses, and still suffer from a lack of accountability (Sayigh 2011a, pp. 33–36).

Article 6.3 of the Change and Reform electoral manifesto similarly vows to "End the intervention of security agencies in the issuing of licenses for publications, research centres, and public opinion polling institutions, as well as their intervention in employment" (Appendix VI in Tamimi 2007, p. 300). This Article, on the one hand, reflects the Islamist belief that polling institutions are pressured by the PA and outside donors to produce polls downplaying Hamas support (personal interviews 2010). On the other hand, it also identifies the rampant nature of nepotism, favouritism and partisanship exhibited throughout the employment sector, especially with regard to the public service and the security forces in particular. Malak (survey 2010), a 21-year-old PFLP voter studying law, for instance, points to "the huge role of nepotism and cronyism in the PA'.

Aside from Hamas' stated goal to 'serve the people' (Milton-Edwards 2008, p. 667), this desire for security reform, again, perhaps, is unsurprising given that Hamas was frequently the target of these apparatuses as an opposition movement. Hamas' security apparatus in the Gaza Strip is presently politicised as well, but it has managed to institute the rule of law and order which had eluded the previous Fatah-led forces, despite the Hamas government employing only a fraction of the resources and personnel (Sayigh 2011b). Indeed, Hamas streamlined the security forces, reducing the number of personnel from 56,887 prior to its armed seizure of the Gaza Strip in June 2007 to around 15,000 today (Sayigh 2011a, p. 58). The Hamas security sector has also been accused of various abuses albeit on a lesser scale; the Haniyeh government in Gaza, however, appears to have instigated measures to ensure greater accountability over recent years (ibid., pp. 33–36). In contrast to its West Bank counterparts, moreover, the Hamas security sector is unambiguously under civilian control in line with Western modes of governance, and is thus, according to Sayigh (ibid., p. 69), more accountable.

At the heart of Hamas' political programme are concerns for social justice (*adala*), leadership accountability and democratic participation (Gunning 2004, p. 241). In essence, its party platform focused on Palestinian society's current circumstances. Hamas' 'Change and Reform' platform ran on promises of tackling poverty, crime and corruption; administrative reform; stronger local government; and a reduction of the central government's power (Hroub 2006b; Klein 2007, p. 441). These were aimed at the shortcomings of Fatah which failed to improve the standard of living in the post-Oslo peace process and was widely perceived to be corrupt and mired in cronyism (Malka 2005, p. 43; Khalidi 2006, pp. 151–152). A 2004 poll, for instance, found that 87 per cent of respondents believed there was corruption in the PA (PCSPR *Poll no. 12* 2004). According to Ali (survey 2010), a 22-year-old Fatah student representative, the PA "is a civilian authority that is devoid of values and correct political principles". In a

118 *Bombs to ballots: political jihad*

similar vein, Mona (survey 2010), a 21-year-old former Hamas sympathiser from Jerusalem, opines that the PA "is full of financial and political corruption.... The PA is an authority which fills people's minds with rules which it doesn't apply to itself." Abdul-Karim (survey 2010), an unaffiliated 21-year-old student studying political science, believes that "the PA is an authority that seeks to achieve some personal interests, but it doesn't seek the liberation of Palestine or the public interest".

Fatah and the PA, moreover, have become synonymous in the minds of many Palestinians. Thus, the public excesses of Fatah and PA leaders were juxtaposed against Islam's traditional emphasis on socio-economic equality, social justice and moderation. According to Gunning (2007, p. 151), "Hamas shaped its election campaign, within the bounds of its ideological framework, around the themes that it thought people would most identify with, and at the same time best exposed Fatah's weaknesses."

In this light, it is important to note the socio-economic status of Hamas' core supporters, most of whom are of the lower and lower-middle classes (that is, most of the Palestinian population) and reside in urbanised areas and refugee camps (Milton-Edwards 1996, p. 43).[6] Most of political Islam's support within the Palestinian Territories derives from those outside the formal labour market, with housewives constituting 52.2 per cent, students 14.1 per cent and the unemployed 9.2 per cent of its support base in 2003 (Hilal 2005, p. 14). At the height of the second intifada in 2003, two-thirds of the Palestinian population lived under the poverty line (ICG 2003, p. 14). Many Hamas leaders originate from similarly humble backgrounds, facilitating identification among the general populace, especially when juxtaposed against their Fatah rivals. Accordingly, Hamas leaders are highly educated and upwardly mobile individuals from outside of the traditional elite with reputations for asceticism, charity and honesty (Tamimi 2007, p. 117; Gunning 2007, pp. 257–258). The prevalence of a refugee support base for Hamas is suggestive of the fact that the PLO has more or less surrendered the refugees' 'right of return' to their pre-1948 homes from which they fled or were expelled in what is today recognised as Israel – as stipulated under UN General Assembly 194 – whereas Hamas has not (Tuastad 2009, pp. 255–256).

In essence, Hamas appealed to ordinary Palestinians disenfranchised by Fatah rule. Hamas' election manifesto advocated "decentralisation, the delegation of authority and sharing the process of decision making" (cited in Tamimi 2007, p. 279). Slogans such as 'partners in blood, partners in decision making' coupled this idea of democratic accountability with the self-sacrifice of the movement and its members throughout the course of the resistance (*Daily Star* 2005). Hamas even played on its pariah status vis-à-vis the United States with one slogan: 'America Says No to Hamas, What Do You Say?' (Farrell 2006).

Fatah, in contrast, has long since struggled to articulate a coherent social or political agenda, instead being described variously as a 'movement of the street', a 'melting pot' or a 'marketplace of ideas' devoid of any clear ideology (personal interviews with Barghouti 2010, Qassam 2010 and Amayreh 2010, respectively). Ahmed (survey 2010), a 22-year-old former Fatah supporter, is less generous, describing a Fatah supporter as "someone who cannot think and lets others think for him". This assertion was vindicated repeatedly throughout the surveys administered by myself. When asked what it means to be a Fatah supporter, Jamila (survey 2010), a 22-year-old Fatah supporter studying business management, explains "I agree on anything the party decides". Itimad (survey 2010), a 20-year-old geography student and Fatah supporter, likewise elucidates that to be a Fatah supporter is "to support every outcome of this movement".

Throughout the course of the electoral campaign, according to Meir Litvak (2005), Fatah was perceived to be lacking a "social agenda, subordinating it to the national struggle and postponing its articulation to the day after liberation". Palestinian journalist Khalid Amayreh (personal interview 2010) further opines,

> Fatah still relies very much upon its legacy, the heritage. Right now, if they want to impress young Palestinians, they remind them of things that happened 40 years ago … Yasser Arafat, the resistance, things like that. They do not use the achievements of people like Mahmoud Abbas because they have no achievements … Hamas' assets, propaganda assets, are here and now. Fatah's propaganda assets are almost anachronistic, you see. In fact, I can say that Hamas has more in common with Fatah's past than Fatah does.

My own surveys at an-Najah, Birzeit and al-Quds universities reflect Fatah's lack of a social or political programme insofar as Fatah supporters refer most frequently to Fatah's historical legacy, Yasser Arafat, slogans and family ties. Some respondents also cited a desire for future employment or economic advancement, again illustrating the neo-patrimonial nature of Fatah's political organisation, rather than any coherent articulation of a social or political programme beyond liberation. For 'Idhar (survey 2010), a 19-year-old member of Fatah, supporting the movement "is one of the incontestable facts in this family". Similarly, Thawab (survey 2010), a 19-year-old Fatah activist from Zawata, explains, "I participated in [Fatah] clubs just to get into college". A third, Muti (survey 2010), a 19-year-old from Bethlehem, rationalises, "because I am studying political science, supporting [Fatah] helps me in my work".

After 20 years of failed negotiations and continued occupation, it is perhaps unsurprising then that Fatah's strategy of relying on its historical record and brand name failed when confronted with an opponent articulating a coherent political programme for the future. As veteran Middle East correspondent Robert Fisk (2006) points out, Palestinians had a choice between the "pro-Western, corrupt, absolutely pro-American Fatah, which had promised to 'control' them … [and] Hamas, which said they would represent them".

The personalisation of politics at a district level

As noted above, it was at a district level where Hamas acquired the majority of its seats, especially in comparison to its Fatah rival. Hamas' domination of the district lists, as at a municipal level, demonstrated its superior conceptualisation

120 *Bombs to ballots: political jihad*

and implementation of strategic voting when confronted with a plurality at large electoral system. Notwithstanding the fact that Hamas was better organised, disciplined and more united than its Fatah rival – for one presenting a unified electoral list – one reason for this discrepancy between the lists and the districts is the personalisation of politics in the Palestinian Territories based on symbolic capital, *wasta* (contacts or 'pull') and reputation. Iyad Barghouti (personal interview 2009), Director of the Ramallah Centre for Human Rights, elucidates this phenomenon:

> People hate Hamas but like Hamas people. People like Fatah but hate their people. So if you ask people which party they want, they will say Fatah. But if you ask them which person they want, they will say the Hamas candidate.

Quite simply, then, Hamas ran a better quality of candidates, including engineers, doctors, university professors, teachers, community activists and businessmen, who were known to be pious, competent and respected throughout their various constituencies. Palestinian society consists of a number of very close-knit, predominantly conservative communities where personal acquaintance and reputation are of vital importance.

Many Fatah candidates, moreover, were quite (in)famous and disliked by the general population. In contrast, Hamas candidates were selected according to merit, aptitude and public service record (Gunning 2007, p. 163). Huda (survey 2010), a Hamas sympathiser studying engineering, votes for Hamas because she wants "a 'moderate' candidate ... who help[s] everyone regardless of who they are". Similarly, Mahmoud (survey 2010), a 27-year-old Hamas member, points to, "good reputation, 'clean hands' and a history of resistance" as ideal characteristics. In short, Hamas candidates were more respected (*ihitram*) by the general population and perceived to be 'clean' (*nathif*) (Tuastad 2009, p. 254).

At the time, Hamas leaders were perceived to lead ascetic lifestyles devoid of excess in line with Islamic thought focusing on socio-economic equality and moderation in all facets of life (Tamimi 2007, p. 117). According to Islah Jad (personal interview 2009), Director of the Women's Centre at Birzeit University and a respected authority on Islamist feminism, the issue of trust was paramount when electing individual candidates at a district level. In a similar vein, the key term employed by the membership to describe the leadership is 'trust' (Gunning 2007, p. 130). Namir (survey 2010), a 23-year-old Hamas supporter, cites "Truthfulness, honesty and paying attention to the interests of the Palestinian cause" as key characteristics. Indicatively, JMCC *Poll no. 57* taken after the election in February 2006 revealed that 38.7 per cent of respondents said they trusted Hamas in comparison to 30.6 per cent for Fatah.

Mustafa Abu Sway (personal interview 2010), Professor of *Sharia* Law at al-Quds University, contends furthermore that Hamas candidates were perceived as incorruptible and, according to the local idiom, in possession of 'clean hands and pockets'. Hamas' reputation for 'clean hands' also allowed it to appeal to non-Muslim voters fed up with corruption (Zweiri 2006, p. 678). In contrast, Fatah

Bombs to ballots: political jihad   121

leaders and candidates are often seen living in expensive villas and driving late model Mercedes (Hass 2010). According to *New York Times* Middle East correspondent Steven Erlanger (2005), conversely, Hamas nominated "well-educated candidates with reputations for probity and piety". Indeed, Fatima's (survey 2010) ideal candidate (represented by Hamas) "believes in God, follows his Prophet and knows what jihad means".

Jereon Gunning (2007, p. 166) argues that the religiosity or the perceived piety of candidates was also an important factor because Islam is associated with integrity in the Palestinian Territories. Hamas candidates are regularly seen attending the mosque and participating in charitable work throughout the community. Moreover, of the 76 Hamas members of the PLC, 55 per cent are university graduates of Islamic *sharia* studies programmes with an additional 11 per cent having worked as "propagandists or preachers" (Barghouti 2007, p. 61). Tamimi (2007, p. 221) points to the increasing Islamisation of Palestinian society as contributing to Hamas' electoral success by facilitating identification with Hamas-backed candidates among pious individuals.

Gunning (2007, pp. 162–168), nevertheless, contends that most Hamas candidates and legislators are professionals possessing temporal qualifications, and these individuals derive social capital from this expertise, as well as their familiarity throughout the community. According to the Washington Institute for Near East Policy (2007), only 12 legislators are listed as been affiliated with mosques; four are imams, one is part of a religious court and three preside on *zakat* (alms) committees. Indicatively, a February 2006 JMCC poll (*no. 57*) found that only 19 per cent of Hamas voters did so for 'religious reasons', suggesting that Islam is not the primary source of Hamas' political (as opposed to ideological) support.

The aftermath

The result of the elections not only stunned Fatah and the international community, but the magnitude of the victory appeared to have also taken Hamas by surprise. Nevertheless, it was clear that Palestinians had enthusiastically embraced this new chance for democratic elections with an estimated 77 per cent turnout in what international observers deemed to be clean and fair elections (Milton-Edwards and Farrell 2010, p. 259).

Hamas offered to form a unity government with all the other factions, but Fatah refused while the other parties prevaricated before coming to the same conclusion. Fatah wanted to see Hamas fail in the face of international aid boycotts, whereas other parties were worried that they would be internationally blacklisted for association with the Hamas-led government. Faced with this refusal, Hamas had no choice but to form a Hamas-dominated government which worked in conjunction with several independents, including a Christian from Bethlehem who was appointed Minister of Tourism (al-Naami 2007).

The international response was self-evidently hypocritical. Despite the fact that Hamas won free and fair elections promoted by the US and the EU, each of

122   *Bombs to ballots: political jihad*

these entities cut off international funding to the new Hamas-dominated administration. Israel, in addition, withheld taxes ostensibly collected on the PA's behalf. The International Quartet, consisting of the US, the EU, Russia and the UN, insisted that the incoming government recognise Israel, renounce violence and adhere to previous agreements between Israel and the PA/PLO.

Unsurprisingly, Hamas refused, as this would have entailed surrendering all its bargaining chips without demanding reciprocity from Israel to recognise Palestinian rights, renounce violence against Palestinians and adhere to previous agreements which Israel had actively been in the process of breaching. One concrete example of Israel's refusal to abide by previous agreements entails the construction of the security/apartheid wall, which snakes its way through the West Bank expropriating Palestinian land. Another example is the continued expansion of 'settlements' on Palestinian territory in the West Bank and East Jerusalem. Both of these actions breach Israel's obligations with the Palestinians and, moreover, are in contravention of international law, most notably the Fourth Geneva Convention, Article 7 of the Rome Statute of the International Criminal Court and multiple Security Council resolutions.

More shocking to Hamas was the perceived duplicity of Fatah, and especially PA President Mahmoud Abbas, which subsequently moved to undermine the incoming Hamas administration. The outgoing Fatah-dominated legislature passed a succession of new laws conferring emergency powers and control of the security forces upon President Mahmoud Abbas before the new Hamas-dominated legislature came into effect. During my own interviews with Islamist Deputies and Ministers of the tenth and eleventh administrations, Parliamentary Speaker Aziz Dweik, Secretary General Mahmoud al-Ramahi, Finance Minister Omar Abdul-Razeq and Women's Minister Mariam Salah all expressed their surprise at the duplicity of Fatah, and the Palestinian President in particular, in undermining the newly installed democratic process. In effect, Fatah refused to hand over control of the Fatah-dominated security forces to the interior ministry which, in turn, sowed chaos and disorder. Tellingly, in a presage of things to come, the PA recruited an extra 13,000 Fatah supporters as policemen during the month prior to the 2006 elections (Milton-Edwards 2008, pp. 663–664). As a result, Hamas was forced to create its own Executive Force (*tanfithya*), an adjunct police unit consisting of 3000 to 3500 men, in the Gaza Strip to effect law and order. The period from Hamas' election in January 2006 until its sole takeover of the Gaza Strip in June 2007 is known as the period of 'security anarchy' (*al-falatan al-amni*) (Sayigh 2011a, pp. 1–2) characterised by the prevalence of "Fatah-linked gangs that engaged in thuggery and criminality" (ICG 2011, p. 16).

In June 2006, a joint Palestinian operation tunnelled under the border wall between Gaza and Israel and attacked an Israeli outpost, resulting in the death of two Israeli soldiers and the abduction of Gilad Shalit. This, in turn, sparked a massive Israeli attack on Gaza, the largest since 1967, code-named 'Operation Summer Rains', attempting to rescue the kidnapped soldier. In addition, the IDF rounded up the recently elected Change and Reform legislators and government officials in the occupied West Bank, thereby paralysing the PLC. After three weeks of continuous bombardment the assault had killed over 400 Palestinians, but failed to free Shalit.[7] In October 2011, Israel agreed to free more than 1000 Palestinian prisoners in exchange for Shalit, including over 300 serving life sentences for orchestrating attacks against Israel.

Ongoing strikes by Fatah-dominated civil servants and teachers directed from Ramallah also crippled the new government's administrative capacity. Following the division of Gaza and the West Bank in June 2007, the Hamas government eventually sacked these civil servants and teachers, setting up new public institutions in their place. In particular, Hamas set up parallel security institutions, namely the Executive Force in Gaza, to step in for the existing forces whose commanders publicly refused to work with a Hamas-run government (Milton-Edwards 2008, p. 172).

Nevertheless, between January 2006 and June 2007, Hamas attempted to maintain a separation between the movement itself and the PA government in order to avoid the same mistakes, excesses and politicisation of civic institutions which characterised Fatah rule (ICG 2011, p. 26). In other words, Hamas attempted to make a distinction between the movement and the government. Fatah and the PA, in contrast, had become synonymous in the eyes of many Palestinians, and therefore Fatah lost its identity and *raison d'être* as a resistance organisation. Indeed, Brown and Hamzawy (2010, p. 172) contend that Hamas "tried to be far more faithful to constitutional procedures and legal mechanisms than Fatah had ever been". After conducting fieldwork in Gaza in 2010, Yezid Sayigh reports that even Fatah critics, former security officers, human rights activists and businessmen in the Gaza Strip confirm a strong work ethic on the part of the Hamas government, providing credibility to the claims by Hamas and the de facto Ministry of the Interior that "the mentality of working in a government institution differs from that in an organization [i.e., Hamas]; we altered the perks and privileges that came with the PASF [Palestinian Authority Security Forces] employment, we seek neither rest nor gain" (Abu Abudallah Lafi cited in Sayigh 2011a, p. 48). Tellingly, even after five years of exclusive Hamas rule in the Gaza Strip, a June 2012 poll found that Palestinians believed that the de facto government in Gaza is substantially less corrupt than the West Bank Authority with 57 per cent of respondents believing there is corruption in the former and 71 per cent in the latter (PCPSR 2012).

Hamas also tended towards technocratic expertise rather than political credentials when appointing key cabinet positions (Brown and Hamzawy 2010, p. 173). Throughout the course of my own interviews, several cabinet members for the tenth and eleventh administrations (for instance, the former Deputy Prime Minister and Minister of Education Nasser al-Din al-Shaer, the former Minister for Planning Sameer Abu Aisha, and former Minister for Women's Affairs Mariam Salah, among others) made it explicitly clear that they were not members of Hamas but rather independent Islamists. Indeed, at least initially, Hamas members were required to resign from any leadership roles within the movement before entering government in an attempt to ensure the separation between the movement and the government (Brown 2012, p. 15).

124 Bombs to ballots: political jihad

Hamas politicians also attempted to portray themselves as not only representatives of the people but also as part of the people. In contrast to their Fatah predecessors, Hamas ministers attempted to publicly disavow themselves from the trappings of public office; for instance, rather theatrically taking public transport to work instead of government vehicles (Brown and Hamzawy 2010, p. 178). Hamas parliamentarians shared taxis for transport and flew economy class on their very rare foreign trips (Brown 2012, p. 15). Secretary General of Parliament Mahmoud al-Ramahi recounted to me in a personal interview his preference for standing in line at Israeli checkpoints rather than using VIP powers.

Nevertheless, conflict between Hamas and Fatah continued incessantly. In February 2007, Saudi Arabia managed to broker a deal for a unity government between the feuding factions known as the Mecca Accord. The Accord consisted of four clauses:

> a ban on the shedding of Palestinian blood … [and] adopting the language of dialogue as the sole basis for solving political disagreements in the Palestinian arena"; "reaching a final agreement on the formation of a Palestinian national unity government"; accelerated progress "in activating and reforming" the Palestine Liberation Organisation (PLO); and reinforcing 'the principle of political partnership' within the Palestinian Authority (PA) "on the basis of political pluralism according to an agreement ratified by both parties.
>
> (ICG 2007, p. 1)

Amidst continued Hamas/Fatah fighting, however, a special force loyal to President Mahmoud Abbas was actively being trained and armed by the United States. Hamas perceived this to be part of an attempted putsch by Fatah and the US, and pre-emptively staged a counter-coup in June 2007, sparking a brief but bloody civil war during which Fatah forces collapsed in the Gaza Strip (Rose 2008; Steele 2007).

In reality however, this conflict centred around Abbas' security adviser Mohammed Dahlan, the PA Preventative Security Apparatus, the General Intelligence Directorate and elements of the Presidential Guard, who had been working with the US to destabilise and ultimately overthrow Hamas rule (Sayigh 2011a, p. 55). As a result, when the fighting broke out, the majority of the existing Fatah-led security forces as well as most Fatah members

> did not see this as their fight, and so remained on the sidelines. The committee appointed by Mahmoud Abbas to investigate the loss of Gaza concluded that no more than 10–15 percent of PASF [Palestinian Authority Security Forces], and maybe fewer than 2000, or 3.5%, fought against Hamas, and noted the "collective military abstention" of local Fatah members "even [those] in leadership echelons".
>
> (Ibid.)

Bombs to ballots: political jihad 125

Reprisals were made against Hamas institutions in the West Bank and, with questionable legality, Abbas appointed a counter-government by Presidential decree led by Salam Fayyad, thus bringing an abrupt end to the short-lived experiment of democratic governance in the Palestinian Territories. In consequence, Hamas increasingly "abandoned many of its pledges to maintain fidelity to resistance and legality", instead choosing to insert itself more directly into many aspects of Gaza's social, political and economic structures (Brown and Hamzawy 2010, p. 174).

While criticised for excessive use of force during the civil conflict and initial law enforcement efforts subsequent to the conflict, Hamas has instituted order which had been hitherto lacking under the previous administrations. According to Milton-Edwards (2008, p. 672), following criticism of violating freedoms and rights, a consensus emerged that the Executive Force, "compared to other [in essence, West Bank] branches of the PSF [Palestinian Security Forces], were disciplined and sincere in their attempts to address ordinary law and order issues." Sayigh (2011a, p. 6) moreover, reports that the de facto government in Gaza has shown itself to be a 'learning organisation' and, in addition, the Haniyeh government has "demonstrated the local 'ownership' so often sought by Western donors in other settings, but rarely attained and usually not successfully induced, whether through the promise of assistance or by imposing conditions on aid". In other words, the de facto government in Gaza, rather than donors, has succeeded in designing, implementing and reviewing its security sector policies and programmes, something which the West Bank authority has conspicuously failed to do (DCAF 2010, p. 2). In this respect, Hamas argues that "good governance is a form of resistance (personal jihad)" (cited in Sayigh 2011a, p. 17).

Conclusions

With the death of Yasser Arafat and consequent liberalisation of the political system, Hamas reframed the concepts of resistance and jihad in order to justify participation in institutionalised politics. Buoyed up by its escalating popularity – which doubled over the course of the second intifada from 2000 to 2005 – Hamas reacted to a war-weary populace, not to mention the heavy price paid by the movement and its leadership, and shifted the emphasis of resistance and jihad to the political track. In effect, a change in the political opportunity structure allowed Hamas to advance its cause via formal national political institutions which, hitherto, had not existed under the autocratic Arafat regime – or at least in theory.

Elections, moreover, provided Palestinians with hope. A February 2006 poll a month after the elections found that 77.9 per cent of Palestinians were either very optimistic or somewhat optimistic about the future performance of the elected government (JMCC 2006). The reaction of the International Quartet, led predominantly by the United States, to Hamas' victory in 2006, however, undermined this optimism and Hamas' shift towards democratic participation.

126 *Bombs to ballots: political jihad*

Dr Hafez Shaheen (personal interview 2010), then Deputy Mayor for Planning and Technical Affairs and Change and Reform councillor in Nablus, for example, is adamant that the 2006 legislative elections were "a political trap" and "a big mistake" for Hamas.

The policies of boycotts imposed upon the Hamas government by the United States, the EU, Israel and the Fatah-led PA in the West Bank, in addition, have been costly on multiple levels. What little credibility United States policy on democratisation in the Middle East still possessed was dealt an almost fatal blow. US and Fatah duplicity aimed at undermining Hamas helped facilitate a brief but bloody civil war in the Gaza Strip, the result of which – namely Palestinian division and the split between Gaza and the West Bank – continues to manifest itself at the time of writing, despite the signing of several putative unity deals from May 2011. While Hamas has shown itself to be vigilant in enforcing ceasefires with Israel, this failed to prevent the carnage of Operation Cast Lead, during which Hamas miscalculated in retaliation to Israeli provocation; Israel responded with disproportionate force, leading to UN accusations of war crimes as enshrined in the Goldstone Report. Following an even bloodier round of conflict in July and August 2014, in part set off by Israeli attempts to undermine Palestinian reconciliation, Hamas and Fatah formed a unity government. At the time of writing it is unclear, however, what this new-found unity will produce and how long it will last.

These boycotts, moreover, have been counter-productive if the intention was to weaken Hamas and/or force it to accept US, UN, Fatah or Israeli dictates. The isolation and siege of Gaza has merely served to entrench Hamas' hegemony within the coastal enclave and forced it to become, by necessity, more self-sufficient, thereby weakening any leverage that outside forces may have possessed. The boycott of the Hamas administration has weakened the moderates within the movement advocating political participation and strengthened hardliners. The isolation of the Gaza Strip has caused it to become more conservative and patriarchal, facilitating a climate conducive to the emergence of al-Qa'ida and ISIS-inspired *salafi* jihadists challenging Hamas' more moderate brand of Islam (ICG 2011; Sayigh 2011a, p. 5). In turn, this has forced Hamas to institute autocratic measures to curb their influence and at least tacitly accede to street-level Islamisation.

Divisions within both the Palestinian polity and Hamas remain acute despite ongoing attempts to build a Palestinian political consensus. Consequently, politics is in danger of being emptied of meaning. At present there is much disillusionment with the Palestinian political factions. From March to May 2010, for instance, my own surveys (n = 131) indicate that around 38 per cent of university students want nothing to do with any political faction. According to Maryam (survey 2010), a 20-year-old law student, for instance, "All candidates are liars and they work for themselves". Similarly, Lulu (survey 2010), an 18-year-old law student from Nablus, explains: "I stopped supporting [Fatah] because I discovered that movements and parties only hinder the process of establishing a Palestinian state." Sajideh (survey 2010), a 20-year-old engineering student, was initially attracted to Hamas because

I believed that they [Hamas] didn't say one thing and do another, but I discovered the opposite ... I stopped supporting them because I did not believe in what they were saying at the end.... There is a lot of hypocrisy among all parties.... It's all slogans in reality.

Sa'ad (survey 2010), a 21-year-old communications student from Beitunia and former Fatah supporter, likewise explains, "I am against the whole idea of 'Palestinian parties' but I encourage resistance in all of its forms", adding that the PA "is hollow and meaningless. It doesn't have power. It doesn't deserve to represent me." All of these statements point to a general disillusionment with politics on both sides of the spectrum. Indicatively, PCPSR (2012) found that 60 per cent of Palestinians blame both Hamas and Fatah for the division between the West Bank and Gaza with only 13 per cent ascribing blame to Hamas, 10 per cent to Fatah and 7 per cent to other parties in June 2012.

If this disillusionment is replicated on a societal level, it may, in turn, have implications for the popular legitimacy of any Palestinian government, as well as any derivative effects produced by governmental policy, such as a negotiated settlement with Israel. A June 2012 poll (ibid.) found that 31 per cent of respondents are either undecided or would vote for a third party in legislative elections. When quizzed about the potential ramifications of legislative elections which were supposed to be held in May 2012, Laila (personal communication 2012), an American educated businesswoman from Ramallah with an inclination towards the PFLP, dismissed the elections as "corrupted people trading chairs". Nevertheless, despite their distrust of the political process, Palestinians still exhibit a healthy enthusiasm, if somewhat counterbalanced by cynicism, for the concept of democratic governance. An October 2014 poll (PCSPR 2014) found that 72 per cent of Palestinians would vote in new elections, even as 52 per cent considered the continued existence of the Palestinian Authority as a burden on the Palestinian cause.

Hamas, in addition, has shown itself to be a relatively pragmatic and flexible governing entity. In this regard, Hamas operates in the context of opportunities, and is cognisant of the needs and desires of the Palestinian population, power relations between competing forces, as well as the practical feasibility of its actions (Mishal and Sela 2000, p. viii). As such, Hamas' shift towards political resistance should be encouraged with the intention of socialisation. Greater links with foreign powers and responsibility to a wider domestic constituency mean that greater leverage may be brought to bear with the intention of moderating Hamas policy. To this end, Hamas has demonstrated the capacity for alliance building and cross-factional cooperation. Hamas has also repeatedly stated its amenability to coexistence with Israel despite its ostensible ideological convictions (see Yousef 2006; Weymouth 2006; Mishal 2006).

It is clear that Hamas is struggling to reconcile the tensions between politics, resistance and government. The ongoing boycotts that allowed Hamas to exercise unlimited control within the Gaza Strip, while severing the population from the outside world, have been neither conducive to democracy nor Palestinian

128 *Bombs to ballots: political jihad*

reconciliation. According to Yezid Sayigh (2011a, p. 76), "The abeyance of electoral democracy in the PA has, moreover, weakened the effect that public opinion previously had on Hamas's inclination to engage in Islamizing practices." As Nathan Brown (2012, p. 18) similarly points out, "A Hamas movement that had to ask for Palestinians' votes would likely behave differently – paying attention to public opinion, articulating its strategic vision, and seeking to persuade those outside of Islamist circles." In this light, 'incentivisation' rather than brutalisation and deprivation may well be a more appropriate course of action.

In 2006, Hamas decided to participate in legislative elections in a process which was supposed to allow Palestinians the right to freely choose their own leadership. Hamas' electoral victory stands to evidence that the Hamas-backed list successfully campaigned on a multi-faceted platform, not only entailing religious conviction but also managing to convince the broader Palestinian public of the merit of its social and political programmes as well. In other words, Hamas was able to reach out to a wider constituency beyond its ideological core, demonstrating its ability to function as a pragmatic political actor when presented with the opportunity to advance its cause via legitimate institutional channels. In this light, Hamas' electoral participation may be viewed as an abortive attempt to reorientate and reframe the concepts of resistance and jihad within the framework of democratic legitimacy.

Hamas, moreover, has attempted to reframe resistance which defines good governance as a personal jihad to act ethically in the eyes of God. The nuance of this shift from bombs to ballots was evidently lost on Israel and the major Western powers which continue to axiomatically associate Islam, jihad and resistance with eschatological violence. Consequently, the viability of alternative social and political agendas predicated upon improving the livelihood of everyday Palestinians, in contrast to armed insurrection, have been undermined. Instead, these alternative agendas continue to be mistakenly categorised under the all-encompassing rubric of 'terrorism' which has not only served to perpetuate the conflict(s) in Palestine but also throughout the entire Middle East region.

This shift towards political resistance should be respected and encouraged, even if Hamas' political platform is derived from Islamist thought and thus, in theory, not consistent with Western conceptions of secular governance. The application of the religious fundamentalist/Orientalist label to Hamas, however, obscures the reality on the ground, especially the movement's institutional presence and popular support. In practice, this essentialised religious label delegitimises Hamas as irrational, extremist and threatening in Western secular eyes (Esposito 1999, pp. 257–258). The applicability of 'secular' governance, however, needs to be problematised, especially within the context of the Muslim Middle East, where the concept of 'secularism' has few historical and/or cultural points of reference. In short, it needs to be recognised that democracy and modernity do not necessarily need to be defined in Western/'secular' terms (Esposito and Piscatori 1991). The alternative, entailing political marginalisation and

Bombs to ballots: political jihad 129

delegitimisation, limits the political opportunities and incentives of movements seeking representation, dignity and self-determination. Marginalisation disenfranchises the substantial proportion of the Palestinian population which supports Hamas and most likely will only push the movement further towards conservatism, autocracy and the potential further radicalisation of the Gaza Strip consequent to its international isolation.

Notes

1 Neutral or apolitical students, on the other hand, often expressed disgust or disillusionment with all of the political factions. Many perceived political factions to be working for parochial interests rather than for the national cause; 51.4 per cent of these students indicated that they would not vote in any elections held in the near future.
2 The electoral system utilised for the first two rounds entailed a plurality at large or a bloc system whereby each voter is able to vote for the number of candidates commensurate to seats available based on districts. The third and fourth rounds, in contrast, utilised a system of proportional representation based on party lists.
3 In a number of areas such as Bethlehem, Ramallah and Jerusalem, there were seats specifically allocated to Christian candidates as part of a quota system. The PLC also provides a quota specifically for women.
4 The district-level voting system was abolished by presidential decree following the split between Gaza and the West Bank in 2007.
5 Barghouti was leader of the Fatah militia *Tanzim* ('Organisation') and is currently serving five life sentences in an Israeli prison for orchestrating attacks against Israel.
6 It is also worth noting that the number of Palestinians living in the Diaspora, mostly in Jordan, Syria and Lebanon, now outnumber those living in the Palestinian Territories. Most of these refugees and their descendants from the 1948/1949 conflict continue to live in refugee 'camps' and are treated as second-class citizens.
7 In the north, Hizbullah, either seeking to take advantage of the chaos or in solidarity with Hamas and the Palestinian people, ambushed an Israeli patrol on the border of Lebanon, killing eight and seizing two mortally wounded or deceased soldiers, which precipitated a month-long offensive claiming over 1400 (mostly civilian) Lebanese lives and 150 (mostly IDF) Israelis, as well as destroying much of Lebanon's civilian infrastructure. Hundreds of thousands of civilians were displaced on both sides of the border. The ensuing denouement of this conflict was the macabre exchange of the bodies of these two soldiers for several prisoners incarcerated in Israeli prisons, as well as the exhumed remains of Hizbullah fighters buried in Israeli soil.

References

Abu Amr, Z. 2007. 'Hamas: From Opposition to Rule'. In *Where Now for Palestine? The Demise of the Two-state Solution*, edited by J. Hilal. London: Zed Books.
al-Naami, S. 2007. 'Hamas versus al-Qa'ida'. *al-Ahram* (Cairo), 12–18 July.
Alshech, E. 2008. 'Egoistic Martyrdom and Hamas' Success in the 2005 Municipal Elections'. *Die Welt des Islams* 48(1): 23–49.
Barghouti, I. 2007. *Religion and State in Palestine*. Ramallah: Ramallah Centre for Human Rights.
Bourdieu, P. 1991. *Language and Symbolic Power*. Cambridge: Polity Press with Blackwell.
Brown, N. 2007. *Requiem for Palestinian Reform: Clear Lessons from a Troubled Record*. Washington, DC: Carnegie Endowment for International Peace.

130 *Bombs to ballots: political jihad*

Brown, N. 2012. *Gaza Five Years On: Hamas Settles In*. Washington, DC: Carnegie Endowment for International Peace.

Brown, N. and Hamzawy, A. 2010. *Between Religion and Politics*. Washington, DC: Carnegie Endowment for Peace.

Burgat, F. 2003. *Face to Face with Political Islam*. London: I.B. Tauris.

Caridi, P. 2010. *Hamas: From Resistance to Governance?* Jerusalem: PASSIA.

Daily Star (Lebanon). 2005. 'Hamas Challenges Fatah in Elections'. 6 May.

DCAF 2010. *Building Ownership in Palestinian Security Sector Reform. Spotlight No. 6.* Ramallah: Geneva Centre for the Democratic Control of Armed Forces.

Denoeux, G. 2002. 'The Forgotten Swamp: Navigating Political Islam'. *Middle East Policy* 9(2): 56–81.

Erlanger, S. 2005. 'Hamas Surges in the Polls; Blow to Fatah'. *New York Times*, 17 December.

Esposito, J. 1999. *The Islamic Threat: Myth or Reality?* New York: Oxford University Press.

Esposito, J. and Piscatori, J. 1991. 'Democratization and Islam'. *Middle East Journal* 45(3): 427–440.

FairVote. 2006. *It's the Election System Stupid: The Misleading Hamas Majority and the System that Created it*. MD: FairVote Program for Representative Government.

Farhat, F. 2006. 'Les Femmes, le Hamas et les elections de janvier 2006'. *Confluences en Mediterranee* 59: 63–68.

Farrell, S. 2006. 'Hamas Tries to Exploit its Pariah Status at the Ballot Box'. *The Times* (London), 24 January.

Fisk, R. 2006. 'The Problem with Democracy'. *Independent* (UK), 28 January.

Foucault, M. [1976] 1990. *The Will to Knowledge: The History of Sexuality*. London: Penguin Books.

Gordan, N. and Filc, D. 2005. 'Hamas and the Destruction of Risk Society'. *Constellations* 12(4): 542–560.

Gunning, J. 2004. 'Peace with Hamas? The Transforming Potential of Political Participation'. *International Affairs* 80(2): 233–255.

Gunning, J. 2007. *Hamas in Politics: Democracy, Religion, Violence*. London: Hurst & Co.

Gutman, M. 2005. 'From Bullets to Ballots?' *The Jerusalem Post*, 15 July.

Hass, A. 2010. 'How Will the Next Palestinian Uprising Look?' *Ha'aretz* (Israel), 3 March.

Hilal, J. 2005. 'Hamas's Rise as Chartered in the Polls 1994–2005'. *Journal of Palestine Studies* 35(3): 6–19.

Hroub, K. 2000. *Hamas: Political Thought and Practice*. Washington, DC: Institute of Palestine Studies.

Hroub, K. 2006a. *Hamas: A Beginner's Guide*. London: Pluto Press.

Hroub, K. 2006b. 'A "New Hamas" Through Its New Documents'. *Journal of Palestine Studies* 35(4): 6–27.

ICG. 2003. *Islamic Social Welfare Activism in the Occupied Palestinian Territories: A Legitimate Target?* Brussels: ICG.

ICG. 2006. *Enter Hamas: The Challenges of Political Integration*. Brussels: ICG.

ICG. 2007. *After Mecca: Engaging Hamas*. Brussels: ICG.

ICG. 2008. *Ruling Palestine I: Gaza under Hamas*. Brussels: ICG.

ICG. 2011a. *Radical Islam in Gaza*. Brussels: ICG.

ICG. 2011b. *Palestinian Reconciliation: Plus Ça Change …* Brussels: ICG.

Bombs to ballots: political jihad 131

Jarbawi, A. and Pearlman, W. 2007. 'Struggle in a Post-charisma Transition: Rethinking Palestinian Politics after Arafat'. *Journal of Palestine Studies* 36(4): 6–21.

JMCC. 2006. *Poll no. 57, February*. Jerusalem: JMCC.

Kalman, M. 2006a. 'Hamas Proving It's Politically Shrewd'. *San Francisco Chronicle*, 29 January.

Kalman, M. 2006b. 'Secret Democracy Elevated Hamas, Underground Campaign Unified Voters'. *San Francisco Chronicle*, 19 February.

Khalidi, R. 2006. *The Iron Cage: The Story of the Palestinian Struggle for Statehood*. Boston, MA: Beacon Press.

Klein, M. 2007. 'Hamas in Power'. *The Middle East Journal* 61(3): 442–459.

Klein, M. 2009. 'Against the Consensus: Oppositionist Voices in Hamas'. *Middle Eastern Studies* 45(6): 881–892.

Legget, K. 2005. 'Odd Allies: Bethlehem Mayor Courts Hamas, Stirring Up Region'. *Wall Street Journal* (New York), 23 December.

Levitt, M. 2006. *Hamas: Politics, Charity and Terrorism in the Service of Jihad*. New Haven, CT: Yale University Press.

Litvak, M. 1997. 'Inside versus Outside: The Challenge of the Local Leadership 1967–1994'. In *The PLO and Israel: From Armed Conflict to Political Solution, 1964–1994*, edited by A. Sela and M. Ma'oz. New York: St Martin's Press.

Litvak, M. 2005. 'Hamas' Victory in Municipal Elections'. *Tel Aviv Notes*, 26 December.

Malka, H. 2005. 'Forcing Choices: Testing the Transformation of Hamas'. *The Washington Quarterly* 28(4): 37–53.

McGeough, P. 2009. *Kill Khalid ... Mossad's Failed Hit and the Rise of Hamas*. Crow's Nest, NSW: Allen & Unwin.

Milton-Edwards, B. 1996. *Islamic Politics in Palestine*. London: I.B. Tauris.

Milton-Edwards, B. 2008. 'Order without Law? An Anatomy of Hamas Security: The Executive Force (Tanfithya)'. *International Peacekeeping* 15(5): 663–676.

Milton-Edwards, B. and Farrell, S. 2010. *Hamas: The Islamic Resistance Movement*. Cambridge: Polity Press.

Mishal, K. 2006. 'We Will Not Sell Our People and Principles for Foreign Aid'. *Guardian* (UK), 31 January.

Mishal, S. and Sela, A. 2000. *The Palestinian Hamas: Vision, Violence and Coexistence*. New York: Columbia University Press.

Pappé, I. 2006. *A History of Modern Palestine: One Land, Two Peoples*. Cambridge: Cambridge University Press.

Pascovich, E. 2012. 'Social–Civilian Apparatuses of Hamas, Hizballah and Other Activist Islamic Organizations'. *Digest of Middle East Studies* 21(1): 126–148.

PCPSR. 2004. *Public Opinion Poll no. 12, June 24–27*. Ramallah: PCSPR.

PCPSR. 2005. *Local Elections Exit Polls, December 15*. Ramallah: PCSPR.

PCPSR. 2006. *Legislative Elections Exit Poll, January 25*. Ramallah: PCPSR.

PCPSR. 2012. *Public Opinion Poll no. 44, June 21–23*. Ramallah: PCSPR.

PCPSR. 2014. *Public Opinion Poll no. 53, October 10*. Ramallah: PCSPR.

Pradhan, B. 2008. 'Palestinian Politics in the Post-Arafat Era'. *International Studies* 45(4): 295–339.

Qur'an, The. 2008. Translated and edited by T. Khalidi. London: Penguin Books.

Regular, A. 2006. 'Hamas Signs Pact on Code of Conduct for PLC Elections'. *Ha'aretz* (Israel), 9 January.

Reinhart, T. 2006. *The Road Map to Nowhere: Palestine/Israel since 2003*. New York: Verso.

132 *Bombs to ballots: political jihad*

Rose, D. 2008. 'The Gaza Bombshell'. *Vanity Fair*, April.

Ross, D. 2006. 'Foreword'. In *Hamas: Politics, Charity and Terrorism in the Service of Jihad*, by M. Levitt. New Haven, CT: Yale University Press.

Roy, S. 2007. *Failing Peace: Gaza and the Palestinian–Israeli Conflict*. London: Pluto Press.

Roy, S. 2011. *Hamas and Civil Society in Gaza: Engaging the Islamic Social Sector*. Princeton, NJ: Princeton University Press.

Rubin, B. 2006. 'A Review that Speaks Volumes'. *The Jerusalem Post*, 26 June.

Sayigh, Y. 2011a. *'We Serve the People': Hamas Policing in Gaza*. Brandeis University: Crown Centre for Middle East Studies.

Sayigh, Y. 2011b. *Policing the People, Building the State; Authoritarian Transformation in the West Bank and Gaza*. Washington, DC: Carnegie Endowment for Peace.

Shikaki, K. 2006. 'Sweeping Victory: Uncertain Mandate'. *Journal of Democracy* 17(3): 116–130.

Steele, J. 2007. 'Hamas Acted on a Very Real Fear of a US-sponsored Coup'. *Guardian* (UK), 22 June.

Tamimi, A. 2007. *Hamas: A History from Within*. Northampton, MA: Olive Branch Press.

Tuastad, D. 2009. *Primary Solidarity: A Comparative Study on the Role of Kinship in Palestinian Local Politics*. PhD thesis. Oslo: University of Oslo.

Turner, M. 2006. 'Building Democracy: Liberal Peace Theory and the Election of Hamas'. *Democratization* 13(5): 739–755.

Van Natta Jr., D. and O'Brien, T. 2003. 'Flow of Saudis Cash to Hamas is Scrutinized'. *New York Times*, 17 September.

Weinburg, L. and Pedahzur, A. 2003. *Political Parties and Terrorist Groups*. London: Routledge.

Weymouth, L. 2006. 'We Do Not Wish to Throw Them into the Sea' (Interview with Ismail Haniyeh). *Washington Post*, 26 February.

WINEP. 2007. *The Palestinian Legislative Council*. Washington, DC: Washington Institute for Near East Policy.

Younis, M. 2000. *Liberation and Democratization: The South African and Palestinian National Movements*. Minneapolis, University of Minnesota Press.

Yousef, A. 2006. 'Pause for Peace'. *New York Times*, 1 November.

Zuhur, S. 2010. *Hamas and Israel: Conflicting Strategies of Group-based Politics*. Carlisle, PA: Strategic Studies Institute.

Zweiri, M. 2006. 'The Hamas Victory: Shifting Sands or Major Earthquake?' *Third World Quarterly* 27(4): 657–687.

Interviews and surveys

Abdul-Razeq, O., former Islamist Finance Minister, elected MP and Professor of Economics at an-Najah National University, Ramallah, February 2010.

Abu Aisha, S., former Minister of Planning for the Tenth 'Hamas' Administration and Professor of Engineering at an-Najah National University, Nablus, March 2010.

Abu Marzouq, M., Deputy Head of the Hamas Political Bureau, US Specially Designated Global Terrorist and Doctor of Engineering, Damascus, May 2010.

Abu Sway, M., Professor of *Sharia* Law at al-Quds University, Abu Dis, January 2010.

Ahmed, a 22-year-old former Fatah supporter, anonymous survey, an-Najah National University, Nablus, March 2010.

Bombs to ballots: political jihad 133

Ali, a 22-year-old Fatah member and student representative, anonymous survey, al-Quds University, al-Quds, May 2010.

al-Ramahi, Mahmoud. Islamist Secretary General of Parliament, elected PLC Deputy and anaesthetist, Ramallah, January 2010.

al-Shaer, Nasser ed-Din, former Deputy Prime Minister and Minister of Education for the Tenth 'Hamas' Administration, Professor of *Sharia* Law at an-Najah National University, Nablus, February 2010.

Amayreh, K., Palestinian freelance journalist, Dura, January 2010.

Barghouti, I., Director of the Ramallah Centre for Human Rights and Professor of Political Sociology, Ramallah, October 2010.

Dweik, Aziz, Islamist Speaker of Parliament, elected PLC Deputy and Professor of Urban Geography, Hebron, May 2010.

Fatima, an 18-year-old Hamas supporter, anonymous survey, an-Najah National University, Nablus, March 2010.

Hatim, a 20-year-old Fatah member from Ramallah, anonymous survey, Birzeit University, Birzeit, April 2010.

Huda, a Hamas sympathiser and American-born engineering student, anonymous survey, Birzeit, University, Birzeit, April 2010.

Hussein, a 22-year-old former student representative of Fatah, anonymous survey, an-Najah National University, Nablus, March 2010.

'Idhar, a 19-year-old Fatah member, anonymous survey, an-Najah National University, Nablus, March 2010.

Itimad, a 20-year-old student studying geography and Fatah supporter, anonymous survey, an-Najah National University, Nablus, March 2010.

Jad, Islah, Director of the Institute of Women's Studies and Assistant Professor of Gender and Development at Birzeit University, Birzeit, October 2010.

Jamal, a 21-year-old Fatah member studying political science, anonymous survey, al-Quds University, Abu Dis, May 2010.

Jamila, a 22-year-old Fatah supporter studying business management, anonymous survey, Birzeit University, Birzeit, April 2010.

Khalid, a 22-year-old member of Hamas studying media and political science, anonymous survey, Birzeit University, Birzeit, April 2010.

Laila, a 31-year-old American-educated NGO project director, Ramallah, 2012.

Lulu, an 18-year-old law student and former Fatah supporter, anonymous survey, an-Najah National University, Nablus, March 2010.

Mahmoud, a 27-year-old Hamas member, anonymous survey, an-Najah National University, Nablus, March 2010.

Malak, a 21-year-old PFLP voter studying law, anonymous survey, Birzeit University, Birzeit, April 2010.

Maryam, an unaffiliated 20-year-old studying law, anonymous survey, Birzeit University, April 2010.

Masri, N., then Islamist Deputy Mayor of Nablus; Member of Board of Trustees, an-Najah University, Nablus; Member of Board of Trustees, Islamic University, Gaza; Member of Management Committee, Al-Tadamon Charitable Society; Member of Royal College of Physicians, UK, MRCP, England and physician, Nablus, April 2010.

Mishal, Shaul, Palestinian-Israeli Professor of Political Science at Tel Aviv University, Tel Aviv, November 2009.

Mona, a 21-year-old former Hamas sympathiser from Jerusalem, anonymous survey, an-Najah National University, Nablus, March 2010.

134 *Bombs to ballots: political jihad*

Nabihah, an unaffiliated 21-year-old student studying political science, anonymous survey, al-Quds University, al-Quds, May 2010.

Namir, a 23-year-old Hamas supporter, anonymous survey, al-Quds University, Abu Dis, May 2010.

Qassam, A.-S., former presidential candidate and Professor of Political Science at an-Najah National University, Nablus, January 2010.

Sa'ad, a 21-year-old student studying communications and former Fatah supporter, anonymous survey, Birzeit University, Birzeit, April 2010.

Sajideh, a 20-year-old engineering student and former Hamas supporter, anonymous survey, Birzeit University, Birzeit, April 2010.

Salah, M., former Islamist Minister for Women's Affairs, elected PLC Deputy, and Professor of *Sharia* Law at al-Quds University, Ramallah, May 2010.

Shaheen, H., then Deputy Mayor of Nablus for Planning and Technical Affairs, local councillor for Change and Reform, and Professor of Engineering at an-Najah National University, Nablus, March/April 2010.

Thawab, a 19-year-old Fatah activist from Zawata, anonymous survey, an-Najah National University, Nablus, March 2010.

5 Charity, community development and civilian jihad[1]

Take from their wealth a freely given alms, to cleanse them therewith and purify their acts.

The Qur'an (9:103)

All these charities that help, that we made, that we built, was built aside from our participation in elections or not.... We expect return from Allah.

Dr Omar Abdul-Razeq (personal interview 2010), Islamist PLC Deputy and former Minister of Finance

Palestinian existence is characterised by a history of dispossession, exclusion and the denial of identity. As a result, Palestinians believe that their continued existence is a form resistance in itself. Central to this resistance is the Palestinian ethos of *summud* or steadfastness. Traditionally, this has been characterised as passive resistance, which entails remaining on the land in the face of Israeli oppression. The adoption of *summud* as an ideology was motivated by a refusal to countenance a second ethnic cleansing akin to the *nakba* in 1948 (Kimmerling 2003, p. 15). Thus, *summud*, both collectively and individually, is a positive action to ensure that history does not repeat itself (Peteet 1991, p. 183). An individual practising *summud* is one of three heroic figures in Palestinian society (Kimmerling and Migdal 2003, p. 243). The elevation of the stoic or survivor to a hero figure helps facilitate broad-based identification with the Palestinian cause among those unwilling or unable to actively fight the Israeli occupation. According to Sara Roy (2007, p. 13), resistance is

> based on the ethos of survival. The imperative [is] to remain steadfast against occupation, to resist all attempts by the occupier to dispossess, expropriate and destroy, and helping (not empowering) society to preserve what it [can].

Summud muqawim, in contrast, is a more activist form of resistance based on community development and institution building to heighten self-sufficiency and lessen dependency on the occupation (Farsoun and Landis 1990, p. 28). This is similar to a strategy described in civil resistance literature as constructive

136 *Charity, community and civilian jihad*

(in contrast to disruptive) non-violent resistance, which consists of building parallel structures in order to reduce dependency on an oppressive regime (Burrowes 1996, pp. 97–99). This is a strategy based on empowerment. The Islamic movement in the Palestinian Territories has long been engaged in this type of resistance. According to Bashir (personal interview 2010), a 44-year-old Hamas member involved in youth activities then based in Damascus,

> there is a civilian concept of resistance as well, which is the action of organisations of charity, building and development. This is another form of resistance or supporting the resistance.

For Hamas, moreover, there is an intertwining of political, religious and social dimensions. Hamas and its sympathisers view charity and community development as both a religious injunction and an act of resistance in itself. To this end, Hamas conceives of social work, charity and institution building as civilian jihad (Stephan 2009), concomitantly aimed at ameliorating the living standards of Palestinian society and working for its reform within an Islamic framework.

While we have seen in previous chapters that the application and emphasis on armed resistance and political jihad are dependent on opportunities, circumstance and popular opinion, civilian resistance, charity and community development have remained a constant endeavour for the Islamic movement in the Palestinian Territories. Indeed, it is important to recall that social activism was the primary concern of Hamas' predecessor, *al-Ikhwan al-Muslimun*. Hence, the Palestinian *Ikhwan*, and by extension Hamas as its successor, largely consist of "a social project motivated by philanthropy and dedicated to charity" (Tamimi 2007, p. 3).

Hamas and its affiliates engage in two disparate yet deeply intertwined types of social work: *da'wa* (proselytising or the 'call' to Islam) and development-orientated institution building aimed at improving the day-to-day living conditions and future opportunities of Palestinians in need. As Sara Roy (2011, p. 70) observes, the original orientation of Islamic social work in the Palestinian Territories, as espoused by Hamas' predecessor the *Ikhwan*, placed an emphasis on religious and educational initiatives largely focused on *da'wa*, whereas the creation of Hamas and the first intifada prompted a shift towards a more broad-based strategy predicated on charity, community development and institution building. The former strategy focuses on the creation of 'sound Muslims' which then, in turn, facilitates the creation of a virtuous, Islamic society (Irving Jensen 2009, pp. 5–6). The latter emphasis on institution building, in contrast, seeks to ameliorate the living conditions of Palestinians within the context of an inefficient and corrupt administrative entity subordinated to the policy impediments of the occupation authorities. This broad-based social work is then further divided between traditional charitable organisations concerned primarily with immediate needs and service providers focused on community development.

Social work situated within the chaos so characteristic of the second intifada, and the consequent free-fall of the socio-economic status of many ordinary Palestinians, was more marked by crisis management than institution building.

Charity, community and civilian jihad 137

To this end, this chapter will interrogate Hamas' provision of social services and institution building on a material basis within the context of difficult socio-economic circumstances attendant on the occupation, whereas Chapter 6 will discuss the ideational aspects of Hamas' social programmes predicated on *da'wa* and education.

Hamas, its predecessor and its affiliates have a long history of providing cheap and efficient social services to the Palestinian community, long suffering from the inadequate provision of services: first from the occupation authorities neglecting its duties as stipulated under international law, and then from a corrupt and inefficient Palestinian Authority. As a result, Hamas was able to build a strong level of trust at a grassroots level which was facilitated by personal involvement within the wider community.

Despite numerous contentions pointing to the centrality of Hamas' social institutions in facilitating its grassroots support, there is surprisingly little in-depth literature dealing with this phenomenon. Khaled Hroub (2000, p. 234), for instance, asserts that:

> Hamas's concern with social issues found expression in the extensive charitable social services the movement established for the poor. Various Palestinian social strata came to depend on the health care, vocational training, and charitable works services that Hamas provided. These activities led to a rise in Hamas's popularity. Subsequently these social services became one of the most important sources of influence that Hamas had with broad strata of the public. Nevertheless, the literature on this subject, either by Hamas or others, remains meagre.

But why exactly does Hamas engage in social work? Mainstream Western discourses often portray Hamas-run charities as mere fronts for promoting terrorism against Israel. Thus, this chapter will first examine the premise that Hamas charities function as a 'womb to tomb' programme facilitating the recruitment and indoctrination of 'terrorists'. Do Islamic social institutions facilitate armed resistance? To what extent, moreover, are Islamic social institutions in the Palestinian Territories formally linked to Hamas at all?

In contrast to the oft-stated assertion that Hamas charities are terrorist-producing factories, the second and third sections contextualise Islamic social work and situate it within the wider political, cultural and socio-economic milieu. In essence, these sections will explore the historical, cultural and socio-economic imperatives which may motivate, or indeed necessitate, the many varied Islamic social institutions in the Palestinian Territories.

To this end, what types of civilian jihad and resistance does Hamas engage in? The fourth section will provide a brief descriptive context of Islamic social institutions within the Palestinian Territories. While an extensive review of Islamic social institutions is beyond the scope of this chapter, it will briefly explore several key institutions dating back to Hamas' *Ikhwan* predecessor, as well as several initiatives which are somewhat unique within the cultural context

138 *Charity, community and civilian jihad*

of the Arab Middle East (see Roy 2011, pp. 97–160 for an extensive review). The fifth section examines Islamic charity as crisis management within the context of the second intifada.

Finally, how do these institutions contribute to Hamas' wider programme of resistance? To what extent do Islamic social institutions contribute to Hamas' popular legitimacy, and why?

It is important to note that charitable endeavours, community development and institution building are neither unique to Hamas as a socio-political actor possessing a militant wing, nor Islamic movements in general. If anything, Islamist movements in other countries freed of occupation provide far more extensive and coordinated social services. According to Harb and Leenders (2005, p. 174), for instance, the Hizbullah in Lebanon provides a 'holistic' array of social services. Indeed, one non-aligned Sheikh describes Hizbullah as "more than just a party. It is the general environment in which we live" (cited in ICG 2007, p. 5; see also Pascovich 2012). Similarly, the Egyptian Muslim Brotherhood, a predominantly non-violent organisation, has a long history of social work within the community. Throughout the course of the Cold War, moreover, a variety of leftist and anti-colonial movements – many of which viewed themselves as governments in waiting – provided social services to their would-be constituents. Indeed, it was the secular communists and the leftist PFLP who institutionalised community work within the Palestinian Territories (Sayigh 1998, pp. 470–484; Rosenfeld 2004, pp. 207–208).

From 'womb to tomb': the received view

The US government and much of the Western mainstream media posit that Hamas' social welfare services play the nefarious role of inciting, supporting and instigating terror against Israel. During the case of the US government vs. the Holy Land Foundation, then the largest Muslim charitable organisation in the US, alleging that the organisation provided funding for Hamas, US prosecutor Barry Jonas described Islamic charities in the Palestinian Territories as part of a 'womb-to-tomb' cycle recruiting terrorists for Hamas (cited in Kovach 2008; see also Levitt 2004).

This near-axiomatic point of view, as actualised and employed by most major Western governments and much of the mainstream media, is aptly expressed by James Brooke and Elaine Sciolino (1995) in a special report for the *New York Times*:

> critics contend that the distinction between Hamas terror and Hamas good works is dubious. Charity, they say, helps raise the political stature of a group that promotes terror.... But in the Israeli-occupied West Bank and in Palestinian controlled Gaza, Hamas has another face. Hamas-run schools offer free classes and Hamas-run clinics charge as little as $1 for private visits to a doctor. During the Islamic holy month of Ramadan last spring, Hamas distributed free meat and clothing to its supporters, while

Charity, community and civilian jihad 139

[Palestinian President] Mr. Arafat complained bitterly to Israeli and American officials that he could barely meet the payroll of his new Palestinian Authority. Hamas also uses schools, mosques, jails and funerals to spread the gospel about their jihad, or holy war, and to recruit young suicide bombers with the lure of martyrdom.

Whilst acknowledging that Hamas does provide these services, the emphasis on charity as a conduit for terrorism is clear without any insightful analysis pertaining to the potential benefits of medical clinics beyond the recruitment of terrorists.

Matthew Levitt (2006, p. 5), a former Deputy Assistant Secretary for Intelligence and Analysis for the US Treasury Department, similarly contends that:

Inside the Palestinian territories, the battery of mosques, schools, orphanages, summer camps, and sports leagues sponsored by Hamas are integral parts of an overarching apparatus of terror. These Hamas entities engage in incitement and radicalize society, and undertake recruitment efforts to socialize even the youngest children to aspire to die as martyrs. They provide logistical and operational support for weapons smuggling, reconnaissance, and suicide bombings. They provide day jobs for field commanders and shelter fugitive operatives.

Thus, the focus of Levitt's unambiguously titled book, *Hamas: Politics, Charity and Terrorism in the Service of Jihad* argues that Hamas is merely a terrorist organisation which utilises "its extensive charitable and educational work to promote its foremost aim: driving Israel into the sea" (Erlanger 2006).

The Intelligence and Terrorism Information Centre (ITIC) (2005) in Israel, a think-tank closely affiliated with the Israeli Ministry of Defence, reaches a similar conclusion depicting Hamas-affiliated charities as mere fronts for effecting terror and violence. Indeed, Levitt is heavily dependent on the ITIC which was "created in memory of the fallen of the Israeli intelligence community" and is staffed by former employees of this establishment.[2] Flanigan (2006, p. 642) likewise argues that Hamas and other "terrorist organizations use charitable service provision as a tool to shift the position of the local population along a 'continuum of community acceptance'", in effect conditioning the community to support political violence. These works almost completely elide the need, impact and benefit of Islamic social work beyond terrorist recruitment. In fact, as Jonathan Benthall (2008, p. 17) points out, there is "no sentence in Levitt's book on Hamas which acknowledges that Islamic charities in Palestine may be even partly motivated by altruism", although Levitt (2006, p. 238) does refer to Hamas' "notorious honesty".

Exactly how such dogmatic views could be argued through a process of causation or even correlation, moreover, is difficult to ascertain, given the apparent lack of firsthand experience with Islamic charities and, indeed, the day-to-day travails attendant upon living under military occupation. An absence of reliable data pertaining to the recipients of aid and subsequent life outcomes also make these arguments difficult, if not impossible, to substantiate on a large-scale basis.

140   *Charity, community and civilian jihad*

These arguments also place an emphasis on (Israeli) security rather than on socio-political phenomena related to foreign occupation and oppression. In addition, they are often heavily conditional on military, government and 'intelligence' sources, and are written from an antagonistic and/or ideologically oppositional point of view (Brown 2008, p. 78). 'Intelligence' sources are especially problematic since, by their very nature, these cannot be independently verified and are prone to deception. As Gunning (2008, p. 101) notes, despite dedicating an entire book to the alleged Hamas charity–terrorism nexus, Levitt "only mentions a few instances where charitable money is believed to have been used for armed activities.... Instead, his argument rests on the overlap in personnel between the political, military and charitable wings." According to Pascovich (2012, p. 133), moreover, "examples of military operatives becoming integrated into Hamas's charitable committees are quite rare. Also, no clear cut-evidence of money transfers from committees to the military wings can be found." As a result, these alarmist arguments postulating a charity–terrorism nexus should be treated with scepticism as they often serve to justify political repression and the targeting of Islamic social institutions.

These analyses also omit the fact that Hamas' military wing responsible for armed attacks, the Qassam Brigades, is operationally independent and deliberately kept separate from other aspects of the movement (Hroub 2006, pp. 120–123). While Hamas does undoubtedly extol the virtues of self-sacrifice, armed resistance and martyrdom, this is by no means unique to Hamas within the context of Palestinian society. All of the major Palestinian factions, and indeed many of the minor ones, for instance, possess armed wings which have engaged in suicide bombings. Hamas, moreover, was inundated by *too many* volunteers for suicide operations throughout the course of the second intifada (Milton-Edwards and Farrell 2010, p. 137). All of this suggests that there were other factors at play beyond the receipt of Islamic charity, namely Israeli brutality and repression and a history of armed struggle, which may cause individuals to gravitate towards militarism.

Nevertheless, these perceptions are not only limited to foreign observers but hold extensive currency within both Palestinian Authority ministries and secular institutions, whether through ignorance, ideological aversion and/or competition (Roy 2011, p. 101). Indeed, there is a strong tendency within the PA and the secular elite to view Islamic as synonymous with Hamas. It is important to note, however, that the aforementioned sources originate in or have strong links with Hamas' principal enemies and competitors – Israel, the United States and the Palestinian Authority – and, as such, must be treated with a grain of salt given the potential policy implications of such opinions. As the late Edward Said (1997) observed, in the Palestinian Territories, as throughout the wider Middle East region, dictatorial secular elites have frequently invoked the spectre of religious fundamentalism to justify autocracy in the eyes of their Western interlocutors and aid sponsors.

Fieldwork-based sources, however, reveal a different story. The most extensive of these works, Sara Roy's (2011) *Hamas and Civil Society in Gaza:*

Charity, community and civilian jihad 141

Engaging the Islamist Social Sector is the latest instalment of some 25 years of field experience studying Gaza's economy and Islamic social institutions in Gaza and the West Bank. Focusing predominantly on the Oslo years (1993–2000), Roy (ibid., p. 164), in contrast to the predominant charity–terrorism nexus that is popular in Western policy and intelligence circles, reveals that, for the most part, Islamic social institutions are decentralised, usually situated at a localised niche level, and staffed by local members of the community which they serve. Lundblad (2008, p. 206) similarly characterises *zakat* (alms) committees as "community-based and rooted in what we could call local Islam" (see also Benthall 2008, p. 6; Brown 2008, p. 78).

Contrary to the common view portraying a closely linked network promoting Islamic militancy, Roy (2011, pp. 134–135) reports that she was surprised by how little formal interaction she discovered between Islamic social institutions, which generally did not extend beyond referrals and sharing needs lists to ensure recipients were not attempting to claim from multiple institutions. In fact, Roy (ibid., p. 135) found that many social institutions possessed stronger organisational and bureaucratic links to the PA than with each other. In other words, there is no consistent, centrally organised, Hamas ideology spread throughout these institutions. Roy (ibid., p. 164) argues that Hamas, as an organisation, simply does not have either the bureaucracy or the expertise to coordinate and run such an extensive, openly public and varied array of Islamic social institutions.

According to Gunning (2008, p. 99), moreover, "charities considered to be affiliated with Hamas are organizationally independent from the political and resistance wings. Each of the charities has its own administration and is answerable to its own board of trustees." Not only is this pragmatic in the face of Israeli repression and Palestinian territorial fragmentation, but ensuring the structural and financial separation between charitable, militant and political activities avoids jeopardising the existence of Islamic social endeavours working to help the needy and reform Palestinian society (Pascovich 2012, pp. 133–134).

Further rebutting the accusations of indoctrinating terrorists, the vast majority of Islamic social institutions were registered with the PA or occupation authorities as relevant. Even prior to the Oslo Accords, Islamic social institutions were registered with the occupation authorities (Brown 2008, p. 74). In similar vein, PA ministries worked actively in conjunction with Islamic social institutions and referred constituents to specialised Islamic institutions with the appropriate expertise (Roy 2011, p. 187).

Islamic social institutions in the Palestinian Territories have also received funding from the UN and various other donors – including Western states and international organisations – because they were deemed to be more transparent and fiscally accountable. Tellingly, this reputation for incorruptibility "has been supported by Hamas's affiliation with various highly regarded NGOs (many of those employed in financial positions by the United Nation's Relief and Works Agency ... are affiliated with Hamas)" (Gunning 2008, p. 100). Save the Children, USAID, Médecins sans Frontières, Medical Aid for Palestine, the World

142 *Charity, community and civilian jihad*

Food Programme and UNDP, among others, are just several examples of international, non-Islamic organisations which have, at a various times, contributed to Hamas-affiliated charities or *zakat* committees, "because they have observed that contributions reach their intended destination" (ibid., p. 100; see also Benthall 2008, p. 11; Lundblad 2008, pp. 206–207). This, in turn, has helped build confidence among the local population.

Given their close cooperation and compliance with most Israeli, PA and international regulations, it would appear unlikely that Islamic social institutions are actively recruiting or socialising terrorists, at least to any noticeable extent. One USAID official with extensive experience in the Palestinian Territories is more direct,

> Provision of services certainly makes Hamas look good, but that does not make the beneficiaries natural candidates to become suicide-bombers. There is no evidence that social services organised by Islamic groups are used to recruit people to conduct attacks. Recruitment happens, but elsewhere, for example in mosques.
>
> (cited in ICG 2003, p. 21)

Physical aid and developmental programmes provided by the Islamic social sector, moreover, do not discriminate based on political, ideological or religious creed. Priority, for the most part, is given to those most in need, not according to partisan interests or ideological affinity – and indeed regardless of whether or not they are Muslim (Roy 2011, p. 186; Lundblad 2008, pp. 206–207).

Tellingly, many foreign governments distinguish, or have previously distinguished, between Hamas' armed wing and its presumed political and social affiliates. The EU, for instance, did not proscribe the latter activities as 'terrorist' in nature until 2003 and only then under intense US pressure (Brown 2008, pp. 73–77). This suggests that the reason for blacklisting Islamic social institutions lies less in objection to their operational capacity and supposed recruitment of 'terrorists' than in the political and ideological agendas of Israel and the United States, especially within the context of the 'global war on terror', because many of these organisations had been operating for years, if not decades prior, in compliance with Israeli and PA regulations. Moreover, the fact that Israel chose to target *both* Islamic and PA social institutions during the second intifada more closely resembles a form of collective punishment than the ostensible preservation of security. These actions, in addition, clearly did little to prevent individuals from gravitating towards militarism within the context of the second intifada. Nor did it prevent Hamas from accumulating more political support as evidenced by its victory in the 2006 legislative elections.

Another extensive fieldwork-based study on Islamic schools in the Palestinian Territories commissioned by Fafo (the Norwegian organisation under whose auspices the Oslo Accords were secretly formulated during the early 1990s) found that there was very little, if any, evidence to suggest that these schools were indoctrinating children to promote Islamic extremism or violence (Hoigilt

Charity, community and civilian jihad 143

2010). Nor was this report able to find any strong evidence suggesting that Hamas was directly involved with the day-to-day operations of these schools, although sympathisers, supporters and members may indeed have been employed as staff. Given that the Hamas-backed party list received 44.5 per cent of the vote during the 2006 elections, the presence of Hamas sympathisers on a wider societal level is almost impossible to avoid. Often parents, including PA employees and wealthy Palestinians, send their children to Islamic schools because of the superior quality of their education and focus on instilling good morals, good behaviour and discipline (Irving Jensen 2009, pp. 118–121; Hoigilt 2010, p. 22; Roy 2011, p. 81). Indeed, as one PA official opined, "the pupils are not in need of incitement; the daily practices of the occupation and what these pupils see with their own eyes is more than sufficient for this purpose" (cited in ICG 2003, p. 22). Similarly, as one secular NGO activist points out, "children are not being told anything they don't already know and do not experience everywhere else" (ibid.). Many Islamic schools also prioritise enrolments for poor families on needs-based criteria.

In a similar vein, the Hamas Administration in the Gaza Strip still retains the PA formulated curriculum (ICG 2008, p. 81). Indeed, education remained one of the few areas of cooperation between the West Bank Palestinian Authority and the Gazan government after the political schism of June 2007, including the standardisation of curricula and coordination of the *tawijhe* (matriculation exams) (Hoigilt 2010, p. 20; Roy 2011, p. 81).

Michael Irving Jensen (2006, p. 67), moreover, reports that during a semester conducting field research at the Islamic University of Gaza – widely considered to be a long-time Hamas bastion – an instructor actually admitted to emphasising the Islamic content of the courses he attended, specifically for *his* benefit and for *his* education. During this time, Irving Jensen (2009, pp. 71–74) also played for an Islamic soccer team through a youth organisation reputedly affiliated with Hamas, concluding that while some players were attracted to the club because of religious motivations, many others were influenced by the opportunity for field time and proximity to home. Thus, while Islamic social institutions espouse Islamic values to varying degrees, this does not necessarily mean that they are controlled by Hamas, let alone used to recruit terrorists or socialise recipients into perpetrating or accepting political violence. More mundane matters are also in play.

Merely identifying organisational affiliation, moreover, is problematic in itself because "although there is considerable overlap in personnel and interests, each charity is operated by its separate Administrative Council. While charity representatives sit on Hamas' *Shura* Council, the charities do not appear to be directly controlled by Hamas" (Gunning 2007, p. 115). Omar Abdul-Razeq (personal interview 2010), former Finance Minister for Change and Reform, told me that, while he does help to fund a kindergarten, for instance, he does not interfere or involve himself with its day-to-day operations, but rather leaves that to the discretion of the staff involved. This is not to say that Hamas does not accumulate social and political capital as a result of these organisations – indeed, the

144   *Charity, community and civilian jihad*

general consensus is that it does, both on an organisational and individual level – but it is necessary to clarify that, although the staff and/or directors may be members or supporters of Hamas, it is likely that "ideological affinity plays a more crucial role in mobilizing Hamas's network than does formal affiliation" (Malka 2007, p. 105). This prevalence of ideological affinity rather than formalised membership is also evident throughout Hamas' political support base and, indeed, political representatives.

Roy notes that affiliation with Hamas is usually designated by the wider population insofar as it is 'known' to be Hamas (see Roy 2011, pp. 146, 159). My own time in the West Bank revealed a similar phenomenon whereby individuals were 'known' to be Hamas by popular designation rather than through any substantive or verifiable evidence. Men, for instance, were often jokingly referred to as 'Sheikh' to convey that they were Islamists. Thus, while it is probable that Hamas does not formally run or control most Islamic social institutions in the Palestinian Territories – and hence these institutions are unlikely to be actively indoctrinating the population to support or perpetrate armed jihad – it is likely that Hamas does accumulate a substantial amount of social and political capital as a result of these organisations. Undoubtedly, Hamas does extol the virtues of resistance, self-sacrifice and martyrdom but there is no unified ideology among Islamic social institutions beyond their own particular interpretation and implementation of 'Islam'. Therefore, while there is no doubt that some recipients of Islamist aid and social services have gone on to become militants, there are also hundreds of thousands who have not, suggesting that terrorist recruitment is not the primary objective of these organisations.

The historical role of charity in the Palestinian Territories

Factional social services originated with the desire to win over the Palestinian 'street' while seeking to ameliorate the living conditions of Palestinians residing under an occupying regime providing minimal services (Rosenfeld 2004, pp. 207–208; Sayigh 1997, p. 243). As a factional politicised activity, social services were first conceived of and offered by the communist and leftist parties. As befitting the then apolitical nature of the *Ikhwan*, Islamic social institutions were not initially politicised, and focused on education, *da'wa* and Islamisation. An absence of adequate state institutions, ostensibly required of the Israeli administration under international law, led to the predominance of local NGOs and civil society of which the Islamists were an integral part. This predominance of civil society was further exacerbated in the late 1980s when an Israeli recession caused severe damage to the Palestinian economy.

By this stage, the Islamists were operating a variety of social institutions, including *al-Mujamma al-Islami* (the Islamic Centre), *al-Jami'yya al-Islamiyya* (the Islamic Society), *Jami'yyat al-Shabbat al-Muslimat* (the Young Women's Muslim Association), *Jami'yyat al-Salah al-Islamiyya* (the Association of Islamic Prayer) and the Islamic University of Gaza. Indeed, Hamas institutions and charities have long been recognised as providers for community

Charity, community and civilian jihad   145

and associated with the *Ikhwan's* services dating back to the 1970s. Islamic social institutions became especially prominent after 1991 when Saudi Arabia and the Gulf States withdrew their funding to the PLO in retaliation for supporting Saddam Hussein's invasion of Kuwait (Mishal and Sela 2000, pp. 88–89; Sayigh 1997, p. 105). As a result, the PLO was faced with a financial crisis and forced to close down many of its social services (Makovsky 1996, p. 108; Younis 2000, p. 163). Some Gulf States also increased funding to Hamas (Milton-Edwards and Farrell 2010, p. 63). Consequently, Hamas stepped into the welfare vacuum left by the financially beleaguered PLO. According to the World Bank, Palestinian charitable NGOs provided 60 per cent of primary health care and 50 per cent of secondary health care prior to the 1993 Oslo Accords (Hroub 2000, p. 241).

The inadequacy of government services continued following the establishment of the Palestinian Authority in 1994. At this stage, Hamas and the Islamists predominantly shied away from overt confrontation with Israel and the PA and instead chose to focus on civilian resistance through institution building. During the Oslo years (1993–2000) Islamic social institutions expanded dramatically and accounted for between 10 and 40 per cent of social institutions in the Palestinian Territories by 1999 according to various sources, ranging from Palestinian ministries to NGOs and Palestinian research institutions, "and in individual sectors such as education, these percentages appeared to be much higher" (Roy 2011, p. 101).

Hamas and its leaders also possess an elevated social status as the result of a long history of mediating personal and clan disputes. This has been especially important in accruing social prestige in a society historically marked by an absence of civil law and a central judiciary (Tuastad 2009, p. 236; Roy 2011, p. 75). During the 1970s and 1980s, Palestinians lost faith in the independence, impartiality and fairness of Israeli courts and turned to more informal and traditional means of mediation. In effect, Palestinians turned to community leaders to resolve disputes through various forms of Islamic and/or customary law (*'urf*) (Sayigh 2011, p. 77). During this period Hamas founder Sheikh Ahmed Yassin and other Hamas leaders carried out the "role of the police and courts by handling small torts, personal real estate, and financial disputes among the population of Gaza" (Hroub 2000, p. 236). In essence, Yassin and other Islamist leaders undertook "the function of adjudication and social regulation during troubled times", thereby accruing them popular authority (ibid., pp. 236–237). These interactions helped establish relations of trust within the community and facilitate a break with the Israeli legal system. Hamas leaders similarly adjudicated disputes throughout the chaos and lawlessness of the second intifada (Tuastad 2009, p. 236). Providing alternate services to an oppressive regime is a form of constructive non-violent or civic resistance. As discussed in the previous chapter, trust and personal relations with individuals were pivotal to Hamas' domination of the local district electoral lists.

146 *Charity, community and civilian jihad*

The Oslo years: institution building

Following the Oslo Accords, Arafat quickly moved to control the vibrant indigenous civil society – which emerged during the 1970s and sustained the population throughout the first intifada – and effectively merged most of it with the PA (Hammami 2000, p. 17; Jad 2007, p. 623). Consequently, leftist NGOs and political parties became dependent on Arafat for financial support because most donor money flowed through PA institutions and, moreover, were dependent on PA acquiescence to operate. The dynamic activism of the political left disintegrated or was co-opted, with many former leftists finding a new home in the burgeoning NGO industry facilitated by the post-Oslo optimism.

The 'NGOisation' of the political left led to its political and civil deterioration because foreign-sponsored NGOs are often perceived by Palestinians to be driven by foreign and elitist interests (Jad 2004; Bornstein 2009). According to Hanafi and Tabar (2004), this resulted in the creation of a new 'globalised elite' within Palestinian society who possess greater ties with international NGOs and donors than with the local community. Adel Samara (2001, p. 158), moreover, contends that Western "NGOs are the new form of the traditional European capitalist missionaries". As a result, the influence of leftist politics continued to wane, especially given the previous loss of its principal benefactor following the disintegration of the Soviet Union, leading to some of those who were traditionally secular or of the left turning to Islamism (O'Leary and Tirman 2007, p. 4). In contrast, Hamas possessed alternate, non-Western flows of funding derived from internal and external *zakat* donations, as well as select foreign governments, predominantly emanating from the Gulf States (Pascovich 2012, p. 131; Gunning 2007, p. 45). As a result, only Hamas and a few large international NGOs remained functionally autonomous, despite the PA's efforts to control their activities.

According to Sara Roy (2007, pp. 251–252), over the course of the post-Oslo 1990s, there was a "pronounced shift in emphasis within the movement away from the political/military action toward social/cultural reform" which reflected "the successful weakening by Israel and the Palestinian Authority of the Islamic political sector and the defeat of its military wing". Several suicide bombing campaigns against Israel also proved to be out of step with public opinion, especially when these led to closures of the Palestinian Territories which, in turn, resulted in severe financial repercussions and military retaliation (Gunning 2009, p. 162). Ever sensitive to public opinion, Hamas predominantly ceased attacks against Israel until the outbreak of the second intifada, aside from several retaliatory suicide bombing campaigns following the massacre of Palestinian civilians and the assassination of Hamas leaders, for instance, in 1994, 1996 and 1998 respectively.

Khalid Hroub (2008) similarly contends that faced with an overwhelmingly asymmetrical military situation, Hamas repackaged the notion of resistance in order to conflate it with socio-political change. As noted above, the primary goal of Hamas' forbears, the *Ikhwan*, however, was indeed this social change, so it is not necessarily so much of a permanent reinterpretation as the turning of the wheel according to political exigencies and practical reality.

While the first intifada impacted negatively upon the socio-economic fabric of the Palestinian Territories, it is imperative to note that this trend *accelerated* during the years of the 'peace process' (Roy 2002). Roy (2007, p. 80) argues that the introduction of the 'closure' policies in the wake of the Oslo Accords has been the single most damaging factor to Palestinian socio-economic life. Closures hermetically seal off the Palestinian Territories, both from the outside world and the other fragments of 'Palestinian-ruled' areas. In other words, these closures isolate the Palestinian Territories from Israel, internal and external markets, as well as restricting the movement of labour and goods. These policies are facilitated by clauses in PLO/PA agreements with Israel, allowing Israel to control borders and perimeters between cantons. These are especially problematic given that much of the Palestinian economy is dependent on agriculture and workers employed in Israel (ibid., pp. 110–111). Thus, closures simultaneously impede the export of Palestinian produce, much of which is ruined, and the entry of Palestinian workers into Israel. The outbreak of the al-Aqsa intifada only served to exacerbate these problems, especially following the Israeli destruction of PA infrastructure, heightening Palestinian dependency on Islamic social services.

In contrast to Hamas' perceived efficiency and honesty was the Palestinian Authority's ineptitude coupled with perceptions of corruption, opulence and nepotism. The Oslo years also saw an increasing gap between the living standards of Fatah leaders and their grassroots constituency. Arafat's regime became increasingly authoritarian and was perceived to be one of "corruption, malfeasance and arbitrariness" (Farsoun and Aruri 2006, p. 206). Conversely, as Gunning (2007, p. 45) observes, "In a field where corruption was rife, Hamas' charities had established a reputation for accountability and transparency, ensuring enduring grassroots support and donations". In brief, all of this caused a growing disconnect between the official Palestinian leadership and the community, whereas Hamas representatives were perceived to be contributing to the society through charitable endeavours.

Socio-economics

The argument that Islamic social work is predominantly a conduit for terrorism also elides the parlous socio-economic circumstances which many ordinary Palestinians confront on a quotidian basis and the practical impact that Islamic charity has upon Palestinian society (ICG 2003, p. 14). In 2011, according to the UNDP, 34.5 per cent of Palestinians in the Occupied Territories lived in poverty.[3] In similar vein, the Palestinian Central Bureau of Statistics recorded unemployment at 26.8 per cent in November 2011 (WAFA 2011). At the same time, the UNRWA estimated that 45 per cent of the Gaza Strip population was unemployed.[4] Indicatively, a large segment of Hamas' support base is derived from lower socio-economic strata of Palestinian society (Hilal 2005, p. 14).

148   *Charity, community and civilian jihad*

In essence, much of Hamas' popular base derives from marginalised, disenfranchised and disillusioned segments of society excluded from formal influence and positions of power. This support is especially acute among refugees, because refugees have, historically, been marginalised and discriminated against by the rest of the population (Gunning 2007, p. 264). The Gaza Strip population, for example, traditionally marginalised and derided by the West Bank elite, consists predominantly of refugees and their descendants from the 1947/1948 *nakba*; conspicuously, it is also Hamas' power base. Indeed, many of Hamas' founding members came from refugee backgrounds (Milton-Edwards 1996, p. 147; Hroub 2006, pp. 123–136).

Hamas similarly derives much support from the urbanised poor who are excluded from the largesse of PA institutions and foreign NGO work. In effect, the urbanisation of the population has entailed the breakdown of the traditional authority structures which allow Fatah to maintain its pre-eminent position in the rural villages (Gunning 2007, pp. 149–150). It is in the urban areas, moreover, where Fatah/PA corruption and ineptitude in providing community services has been most visible, thus creating resentment and disillusionment among the lower socio-economic strata of the urbanised population. Hamas clearly outperformed Fatah within these urban areas and crowded refugee camps during the 2004/2005 municipal and 2006 legislative elections.

Furthermore, these observations which axiomatically contend that Hamas' charitable endeavours are dedicated to perpetrating terror fail to account for what is arguably the most defining feature of the Palestine/Israel conflict: the absence of an independent Palestinian state. The administrative entity under nominal Palestinian control has proven itself to be inept, inefficient and opaque, as well as mired in corruption, malfeasance and nepotism. In effect, the creation of the Palestinian Authority and the return of the Fatah elite created a new rich class ignorant of the historical and everyday experiences of the majority of the population. This ignorance was repeatedly conveyed to me by the children of prominent PLO officials during my own time in the West Bank. One Ramallah-based Fatah member and businessman, Fadl, even opined to me that "Palestine is not poor", citing his own wealth as evidence (personal communication 2010). Similarly, the daughter of a PLO ambassador to Europe, Amirah, explained that she could not understand why people treated her as an outsider as she stepped drunkenly into her late model luxury car (personal communication 2010). To this end, the Ramallah-based elite cocooned within vested interests appear to be deeply out of step with large segments of the society which they purport to lead.

This disconnect and the failure of the elite to improve the living standards of the general public provides another explanation behind a progressive inclination towards Hamas which reached its apparent zenith in 2006. Indeed, this 'insider' (grassroots activists living under occupation who rose to prominence during the first intifada) versus 'outsider' (in essence, the PLO leadership and their families who returned to the Palestinian Territories following the Oslo Accords) division is keenly felt throughout Palestinian society (Pradhan 2008, pp. 313–317). This divide often ascribes Hamas immense 'insider' credibility (Sayigh 2011, p. 11).

Charity, community and civilian jihad   149

The arguments that Islamic social institutions are solely geared towards terrorism, moreover, glaringly omit the culpability of the Israeli occupation in contributing to the precarious socio-economic situation of the Palestinian population and fuelling resentment through repressive policies. Occupation policy has (1) conspicuously failed to provide adequate community services as required of the occupier under international law, and (2) implemented policies actively aimed at preventing the emergence of an independent indigenous economy. Indeed, the occupation and its policies are characterised by what Sara Roy (1995, p. 4) coined "de-development" which entails "the deliberate, systematic deconstruction of an indigenous economy by a dominant power", resulting in the "total regression of political institutions, social structures, and economic infrastructures necessary to facilitate economic growth and independence" (Farsoun and Aruri 2006, pp. 221–222). According to Israeli journalist Amira Hass (2011),

> the blocking of Palestinian economic development derives from the colonialist tendency of the Israeli occupation ever since 1967: exploitation of natural resources coupled with a desire to keep the Palestinian economy from competing with the Israeli one.

As a result, the Palestinian economy has been reduced to almost complete dependency on Israel and subject to the whims of Israeli policy, especially Israeli closures and the arbitrary checkpoint regime, which have repeatedly devastated the Palestinian economy.

Amid what the late Edward Said (1993) called the "disabling discontinuity" attendant on the Oslo process, cantonising the West Bank into over 100 Bantustans under varying jurisdictions, this process of de-development actually accelerated following the Oslo Accords (Roy 1999). Gaza, moreover, has been almost completely sealed off from the rest of the world since the early 1990s. The result, according to Gunning (2007, p. 249), meant that "The working class was weakened in material terms by the effect of post-Oslo closures, causing unemployment to rise steeply and GNI to drop sharply". The exact cost of the Israeli occupation was documented in a report prepared by the Palestinian Ministry of National Economy and the Applied Research Institute, Jerusalem (2011, p. vi) to be around $6.9 billion per annum; that is to say, about 84.9 per cent of Palestinian GDP in 2010.

Consequently, many Palestinians became increasingly dependent on social services provided by Islamic social institutions which, in turn, contributed to facilitating trust between Hamas and the grassroots community. In light of the continued deterioration of the socio-economic situation in the Palestinian Territories, it is thus unsurprising that a mass actor concerned with community welfare – indeed, inspired by a religion expounding the ethos of charity – would seek to ameliorate the living conditions of Palestinian society without needing to axiomatically assert that all such actions must be predicated on recruiting 'terrorists'.

150 *Charity, community and civilian jihad*

Charity and volunteerism in Islam

Hamas' social endeavours throughout the community reflect the centrality of socio-economic equality, social justice (*adala*) and charity (*khayr*) in Islam. According to Azim Nanji (2012), "the Qur'an articulates through a variety of terms, especially *sadaqa* and *zakat*, a very textured and multivalent conception of giving which draws upon the ideals of compassion, social justice, sharing and strengthening the community". While *sadaqa* and *zakat* are often used interchangeably throughout the broader context of *The Qur'an*, *sadaqa* relates more to voluntary charity, whereas *zakat* is, theoretically, obligatory to all Muslims. Since taking control of Gaza in 2007, the de facto Hamas government has passed legislation requiring all Muslims (including non-nationals) to pay *zakat* and, to this end, has set up a *Zakat* Authority to collect and distribute alms (Sayigh 2011, p. 102).

Zakat is one of five pillars of Islam and mandates that Muslims who possess *nisab* (adequate wealth) donate a certain percentage of their property and income to the poor and needy. Traditionally, *zakat* committees in the Palestinian Territories are localised entities caring for the needs of their immediate community (Lundblad 2008, p. 206). Since December 2007, however, the West Bank PA has embarked on a campaign to bring the committees under centralised control by appointing Fatah loyalists to their boards because many *zakat* committees are perceived to be sympathetic to Hamas (Benthall 2008, p. 7).

Zakat, derived from the word *zara* (to be pure), literally means 'purity' but also designates religious charity or alms. Thus, when Hamas member Bashir (personal interview 2010) describes his "work with charities like the one for poor families, such as money collection and collection of *zakat*, and then distributing this money and *zakat* and giving it to people in need", he is not only describing the physical act of giving charity, but a metaphysical journey of purification based on religious precept. According to Benthall (2008, p. 6), moreover, *zakat* "is closely associated with prayer – which without the observance of zakat is considered of no avail". Indeed, consider the following passage from *The Qur'an* (2:177):

> Who dispenses money, though dear, to kinsmen, orphans, the needy, the traveller, beggars and for ransom; Who performs the prayer and pays the alms; Who fulfil their contracts when they contract; Who are steadfast in hardship, calamity and danger; These are the true believers. These are truly pious.

Here, it is possible to discern the intertwining of prayer and almsgiving as well as the correlation between charitable giving and piety. The injunction advocating steadfastness in the face of adversary is especially resonant within the Palestinian context.

Volunteerism is also a key tenet of Islam and community work in general. According to Sarah Roy (2011, p. 68), "the role of the individual and of individuals in the renewal of Islamic society is recognized and cannot be violated,

Charity, community and civilian jihad 151

underlining the importance of voluntary belonging and voluntary action". This ethos of volunteerism is especially important when one considers that the total amount of aid and services provided by the Islamists is dwarfed by the Palestinian Authority, at least in times of peace. In this regard, the Islamist Speaker of Parliament Aziz Dweik (personal interview 2010) contends that:

> the social work of the Islamists, despite its very minor percentage compared to the total GDP, we could really serve the population, the public.... By themselves, people will carry everything on their shoulders to take it to the houses of the people and give it to them, with a good word, with a smile, and telling them that you are doing that because of our belief.

Here, Dweik concomitantly highlights the importance of religious motivation and volunteerism in Islamic social work. Dweik's reference to a good word further reflects the Qur'anic (2:263) verse: "A kind word followed by magnanimity is better than charity followed by rudeness."

Palestinian society, in addition, is characterised by a system of patronage based on *wasta* ('pull' or contacts). As such, many Palestinians see the social services and aid provided by the PA and the international community via the UNRWA and other NGOs less as a charity than an entitlement (Feldman 2007, p. 144). According to former Ararat security adviser and lecturer at Birzeit University William Nasser (personal interview 2010), this system of patronage, as embodied by the father figure of Arafat, engendered the perception among the wider community that government hand-outs were the natural order of things, whereas the charity provided by Islamist social institutions (often equated to Hamas) were perceived to be derived from religious piety and volunteerism. In other words, Arafat's rule was intensely "neo-patrimonial" (Shamir and Shikaki 2010, p. 48). In effect, the PA functioned as a 'quasi-rentier' state predicated on aid money rather than a rentier state's traditional reliance on natural resources (for instance, oil in Saudi Arabia) (Robinson 1997, pp. 198–200; Hanafi and Tabar 2004).

PA and donor money, moreover, is viewed as 'dirty' or 'tainted', devoid of either honourable intentions or origins. Aid money also allowed the PA to reduce its reliance on grassroots support (Gunning 2007, p. 44). In contrast, Islamic charity (at least until its takeover of Gaza in June 2007) was seen as 'clean' money earned by hard work and motivated by religious piety. Indeed, *zakat* committees are the second most trusted institutions in the Palestinian Territories after universities (Benthall 2008, p. 17). According to Nathan Brown (2003, p. 160), "Zakat committees enjoy a tremendous amount of legitimacy. Even secular leftists admire their authenticity and ability to operate without reliance on Western funding."

As discussed in Chapter 4, Hamas was at least partially elected because it possessed a reputation for what the local idiom describes as 'clean hands' or incorruptibility. These perceptions, in turn, accorded Hamas more prestige and symbolic capital than the services provided by other actors, despite the

152   *Charity, community and civilian jihad*

comparatively minor amount delivered by these institutions in times of peace, because Hamas' actions were perceived to be *voluntary*; that is to say, motivated by a genuine desire to serve the people rather than buy them off. By 1998, moreover, "Although *zakat* committees provide[d] a smaller amount of assistance, they reach[ed] a larger portion of the population" than the UNRWA or the PA Ministry of Social Affairs (Hilal *et al.* 1998, p. 13).

Building a rapport with the wider community is an essential strategy for any socio-political movement attempting to bring about societal change. Thus, as Omar Abdul-Razeq (personal interview 2010) explains,

> In any change movement, in any movement that needs to change the situation, the environment that they live in, you have to build bridges with the society itself. The actors, the people who will, those who will bring the change are the people themselves. I cannot change people from my desk, from my office. I cannot get their confidence just talking to them from my office. I must be involved. I have to ... build up on that capital, social capital, the relations, the service. And you know what helps that? It's part of our religion. There are sayings from the Prophet Mohammed that say a Muslim who does not help his neighbour is not a Muslim. A Muslim who sleeps knowing that his neighbour is hungry is not a Muslim. It's also part of your religion. It's part of your belief that you are gaining in the other life, that you are practising these practices. So also, I guess, [this] distinguishes us from others that we do these services not waiting for return.

Here, Abdul Razeq reiterates the importance of volunteerism and selflessness in Islamic thought. These ideas of charity and selflessness are infused throughout *The Qur'an*, for instance, Sura 2.264: "O'believers, nullify not your alms-giving by demanding gratitude or causing offence, like one who spends his wealth in order to flaunt it before people but believes neither in God nor in the Last Day." Abdul Razeq's comments also point to "the absence [in Islam] of a dichotomy between spiritual and material endeavours in human life, i.e. acts sanctioned as a part of faith are also linked to the daily conditions of life in this world" (Nanji 2012). Hence, the act of charitable giving not only helps needy members of society but it is also believed to facilitate an individual's ascent to Paradise.

Dr Hafez Shaheen (personal interview 2010), then Islamist Deputy Mayor of Nablus for Planning and Technical Affairs, Change and Reform councillor and Professor of Engineering, similarly highlights the religious imperative motivating charitable giving and community work: "Our Prophet says, 'Working for the interest[s] and the need[s] of a person is much better than worshipping Allah in Mecca for three years.' " The act of giving thus "aims at being both a social corrective and a spiritual benefit, it reflects the ethical and spiritual values which are associated with wealth, property, resources and voluntary effort in personal as well as communal contexts" (Nanji 2012). According to Gunning (2007, p. 123), moreover, "Participation signifies piety and public-spiritedness as well as social networking capital." In essence, social institutions allow for the creation of

Charity, community and civilian jihad 153

personal, emotional and psychological connections (Roy 2011, p. 122; ICG 2003, p. 21). These social networks are important on a political level because, as demonstrated in the previous chapter, personal connections, *wasta* and reputation were key factors facilitating Islamist electoral dominance at a local district level. Hence, social work, politics and resistance are not mutually exclusive but interact and intertwine with each other to create the movement that Hamas is today.

A brief descriptive context of key and novel institutions

This section provides a brief descriptive account of the activities of several key Islamist social institutions considered to be associated with Hamas. It will also detail several other Islamist institutions whose operations may be considered novel, or even unique, within the cultural context of the Arab Middle East. This is by no means a comprehensive or complete list but seeks rather to capture a brief snapshot of the scope and complexity of Islamist social activities within the Palestinian Territories.

As noted above, these institutions may be divided into two general categories: traditional needs-based charity and community development. The former not only provide items as mundane as food, clothing, medicine, money for transport and utilities, welfare payments for those who have lost family members in the struggle against Israel, and even nappies, but also engage in other activities such as organising communal weddings for destitute young couples and identifying local donors or sponsors for those in need (Milton-Edwards and Farrell 2010, pp. 178–179; Roy 2011, p. 106). Islamists also operate mobile medical units which provide free medical services and visit rural areas on a regular basis, while Islamist pharmacists often dispense medicine at cost or lower (Tamimi 2007, p. 38). Mu'minah (survey 2010), a 21-year-old Hamas supporter studying electrical engineering, similarly elucidates her work in "social clubs helping the homeless, raising social awareness, [and] spreading Islam".

Islamic social organisations engage in a wide variety of initiatives aimed at providing Palestinian society with the skills, institutions and civil infrastructure needed for long-term community development. Hamas' social welfare network, or rather institutions commonly attributed to Hamas and its supporters, engage in a wide variety of development projects including, for example, schools, orphanages, medical clinics, hospitals, sports and youth clubs, women's committees, a blood bank, and the Islamic University in Gaza (Hroub 2006, p. 19). These institutions have been indispensable in ameliorating the living conditions of ordinary Palestinians living under the twin conditions of a foreign occupier and a corrupt and inefficient administrative authority.

Hamas' premier flagship social institution, unambiguously considered to be associated with the movement, is *al-Mujamma al-Islami*. *Al-Mujamma* was founded in 1973 as an umbrella organisation for the *Ikhwan*'s activities in the Gaza Strip by Hamas founder Sheikh Ahmed Yassin, in addition to other prominent Hamas figures such as physicians Abd al-Aziz al-Rantisi and

154 *Charity, community and civilian jihad*

Mahmoud al-Zahar (Abu Amr 1994, p. 16). *Al-Mujumma's* leadership consisted of men from refugee families, meaning that they were excluded from internal political structures which remained the domain of the traditional landed elite (Roy 2011, p. 72). The leadership consisted of highly skilled individuals educated in Egypt and the United States in secular fields, including medicine, engineering and education; skills for which poverty-stricken Gaza was in desperate need. Interestingly, the leadership of *al-Mujamma*, and subsequently Hamas, possessed very little formal religious training; rather they operated as lay preachers. Nevertheless, *al-Mujumma* was initially more Muslim than Palestinian and it was only following the end of the first intifada that *al-Mujamma* and Hamas in general shifted its focus from what Menachem Klein (1996, p. 113) calls "Islamicizing Palestine" to "Palestinianizing Islam".

Al-Mujamma, however, insists that its 250 employees and additional 100 teachers are completely separate from the militant aspects of Hamas. According to the organisation's head, Sakkar Abu Hein (cited in Milton-Edwards and Farrell 2010, p. 177), "We work in everything except politics and the military. We provide social, medical, educational and charities for poor people, orphans and others. All kinds of charitable services."

Indeed, *al-Mujamma* "was primarily established as mosque, but attached to it were a medical clinic, a youth sports club, a nursing school, an Islamic festival hall, a *zakat* committee, and a center for women's activities and for training young girls" (Abu Amr 1994, p. 16). Within this framework *al-Mujamma* worked to combine "worship, education, and social welfare with subsidized services such as medical treatment, children's day care, free meals, and sports clubs" (Mishal and Sela 2000, p. 20). *Al-Mujamma* has a noted focus on sports which serves to occupy the time and normalise the lives of the youth of Gaza in an environment where overcrowding, violence and despair are such prevalent occurrences.

Throughout the 1970 and 1980s, *al-Mujamma* proceeded to establish branches throughout the Gaza Strip, and indeed in 1978/1979 was granted operating licences by the occupation authorities who, ironically considering the present status of affairs, saw it as a useful counterbalance to the militant secular nationalism led by the PLO (Milton-Edwards and Farrell 2010, p. 44; McGeough 2009, p. 41). The acquisition of legal documentation authorising its activities allowed *al-Mujamma* to publicly situate, embed and institutionalise its operations within the community, thereby creating a public profile for the Islamists and augmenting their influence on the public agenda (Roy 2011, p. 75). Indeed, in the decades following its inception, *al-Mujamma* has provided care, education and community services to tens of thousands of Palestinians in need. As a result, *al-Mujamma*, the *Ikhwan* – and later by extension Hamas – succeeded in establishing an "infrastructure of social institutions based on personal friendships, trust, and group solidarity, cementing its presences and influence at the grassroots level in a manner other political groups found difficult to match, let alone surpass" (ibid., p. 73). Since its inception, *al-Mujamma* has also set up a variety of other affiliated organisations such as *al-Jami'yya al-Islamiyya* in 1976 and *Jami'yyat al-Shabbat al-Muslimat* in 1981.

Al-Jami'yya focuses on providing care for orphans as well as distributing items such as food, clothing and school bags to Palestinians in need. Local volunteers identify the needy and then distribute such items; an instalment, for instance, could be as basic as, "5 kg of sugar, 2 kg of tea, 2 kg of lentils, 3 kg of beans, 2 kg of hummus, 6 kg of rice, 4 litres of cooking oil, two cans of meat, tomato sauce and 25 kg of flour" (Milton-Edwards and Farrell 2010, p. 175). *Al-Jami'yya* also runs a blood bank. According to article 3 of its statute,

> The aim [of *al-Jami'yya al-Islamiyya*] is to lead the people to the True Islam [*al-Islam al-hanif*] and to work spiritually through worship, and intellectually through science, and physically through sports, as well as socially through charity.
>
> (cited in Roy 2011, p. 74)

Its manager, Mohammed Shabab (cited in Milton-Edwards and Farrell 2010, p. 175), similarly asserts that the goal of the organisation

> is to bring people to the Islamic religion and to build a full Palestinian life, bringing them mosques, faith and education by introducing them to science, physically by offering them sports, socially by lifting their spirits and morally by bringing them employment.

Since the 1980s, *Jami'yyat al-Shabbat al-Muslimat* has not only provided training and instruction for women in traditional vocations such as sewing and embroidery, but also in previously male-orientated domains such as computer skills, religious instruction and literacy (Roy 2011, p. 74).

Unsurprisingly in light of decades of conflict, one of the main focus areas for Islamic social institutions is the provision of care for orphaned children.[5] Not only is this practical within the context of the Palestinian Territories given the high number of orphans present, but the care of orphans is accorded a special place within Islamic tradition (Benthall and Bellion-Jourdan 2003, pp. 102–104). As Montgomery Watt (1961, p. 207) explains, "The Qur'an shows concern for orphans and other persons liable to be oppressed by the wealthy." The Prophet Mohammed himself is said to have been an orphan. According to a *hadith* narrated by Sahl bin Sa'd (cited in Lundblad 2008, p. 207), moreover, the Prophet Mohammed decreed: "I and the person, who looks after an orphan and provides for him will be in Paradise like this." Thus, when viewed in conjunction with the Qur'anic verses, the care of orphans would appear to be a religious and practical imperative among Palestinian Islamists. Significantly, the PA has no orphanage programme so it typically refers orphans to Islamic social institutions (Roy 2011, p. 117). By 1995, 7000 to 10,000 orphans in the Gaza Strip received assistance from various Islamic social institutions (ibid., p. 80). *Al-Mujamma* alone provided for 500 orphans in 1990, which increased to around 5000 orphans receiving a monthly stipend by 2006 (Milton-Edwards and Farrell 2010, p. 177). Islamic institutions may not even directly care for or fund orphans themselves

156 *Charity, community and civilian jihad*

but rather act as facilitators identifying potential donors among the community and persuading them to sponsor a needy teenager.

In addition to traditional charitable endeavours, Sara Roy (2011) reports of several novel, perhaps even unique, Islamic social institutions within the cultural context of the Arab Middle East. One such institution, *al-Rahma* (mercy), cares for what are euphemistically called 'parentless' – that is to say, illegitimate – children and tries to reintegrate them into Palestinian society (ibid., p. 128). Within the cultural context of the Arab Middle East, illegitimate children are considered to be an aberration whose existence is scorned, ostracised and denied. Thus, the existence of such an organisation marks a significant divergence from pre-existing cultural norms, whilst concomitantly demonstrating that Islamic organisations in the Palestinian Territories can be a force for social progress.

Several other Islamic social organisations focus on the rehabilitation of families possessing members who have collaborated with the occupation (ibid., p. 132). Collaborators and, by association, their families, are especially abhorred in Palestinian society. This rehabilitation of 'collaborator' families is especially significant given Hamas' extensive targeting of collaborators during the first intifada (although the targeting of collaborators was by no means unique to Hamas). Again, the existence of these organisations – unique among the Palestinian factions, secular or otherwise – demonstrates the potentially progressive nature of Islamic social institutions. It also demonstrates the needs rather than partisan-based approach taken by Islamic charities. Sheikh Husni Abu Awad (cited in ICG 2003, p. 24), then Head of the Ramallah *zakat* committee, explains:

> we do not ask how the death happened but only ask for the death certificate; the social worker decides based on the family's need for assistance. We have 100 sponsored children whose fathers have been killed for collaborating with the occupation. This does not concern us.

Another example of an Islamic social institution commonly perceived to be Hamas, *al-Wafa* Medical Rehabilitation Hospital in Gaza, is considered to be one of the most sophisticated medical institutions in the Palestinian Territories. *Al-Wafa* predominantly treats patients suffering from acute chronic physical and cognitive disabilities, but it is also involved in educational and community outreach programmes (see Roy 2011, pp. 151–160). One of the more surprising aspects of *al-Wafa*, which shatters preconceived stereotypes associated with Islam, is that it runs sexual health sessions. These sessions, for example, include discussions on erectile dysfunction and increasing the length and pleasure of intercourse, among others (ibid., pp. 158–159). The existence of such a programme is somewhat surprising given the sexually conservative culture of the Arab Middle East. *Al-Wafa* is just another example of the wide and sometimes startling array of social services offered by Islamic social institutions in the Palestinian Territories. *Al-Wafa's* concern with the chronically ill and sexual health sessions would also seem to debunk the proposition that this organisation is

Charity, community and civilian jihad 157

involved in the recruitment of militants or associated military propaganda, despite the fact that Hamas derives social and by extrapolation political capital from the organisation.

The second intifada: crisis management

The outbreak and militarisation of the second intifada led to the dramatic deterioration of living conditions in the Palestinian Territories. Israeli policies entailing the destruction of PA infrastructure and collective punishment of the population further exacerbated these conditions. Examples of such collective punishment included the punitive suspension of utilities, including electricity, water and sewerage, as well as closures and even 24-hour curfews. By 2003 two-thirds of the Palestinian population were living beneath the poverty line, three times the amount documented at the beginning of the intifada (ICG 2003, p. 14). By 2002, moreover, the World Bank estimated that 75 per cent of the Gaza Strip were living beneath the poverty line (defined as \$2.10 per person per day) (Human Development Group 2003, p. 2). Following the outbreak of the second intifada, NGOs and charitable institutions rapidly became the largest providers of welfare, accounting for 60 per cent of beneficiaries compared to 34 per cent from UNRWA and 6 per cent from the PA (OCHA and UNSO 2001, p. 18).

Whereas during the Oslo years Islamic social work had focused on community development and institution building, the years of the second intifada were preoccupied more with crisis management within the context of high-intensity conflict, closures and curfews. The Israeli destruction of PA infrastructure drastically curtailed its ability to provide basic services to the Palestinian population, thereby rendering the population more dependent on Islamic social institutions than ever before.

During this time Hamas worked to alleviate the suffering of the population, including, for example, food runs to isolated areas in defiance of prolonged curfews and closures enforced by the Israeli army (Milton-Edwards and Farrell 2010, p. 105). Indeed, during the second intifada, after the UNRWA, Islamic social institutions were the second largest providers of emergency and relief provision to the Palestinian population, accounting for some 10 to 18 per cent in total depending on the period, in contrast to the 6 per cent provided by the Palestinian Authority (Gordon and Filc 2005, p. 553). Likewise, the International Crisis Group (ICG 2003, p. 15) estimates that over one in six Palestinians received food from Islamic social institutions and, by 2001, were collectively the second largest providers of food after the UNRWA. Islamic social institutions, moreover, similarly outperformed PA institutions in terms of emergency services and financial relief, whereas the impact of secular NGOs was so insignificant that it was categorised under 'other' (Gordon and Filc 2005, p. 553). Hence, during this period of a heightened risk society, Palestinians turned increasingly to Hamas not only for the provision of services but also for an ethos of resistance and solidarity. Community solidarity is also a central tenet of Islam. Thus, during the second intifada, not only did Hamas act as a security provider in the

158 *Charity, community and civilian jihad*

sense of a de facto social contract predicated on armed protection, as discussed in Chapter 2, but also as a provider of human security in the form of its relief works.

The extensive checkpoint regime employed by the occupation during the al-Aqsa intifada isolated and cut off different areas of the West Bank from each other, resulting in long periods characterised by an absence of central authority or sense of security. This resulted in an increased sense of localism and a return to traditional values (*taqlid*). In the absence of a functioning judiciary, for example, Hamas notables chaired *sulha* (reconciliation) committees to resolve disputes in accordance with Islamic practice and customary law (Sayigh 2011, p. 77). *Sulha*, as practised by Hamas, was perceived as a sign of stability in contrast to the anarchy so characteristic of the al-Aqsa intifada (Tuastad 2009, p. 236). As a result, these committees increased Hamas' reputation and social status as fair-minded community leaders. In a similar vein, mosques, predominantly associated with Hamas at the time, represented stability, purity and control (ibid,. p. 238). According to Khalil Shikaki (personal interview 2009), moreover, Director of the Palestinian Centre for Survey and Policy Research, the higher an individual's commitment to traditional values, the more likely they are to support Hamas. Notably, during this period of violence and sustained unrest, Hamas was the only indigenous institutional force perceived to possess the capability or, perhaps more importantly the volition, to provide effective social services to the Palestinian community.

Conclusions

Islamic social institutions have existed in the Palestinian Territories for decades and are considered to be among the most prolific, efficient and professional providers of social work, charity and community development. From its *Ikhwan* beginnings, Hamas has been associated or equated with such institutions regardless of its actual direct control or management of such institutions. While the inception of Hamas actively politicised the Islamic movement in the Palestinian Territories and pushed it towards active resistance against the Israeli occupation, an unfavourable political and security environment following the Oslo Accords prompted the movement to reinterpret resistance to equate it with community development and social reform until the outbreak of the second intifada in 2000. As such, this again demonstrates Hamas' ability to reframe its struggle, outlook and operations according to the practical exigencies and opportunities, yet still within the framework of resistance and jihad. In contrast to militant resistance, Islamic social institutions espouse a discourse of empowerment pertaining to constructive civil resistance, or *summud muqawim*, based on institution building and community development. As Hamas MP Mushir al-Masri (cited in Milton-Edwards and Farrell 2010, p. 157) points out, "We build for you and we also resist for you". This again ties into pre-existing religious, historical and situational frames which resonate with wide segments of a predominantly traditional society.

Charity, community and civilian jihad 159

Nevertheless, Hamas continues to be equated with existential armed jihad despite the heterogeneous nature of its overall programme of resistance, as well as its supporters and sympathisers. With regard to Islamic social institutions, there is a tendency to view these as solely dedicated to recruiting militants. The policies of major Western governments, Israel and, to a lesser extent, the West Bank Palestinian Authority reflect this conviction. However, while it is likely that there is an element of truth in the claim that some Islamic social institutions believe social work represents "not so much a donation as an investment" (Milton-Edwards and Farrell 2010, p. 176), the most extensive fieldwork analysis by Sara Roy (2011, p. 164) suggests a decentralised network of networks with no unified ideology beyond varying interpretations of 'Islam' (see also Lundblad 2008, p. 206; Brown 2008, p. 76; Malka 2007, p. 105). This implies that these institutions are not engaged in the production of militants in any systematic fashion.

The long-standing compliance of the majority of Islamic social institutions with Israeli and PA regulations – and indeed, active referrals of the PA to specialist Islamic institutions – point to a similar conclusion. In similar vein, the separation of Hamas' social and political aspects from its militant wing by various foreign governments including the EU Bloc until put under immense pressure by the US in 2003 indicates a similar level of confidence in Islamic social institutions among large segments of the international community. Indeed, modern Islamic social institutions in the Palestinian Territories substantially predate their militant counterparts embodied by Hamas and Islamic Jihad. As Jereon Gunning (2008, p. 101) points out, moreover, "it is in both the charities' and Hamas's interests to keep humanitarian and 'military' fundraising apart". Similarly, according to the International Crisis Group (ICG 2003, p. 21),

> Hamas seeks to derive prestige and political profit from social welfare activism precisely by maintaining the professionalism and integrity of such institutions rather than politicizing them. It appears to understand better than others that if schools and medical clinics developed a reputation as recruitment centres, and services were provided in exchange for support, the crown jewels of the Islamist movement would be irretrievably debased in exchange for short-term gains of dubious value.

As such, it would appear that targeting these institutions is more predicated on political calculations rather than genuine security threats, especially if one considers the widespread Islamophobia characteristic of the 'war on terror'.

This is not to say that these institutions are not sometimes used to recruit militants but the varied, decentralised and niche-driven nature of these institutions suggests that the recruitment of militants is not a prominent, let alone primary, concern. It is natural that the recipients of aid from these institutions would feel grateful, but connecting a packet of pampers or bus money, for instance, to militancy and suicide bombings is a bit of a stretch of the imagination to say the least. It seems, moreover, that developmental organisations providing education, vocational training and other long-term skill sets would be

160   *Charity, community and civilian jihad*

a very expensive, wasteful and inefficient method of military recruitment should the primary aim be the potential early death of the recipient through militant attacks against a vastly more powerful enemy.

In addition, the very existence of these Islamic social institutions, and such varied and extensive networks at that, is indicative of the governmental and administrative failures of both the PA and the occupation authorities. Given the trying socio-economic circumstances of many Palestinians, it is natural that individuals would approach charitable institutions because they are destitute. Similarly, it is a normal response that these people would feel grateful, but the numbers who would then turn to active militarism would be miniscule. In other words, Islamic social institutions accrue support and public legitimacy for Hamas indirectly through voluntary good deeds rather than in the expectation of political or military support (Pascovich 2012, p. 133). The amount of political support Hamas derives from social work is, to my knowledge, difficult if not impossible to quantify from the available sources.

Targeting these institutions merely serves to deprive the most vulnerable segments of society which rely on these institutions to survive. Deprivation and further impoverishment, moreover, could potentially be counter-productive and radicalise those who are already on the brink of despair. Ironically, targeting Islamic social institutions has the potential to recruit rather than deter militants. As James Baldwin observes (1963, p. 90), "The most dangerous creation of any society is the man who has nothing to lose." Echoing this notion are comments from ordinary Palestinians; for example:

> I don't want my land back. Land belongs to God. I want to work and live.... Doesn't Israel understand how dangerous poverty is to everyone? Does Israel think it can throw us out? This situation makes everyone want to explode. I'm convinced that everyone that blew himself up has an unemployed brother.
>
> (cited in Hass 2002)

Targeting legitimately run Islamic institutions in the Palestinian Territories or abroad, moreover, has the potential to drive charitable donations underground away from the scrutiny of banking regulators and watchful pro-Israeli organisations, thus making the money harder to trace and increasing the possibility that it may be diverted to military ends (Benthall 2008, p. 9; Gunning 2008, p. 101).

The targeting of these institutions by the PA has also caused significant civil unrest between the PA and the Palestinian population. Indeed, the targeting of Hamas by PA forces in general tends to be deeply unpopular among the majority of the wider population who harbour a profound antipathy to *fitna* (internal civil conflict). Perhaps this is unsurprising given that over 120,000 Palestinians benefit from monthly payments from Islamic social institutions, with another 30,000 receiving annual aide (Hroub 2008b, pp. 109–110).

On a more mundane level, activities and sports give children and youth an outlet for a normal life. As Irving Jensen (2009, pp. 71–74) reports, there are a

Charity, community and civilian jihad 161

variety of other reasons which may guide an individual's decision to join an Islamic sports club such as proximity and opportunity, instead of motivations predicated on an Islamic ethos.

The same may be said about Islamic schools where enrolment is often decided by the quality of education rather than by religious piety. In Australia, for instance, secular families often send their children to religious private schools even though neither the child nor the parents are religious.

Nevertheless, it would seem evident that the prolonged engagement of Islamic social institutions with the community has established a variety of personal, psychological and emotional connections based on trust, charity and goodwill. These connections, in turn, have accumulated social capital and established reputations for piety, probity and fiscal transparency among large segments of the wider population. Indeed, during my own time in the West Bank, a common reply I received regarding Islamic social institutions was "at least they help people", even if the individual totally disagreed with Hamas and Islamist ideologies in general. In contrast, the PA is often colloquially referred to as the 'mafia' (ICG 2011, p. 17; Milton-Edwards and Farrell 2010, p. 176). Given that the main issue for the 2006 elections was corruption, it would appear that the fiscal transparency of Islamist social institutions, and their reputations for professionalism and efficiency, allowed Hamas and its political leaders to translate this social capital into political support.

Finally, while it would appear likely that to a certain degree some of these institutions are limited sources of military recruitment, and thus it would be wise to be vigilant in this regard, the blanket demonisation, dehumanisation and targeting of Islamic social institutions in the Palestinian Territories is unhelpful and likely to engender negative repercussions for the most vulnerable segments of Palestinian society. Some militants, would undoubtedly have been recruited either directly or indirectly through Islamic social institutions, but hundreds of thousands of beneficiaries did not turn to militancy. As such, a more nuanced approach should be taken when analysing and potentially taking punitive action against Islamic social institutions in order to avoid exacerbating the already precarious economic situation experienced by the recipients of Islamic aid and social services in the Palestinian Territories.

Notes

1 Parts of this chapter are drawn from Dunning, T. 2015. 'Islam and Resistance: Hamas, Ideology and Islamic Values in Palestine'. *Critical Studies on Terrorism* 8(2): 284–305. Reproduced with permission of Taylor and Francis.
2 See the ITIC website at www.terrorism-info.org.il/site/content/T1.asp?Sid=18&pid=121.
3 See UNDP: Programme of Assistance for the Palestinian People for up-to-date statistics at www.undp.ps/en/index.html.
4 See UNRWA at www.unrwa.org/etemplate.php?id=902.
5 An 'orphan' is generally defined as a child who has lost his or her father/breadwinner but the term is sometimes used to describe a child born out of wedlock and rejected by the family.

162 *Charity, community and civilian jihad*

References

Abu Amr, Z. 1994. *Islamic Fundamentalism in the West Bank and Gaza: Muslim Brotherhood and Islamic Jihad*. Bloomington: Indiana University Press.

Applied Research Institute – Jerusalem and the Palestinian Ministry of National Economy. 2011. *The Economic Costs of the Israeli Occupation for the Occupied Palestinian Territory*. Jerusalem: ARIJ.

Baldwin, J. 1963. *The Fire Next Time*. New York: The Dial Press.

Benthall, J. 2008. *The Palestinian Zakat Committees 1993–2007 and Their Contested Interpretations*. Geneva: Graduate Institute of International and Development Studies.

Benthall, J. and Bellion-Jourdan, J. 2003. *The Charitable Crescent: Politics of Aid in the Muslim World*. London: I.B. Tauris.

Bornstein, A. 2009. 'In-betweenness and Crumbled Hopes in Palestine: The Global in the Local in the Occupied Territories'. *Dialectical Anthropology* 33(2): 175–200.

Brooke, J. and Sciolino, E. 1995. 'Bread or Bullets? Money for Hamas'. *New York Times*, 16 August.

Brown, N. 2003. *Palestinian Politics after Oslo: Resuming Arab Palestine*. Berkeley: University of California Press.

Brown, N. 2008. 'Principled or Stubborn? Western Policy towards Hamas'. *International Spectator* 43(4): 73–87.

Burrowes, R. 1996. *The Strategy of Nonviolent Defense: A Ghandian Approach*. Albany: State University of New York Press.

Erlanger, S. 2006. 'Militant Zeal'. *New York Times*, 25 June.

Farsoun, S. and Aruri, N. 2006. *Palestine and Palestinians: A Social and Political History*. Boulder, CO: Westview Press.

Farsoun, S. and Landis, J. 1990. 'The Sociology of an Uprising: The Roots of the Intifada'. *Intifada: Palestine at the Crossroads*, edited by J. Nasser and R. Heacock. New York: Praeger.

Feldman, I. 2007. 'Difficult Distinctions: Refugee Laws, Humanitarian Practices, and Political Identification in Gaza'. *Cultural Anthropology* 22(1): 129–169.

Flanigan, S. 2006. 'Charity as Resistance: Connections between Charity, Contentious Politics, and Terror'. *Studies in Conflict and Terrorism* 29(7): 641–655.

Gordon, N. and Filc, D. 2005. 'Hamas and the Destruction of Risk Society'. *Constellations* 12(4): 542–560.

Gunning, J. 2007. *Hamas in Politics: Democracy, Religion, Violence*. London: Hurst & Co.

Gunning, J. 2008. 'Terrorism, Charity and Diasporas: Contrasting the Fundraising Practices of Hamas and al Qaeda among Muslims in Europe'. In *Countering the Financing of Terrorism*, edited by T.J. Biersteker and S.E. Eckert. London: Routledge.

Gunning, J. 2009. 'Social Movement Theory and the Study of Terrorism'. In *Critical Terrorism Studies: A New Research Agenda*, edited by R. Jackson, M. Smyth and J. Gunning. New York: Routledge.

Hammami, R. 2000. 'NGOs Since Oslo: From NGO Politics to Social Movements'. *Middle East Report* 214: 16–48.

Hanafi, S. and Tabar L. 2004. 'Donor Assistance, Rent-seeking and Elite Formation'. In *State Formation in Palestine: Viability and Governance during Social Transformation*, edited by G. Giacamen and. A. Mustaq Khan. London: Routledge-Curzon.

Harb, M. and Leenders, R. 2005. 'Know Thy Enemy: Hizbullah, Terrorism and the Politics of Perception'. *Third World Quarterly* 26(1): 173–197.

Hass, A. 2002. 'Jobless in Gaza'. *Ha'aretz* (Israel), 27 June.

Charity, community and civilian jihad 163

Hass, A. 2011. 'The Real Cost of Israel's Occupation of the Palestinians'. *Ha'aretz* (Israel), 16 November.

Hilal, J., Malki, M., Shalabi, Y. and Ladaweh, H. 1998. *Towards a Social Security System in the West Bank and Gaza*. Ramallah: Palestine Economic Policy Research Institute.

Hoigilt, J. 2010. *Raising Extremists? Islamism and Education in the Palestinian Territories*. Oslo: FAFO.

Hroub, K. 2000. *Hamas: Political Thought and Practice*. Washington, DC: Institute of Palestine Studies.

Hroub, K. 2006. *Hamas: A Beginner's Guide*. London: Pluto Press.

Hroub, K. 2008a. 'Palestinian Islamism: Conflating National Liberation and Sociopolitical Change'. *International Spectator* 43(4): 59–72.

Hroub, K. 2008b. *Le Hamas*. Paris: Demipolis.

Human Development Group. 2003. *Supplemental Trust Fund Grant to the Second Emergency Services Support Project*. World Bank.

ICG. 2003. *Islamic Social Welfare Activism in the Occupied Palestinian Territories: A Legitimate Target?* Brussels: ICG.

ICG. 2007. *Hizbullah and the Lebanese Crisis*. Brussels: ICG.

ICG. 2008. *Ruling Palestine I: Gaza under Hamas*. Brussels: ICG.

ICG. 2011. *Palestinian Reconciliation: Plus Ça Change …* Brussels: ICG.

Irving Jensen, M. 2006. 'Re-Islamising Palestinian Society "From Below": Hamas and Higher Education in Gaza'. *Holy Lands Studies* 5(1): 57–74.

Irving Jensen, M. 2009. *The Political Ideology of Hamas: A Grassroots Perspective*. London: I.B. Tauris.

ITIC. 2005. *'Charity' and Palestinian Terrorism – Spotlight on Hamas-run al-Tadahmun Charitable Society in Nablus, Special Information Bulletin*. Israel: Intelligence and Terrorism Information Centre.

Jad, I. 2004. 'The NGO-isation of Arab Women's Movements'. *IDS Bulletin* 35(4): 34–42.

Jad, I. 2007. 'NGOs: Between Buzzwords and Social Movements'. *Development in Practice* 17(4–5): 622–629.

Kimmerling, B. 2003. *Politicide: Ariel Sharon's War against the Palestinians*. New York: Verso.

Kimmerling, B. and Migdal, J. 2003. *The Palestinian People: A History*. Cambridge, MA: Harvard University Press.

Klein, M. 1996. 'Competing Brothers: The Web of Hamas–PLO Relations'. *Terrorism and Political Violence* 8(2): 111–132.

Kovach, G. 2008. 'Five Convicted in Terrorism Financing Trial'. *New York Times*, 24 November.

Levitt, M. 2004. 'Hamas from Cradle to Grave'. *Middle East Quarterly* 11(1): 3–15.

Levitt, M. 2006. *Hamas: Politics, Charity and Terrorism in the Service of Jihad*. New Haven, CT: Yale University Press.

Lundblad, L. 2008. 'Islamic Welfare, Discourse and Practice: The Institutionalization of Zakat in Palestine'. In *Interpreting Welfare and Relief in the Middle East*, edited by N. Naguib and I.M. Okenhaug. Leiden: Brill.

Makovsky, D. 1996. *Making Peace with the PLO: The Rabin's Government's Road to the Oslo Accord*. Boulder, CO: Westview Press.

Malka, H. 2007. 'Hamas: Resistance and Transformation of Palestinian Society'. In *Understanding Islamic Charities*, by J. Alterman and. K. von Hippel. Washington, DC: Centre for Strategic and International Studies.

164 *Charity, community and civilian jihad*

McGeough, P. 2009. *Kill Khalid ... Mossad's Failed Hit and the Rise of Hamas.* Crow's Nest, NSW: Allen & Unwin.

Milton-Edwards, B. 1996. *Islamic Politics in Palestine.* London: I.B. Tauris.

Milton-Edwards, B. and Farrell, S. 2010. *Hamas: The Islamic Resistance Movement.* Cambridge: Polity Press.

Mishal, S. and Sela, A. 2000. *The Palestinian Hamas: Vision, Violence and Coexistence.* New York: Columbia University Press.

Nanji, A. 2012. 'Almsgiving'. In *Encyclopaedia of the Qur'an*, edited by J.D. Auliffe. Washington, DC: Georgetown University/Brill Online.

OCHA and UNSO. 2001. *Food and Cash Assistance Programmes, October 2000–August 2001: A Brief Overview.* Jerusalem: OCHA.

O'Leary, B. and Tirman, J. 2007. 'Thinking about Durable Political Violence'. In *Terror, Insurgency and the State: Ending Protracted Conflicts*, edited by M. Heiberg, B. O'Leary and J. Tirman. Philadelphia: University of Pennsylvania Press.

Pascovich, E. 2012. 'Social–Civilian Apparatuses of Hamas, Hizballah and Other Activist Islamic Organizations'. *Digest of Middle East Studies* 21(1): 126–148.

Peteet, J. 1991. *Gender in Crisis: Women and the Palestinian Resistance Movement.* New York: Columbia University Press.

Pradhan, B. 2008. 'Palestinian Politics in the Post-Arafat Era'. *International Studies* 45(4): 295–339.

Qur'an, The. 2008. Translated and edited by T. Khalidi. London: Penguin Books.

Robinson, G. 1997. *Building a Palestinian State: The Incomplete Revolution.* Bloomington: Indiana University Press.

Rosenfeld, M. 2004. *Confronting the Occupation: Work, Education, and Political Activism of Palestinian Families in a Refugee Camp.* Stanford, CA: Stanford University Press.

Roy, S. 1995. *The Gaza Strip: The Political Economy of De-development.* Washington, DC: Institute for Palestine Studies.

Roy, S. 1999. 'De-development Revisited: Palestinian Economy and Society since Oslo'. *Journal of Palestine Studies* 28(3): 64–82.

Roy, S. 2002. 'Ending the Palestinian Economy'. *Middle East Report* 9(4): 122–165.

Roy, S. 2007. *Failing Peace: Gaza and the Palestinian–Israeli Conflict.* London: Pluto Press.

Roy, S. 2011. *Hamas and Civil Society in Gaza: Engaging the Islamic Social Sector.* Princeton, NJ: Princeton University Press.

Said, E. 1993. 'The Morning After'. *London Review of Books* 15(20), 21 October.

Said, E. 1997. *Covering Islam: How the Media and the Experts Determine How We See the Rest of the World.* New York: Vintage Books.

Samara, A. 2001. *Epidemic of Globalization: Ventures in World Order, Arab Nation and Zionism.* Glendale: Palestine Research and Publishing Foundation.

Sayigh, Y. 1997. 'The Armed Struggle and Palestinian Nationalism'. In *The PLO and Israel: From Armed Conflict to Political Solution, 1964–1994*, edited by A. Sela and M. Ma'oz. New York: St Martin's Press.

Sayigh, Y. 1998. *Armed Struggle and the Search for State: The Palestinian National Movement 1949–1993.* Oxford: Clarendon Press.

Sayigh, Y. 2011. *'We Serve the People': Hamas Policing in Gaza.* Brandeis University: Crown Centre for Middle East Studies.

Shamir, J. and Shikaki, K. 2010. *Palestinian and Israeli Public Opinion: The Public Imperative in the Second Intifada.* Bloomington: Indiana University Press.

Stephan, M. 2009. *Civilian Jihad: Nonviolent Struggle, Democratization and Governance in the Middle East*. New York: Palgrave Macmillan.

Tamimi, A. 2007. *Hamas: A History from Within*. Northampton, MA: Olive Brach Press.

Tuastad, D. 2009. *Primary Solidarity: A Comparative Study on the Role of Kinship in Palestinian Local Politics*. PhD thesis. Oslo: University of Oslo.

Wafa – Palestinian News and Info Agency (Ramallah). 2011. 'PCBS: Unemployment up to 26.8% in Third Quarter', 21 November.

Watt, W.M. 1961. *Muhammad: Prophet and Statesmen*. London: Oxford University Press.

Younis, M. 2000. *Liberation and Democratization: The South African and Palestinian National Movements*. Minneapolis: University of Minnesota Press.

Interviews and surveys

Abdul-Razeq, Omar, former Islamist Finance Minister, elected MP and Professor of Economics at an-Najah National University, Ramallah, February 2010.

Amirah, the daughter of a PLO ambassador to Europe, Ramallah, April 2010.

Bashir, a 44-year-old Hamas member and youth activities officer, Damascus, May 2010.

Dweik, A., Islamist Speaker of Parliament, elected PLC Deputy and Professor of Urban Geography, Hebron, May 2010.

Fadl, a Ramallah-based Fatah member and businessman, Ramallah, April 2010.

Mu'minah, a 20-year-old Hamas supporter, anonymous survey, Birzeit University, Birzeit, April 2010.

Shaheen, H., then Deputy Mayor of Nablus for Planning and Technical Affairs, local councillor for Change and Reform, and Professor of Engineering at an-Najah National University, Nablus, March/April 2010.

Shikaki, K., Director of the Palestinian Centre for Policy and Survey Research, Ramallah, November 2009.

6 Ideational jihad, education and Islamic values[1]

> [We] find some kind of ease in the ideology of Islam.... We refer to it as the religion of the true nature of the human being. It is deep within the heart of the human being, believing in the one who created you, doing good to the others, living as a free human being without any kind of repression.
>
> Islamist Speaker of Parliament, Dr Aziz Dweik (personal interview 2010)

"Islam is the solution" and "the Qur'an is our constitution" have been common catch cries for Islamist opposition for decades, not only within the Palestinian Territories but also throughout the wider Muslim world. Indeed, at the heart of *The Qur'an* is the struggle for justice (*adl'*) and resistance to oppression. In this regard, according to Deputy Head of the Political Bureau, Mousa Abu Marzouq (personal interview 2010), "Islam is a self-engine ... against oppression and occupation, and against all the features that oppress people and offend them ... Islam is a strong engine for people to refuse oppression, occupation, discrimination and so on." Within the Palestinian context this not only refers to resistance to foreign domination but, as with the wider Muslim Middle East, a struggle to preserve traditional notions of identity, culture and values. This is, in effect, a cultural struggle aimed at reasserting local identity in the face of what is perceived to be an encroaching Western world bent on secularisation (Kepel 2002, pp. 23–42; Crooke 2009). Indicatively, Article 10.2 of the Change and Reform electoral manifesto seeks to "Immunize the citizens, especially young people, against corruption, Westernization, and intellectual invasion" (Appendix VI in Tamimi 2007, p. 305).

Islam is predicated on five main tenets or pillars (*arkan al-Islam*): *shahada* (bearing witness to God), *salah* (prayer), *sawm* (fasting, in essence, during Ramadan), *zakat* (alms) and *hajj* (pilgrimage). The Shi'a also include jihad (striving or exerting oneself in the name of God) as a sixth pillar, and although the concept of jihad is clearly central to Sunni Islamism(s) in practice, as demonstrated throughout this project, to consider it as a sixth pillar is generally beyond the purview of mainstream Sunni Islam. Nevertheless, as Aziz Dweik (personal interview 2010), the Islamist Speaker of Parliament, points out, "In Shiite Islam, they add to it [the pillars], jihad, which is to fight for the cause of God, and in

Jihad, education and Islamic values 167

Sunni Islam they say it is the highest point in Islam where you have to fight to defend your religion."

The influence of these pillars on the actions of Hamas has been evident throughout the course of this project. Chapter 3, for instance, examined the heroic figure of the *shahid* (martyr or 'witness to God') so central to Palestinian culture. Indicatively, the word *shahid* is derived from the first pillar, *shahada* (to watch or to witness). Chapters 4 and 5, furthermore, explored the impact of public manifestations of piety in accumulating symbolic capital facilitating public identification and popular support for Hamas. Public manifestations of piousness include visiting the mosque for prayers, fasting during Ramadan, conducting charitable works, the collection of *zakat* for the needy and pilgrimage to Mecca. This is important because, according to Palestinian professor Sameer Hammoudeh (personal interview 2009), there was a marked increase in Islamic practice (as opposed to belief) following the Iranian Revolution indicative of a social trend towards public Islamisation in the Palestinian Territories.

Islam is a public religion which imbues its values within the societal fabric: a collective rather than an individual endeavour. Indeed, Islam is predicated on the notion of the *umma*, or community of believers, whereby social space is considered communal (Kadayifici-Orellana 2007, p. 48). As such, public displays of piety are especially important in terms of establishing networks and accumulating social capital. Hamas, Hammoudeh (personal interview 2009) continues, portrays itself as the embodiment of Islamic practices in the Palestinian Territories and attempts to use this social trend in order to attract popular support. Mu'minah (survey 2010), a 21-year-old Hamas supporter studying electrical engineering, believes that the movement represents "Islamic values like working, struggling [jihad], defending the homeland and not giving our land away". Fatima (survey 2010), an 18-year-old Hamas supporter studying information technology, similarly elucidates: "From what I've seen, the movement is really close to the Islamic religion; what attracted me is their belief in God and victory." Social endeavours such as the collection of *zakat* and charity also tie into Islam's traditional focus on social justice or *adala*. The historically modest living arrangements of Islamist political leaders, many of them of refugee origin, similarly resonate with traditional Islamic notions preaching moderation, a lack of excess and what former Islamist Finance Minister Omar Abdul Razeq (personal interview 2010) describes as *wasatiya* or the 'middle way'.

Patience (*sabr*), endurance and steadfastness (*summud*) are also recurring themes in both Islam and the Palestinian consciousness evident throughout the preceding chapters. During the *hijra* (the migration from Mecca to Medina), for instance, the Prophet Mohammed waited patiently in Medina for ten years before finally conquering Mecca. Mariam Salah (personal interview 2010), the former Minister for Women's Affairs and Professor in *Sharia* Law, argues that "Besides liberating our lands, we also should learn how to be patient in case we lose a dear person as a martyr or prisoner or injured ... all of this comes from the core of our religion, so we are patient and endure". Indicatively, there are over 200 verses in *The Qur'an* focusing on patience and many others that refer to it

168 *Jihad, education and Islamic values*

indirectly (Kadayifici-Orellana 2007, p. 113). Maulana Wahiduddin Khan (1998, p. 1) argues, furthermore, that patience is among the highest of Islamic values. Thus one can perceive the influence of Islamic thought in informing, guiding and legitimating the political thought and practice of Hamas and its supporters.

But what exactly are the historical antecedents influencing Hamas' interpretations and reinterpretations of Islam, jihad and resistance? To this end, this chapter will first examine the historical influence of Islamic thought, not only within the Palestinian Territories but also throughout the wider Middle East region. How have these histories contributed to Hamas' polysemic conceptions of jihad and resistance, and their implementation thereof?

Second, this chapter will explore one of the more persistent arguments, fed by Islamists and Orientalists alike, that Islam is exceptional among religions insofar as *The Qur'an* is believed to be the direct word of God and thus purports to be holistic in its scope. Do these arguments stand up to scrutiny? In what way does Hamas interpret Islam and justify the evolution of its application? How flexible are Hamas' seemingly dogmatic ideological convictions? Specifically, this section interrogates some of the more controversial aspects of *sharia* law and Hamas' charter/covenant (*mithaq*).

Third, how does Islam influence the individual and collective behaviour of Hamas members and supporters? What role do values play in eliciting popular support and legitimacy for Hamas? To this end, this section investigates the ideational base of resistance through individual renewal and pious behaviour.

Fourth, what role does Islam, jihad and resistance play in the current and future visions of Hamas? This section examines the centrality of education, both in its practical and spiritual senses, to Hamas' long-term goals pertaining to the creation of an Islamic society.

The historical influence of Islamic thought

As the power of the Ottoman Empire waned and the Muslim Middle East struggled to match the social and technological revolutions of the European world during the Age of Enlightenment, some Muslim philosophers called for a 'return' to Islam to combat civilisational atrophy. Historically, prominent thinkers critical of the Muslim world's blind imitation of Western forms of governance and advocating 'Islam as the solution' include Jamal al-Din al-Afghani (1838–1897), Muhammad Abduh (1849–1905), Rashid Rida (1865–1935), Mustafa Kamil (1874–1908) and Shakib Arsalan (1869–1946). These thinkers did not reject Western modernity out of hand, but rather sought to reinterpret Islam in order to reconcile concepts such as democracy and constitutionalism with Islamic values. These thinkers were a rebellion against the ossified teachings or *taqlid* of the established *ulema* (religious scholars) (Kurzman 2002, pp. 10–11).

Regional trends also need to be taken into account when examining the development of Islamic thought in Palestine. Repeated international conflicts demonstrate that the Palestine/Israel conflict is regional in its scope. The Middle East

Jihad, education and Islamic values 169

has also been home to a variety of regional political movements, including pan-Arabism and pan-Islamism. Indeed, Hamas and the Muslim Brotherhood (*al-Ikhwan al-Muslimun*) in Palestine were initially part of this pan-Islamic movement before moving from what Klein (1996, p. 113) described as "Islamicizing Palestine" to "Palestinianizing Islam".

Ideological tendencies, moreover, do not occur in a vacuum, but rather diffuse across borders. This is especially the case given that Hamas' political bureau is located outside of Palestine and thus is susceptible to external change. Hamas' relocation of its political bureau away from Syria in 2012 is one example whereby external changes affected the alignment of Hamas' political and ideological choices. In other words, political and ideological ideas are not hermetically sealed entities but part of a process of borrowing and synthesis. Multiple interviewees made reference to me about external events and contemporary figures (for instance, Yousef Qaradawi) as influential factors in determining the movement's evolution.

Historically, Islam has been central to Palestinian resistance against foreign rule in all of its forms. The first celebrated preacher, militant and martyr to the Palestinian cause, Sheikh Izz al-Din al-Qassam (1882–1935), in honour of whom Hamas' armed wing and makeshift rockets are named, was one of the first to actively resist British Mandate rule and Zionist immigration during the 1930s. Already known as a firebrand preacher instrumental in fomenting the Syrian uprising against French rule in 1921, al-Qassam fled to Haifa where he worked as a preacher in the *istiqlal* (independence) mosque providing education, social services and spiritual guidance for the poor. In essence, al-Qassam was:

> An individual deeply imbued with what we might wish to call the Islamic social gospel and who was struck by the plight of Palestinian peasants and migrants. Al-Qassam's pastoral concern was linked to his moral outrage as a Muslim at the ways in which the old implicit social compact was being violated in the circumstances of British mandatory Palestine. This anger fuelled a political radicalism that drove him eventually to take up arms and marks him off from the Palestinian notable politicians.
>
> (Burke 1993, p. 164)

Although initially focused on social endeavours, al-Qassam took up arms in 1930 and created a paramilitary organisation called the Black Hand which periodically attacked British forces and Jewish settlements. In 1935, he was surrounded by British troops in a cave near Jenin and killed in the ensuing fire-fight. Although al-Qassam was killed, his ethos of resistance to foreign rule lived on. According to Schleifer (1993, p. 166):

> Called upon to surrender al-Qassam told his men to die as martyrs, and he opened fire. Al-Qassam's defiance and manner of his death (which seemed to stun the traditional leadership) electrified the Palestinian people. Thousands forced their way past police lines at the funeral in Haifa, and the

170 *Jihad, education and Islamic values*

secular Arab nationalist parties invoked his memory as the symbol of resistance. It was the largest political gathering ever to assemble in mandatory Palestine.

Al-Qassam's actions are credited with inspiring the 1936 to 1939 Palestinian revolt against British rule and Jewish immigration. The revolt was of such intensity that more British troops were stationed in the British Mandate Palestine than the entire Indian subcontinent (Pappé 2006, p. 121). While partially successful insofar as the British abrogated the Balfour Declaration and substantially curbed Jewish immigration, the Palestinian national movement was brutally suppressed by British forces and never recovered in time for its disastrous confrontation with Zionist forces in 1947/1948.

The parallels between al-Qassam and Hamas are clear. Both Hamas and al-Qassam consist of individuals outside of the traditional elite. Both Hamas and al-Qassam were initially concerned with education, societal renewal and the welfare of the community based on Islamic thought. Both turned to armed resistance against foreign rule. In many ways, al-Qassam acts as a model for Hamas who has attempted to claim him as their own (Filui 2012, p. 54). The name of Hamas' armed wing, *Kata'ib al-Shahid al-Izz al-Din al-Qassam* (the Brigades of the Martyr Izz al-Din al-Qassam), may be viewed as an attempt to establish historic continuity with the symbol and ethos of one of Palestine's first recognised resistance figures and martyrs. This is an example of what Hobsbawm and Ranger (1992) coined the "invention of tradition"; in this case, a historical tradition of resistance.

The most recognisable modern movement advocating political reform in line with Islamic principles is Hassan al-Banna's (1906–1949) *al-Ikhwan al-Muslimun*, which was founded in Egypt in 1928 and soon spread to the wider region, including Palestine in 1935. The *Ikhwan* initially advocated reform through Islamisation rather than armed struggle. Although focused on societal renewal and reform through Islam, members of the *Ikhwan* nevertheless fought against Zionist forces over the course of the 1948/1949 conflict (Mayer 1982). Islamic brigades also fought under the banner of Fatah during the late 1960s, operating from guerrilla bases dubbed the 'Camps of the Sheikhs' in Jordan.

While the political influence of Fatah and the PLO rapidly eclipsed the Islamists following the crushing defeat of the Arab armies in the 1967 Six Day War, it is nevertheless difficult to understate the influence of the *Ikhwan* on the Palestinian national movement, both for Fatah and Hamas. According to Aziz Dweik (personal interview 2010),

> many of the leaders of Hamas, not all of them, studied in Egypt ... so the incubator of the Muslim Brotherhood ... gave birth to two things: the nationalist movement in Palestine ... [Fatah founders] Abu Iyad, Abu Jihad, Abu Mazen ... all of these fathers – Abu meaning the father of – graduated from the Muslim Brotherhood incubator. Also, the Islamists in Hamas, many of them ... graduated from the same incubators.

Jihad, education and Islamic values   171

Following *al-nakba* in 1947/1948, however, the majority of the Palestinian *Ikhwan* believed that only after the creation of a virtuous, Islamic society would the Palestinians be strong enough to throw off the Israeli occupation. As a result, the Islamists in Palestine focused on *da'wa* (proselytising or the 'call' to Islam) in preparation, while remaining militarily passive in the face of Israeli occupation. This, in turn, led to the creation of Fatah in 1954. Indeed, aside from Yasser Arafat, the founding members of Fatah were former Palestinian *Ikhwan* disenchanted with the *Ikhwan*'s passivity and lack of military resistance against Israel (Tamimi 2007, p. 18). Ironically, it was in 1974 when Arafat and the PLO started moving towards accommodation with Israel and a two-state solution that the Islamists began to drift away from Fatah and eventually towards armed resistance.

As a result, it is common to find that many Palestinians – whether these are inclined towards Fatah, Hamas or neither – believe that Fatah itself is an Islamic organisation, despite common assertions of Fatah secularity in mainstream international discourses. Khatib (survey 2010), a 20-year-old Fatah supporter studying political science, for instance, describes Fatah as the "one who combined love of Islam and the country" and whose priorities are "Islam, Allah and the land".

While Fatah is part of the PLO, which indeed does possess a 'secular' constitution, it is important to note that Fatah is a movement bereft of strong ideological commitments. According to Arafat security adviser and long-time PLO official William Nasser (personal interview 2010),

> Fatah was never a secular movement ... Fatah was a national movement that has secular and religious within this framework, ... The mainstream consider that this is a national movement where all the trends should meet ... it was a melting pot of all national trends, especially after the Karameh battle in 1968 people started joining in [their] thousands.... They all agreed on main issues, main principles: armed struggle, liberation of Palestine, democratic society ... [but] the only thing they agreed upon was a democratic state, not a secular democratic state.

Accordingly, Fatah does not work to secularise Palestinian society in the manner that Hamas works for Islamisation. Indeed, on the contrary, Iyad Barghouti (2007, pp. 14–15) argues that it was the Fatah-dominated Palestinian Authority which Islamised the laws in order to try to undercut Hamas. It was Arafat, for example, who created a Minister of Religious Affairs, a position which had hitherto been unheard of in the Levant (*al-mashriq al-'arabiyy* in Arabic). In this regard, Barghouti (ibid., p. 45) continues, Hamas' electoral participation was more designed to maintain the status quo rather than further Islamise the laws.

Palestinian basic law, the de facto constitution, moreover – like most Muslim majority constitutions – already derives its basic principles from *sharia* law. Thus, one can witness the centrality of Islam to much of Palestinian society even among the ostensibly 'secular' factions. Nasir al-Din (survey 2010), an unaffiliated 20-year-old studying political science, for example, believes that Hamas is

172   *Jihad, education and Islamic values*

a religious organisation and attaches significance to this because "it is important to achieve peace in the light of religion". To this end, it is vital to recognise the profound influence that Islam exercises in Palestinian society. It is, therefore, imperative not to treat Hamas and Islam as synonymous within the Palestinian Territories and to exceptionalise Hamas in consequence, because Islam is a central tenet for other movements and, indeed, the wider society as a whole.[2] Nevertheless, between the 1967 Six Day War and the creation of Hamas in 1987, the political influence of the Islamists took a back seat to the militant nationalism of the Fatah-led 'secular' PLO.

A variety of external structural changes helped facilitate the regional rise of Islamism. This commenced with the demise of secular Arab nationalism in the wake of the 1967 Six Day War, during which the West Bank, Gaza, the Sinai Peninsula and the Golan Heights were occupied by Israel (Milton-Edwards 2000, p. 123; Knudsen 2005, p. 1374). During the 1970s, there was a marked increase in Islamist support culminating in the 1979 Iranian Revolution and Soviet invasion of Afghanistan, both of which provided inspiration and galvanisation for Islamic activism (Tamimi 2007, p. 48; Mishal and Sela 2000, pp. 29–30). According to the Islamist Secretary General of Parliament Mahmoud al-Ramahi (personal interview 2010),

> the Islamic Revolution in Iran showed the people an experience with religion [that] maybe we can make a revolution and change the situation ... Iran and the mujahedeen of Afghanistan showed the people that with the resistance and the revolution maybe we can change our life.

Contemporaneous to these events was the sharply growing oil wealth of Saudi Arabia and the Gulf States which facilitated the establishment and institutionalisation of communal Islamic activities throughout the region (Irving Jensen 1998, p. 204; Mishal and Sela 2000, p. 28). William Nasser (personal interview 2010), furthermore, contends that the 1989 Soviet withdrawal from Afghanistan

> changed the mood of the people and people again felt this impression of having a struggle movement, not just puppets of regimes.... But those who came back started forming their own groups and this actually had its effect all over the Arab world, not only in Palestine. So the religious mood was raised, actually, to appease this coming back of jihadi thinkers and jihadi groups.

In addition, the fall of the Soviet Union and the 1991 defeat of Iraq ideologically discredited both Communism and the pan-Arabism espoused by Saddam Hussein (Juergensmeyer 2008, pp. 69–70; Roy 2007, p. 40). These events resulted in an ideological and financial vacuum for the then hegemonic Palestinian Liberation Organisation, leading some of those who were traditionally secular or of the left turning to Islamism (O'Leary and Tirman 2007, p. 4). In effect, the failure of 'imported' ideas, such as secular nationalism, communism and, more recently, as evidenced by the ongoing Arab uprisings, neoliberal market capitalism, has led large segments of population to 'return' to traditional indigenous reference points in order to modernise their societies for the benefit of the wider community. In this light, ideological trends in Palestine follow regional trends. As such, Hamas is a local manifestation of the regional trend towards Islamism, albeit under unique circumstances, namely Israeli occupation.

There are also a variety of structural changes specific to Palestine which account for the rise of Hamas. During the 1970s and 1980s, the *Ikhwan* in Palestine established a variety of social and charitable networks, as well as a nascent military structure (Zuhur 2010, p. 6). According to its 1988 charter, Hamas is the armed offshoot of the *Ikhwan*. During this time, moreover, the construction of mosques increased exponentially in the Palestinian Territories. Between 1967 and 1987, the number of mosques in the West Bank increased from 400 to 750, while the number in the Gaza Strip tripled from 200 to 600 (Abu Amr 1993, p. 8). This increase in the construction of mosques would seem to be indicative of an increase in religiosity. As noted, however, it was the emergence of a militant Islamist competitor, Palestinian Islamic Jihad, during the 1980s which pushed the *Ikhwan* to create Hamas as its resistance arm in order to establish its resistance credentials and, thus, compete for popular support within the context of the first intifada.

Following the intifada, Hamas and the Islamist movement in the Palestinian Territories spent their time focused on community development, Islamic education and *da'wa*. As Sara Roy (2011, p. 143) points out, during the Oslo period, "The battle was not military but ideational, over ideas and values" with one Islamist leader explaining, "we fight by changing ideas through Islam". During this period, the social dominance and moral authority of the Islamists were unchallenged even if their political influence remained relatively marginal until the outbreak of the second intifada in 2000. In effect, the Islamists possessed a moral authority lacking among members of the Fatah-dominated elite.

Following the outbreak of the second intifada and the consequent carnage that this unleashed, many Palestinians sought refuge in Islamic thought. Some turned to Islam for motivation, others for solace. The *shahid* complex, for instance, not only provided a driving force for armed operations, but also acted as a source of solace whereby all of those perceived to be lost to the occupation were honoured as martyrs, regardless of whether they were active combatants or not. Thus, the certainty of religion and faith in God concomitantly acted as both an inspiration and a refuge. According to Yasmin (survey 2010), an 18-year-old IT student and Hamas supporter, the movement "provides psychological and mental support".

The destruction resulting from the intifada also prompted a further shift towards moral conservatism and traditional values based on Islam. Hamas, as the principal movement identified with Islam in the Palestinian Territories, was the main beneficiary of these shifts. Indeed, Khalil Shikaki (personal interview 2009), Director of the Palestinian Centre for Policy and Survey Research, contends that the greater importance an individual attaches to traditional values, the more likely they are to support Hamas. Tellingly, Hamas popularity doubled

174 *Jihad, education and Islamic values*

throughout the first four years of the second intifada and eclipsed Fatah for the first time in 2004 (Araj and Brym 2010, p. 855). This popularity was then translated into more concrete political dividends throughout the course of the 2004/2005 municipal and 2006 legislative elections.

Islamic exceptionalism, *ijtihad* and *sharia* law

There is a tendency among both Orientalists and Islamists alike to exceptionalise Islam. In essence, both proponents and critics of Islamic thought argue that it is unique among faiths insofar as it purports to offer a comprehensive belief system which regulates all of the human condition (*minhaj al-hayat*). According to Mousa Abu Marzouq (personal interview 2010),

> Islam is not like the other religions. The nature of Islam is a political, social and economic movement. Islam is a comprehensive movement. Thus, if you decide to stick to Islam, it will be something inevitable to have a political orientation, social orientation, and economic orientation, besides a commitment to Islam's teachings.

This notion is echoed by Orientalists who then extrapolate that Islam is defined by immutable, unchanging characteristics dating back to the time of the Prophet Mohammed. As such, Orientalists argue that Islamic thought is an archaic, oppressive and stagnant force in society. Prescribed punishments, or *hudud*, based on corporal punishment are held up as exemplars of this regressive force.

Part of these understandings stems from the belief that *The Qur'an* is considered to be the direct words of God. Aziz Dweik (personal interview 2010) contends that

> the Holy *Qur'an* speaks to the human being directly. According to our understanding, we say that the Holy *Qur'an* is the words of God so we go and think of these words where God is talking to us directly … you will feel, according to our understanding, that God is talking to you.

Mahmoud al-Ramahi (personal interview 2010) goes a step further, arguing that "as Muslims, we have direct relations with God himself through *The Qur'an*". The implication here is that other religions do not possess such relations.

But these arguments belie the complexity and evolution of the Islamic world throughout the centuries. These arguments also elide the multiple interpretations and applications of Islamic thought throughout the Muslim world stretching from Indonesia to Morocco. To suggest that Muslims, consisting of over one billion believers derived from a multitude of histories, cultures, identities and ethnicities, are all the same is preposterous. It is clear that there are many competing forces and ideologies within Islam, not only *between* traditions (for instance, Sunni and Shiite Islam), but *within* traditions as evidenced by al-Qa'ida-inspired Wahabbi Salafi jihadists and reformists like the Muslim Brotherhood.

Jihad, education and Islamic values 175

There is, moreover, a contradictory consciousness among the various strains of Islamic thought and Islamist ideologies. While *The Qur'an* is believed among Muslims to be the direct word of Allah regulating all worldly affairs, it is recognised that it does not necessarily specify a course of action for the complexities of the modern world. In this regard, the Islamic concept of *ijtihad* (independent reasoning) allows for the interpretation and reinterpretation of *The Qur'an*, *sunnah* (Prophetic tradition) and *hadith* (sayings of the Prophet) in order to better deal with the modern world. Tellingly, *ijtihad* is derived from the word 'jihad', or to strive in the name of God. The notion of *qiyas* (analogy) is similarly used to deal with specific circumstances not mentioned in *The Qur'an*. Finally, practitioners strive for *ijma'* (consensus) wherever possible (Kadayifici-Orellana 2007, pp. 47–62). As such, Islam is traditionally syncretic and often incorporates local belief systems under the wider framework of 'Islam'.

Islam also incorporates values from other belief systems, including secularism. Thus, according to Hafez Shaheen (personal interview 2010), then Islamist Deputy Mayor of Nablus for Planning and Technical Affairs, "Islam does not prohibit Muslims from taking good things and good values from other cultures as long as this does not contradict the main values or pillars of Islam". Similarly, al-Ramahi (personal interview 2010) contends that "the forbidden in our life is not more than ten things but there [are] millions of things shared not only with the secular but with Jewish and the Christians and the others". Hence, these statements would appear to contradict the claim both by Orientalists and Islamists alike that, on a practical level, Islam is all-encompassing, holistic or especially different from other belief systems.

The Qur'an, moreover, was revealed over the course of 23 years and contains practical and political guidance pertaining to the evolution of contemporary events during the time of the Prophet Mohammed (Khalidi 2008, p. xiv; Kadyifici-Orellana 2007, p. 57). As a result, *The Qur'an* contains contradictory passages, thus requiring human interpretation to assess which verse takes precedent.

Mariam Salah (personal interview 2010) explains:

> *The Qur'an, sunnah* and the Prophet's sayings are the most accurate and right sources in Islam, but anything else comes from human beings and we humans make mistakes. Even the Islamic scientists could make mistakes. In *The Qur'an* we have clear and direct rules and also indirect ones where people and specialists try to elicit their meaning or significance. We have gatherings of Islamic jurisprudence for this purpose. If, for example, in Europe and America there were rules that do not contradict with *The Qur'an* and *sunnah*, I would take those rules. For example, we took the way how to drive a car from the West, driving a car does not contradict with Islam.

Indeed, within *The Qur'an* certain verses are considered to be *muhkam* (explicit, clear cut or fully intelligible), whereas others are considered *mutashabih* (indeterminate, ambiguous or with multiple meanings) (Khalidi 2008, pp. xi–xii).

176 *Jihad, education and Islamic values*

According to Tarif Khalidi (ibid.), the *mutashabih* are deliberately designed by God to stimulate thinking; *The Qur'an*, moreover, is filled with repeated exhortations to reflect upon the universe created by God and humankind's place within it. Thus, not only is there a process of contestation and interpretation within Islamic thought but *The Qur'an* actively encourages this process.

Salah (personal interview 2010), for instance, continues, "there are Muslims in Saudi Arabia but their kings follow the Western style, life and rules". Here, Salah appears to be pointing to the discrepancy between the austere Wahabbi Islam propagated throughout the Kingdom and the notorious playboy antics of various members of the royal family while abroad.

Hamas and 'moderate' Islamists in the Palestinian Territories take great pains to differentiate themselves from what they perceive to be extremist or false interpretations of Islam, for instance, al-Qa'ida, the Taliban and Saudi Arabia. According to Jibril (personal interview 2010), a former member of the planning committee for the intifada, for example, "al-Qa'ida itself and others, they take a small part of the religion and said okay, this is our part and they started to practise it in a wrong way. But we, as Hamas, we look regarding the religion but [also] the actual situation." Here, the informant grounds Hamas' ideology and actions in temporal rather than metaphysical terms. Indicatively, Bashir (personal interview 2010), a Hamas youth activities officer in Damascus, argues that "we precede the political platform rather than the ideology ... the political platform is more important than the ideology". So, as Shaheen (personal interview 2010) points out, while Islam

> is a religion that interpret[s] ... all the affairs of human beings ... when it comes to general things like regulating, like governing, like economy, like politics and such things, Islam did define general rules and general frames within which you can move and you can interpret.

But then where does Hamas derive its particular interpretation of Islam? According to Bashir (personal interview 2010),

> Hamas does not deal with the traditional reference, and even the concept of traditional reference in the Islamic world differs from references of the other religions and ideologies. According to Hamas, it considers *ijtihad* and *fiqh* [jurisprudence] as its reference. Thus, Hamas asks the scientists, considers the opinion of jurists and politicians, and listens to everyone who is in the Islamic domain but not the domain of a [singular] university or city or organisation ... [even if] that organisation is huge or well known. Hence, the reference for Hamas is the reference of Islamic thought, Islamic *ijtihad*, and the Islamic culture of well-known scientists. So Hamas doesn't comply with any particular part. It does not comply with any particular direction even in the religious standpoint.

Thus, Hamas' interpretation of Islam may be conceived of as a rebellion against traditional, official establishments, such as Mecca in Saudi Arabia and al-Azhar

Jihad, education and Islamic values 177

in Cairo, which are believed to have been co-opted by corrupt and autocratic regimes. In this light, moderate Islamism as expounded by Hamas is a rearticulation of modernity within an organic, endogenous framework, which concomitantly attempts to preserve traditional cultural reference points while allowing enough flexibility to adapt to the complexities of the modern world. According to Kadayifici-Orellana (2007, p. 35), it is a "theory of cultural rupture with nationalists and *ulemas* [religious scholars] alike".

Salah (personal interview 2010) supports this assertion insofar as "laws and everything that do not contradict with our identity and Islamic culture; we don't reject it. Logic is logic." Through these statements one may clearly perceive a substantial amount of intellectual rationalisation, based on both practicality and principles, indicative of flexibility regarding the pragmatic interpretation and application of Islamic thought. According to al-Ramahi (personal interview 2010), "We understand that our religion gives us the chance to deal with others, not be separated from the others." Below we examine Hamas' practical flexibility with regard to two controversial subjects: Hamas' 1988 charter and the implementation of *sharia* law.

Hamas' charter, Israel and the peace process

Hamas' 1988 charter is a controversial document undoubtedly replete with anti-Jewish references, including tracts emanating from the infamous 'Protocols of the Elders of Zion' purporting to describe a worldwide Jewish conspiracy to dominate the world. The charter also lists Hamas' putative ideological goal of liberating all of historical Palestine – that is to say, including what is today recognised as Israel – which has led to the common assertion that Hamas is a racist, anti-Semitic organisation whose chief goal is to drive the Jews into the sea. In an interesting parallel to Jewish conceptions of the 'Promised Land', Hamas' charter also defines the territories of British Mandate Palestine as *waqf* or Islamic endowment entrusted to Muslims until Judgement Day. Hamas' refusal to recognise Israel's right to exist is seen as evidence that Hamas would be unable or unwilling to coexist with Israel, thereby revealing its ostensibly genocidal intents.

The reality, however, is far more nuanced and much less literal than critics would have us believe. The charter, for one, is cited exponentially more by Hamas' critics than by its supporters. Indeed, the charter is not mentioned in any of its political texts and has rarely been cited by Hamas leaders since the early 1990s (Klein 2007, p. 450). In other words, Hamas does not invoke its charter as a reference point to guide or legitimate its actions. Rather, the charter surfaces predominantly within Western and Israeli criticisms of the movement. It appears, thus, that Hamas' critics place more salience on the role of the charter than on the movement itself. The charter is regarded by Hamas leaders as an anachronistic remnant of an earlier, more immature stage of the movement which has been steadily sidelined since the 1990s.

A 1990s document entitled 'This Is What We Struggle For' delivered to Western diplomats in Amman, Jordan, and a 2000 document, *The Islamic*

178 *Jihad, education and Islamic values*

Resistance Movement, are just two of the many attempts Hamas has made to outline its contemporary motivations and goals (see Appendices I and II in Tamimi 2007). Usama Hamdan (2011), Hamas' representative in Lebanon, dismisses discussion of the charter as 'boring'. In short, the charter is a historical document which has very little relevance to Hamas' current political programme. Hamas' 2006 electoral manifesto and subsequent government policy documents are more accurate representations of Hamas' political trajectory.

Although there are certainly elements of racism in Hamas' charter, the movement has attempted to exorcise references to the 'Jews' in favour of 'Zionists' or 'Israelis' since the 1990s. Among the older generation of Palestinians, moreover, Jews and Israelis are often treated as synonymous. This is not due to classic European anti-Semitism based on notions of blood libel but a result of decades of dispossession, discrimination and oppression perpetrated by the Israeli state which, incidentally, attempts to define itself as the incarnation of world Jewry. According to Mousa Abu Marzouq (personal interview 2010),

> Hamas does not recognise Israel. But it does not recognise Israel, not because the Israelis are Jews, or because of the Israelis' religion. No. I do not recognise Israel even if the ruler of Israel were a Muslim, who took the others' land, my land, my field, and kicked me out of it.

Traditionally, within Islamic tradition, Jews and Christians are defined as *Ahl al-Kitab* (People of the Book), especially during Ottoman times, and accorded the status of protected minorities. As Mariam Salah (personal interview 2010) points out, "As Muslims, we don't have a problem with other religions such as Christianity and Judaism. We respect the religions and all prophets. If even anyone curses [swears] Jesus or Moses we consider him as *kafir* [unbeliever]."

But then why does Hamas insist on retaining its charter given the furore concerning its contents? Ala' al-Din (personal interview 2010), a high-ranking West Bank parliamentarian, explains:

> This comes to our internal politics. Why? Within our internal politics Abu Amr [Yasser Arafat] cancelled the PLO charter ... which had some kind of consensus among the Palestinians, and he offered that cancellation to the Israelis: "Israel has the right to live, we have to share peace with Israel, we have to cooperate with the Israelis".... And we, as Palestinians, were watching this over, and the Israelis did not give him anything in [the] way to reciprocate his project, so Hamas could not go to the same mistake. You see? This is the real incentive for the Hamas people not to give up their charter, but, in practice, they have given up the charter by saying, "We do accept a sovereign Palestinian state within the West Bank [and Gaza] with East Jerusalem as its capital."

In this regard, Mahmoud al-Ramahi (personal interview 2010) explains, "We have to differentiate between the right to exist and existence. Israel as a state

Jihad, education and Islamic values 179

exists, but we will never recognise the right of Israel to exist in our land." In effect, Hamas accords Israel de facto in contrast to de jure recognition; that is, while not recognising the *legitimacy* of Israel's existence, Hamas recognises that Israel *does* exist and indicates its willingness to deal with Israel accordingly. On the other hand, Hamas and its supporters do not recognise the legitimacy of Israel's founding because it implicitly legitimises Palestinian dispossession stemming from 1947/1948. Among Palestinians, this viewpoint is by no means specific to Hamas. Zahrah (survey 2010), an unaffiliated 20-year-old studying media, for instance, opposes recognition of Israel "because it would change history and twist the truth".

Nevertheless, as assassinated Hamas leader and co-founder, Ismail Abu Shanab (2003) bluntly pointed out,

> Forget about the rhetoric, we cannot destroy Israel.... The reality is that Palestinians can create a state that would live by Israel. We will respect any American effort that will stop Israeli settlements and settlers and bring Israelis to withdraw up to 1967 borders.

Thus, in the case of Hamas, there is a need to differentiate between symbolic recognition and coexistence. The behaviour and practice of Hamas suggest somewhat more flexibility and pragmatism than an implacable hatred driven by anti-Judaism and divine endowment of the land. Recent attempts by the de facto government in Gaza to introduce Hebrew into the school curriculum as an elective are similarly indicative of Hamas' realism when it comes to the permanency of Israeli Jews within the region (Brown 2012, pp. 14–15). Ironically, it was the pro-Western PA in Ramallah which vetoed the initiative.

Most poignant, perhaps, is the long-standing policy of Hamas dating from the 1990s to enter into a *hudna* (often translated as ceasefire) and let future generations resolve the conflict. Despite its charter, a *hudna* is rationalised by historical precedent whereby the Prophet Mohammed entered into a truce with the polytheists of Mecca (who are subsequently said to have broken it). Before his assassination, Hamas founder Sheikh Ahmed Yassin spoke of a 10-year *hudna* which would be automatically renewed (Klein 2007, p. 455). But a *hudna* is more than a ceasefire. In an op-ed piece published in the *New York Times*, Ahmed Yousef (2006), a former Deputy Foreign Minister of the Islamist government in Gaza and Hamas spokesman, describes a *hudna* as:

> typically cover[ing] 10 years and recognised in Islamic jurisprudence as a legitimate and binding contract. A *hudna* extends beyond the Western concept of a ceasefire and obliges the parties to use the period to seek a permanent, non-violent resolution to their differences.

Hamas has also repeatedly and publicly committed itself to accepting a popular referendum on any peace agreement reached by Palestinian President Mahmoud Abbas (Carter 2006, p. 213). Instances of this may be found in the Prisoner's

180 *Jihad, education and Islamic values*

Document drawn up by all of the Palestinian factions and Hamas' acceptance of the Arab League initiative, entailing full normalisation with Israel in return for a withdrawal from Arab territories captured in 1967 and the establishment of a Palestinian state (Chehab 2007, pp. 201–202). Moreover, the movement has publicly supported the realisation of partial goals based on a two-state solution, including statements by present luminaries such as Khalid Mishal (2006), Ismail Haniyeh (Weymouth 2006), Mousa Abu Marzouq (2006) and Ahmed Yousef (2007).

While Hamas may never commit to recognise Israel's *right* to exist, if one looks beyond the virulent and often uncompromising populist rhetoric, it has already publicly committed itself to coexistence (Agha and Malley 2008; McCarthy 2008). Indeed, Hamas and Israel do coexist, albeit uneasily, on a day-to-day basis through the (limited) import of goods into Gaza, as well as the cooperation evident among municipalities run by Hamas-backed councillors in the West Bank and the occupation authorities. As Dhakiy (survey 2010), a Fatah activist studying sport, astutely points out, coexistence with Israel "is what Hamas looks for. But it wants an approach that doesn't embarrass it."

Hamas, in essence, sees its charter as a bargaining chip rather than as a rigid set of guidelines, especially when it comes to political practicalities. Indicatively, its political actions have often diverged from the principles outlined in the charter. As the Head of the Political Bureau Khalid Mishal (cited in Tamimi 2007, p. 149) explains, the charter "should not be regarded as the fundamental ideological frame of reference from which the movement takes its positions, or on the basis of which it justifies its actions". Hamas leader Ibrahim Ghoshesh (ibid., p. 149) similarly elucidates that "it goes without saying that the articles of the charter are not sacred … they are subject to review and revision". For an accurate representation of Hamas' practical trajectory it is thus necessary to investigate its 2006 electoral platform and subsequent government policy.

Sharia law and prescribed punishments

The putative desire to install *sharia* law is often viewed as threatening in the eyes of many secularists, elites and Westerners alike. The literal interpretations of certain aspects of *sharia*, namely *al-hudud* (singular *hadd*, literally 'restrictions'), or prescribed punishments, based on corporal or capital punishment, are often viewed with consternation. Being stoned (*rajm*) to death for adultery (*zina'*) or having a hand cut off for theft (*sariqa*) are two common instances cited by critics of *sharia* law. And, indeed, there are instances and institutions where these punishments are literally enforced, not only under 'extremist' regimes such as the Taliban in Afghanistan and the Islamic Republic of Iran, but also under the auspices of putative 'moderate' Western allies, including Saudi Arabia. In similar vein, other aspects of *sharia* law, such as the divorce laws which privilege men, are often portrayed as an affront to liberal values.

In reality, however, very few people call for such a literal interpretation of *sharia*. *Al-hudud*, moreover, constitutes a very short component of the wider

Jihad, education and Islamic values 181

field of *sharia* law based on Islamic jurisprudence. Only 350 of *The Qur'an*'s over 6000 verses are considered to be legal in nature (Kamali 1991, pp. 19–20). *Sharia* law, in general, comprises a wider set of principles which allow for interpretation depending on the time, place and circumstances. In effect, there is a difference between *sharia* as a legal system and *sharia* as a set of guiding principles. Indeed, most legal systems and constitutions in Muslim majority regimes in the Middle East, including the Palestinian Authority in the West Bank, already derive their principles from and are based on the latter understanding of *sharia* law. Thus, this latter conception may be interpreted as akin to Western notions of natural law (Burgat 2003, p. 134).

Even the few legal aspects prescribed as necessitating *al-hudud* need to be treated with more nuance because these punishments are neither immutable nor obligatory in spite of common perceptions. The interpretation and application of these punishments are subordinated to a specific set of criteria and dependent on circumstances in the same manner as Western conceptions of law. Self-defence, for instance, is a mitigating fact for murder. *Sharia* law is applied with similar caveats.

Mariam Salah (personal interview 2010), the former Minster for Women's Affairs and Professor of *Sharia* Law, explained to me that the *hadd* for theft, for instance, would only be applied if one stole for gratuitous purposes. There appears to be an almost utopian belief among Palestinian Islamists that should an Islamic state be established according to the 'correct' interpretation of Islam (although where this interpretation derives from is somewhat unclear), then no one in society would want for anything, and thus theft would be superfluous (ibid.). Therefore, only if an individual stole under these circumstances (in practical terms an almost certain impossibility) would the *hadd* be applied because the individual would be stealing purely out of greed. There are, moreover, a multitude of further criteria which need to be fulfilled for the punishment to be applied, all of which are predicated on the presumption of innocence, giving the accused the benefit of the doubt and ensuring that the crime was a grave offence.

Islamists also cite historical precedents to justify the abrogation of *al-hudud*. During the reign of the second Rightly Guided Caliph Omar Ibn al-Khattab (*c.*586–644), for instance, there was a drought which caused a famine. As a result, the Caliph abrogated the *hadd* severing one's hand for theft in order to account for the fact that people sometimes needed to steal food to ensure the survival of themselves and their family (Gunning 2007, pp. 77–81).

Other prescribed punishments feature similar caveats among moderate Islamists. Only eyewitness accounts and confessions, for example, are deemed to be admissible evidence for *al-hudud*, meaning that the practical application of such punishments is exceedingly difficult. A lack of consensus among the interpretation and application of *al-hudud* has caused high-profile Islamic theologians such as Tariq Ramadan (2005), the grandson of *Ikhwan* founder Hassan al-Banna and leading critic of authoritarian regimes in the Islamic world, to call for a moratorium on *al-hudud* in the Islamic world until a consensus can be reached.

182 *Jihad, education and Islamic values*

One may thus witness the selective interpretation and application of these laws in a manner akin to Western legal systems, instead of the common stereotype of mandatory punishments which do not account for extenuating circumstances.

As a set of guiding principles, there are also a variety of attempts to reinterpret various aspects of *sharia* law in order to innovate and make it more relevant to the modern world. Nasser al-Shaer (personal interview 2010), for example, the former Deputy Prime Minister and former Minister of Education, indicated his desire to include aspects of environmentalism and human rights within the *sharia* law curriculum while Dean of *sharia* law at an-Najah National University in Nablus. Indeed, proponents of *sharia* law argue that it already incorporates provisions for environmentalism and twenty-first-century conceptions of human rights.

Similarly, *The Qur'an* defines men and women as equally responsible moral agents (Khalidi 2008, p. xviii). Hamas has been active in the field of women's rights and women's education. Mariam Salah (personal interview 2010) argues that

> there is no religion nor law that honours the woman as Islam does. This is not only a personal belief but it is also a fact. Who reads Islam and understands it and who reads *The Qur'an, sunnah* and the Islamic Jurisprudence realises that the woman is honoured and that she has rights. If these rights were given to her and Islam was applied, the woman would just be much happier than in any other religion, culture, history or place.

Salah blames the ill-treatment and oppression of women in the Middle East on a misinterpretation of *The Qur'an* as well as inherited traditions and customs. In order to try to improve the status of women, Salah (ibid.) explains:

> I created a committee in the Ministry [of Women's Affairs] and called it "The Supreme National Committee to Confront Violence against Women". I tried to present some proposals of some projects concerned with the rehabilitation of rural women but there was not the financial support to implement the project [because of the international boycott of the elected government].

Indeed, there is a burgeoning Islamist feminist movement throughout the Muslim world working to reinterpret *The Qur'an* in accordance with twenty-first-century conceptions of women's rights (for women of Hamas specifically, see Holt 1997; Jad 2005; Amayreh 2010).

Nevertheless, it is important to emphasise that *sharia* law in its broader scope (as opposed to its limited specific legal scope) is a set of general principles or values which provide a framework for action but are interpreted and applied according to the surrounding environment. In brief, as Mahmoud el-Tagini (1988, p. 63) points out, "Shariah is a fundamental source of legislation rather than a temporal political authority". *Ijtihad, qiyas* and *ijma'*, on the other hand, are the tools with which to interpret and apply *sharia* law in any given context.

Values, behaviour and individual renewal

It is evident that Hamas, and indeed Muslim cultures in general, absorbs and incorporates various ideas and concepts emanating from beyond the Islamic world. At the same time, however, it is clear that Islamism is at least in part driven by competing values, ideology and associated behaviours. To be precise, Islamism is sometimes conceived of as a reaction to what is perceived to be an encroaching Western world. This derives from various measures instituted as a result of European imperialism, especially that of the United Kingdom, France and – from the latter half of the twentieth century – the United States, including the imposition and support of an autocratic, corrupt and 'secularised' elite.

Secularism, furthermore, is often perceived in parts of the Muslim Middle East as atheist or directly *against* God rather than plurality based on the separation of religion and state. However ridiculous it may seem to an outsider, moreover, it is not uncommon to hear Muslims cite the Crusades as an example of European and Christian expansionism. US President George W. Bush's (2001) unfortunate reference to the 'war on terror' as a 'Crusade' did not help matters. Couple this with the historical viewpoint depicting the Prophet Mohammed as the Antichrist and it is little wonder that there is ample suspicion of the purportedly progressive nature of European Enlightenment values.[3] Indeed, secularisation of the state and liberalisation of the economy have been experienced by the vast majority of Muslims in the former protectorates of the Middle East as the imposition and support of corrupt, dictatorial regimes which have curtailed any meaningful attempts at political freedom and widespread economic advancement in furtherance of their own agendas. The creation of the State of Israel, furthermore, continues to be viewed as a settler colonial project attempting to divide the Muslim Middle East in an effort to serve Western interests.

According to Aziz Dweik (personal interview 2010), moreover, "it is the nature of the people to resist ... any kind of values and principles which come from outside". Thus, there is an element of cultural contestation embodied in the rise of Islamism, but there is also a more specific set of experiences relating to imperial foreign policy packaged under the rhetoric of progressive enlightenment values. In consequence, the divergence between the putative goals of these values and the reality of their supposed implementation, as actualised by colonial foreign policy and their later client regimes, is such that the notion of these values has been sullied among the wider populace.

The failure of foreign ideologies, and their loss of credibility, has caused large swathes of the wider community to look to their own symbols, values and traditions in an attempt to modernise the state (or lack thereof in the Palestinian context) within an endogenous framework. As former Minister for Planning Sameer Abu Aisha (personal interview 2010) points out,

> not only here in Palestine but in the region and in the world, there has been a trend towards being more involved, being more supportive of the Islamic movements, especially the moderate ones, especially after the failure of the

184 *Jihad, education and Islamic values*

> pan-Arab movements, the Communists, and that stuff, socialists. They failed so people became more looking for a change and they [the Islamists] are close to the people. They are not far from what people think in mind. Close to the values of the people. Close to the religion of the people. People are by nature religious here ... those in the country as well as in the cities.... [The Islamists are] not something far away ... being close to the good acts and ... the moral issues.

The failure of the Westernised elite to end the occupation and establish an independent sovereign state through negotiations are additional factors accounting for this drift towards Islamism and Hamas in the Palestinian Territories.

Hamas is at the forefront of a regional trend moving away from the autocratic, 'secularised' elite detached from their respective societies towards what is perceived to be a more egalitarian strand which, while imbued with a strong religious flavour, has been at the forefront of the drive for democratisation and electoral reform within the Muslim Middle East for decades. Palestinian-Israeli professor Shaul Mishal (personal interview 2009) opines that Palestinians identify with Hamas because "Hamas is more Palestinian from their point of view". Furthermore, with its history as a grassroots organisation in touch with the wider community, "Hamas is aware of people's needs ... their agonies". Fatah, in contrast, Mishal (ibid.) continues, "is not an authentic, organic representation with deep affiliations to traditional Palestinian notions". In essence, many of these traditional notions are derived from Islam and based on what would generally be considered as moral and social conservatism in Western societies.

Returning to the three heroic figures of Palestinian society, the *feda'i*, the *shahid* and the survivor, or one who practises *summud* (steadfastness), *summud* is also a sign of moral conservatism and thus more identifiable with Hamas (Tuastad 2009, p. 263). In essence, Hamas frames the notions of resistance and jihad within a familiar indigenous framework so that it resonates with the wider population. In effect, this ostensible cultural resistance is framed as jihad and positioned within traditional cultural reference points so as to portray itself as the 'authentic' representation of the Palestinian people.

But what, exactly, are the values of Islam according to Hamas? According to youth worker Bashir (personal interview 2010),

> The values in Islam are of many kinds. Some kinds relate to the fundamentals of the religion like Theism, Faith in the Judgement Day, Faith in all Messengers, and Faith in the Angels and so on. These are the values of Belief and convictions. There are other values of behaviours and manners. And there are values of society and life. Islam has a great effect on Muslims concerning everything in their lives – everything. It is a religion that we find ... balanced, which responds to proper and correct needs; and it deals with all human beings in justice, even with the aggressor.... So, there are Islamic values in wartime, Islamic values in economics, and Islamic values in social life ... Islam is a complete system which includes punishments.

Jihad, education and Islamic values 185

Similarly, Mariam Salah (personal interview 2010) explains,

> *The Qur'an* and *sunnah* are not only about the Muslim rites such as prayer, fasting, *zakat* and *hajj*. These are just a part of Islam. Islam also has the part about treatment of others, the part about ethics and the part about thought. So for me, being a Muslim is not only about practising the Islamic rites but also having and relating my treatment of others, ethics and thought to Allah's orders in *The Qur'an* and *sunnah*.

And yet, as discussed in the previous sections, these values are far more flexible and potentially inclusive than is commonly portrayed. A common theme, however, is not just the *belief* in Islam but the *practice* of Islam as embodied by behaviour. These practices may be as seemingly innocuous and cosmetic as a woman wearing a *hijab* and dressing modestly. As demonstrated in previous chapters, the public behaviour of Islamist leaders, as embodied, for instance, by observance of Islamic principles or engagement in charitable endeavours, has been a major source of social and political capital for Hamas. Thus, *The Qur'an* and the *sunnah* not only possess a spiritual value but also a *practical* value concerning one's understanding of, and behaviour in, the temporal world.

As befitting the notion of cultural resistance, Islamic behaviours and values are often compared and contrasted to the perceived failings of Western existence. Outwardly understanding, yet nevertheless condescending, references were repeatedly made to me pertaining to the ostensibly promiscuous, profligate and spiritually devoid nature of Western existence. The putative failure of the family unit was a particular favourite. Unsurprisingly, the overt sexualisation of society was another.

In each case, however, there tended to be at least an outward attempt at acceptance given that it was 'your' culture based on a specific set of cultural, historical and social circumstances. In a rare display of Islamist humour, Ala' al-Din (personal interview 2010), who incidentally completed his doctoral studies in the United States, cheekily described this perceived cultural divergence and associated behaviour thus:

> the Islamists showed every kind of transparency. In terms of behaviour, our conduct, we are, I can tell and assure you, that we are 100 per cent clean. I know my wife only. God knows I did not know a single woman other than my wife. You will be astonished by that because of, you know, where you were raised but this is fact.... So we told the people our pockets are tight and closed, we would never allow money which [is] not allowed for us to come inside our pockets. And our zips are really closed for any kind of misconduct and behaviour.

Behaviour is of paramount importance to Hamas because it believes that societal reform begins with individual renewal (Klein 2009, p. 885; Malka 2007, p. 101). Although this belief is hardly unique to Hamas as a social movement, central to

186 *Jihad, education and Islamic values*

this renewal in Hamas' eyes is an increased knowledge and practice of Islam. According to Hamas youth worker Bashir (personal interview 2010), "Hamas has worked on the issue of increasing the religiosity of people – the politicised religiosity – which means it has worked on the issues of politics, religion, behaviour, manners, social and moral institutions, and charities". As Fatima (survey 2010), an 18-year-old Hamas supporter, points out, the movement "started by reforming souls and leading them away from sins, so they can resist in the name of God". In a similar vein, Rashid (survey 2010), a 22-year-old Hamas supporter studying media, believes involvement with Hamas contributes to "self-development, enhancing my morals and supporting my political stand". Manar (survey 2010), a 21-year-old Hamas supporter studying geography and political science, concurs insofar as Hamas works "to preserve the moral character and value of society which are declining and receding gradually these days", adding that the movement acts as a "moral utility". In short, contends Abrar (survey 2010), a 22-year-old Hamas supporter, association with the movement "makes you a better person".

As a regional branch of the ostensibly pan-Islamic *Ikhwan*, Hamas and its predecessor were initially more concerned with Islamisation than with liberation and, as such, subject to criticism from the nationalist PLO movements. As the nationalist sentiment grew over the course of the first intifada, Hamas focused increasingly on localised national issues rather than on pan-Islamism. In other words, Hamas increasingly used Islam to augment its nationalist credentials rather than pull Palestinians into the wider pan-Islamic orbit. Despite its putative pan-Islamic agenda, regional branches of the Muslim Brotherhood have similarly evolved according to the local social, political and cultural milieux and possess their own modus operandi, goals and tactics, despite sharing a common worldview.

Indeed, when confronted about the implicit tension between universalism (as embodied by Islam) and localism (in essence, the liberation of Palestine), Mousa Abu Marzouq (personal interview 2010) argued that there is "no problem between the national element and the religious element because patriotism is part of Islam". Bashir (personal interview 2010), a biologist by training, further elucidates:

> Hamas is a national Islamic movement ... there is no problem between both definitions because, according to us and Palestinians in general, nationalism means al-Quds [Jerusalem] and al-Aqsa, and so there is no difference. It is like separating oxygen and hydrogen, can you say determine which one of them is the water? No, water (H_2O) is both oxygen and hydrogen together by certain amounts.

Thus, Hamas seems to infer that there is no strict separation between Islam and Palestine (and, indeed, this is somewhat reinforced by Hamas' charter which defines the territories of British Mandate Palestine as Islamic *waqf* or endowment).

Jihad, education and Islamic values 187

In practice however, Hamas is a localised movement devoid of transnational intentions. It is true that Hamas operates in foreign arenas but it has a strict policy of non-interference in their internal affairs and limits itself to working on issues pertaining to Palestinians. Indicative of this localism is the fact that Hamas has never perpetrated attacks outside of Israel and the Palestinian Territories.

This localism is in marked contrast to the ideologies of transnational jihadi organisations such as al-Qa'ida (and indeed the previous transnational scope of PLO militancy). As a former senior aid to the Head of the Israeli Security Agency (cited in ICG 2011, pp. 6–7), and thus no friend of Hamas, points out,

> Hamas and the Muslim Brotherhood strike a balance between universalism (Islam) and localism (nationalism/Palestine). Their focus is *da'wa*. They spring from the centre of the society, which they wish to occupy. In order to achieve this, they must be moderate. Al-Qa'ida is the opposite. It wishes to distance itself from society – to create a counter-society – in order to attack it.

The localism and temporal aims of Hamas indicate a striking divergence between the ideologies, values and intentions of Hamas and al-Qa'ida-inspired entities, in spite of Israeli, US and, to a lesser extent, European efforts to tie these organisations together. The primary methods Hamas uses to disseminate and instil these values is *da'wa*, predominantly through the mosques and education, both within formal and extra-curricular contexts.

The role of education

Hamas has long since focused on education as a way of disseminating Islamic values among society. On the one hand, Hamas is fixated on formal education, with a particular emphasis on hard sciences, and, on the other, it advocates a spiritual education which equips the individual to deal with the practicalities of everyday life.

Hamas' focus on education is defined in one of the less controversial parts of its charter. Articles 15 and 16 read:

> When an enemy usurps a Muslim land, then jihad is an individual religious duty on every Muslim.... That requires that Islamic education be given to the masses locally and in the Arab and Islamic sphere.... The education process must involve scholars, teachers, educators, communicators, journalists, and the educated, especially the youth of the Islamic movement.... Fundamental changes must be made in the educational system to liberate it from the effects of the ideological invasion that was brought by the Orientalists and missionaries.... We must train the Muslim generation in our area, an Islamic training based on performing religious duties, studying God's book very well, and studying Prophetic tradition (*sunnah*), Islamic history

188 *Jihad, education and Islamic values*

and heritage from its authenticated sources with the guidance of experts and scholars, and using a curriculum that will provide the Muslim with the correct worldview in ideology and thought.

Indeed, according to Jeroen Gunning (2007, p. 85),

> Hamas has an explicit programme of socialising people into willing the Islamic state. Hamas' extensive charity network is part of this programme of da'wah (calling people to Islam), as is its network of Kindergartens, orphanages, and schools, including the Islamic University of Gaza.

Here, one can again witness Hamas' polysemic interpretations of jihad in the name of liberation, in both their cognitive and physical senses. The pursuit of knowledge and the struggle against ignorance is considered by some to be the highest form of jihad (Tibi 1996, pp. 136–137).

This cognitive aspect, moreover, leads back the concept of the 'greater' jihad (*jihad al-akbar*) predicated on an inner struggle with oneself, whereas resistance to occupation ties back to the 'lesser' jihad conceived of as a defensive war. As Jibril (personal interview 2010) explains, "our first priority is to educate the people ... we have to make them understand that it is a transient period and after that we want to liberate our country". In brief, Nidal (survey 2010), a 22-year-old Hamas supporter, opines that movement possesses an "ideology that supports traditional and religious values towards liberating Palestine from occupation". In this way, Islamic education is designed to 'fortify' Palestinian society; that is to say, not only against physical dangers, as embodied by the Israeli occupation, but also the potentially 'pernicious' cognitive influence of certain outside forces (Hroub 2000, p. 239).

Education and *da'wa* are the primary means used to disseminate these values. Indeed, it was an increase in education and literacy during the nineteenth and twentieth centuries that allowed more people direct access to the text of *The Qur'an* – which had hitherto been the domain of the *ulema* and official religious establishments – and, therefore, the ability to interpret its words for themselves. This, in turn, led to the formation of *tajdid* (renewalist) and *islah* (reformist) movements, such as Hamas, challenging the interpretations of the traditional *ulema* who have accorded religious legitimacy to oppressive regimes (Kadayifici-Orellana 2007, p. 98).

Mosques

Mosques are key institutions at the forefront of spiritual education concerned with instilling and disseminating Islamic values and good behaviour. According to Iyad Barghouti (personal interview 2010), Director of the Ramallah Centre for Human Rights, the importance of the mosque is such that people essentially receive a moral lecture five times a day which places them within a "psychological situation where it seems that God is talking to them".

Mosques, in addition, are not only places of worship but also provide a vital social space in the Palestinian Territories where it is possible to discuss social, economic and political matters in a public forum (Roy 2007, pp. 180–186). Mosques are areas for networking and building rapport with the community through familiarity and public demonstrations of piety which, in turn, help accrue social and symbolic capital with potential political dividends. Writing within the Egyptian and Jordanian contexts, for instance, Janine Clark (2004, p. 31) argues that Islamic social welfare is less about ideology or welfare than about networking. Mosques are also sites of political mobilisation and recruitment for Hamas (Farsoun and Arruri 2006, p. 218) which, until recently, had remained relatively unmolested by Israeli security forces (in recent years, however, Israel has begun to target mosques directly, as evidenced in the 2008/2009 Israeli attack on Gaza).

Mosques are centres of practical education as well. During the first intifada, for instance, mosques were used as a forum for public education (Hroub 2000, p. 238). Indeed, many mosques today have kindergartens attached to them. It is difficult to understate the influence of mosques because, according to Barghouti (personal interview 2010), mosques are one of the two most important institutions in the Palestinian Territories (the other being the security forces). Sympathetic imams are also able to issue *fatwa*s supporting Hamas, thereby providing religious legitimacy for its actions.

International education

The role of education, and especially external education, figures prominently in the advent and rise of Hamas as a social movement. Many young students completed their studies overseas where they were exposed to new texts and philosophies, such as those espoused by Hassan al-Banna and Sayyid Qutb. Many Hamas and, indeed, Fatah leaders were involved with the Muslim Brotherhood in Egypt, but also elsewhere such as the Gulf States. Similarly, the opening of universities in the Palestinian Territories during the 1970s provided sites for politicisation and political activism (Rosenfeld 2004, p. 126). Student politics, in effect, are used as 'proxy' battles between rival factions and treated as sites of recruitment.

It seems evident that many of Hamas' forbears, founders and present luminaries became politically active as students, especially in Egypt, where students were exposed to the ideology of *al-Ikhwan al-Muslimun*, and oil-rich Kuwait from which millions of dollars of remittances were sent to the Palestinian Territories by migrant workers. Interestingly, it seems that as students overseas, Palestinian Islamists were also concerned with rectifying Arab and Muslim misconceptions of the Palestinian plight. Mariam Salah (personal interview 2010), for instance, worked in Saudi Arabia to spread public awareness of the question of Palestine because "There was a negative stereotypical image about the Palestinians. People used to believe that the Palestinians sold their lands and that we – the refugees – and our parents sold our lands and left." In a similar

190   *Jihad, education and Islamic values*

manner, Bashir (personal interview, Damascus, May 2010) describes some of his student activities in Damascus, which included holding "Festivals, demonstrations, and marches inside the campus and even outside. Some other activities like handing out papers/publications, holding lectures about the Palestinian issues and about some other Islamic issues."

On a more material level, Palestinian Islamist students set up a variety of student political parties and social networks providing political and financial support to the Islamic movement in the Palestinian Territories. Indeed, prior to the expulsion of Palestinian workers from Kuwait in the aftermath of the 1991 Gulf War, the present Head of the Political Bureau, Khalid Mishal, set up an extensive array of networks financing Islamist activities in the Palestinian Territories (Tamimi 2007, pp. 29–34).

But not all of these activities and youth work are strictly political. Hafez Shaheen (personal interview 2010) illustrates this intertwining of political, religious and social dimensions by describing some of the activities that he participated in while he was studying his undergraduate degree in engineering. While serving as a student representative on the Engineering Faculty Committee at the University of Jordan, Shaheen (ibid.) recounts that:

> Some of the activities, for example, were involved in having journeys. We did arrange to go to Mecca for having *umrah* [pilgrimage outside of *hajj*] and visiting Mecca, the Kabaa. We did have activities like camping during the semester break, two weeks camp and camping activities. We did have like supporting the weak students by arranging educational workshops and such things.... Such activities, in addition, of course, to the political activities where there is, for example, a hot issue and needs to make ... a *mudara* [strike], where there are people walking and demonstrating, we were involved, we were representing. And of course the discussions with the deans and the university presidents about such things.... So it has both political and social dimensions.

In similar vein, Bashir (personal interview 2010) depicts part of his role as "Working with students as a kind of guidance for these students. A moral and behavioural guidance. A political guidance." To this end, "*The Qur'an* and the *sunnah* have a *practical* value in addition to a spiritual one; understanding them is the key to understanding the rest of the world" (Hoigilt 2010, p. 37).

Education in the Palestinian territories

While all schools in the Palestinian Territories are bound to the national curriculum, whether these are public, private or UNRWA schools for refugees, Islamic private schools tend to devote extra time to studying *The Qur'an* and *sunnah*. According to Hoigilt (2010, p. 37), the idea is to "instil positive values in the student and prevent bad habits from developing" with the intent of "highlighting religion as the safeguard of a morally superior identity".

Jihad, education and Islamic values   191

Within the West Bank around 10 per cent of schools are private, the majority of which are Islamic (in contrast to 81 per cent of government schools and 9 per cent run by the UNRWA) (ibid., p. 15). By 2000 in the Gaza Strip, however, around 65 per cent of educational institutions (which apparently includes nurseries and kindergartens) were deemed to be of an 'Islamic' hue (Roy 2007, pp. 299–300). Whereas the schools in the West Bank purported to be apolitical, schools in the Gaza Strip tended to align themselves with Hamas' theme of resistance (Hoigilt 2010, p. 28). This is due to the divergent historical, economic and social experiences of the West Bank and Gaza Strip which has concomitantly rendered the latter more socially conservative yet politically radical. Two-thirds of the Gaza Strip, for instance, are refugees or their descendants who fled or were expelled from what is today recognised as Israel. In addition, the Gaza Strip has been largely isolated from the rest of the world since the early 1990s which has increased its conservatism and religiosity in comparison to the West Bank.

This division has, in turn, led to diverging political, social and cultural norms. According to Sameer Abu Aisha (personal interview 2010), Gaza has not been "open enough to the world for a long, long, time and whoever, like me and others in the West Bank were more open to the world and whoever gets the education abroad, of course, that helped him in shaping his ideas". In similar vein, one liberal Hamas activist in Nablus opined,

> Gaza is generally more conservative than the West Bank. When I speak to a Fatah activist from Gaza, it is like speaking to a Hamas activist in the West Bank – I am more in tune with the Fatah man in Gaza than the Hamas sympathiser in Gaza.
>
> (cited in Hoigilt 2010, p. 28)

As discussed in the previous chapter with regard to social institutions, there is no one homogeneous ideology within the Islamic movement in the Palestinian Territories and Hamas but rather a variety of competing and intertwining interpretations framed within a similar worldview. This heterogeneity is similarly reflected throughout Islamic schools and educational institutions. As a result, some institutions are much stricter in their interpretation, dissemination and application of *The Qur'an* and *sunnah* than others.

Islamic schools are not-for-profit institutions run by *zakat* committees, private sector charitable institutions and individual donors. As with other Islamic social institutions, Islamic schools place a particular emphasis on the education and care of orphans. Islamic education is segregated along gender lines after year four but rather than being a strictly repressive policy, as it would be generally portrayed in the West (despite the existence of ample amounts of gender-specific private schools within the developed world), this segregation has, on the contrary, promoted women's education in many cases. Sara Roy (2011, p. 171), for instance, reports that it was the policy of gender segregation at the Islamic University in Gaza (IUG) which allowed many women from conservative families

192 *Jihad, education and Islamic values*

to pursue a tertiary education. As former Finance Minister Omar Abdul-Razeq (personal interview 2010) points out, "Our religion says, very direct, that education is a right for both men and women, males and females, and the environment has to provide it". Indicatively, these schools do not seek to promote new or radical values but rather tap into existing values and ideas which already resonate with large segments of Palestinian society (Hoigilt 2010, p. 35).

Established in 1978, the Islamic University of Gaza is, perhaps, the most influential institution associated with Hamas in terms of social penetration in the Palestinian Territories. Early on, in particular, the IUG educated a new generation of Muslim leaders, including preachers for local mosques in the West Bank and Gaza, thereby extending the influence of the Islamic movement. Indeed, Ismail Haniyeh, the current de facto Prime Minister of the government in Gaza, was appointed Dean of IUG in 1993 before becoming an assistant to Hamas founder Sheikh Ahmed Yassin in 1997. In this way, according to Roy (2011, p. 76), "the Islamic movement was able to reach further and deeper into the Palestinian community by providing needed services in employment and training as well as education". Currently, there are over 20,000 students enrolled in the Islamic University.

The Islamic University fulfils ideological, social and practical roles in the Gaza Strip (Hoigilt 2010, p. 35). According to Michael Irving Jensen (2006, p. 73), "The general aim of the IUG is, through education, to lead the Palestinian youth out of the crisis that both Islam and Palestinian society are facing – by revitalising Islam and by recreating a space for Islamic cultural and political autonomy." Jacob Hoigilt (2010, p. 41), furthermore, argues that Islamic schools, and by extension IUG, "were conceived as religiously conditioned answers to a difficult education situation, as a means to strengthen civil society". To this end, Irving Jensen (2009, p. 112) continues, the teaching he witnessed at Islamic University "consisted principally in raising students' awareness of the difference between the Islamic world and the West". Through these activities it is possible to discern Islamist resistance aimed at cultural, political and individual autonomy.

However, there is undoubtedly a strong focus on acquiring practical skills and knowledge within Islamic education. Palestinian Islamists have a tendency to focus on education concerned with the temporal world, including medicine, education, engineering and the 'hard' sciences. As with the sports clubs discussed by Irving Jensen in Chapter 5, enrolments in Islamic schools and the IUG are driven by more than spiritual and behavioural guidance. Islamic schools and the IUG possess strong reputations for quality and this is one of the primary reasons, among parents and university students alike, for enrolment in these institutions (Hoigilt 2010, p. 22; Irving Jensen 2006, pp. 118–121). Nasser al-Shaer (personal interview 2010), former Deputy Prime Minister and former Minister of Education, bemoans the state of higher education in the Palestinian Territories citing unprofessionalism, laziness, apathy, mediocrity, nepotism and problems of etiquette among the PA-run institutions in the West Bank. Islamic institutions, in contrast, possess reputations for discipline, efficiency, transparency and quality.

This reputation extends throughout the Islamist student body as well and was repeatedly mentioned to me throughout the course of my own fieldwork. To this end, Hamas focuses on recruiting the best and brightest of students, and the high number of doctors, engineers, academics and teachers within the ranks of its founders, as well as the political representatives of the Change and Reform list, suggests that it has been quite successful in this endeavour. During my own discussions with academics in the West Bank, the general consensus among academics seemed to be that Islamist students are much more serious vis-à-vis their studies than their nationalist counterparts.

Reputation is an important social and political marker within Palestinian society which facilitates the accumulation of social and political capital. Hence, at IUG, "the students through the study of *Islam(icum)* gained 'cultural capital' – in a Bourdieuan sense – as they learned the cultural codes of Islam, and how to form their world view based on this knowledge" (Irving Jensen 2006, p. 73). This cultural capital has helped ensure the success of Islamic charitable organisations and their political counterparts.

Conclusions

Islam forms the bedrock of Hamas' programme of resistance in the Palestinian Territories, whether it be political, charitable or armed. But Islam is more than a call to resistance; Islam serves as a prism through which many Palestinians perceive, interpret and behave in the temporal world. As such, the Islamism of Hamas and the public piety of its leading figures resonate with large segments of the population. As Khalid (survey 2010), a 22-year-old Hamas supporter studying media and political science, points out, Hamas "emphasises the basic constants of historical Palestine, taking into consideration an Islamic reference, as Islam is a fundamental ingredient of these lands".

Hamas' ultimate goal entailing the creation of a virtuous Islamic society is based on the idea of individual renewal through an enhanced knowledge and practice of Islamic precepts. As such, Palestinian Islamists have been highly active throughout the community, both in terms of education and charitable endeavours. This education not only serves to equip Palestinian society with practical skills applicable to the temporal world, but also a spiritual education aimed at being a better person, in the eyes of God as well as the wider society; that is to say, the greater jihad or struggle within. Education seeks to promote traditional Islamic reference points which resonate with large segments of the wider population.

This Islamic reference point however, like all symbols and ideologies, is open to contestation and varying interpretations. These interpretations are not static but rather fluid, dynamic and evolutionary. In this respect, Hamas is a *tajdid* organisation which believes in "restoring the society from within via education, combining scientific and technological advances of the West with traditional Islamic values and principles" (Kadayfici-Orellana 2007, p. 67). As such, Hamas is a distinctly modernist phenomenon whose base is firmly

194 *Jihad, education and Islamic values*

situated in an urbanised lower-middle class despite being of an Islamic hue (Gunning 2007, p. 148).

As long-time political exile Rachid Ghannouchi (1993, p. 39), whose Islamist *al-Nahda* party emerged victorious in Tunisia's first post-revolutionary elections in 2011, points out:

> We want modernity, contrary to the ridiculous allegations made by those adversely inclined against political Islam, but only insofar as it means absolute intellectual freedom; scientific and technological progress; and promotion of democratic ideals. However, we will accept modernity only when we dictate the pace with which it penetrates our society and not when French, British, or American interpretations impose it upon us. It is our right to adopt modernity through methods equitable to our people and their heritage.

Kadayifici-Orellana (2007, p. 68) describes Hamas' approach as "Islamicized modernity" while noting that the movement "argues in favor of democracy, and even a free-market economy, as long as fair distribution is guaranteed".

In this regard, Islamism need not be strictly conceived of as reactionary, but rather as an authentic, endogenous attempt to modernise Muslim majority societies where other imported ideologies have failed. Hamas is part of a regional wave of popular resistance against an established order which adheres to a different set of reference points than everyday members of the wider society. The importance of Islam in the Palestinian Territories long precedes Hamas and will continue even if it disappears. An acceptance of the ongoing resilience of this strain of Islamic politics is essential if there is to be peace in Palestine and Israel.

Notes

1 Parts of this chapter are drawn from Dunning, T. 2015. 'Islam and Resistance: Hamas, Ideology and Islamic Values in Palestine'. *Critical Studies on Terrorism* 8(2): 284–305. Reproduced with permission of Taylor and Francis.
2 Not all Palestinians are Muslims of course. Bethlehem, Ramallah and Jerusalem, for instance, possess sizeable Christian minorities.
3 Specifically, the Prophet was recast as Mahound, the Prince of Darkness. Dante's description of the Prophet Mohammed in *The Divine Comedy: Inferno* located Mohammed in the Eighth Circle of Hell. Voltaire's *Le Fanatisme Ou Mahomet le Prophète*, (*Fanaticism or the Prophet Mohammed*) similarly depicts the Prophet as a savage, bloodthirsty and treacherous despot. A more modern instance depicting the Prophet Mohammed in a derogatory light is the Danish cartoon controversy in 2006, one of which pictured the Prophet hiding a bomb in his turban, resulting in widespread anti-Western violence across the Muslim world. Similarly, a 2012 film made in the US characterised the Prophet Mohammed as a child molester and Islam as a cancer, which, in turn, led to attacks on US embassies throughout the Muslim world, including the storming of embassies in Benghazi, Libya and Yemen. The US ambassador to Libya, Chris Stevens, was killed in the assault in Benghazi.

References

Abu Amr, Z. 1993. 'Hamas: A Historical and Political Background'. *Journal of Palestine Studies* 22(4): 5–19.

Abu Marzouq, M. 2006. 'What Hamas is Seeking'. *Washington Post*, 31 January.

Abu Shannab, I. 2003. 'The Hamas Strategy'. *Toronto Star*, 29 June.

Agha, H. and Malley, R. 2008. 'Into the Lion's Den'. *New York Review of Books* 55(7), 1 May.

al-Ghannouchi, R. 1993. 'The Battle against Islam'. *Middle East Affairs Journal* 1(2): 34–42.

Amayreh, K. 2010. *Islamist Women's Activism in the Occupied Territories: Interviews with Palestinian Islamist Women's Leaders on Women's Activism in Hamas*. Beirut: Conflicts Forum.

Araj, B. and Brym, R. 2010. 'Opportunity, Culture and Agency: Influence on Fatah and Hamas Strategic Action During the Second Intifada'. *International Sociology* 25(6): 842–868.

Barghouti, I. 2007. *Religion and State in Palestine*. Ramallah: Ramallah Centre for Human Rights.

Bhasin, T. and Hallward, M. 2013. 'Hamas as a Political Party: Democratization in the Palestinian Territories'. *Terrorism and Political Violence* 25(1): 75–93.

Brown, N. 2012. *Gaza Five Years On: Hamas Settles In*. Washington, DC: Carnegie Endowment for International Peace.

Brym, R. and Araj, B. 2006. 'Suicide Bombing as Strategy and Interaction: The Case of the Second Intifada'. *Social Forces* 84(4): 1969–1986.

Burgat, F. 2003. *Face to Face with Political Islam*. London: I.B. Tauris.

Burke, E. (ed.). 1993. *Struggle and Survival in the Modern Middle East*. Berkeley: University of California Press.

Carter, J. 2006. *Palestine: Peace not Apartheid*. New York: Simon & Schuster.

Chehab, Z. 2007. *Inside Hamas: The Untold Story of Militants, Martyrs and Spies*. London: Nation Books.

Clark, J. 2004. *Islam, Charity and Activism: Middle Class Networks and Social Welfare in Egypt, Jordan and Yemen*. Indianapolis: Indiana University Press.

Crooke, A. 2009. *Resistance: The Essence of Islamist Revolution*. New York: Pluto Press.

El-Tigani, M. 1998. 'Islamic Law, Human Rights and International Law: A Critique of Mahmoud Tab and an-Naim, Part II'. *Islamica: The Journal of Islamic Society of the London School of Economics in Association with the Muslim Academic Trust* 2(4): 62–71.

Filui, J-P. 2012. 'The Origins of Hamas: Militant Legacy or Israeli Tool?' *Journal of Palestine Studies* 41(2): 54–70.

Gunning, J. 2007. *Hamas in Politics: Democracy, Religion, Violence*. London: Hurst & Co.

Hamdan, U. 2011. 'Hamas "Foreign Minister" Usama Hamdan Talks about National Reconciliation, Arafat, Reform and Hamas's Presence in Lebanon'. *Journal of Palestine Studies* 40(3): 59–73.

Hobsbawm, E. and Ranger, T. (eds). 1992. *The Invention of Tradition*. Cambridge: Cambridge University Press.

Hoigilt, J. 2010. *Raising Extremists? Islamism and Education in the Palestinian Territories*. Oslo: FAFO.

Holt, M. 1997. 'Palestinian Women and the Contemporary Islamist Movement'. *Encounters* 3(1): 64–75.

196 *Jihad, education and Islamic values*

Hroub, K. 2000. *Hamas: Political Thought and Practice*. Washington, DC: Institute of Palestine Studies.

ICG. 2011. *Radical Islam in Gaza*. Brussels: ICG.

Irving Jensen, M. 1998. 'Islamism and Civil Society in the Gaza Strip'. In *Islamic Fundamentalism: Myths and Realities*, edited by Ahmed S. Moussalli. Ithica, NY: Ithica Press.

Irving Jensen, M. 2006. 'Re-Islamising Palestinian Society "From Below": Hamas and Higher Education in Gaza'. *Holy Lands Studies* 5(1): 57–74.

Irving Jensen, M. 2009. *The Political Ideology of Hamas: A Grassroots Perspective*. London: I.B. Tauris.

Jad, I. 2005. 'Between Religion and Secularism: Islamist Women of Hamas'. In *On Shifting Ground: Muslim Women in the Global Era*, edited by F. Nouraie-Simone. New York: Feminist Press at the City University of New York.

Juergensmeyer, M. 2008. *Global Rebellion: Religious Challenges to the Secular State from Christian Militias to al Qaeda*. Berkeley: University of California Press.

Kadayifici-Orellana, S.A. 2007. *Standing on an Isthmus: Islamic Narratives of War and Peace in Palestinian Territories*. New York: Lexington Books.

Kamali, M. 1991. *Principles of Islamic Jurisprudence*. Cambridge: Islamic Texts Society.

Kepel, G. 2002. *Jihad: The Trail of Political Islam*. London: I.B. Tauris.

Khalidi, T. 2008. 'Introduction'. In *The Qur'an*, translated and edited by T. Khalidi. London: Penguin Books.

Klein, M. 1996. 'Competing Brothers: The Web of Hamas–PLO Relations'. *Terrorism and Political Violence* 8(2): 111–132.

Klein, M. 2007. 'Hamas in Power'. *The Middle East Journal* 61(3): 442–459.

Klein, M. 2009. 'Against the Consensus: Oppositionist Voices in Hamas'. *Middle Eastern Studies* 45(6): 881–892.

Knudsen, A. 2005. 'Crescent and Sword: the Hamas Enigma'. *Third World Quarterly* 26(8): 1372–1388.

Kurzman, C. 2002. 'The Modern Islamist Movement'. In *Modernist Islam, 1840–1940: A Sourcebook*, edited by C. Kurzman. Oxford: Oxford University Press.

Malka, H. 2007. 'Hamas: Resistance and Transformation of Palestinian Society'. In *Understanding Islamic Charities*, edited by J. Alterman and. K. von Hippel. Washington, DC: Centre for Strategic and International Studies.

Mayer, T. 1982. 'The Military Force of Islam: The Society of the Muslim Brethren and the Palestine Question, 1945–1948'. In *Zionism and Arabism in Israel and Palestine*, edited by E. Kedourie and. S. Haim. London: Frank Cass.

McCarthy, R. 2008. 'We Can Accept Israel as Neighbour, Says Hamas'. *Guardian* (UK), 21 April.

Milton-Edwards, B. 2000. *Contemporary Politics in the Middle East*. Cambridge: Polity Press.

Mishal, K. 2006. 'We Will Not Sell our People and Principles for Foreign Aid'. *Guardian* (UK), 31 January.

Mishal, S. and Sela, A. 2000. The Palestinian Hamas: Vision, Violence and Coexistence. New York: Columbia University Press.

O'Leary, B. and Tirman, J. 2007. 'Thinking about Durable Political Violence'. In Terror, Insurgency and the State: Ending Protracted Conflicts, edited by M. Heiberg, B. O'Leary and J. Tirman. Philadelphia: University of Pennsylvania Press.

Pappé, I. 2006. *A History of Modern Palestine: One Land, Two Peoples*. Cambridge: Cambridge University Press.

Ramadan, T. 2005. 'Call for a Moratorium on Hudud'. Available at http://tariqramadan. com/arabic/2005/04/05/dialogue-with-tariq-ramadan-about-the-call-for-moratorium-on-hudud/ (accessed 11 February 2014).

Rosenfeld, M. 2004. *Confronting the Occupation: Work, Education, and Political Activism of Palestinian Families in a Refugee Camp.* Stanford, CA: Stanford University Press.

Roy, S. 2007. *Failing Peace: Gaza and the Palestinian-Israeli Conflict.* London: Pluto Press.

Roy, S. 2011. *Hamas and Civil Society in Gaza: Engaging the Islamic Social Sector.* Princeton, NJ: Princeton University Press.

Schleifer, A. 1993. 'Izz al-Din al-Qassam: Preacher and Mujahid'. In *Struggle and Survival in the Middle East,* edited by E. Burke III. Berkeley: University of California Press.

Tamimi, A. 2007. *Hamas: A History from Within.* Northampton, MA: Olive Branch Press.

Tibi, B. 1996. 'War and Peace in Islam'. In *The Ethics of War and Peace: Religious and Secular Perspectives,* edited by T. Nardin. Princeton, NJ: Princeton University Press.

Tuastad, D. 2009. *Primary Solidarity: A Comparative Study on the Role of Kinship in Palestinian Local Politics.* PhD thesis. Oslo: University of Oslo.

Wahiduddin Khan, M. 1998. 'Non-violence and Islam'. In *Forum on Islam and Peace in the 21st Century.* Washington, DC: American University.

Weymouth, L. 2006. 'We Do Not Wish to Throw Them Into the Sea'. Interview with Ismail Haniyeh. *Washington Post,* 26 February.

Yousef, A. 2006. 'Pause for Peace'. *New York Times,* 1 November.

Yousef, A. 2007. 'Open Letter to the Secretary of State'. *New York Times,* 10 December.

Zuhur, S. 2010. *Hamas and Israel: Conflicting Strategies of Group-based Politics.* Carlisle, PA: Strategic Studies Institute.

Interviews and surveys

Abdul-Razeq, Omar, former Islamist Finance Minister, elected MP and Professor of Economics at an-Najah National University, Ramallah, February 2010.

Abrar, a 22-year-old Hamas supporter, anonymous survey, Birzeit University, Birzeit, April 2010.

Abu Aisha, Sameer, former Minister of Planning for the Tenth 'Hamas' Administration, and Professor of Engineering at an-Najah National University, Nablus, March 2010.

Abu Marzouq, Mousa, Deputy Head of the Hamas Political Bureau, US Specially Designated Global Terrorist and Doctor of Engineering, Damascus, May 2010.

Abu Sway, Mustafa, Professor of *Sharia* Law at al-Quds University, Abu Dis, January 2010.

Ala' al-Din, a high-ranking PLC Deputy representing Change and Reform, the West Bank, May 2010.

al-Ramahi, M., Islamist Secretary General of Parliament, elected PLC Deputy and anaesthetist, Ramallah, January 2010.

al-Shaer, N., former Deputy Prime Minister and Minister of Education for the Tenth 'Hamas' Administration, Professor of *Sharia* Law at an-Najah National University, Nablus, February 2010.

Barghouti, I., Director of the Ramallah Centre for Human Rights and Professor of Political Sociology, Ramallah, October 2010.

198 *Jihad, education and Islamic values*

Bashir, a 44-year-old Hamas member and youth activities officer, Damascus, May 2010.

Dhakiy, a Fatah activist studying sport, anonymous survey, an-Najah National University, March 2010.

Dweik, A., Islamist Speaker of Parliament, elected PLC Deputy and Professor of Urban Geography, Hebron, May 2010.

Fatima, an 18-year-old Hamas supporter, anonymous survey, an-Najah National University, Nablus, March 2010.

Hammoudeh, S., Professor of Political Science at Birzeit University, Birzeit, November 2009.

Jibril, PLC Deputy and former member of the Hamas planning committee for the second intifada, the West Bank, February 2010.

Khalid, a 22-year-old member of Hamas studying media and political science, anonymous survey, Birzeit University, Birzeit, April 2010.

Khatib, a 20-year-old Fatah supporter studying political science, anonymous survey, Birzeit University, Birzeit, April 2010.

Manar, Mishal, Shaul, Palestinian-Israeli Professor of Political Science at Tel Aviv University, Tel Aviv, November 2009.

Mu'minah, a 20-year-old Hamas supporter, anonymous survey, Birzeit University, Birzeit, April 2010.

Nasir al-Din, an unaffiliated 20-year-old studying political science, anonymous survey, al-Quds University, Abu Dis, May 2010.

Nasser, William, a former security adviser for Yasser Arafat and lecturer in political and cultural studies at Birzeit University, Birzeit, April 2010.

Nidal, a 22-year-old Hamas supporter, anonymous survey, Birzeit University, Birzeit, April 2010.

Rashid, a 22-year-old Hamas supporter studying media, anonymous survey, Birzeit University, Birzeit, April 2010.

Salah, Mariam, former Islamist Minister for Women's Affairs, elected PLC Deputy, and Professor of *Sharia* Law at al-Quds University, Ramallah, May 2010.

Shaheen, Hafez, Deputy Mayor of Nablus for Planning and Technical Affairs, local councillor for Change and Reform, and Professor of Engineering at an-Najah National University, Nablus, March/April 2010.

Yasmin, a 20-year-old Hamas supporter studying information technology at Birzeit University, anonymous survey, Birzeit, April 2010.

Zahrah, an unaffiliated 20-year-old studying media, anonymous survey, an-Najah National University, Nablus, March 2010.

Conclusion

Revolution, counter-revolution and war

Hamas' polysemic interpretations and reinterpretations of the twin concepts of resistance and jihad are the watchwords which inform, legitimise and guide the actions of the many overlapping and evolving identities which comprise the movement in Occupied Palestinian Territories. Resistance and jihad, in essence, are ambiguous terms which are conceptualised and employed according to practicality, circumstance, opportunity and/or exigency. As Beverley Milton-Edwards (1996, pp. 192–193) observes,

> Hamas' call to jihad is also cast in nationalist hues and is customised to the specificity of the Palestinian milieu. Hamas writing on the subject then reveals a view of jihad that is particularly Palestinian ... Hamas often presents a vague concept of jihad that means many things, from a war against the enemy fought through armed struggle to the notion of jihad as striving and individual contribution through areas like education, art or literature. Thus jihad becomes all things to all people.

Similarly, the concept of resistance extends far beyond the one-dimensional fixation on militancy which tends to dominate mainstream Western analyses of not only Hamas, but also Islamism, Islam and sub-state activism in general. Hamas resistance includes armed, symbolic, political, social and ideational aspects, all of which are predicated on the notion of jihad or striving in the name of God. In brief, according to Khaled Hroub (2000, p. 239), Hamas has "combined Islamic socio-instructional discourse with the discourse of nationalist resistance". Jihad is thus used to articulate a predominantly nationalist agenda centred on self-determination rather than eschatological goals. Khalid Mishal, Head of the Hamas Political Bureau, further demonstrated the flexibility of these concepts in December 2011 when he announced a (temporary) cessation of armed attacks in favour of *muqawama al-shabiye* (popular resistance) (Levy 2012; Daraghmeh 2011).

While the ambiguity of such terms may be considered problematic given their centrality to Hamas' discourse, these polysemic conceptions of resistance and jihad have allowed the movement to be politically pragmatic in temporal, real world terms, yet ostensibly remain true to its ideological convictions. On the one

200   *Conclusion*

hand, this has allowed the movement the flexibility to function as an effective, pragmatic and adaptable political entity, while, on the other, it has allowed the movement to remain intellectually coherent and unified as a mass socio-political actor. Hamas' ability to reconceptualise and then practically apply these varying conceptions of jihad and resistance – sometimes in seeming opposition to certain aspects of its core ideological tenets – demonstrates that the movement is not an adherent to existential violence as posited by many of its detractors.

In effect, my analysis has exposed some of the ideological, political and religious prejudices which inform many of the dominant representations and misrepresentations of Hamas. Specifically, this project has highlighted the West's politically driven application of the pejorative 'terrorist' label. Indeed, as George Orwell (1945, p. 51) once pointed out, "Actions are held to be good or bad, not on their own merits, but according to who does them." Often, in brief, the 'terrorist' appellation is not applied on the basis of the empirical *actions* of an organisation or individual but rather according to *who* engages in these activities. In the case of Hamas, for instance, the 'terrorist' label has been extended to the provision of social services, including caring for orphans and bereaved families who have lost loved ones in the conflict, among others.

Importantly, this project makes a significant contribution to the field insofar as it incorporates substantial evidence derived from direct primary research with the 'terrorist' organisation under investigation – an approach so often lacking in terrorism studies – while situating the movement within its wider social, cultural and political environments. Given that terrorism is fundamentally driven by political rather than by military phenomena, it is important to engage directly with the individuals involved in order to better understand both the motivations of the individuals involved and the underlying causes of conflict. This, in turn, will lead to an improved understanding of the conflict and better informed policy decisions based on empirical evidence rather than on ideological proclivities and/or hubristic Orientalist stereotypes.

My analysis of Hamas' ability to evolve thus helps open up new space for dialogue, negotiations and compromise, which is ultimately aimed at peaceful coexistence between Hamas and Israel. This is important because, as the International Crisis Group (ICG 2012a, p. 33) points out,

> the neglect suffered by certain constituencies [on the Palestinian side] has undermined the [peace] process. Islamists, the diaspora and even Palestinian citizens of Israel have had no meaningful voice in the proceedings. Insofar as those groups collectively represent the majority of the Palestinian people, it is hard to imagine how a process that ignores their interests might succeed.

In short, there is a need to shift the terms of negotiations to include *all* of the central actors to the conflict, however negative their ideologies may be regarded by other antagonists.

Hamas' empirical pragmatism diverges from the dominant Orientalist, security-orientated and mainstream Western approaches to Islamism, especially

Conclusion 201

within the context of the 'war on terror' and the ensuing rise of ISIS and its affiliates. These approaches are often essentialist, and depict Hamas and other Islamist movements as being driven by eschatological or millenarian objectives arguing that the movements are inherently unamenable to compromise. While this may seem academic in exercise, the combined application of the Orientalist and terrorist labels – on the one hand positing an immutable worldview based on the seventh century, while on the other arguing that Hamas engages in irrational, religiously based violence – has profound real world consequences because it is deeply limiting in terms of constructive engagement and, ultimately, achieving peaceful reconciliation between the warring parties. These essentialist analyses give rise to a tautology: the movement is, a priori, defined as inimical to compromise; thus a policy maker faced with such an implacable adversary driven by existential violence has little option but force – an option that has been used far too frequently when dealing with Islamist movements rebelling against the status quo. Indeed, Francois Burgat (2004) contends that these approaches are aimed at the 'criminalisation' of resistance to the established international order.

In this regard, Israeli PM Benjamin Netanyahu's 2014 assertion that "ISIS is Hamas and Hamas is ISIS" is not only disingenuous given the Israeli government's ongoing negotiations with Hamas, but dangerous (Brown 2014). Even the US State Department quickly rejected Netanyahu's assertions comparing Hamas to ISIS (Wilner 2014). Among ISIS' stated goals is the erasure the borders set by the post-First World War dissolution of the Ottoman Empire. At the time of writing (May 2015), ISIS had all but erased the borders between Syria and Iraq. Jihadi movements in Libya, the Sinai Peninsula, Somalia and Boko Haram in Nigeria, among others, have pledged allegiance to ISIS. Hamas' pragmatic localised political goals are in marked contrast to movements such as ISIS which portray themselves as undertaking some kind of eschatological conflict. Netanyahu's hyperbole conflating Hamas with ISIS renders the possibility of compromise all the more difficult.

Contrary to accusations of existential violence carried out against Israel, violence instigated by Hamas does not occur in a vacuum but, rather, is predominantly a reaction against foreign occupation. The omnipresence of the occupation and its effects extend well beyond explicit outbreaks of violence, including feelings of humiliation, frustration and despair that simmer below the surface; all of which can lead to resistance, violent or otherwise. According to James Scott (1990, pp. 111–112), resistance and humiliation are closely intertwined; in his words,

> Just as a traditional Marxist analysis might be said to privilege the appropriation of surplus value as the social site of exploitation and resistance, our analysis here privileges the social experience of indignities, control submission, summation, forced deference, and punishment. The very process of appropriation, however, unavoidably entails systematic social relations of subordination that impose indignities of one kind or another on the weak. These indignities are the seedbed of the anger, indignation, frustration, and

202   Conclusion

swallowed bile that nurture the hidden transcript.... Resistance, then, originates not simply from material appropriation but from the pattern of personal humiliations that characterize exploitation.

As Jereon Gunning (2007, p. 15) also points out, many analyses understate the
role of the state or status quo power in fomenting political violence. The claims
of Syrian President Bashar al-Assad and the late Muammar Gaddafi of Libya,
for instance, to be fighting al-Qa'ida with regard to their respective uprisings
turned into self-fulfilling prophecies as the regimes responded to rebellion with
violent crackdowns. These crackdowns led to radicalisation and militancy. Large
chunks of Syria are now held by the al-Qa'ida affiliate, al-Nusra Front, and ISIS,
the radical outgrowth of al-Qa'ida in Iraq. In Libya, Islamist groups backed by
NATO airstrikes were instrumental in overthrowing the Gaddafi regime. The
security vacuum of the post-Gaddafi era has been marked by ongoing chaos and
violence between rival militias, including ISIS and al-Qa'ida affiliates. Indeed,
in February and April 2015, an Islamist group pledging itself to ISIS executed
dozens of Christians in Libya (Kirkpatrick 2015).

The security vacuums that have enabled the rise of Islamist groups in Libya
and Iraq were created by Western intervention in Libya in 2012 under the guise
of the Responsibility to Protect doctrine that morphed into regime change, and
Iraq's putative breach of Security Council resolutions regarding (non-existent)
weapons of mass destruction in 2003. As Glenn Greenwald (2015) observes,
from Afghanistan to Iraq to Libya: "What we see here is what we've seen over
and over: the West's wars creating and empowering an endless supply of
enemies, which in turn justify endless war by the West." The chaos engulfing the
Middle East is by no means, of course, the sole responsibility of Western interventions; the absolutist, corrupt and venal regimes of the region have all made
major contributions. In Iraq, the discriminatory policies instituted by the Shi'a-
dominated government led by Nouri al-Malaki resulted in the impoverisation
and alienation of Iraqi Sunni Arabs (Cockburn 2014). This, in turn, provided
fertile recruiting ground for ISIS. In a striking resemblance to both the modus
operandi and eventual outcome in Afghanistan during the 1980s, the irresponsi-
ble arming and funding of unaccountable Islamist rebels by Saudi Arabia and the
Gulf states in Syria (with the acquiesce of the West and assistance of Turkey)
has facilitated the inexorable rise of the al-Nusra Front and ISIS, thereby providing a safe haven and training ground for a new generation of transnational
ostensibly eschatological jihadists.

Hamas, in contrast, engages predominantly in controlled violence based on
cost–benefit analyses employed according to circumstance, opportunity and exigency (Mishal and Sela 2000, pp. 19–82). It is clear, however, that political violence against Israel can also serve to boost a movement's popular legitimacy
within the context of the Palestinian polity because it has the potential to tap into
latent Palestinian values pertaining to resistance, self-sacrifice and *summud*
(steadfastness) in the face of oppression. According to Halim Rane (2009,
p. 123), armed resistance is viewed as an honourable path at the end of which

God has promised victory. Nevertheless, Hamas violence is not immutable, as demonstrated by its many ceasefires with Israel, but it is, rather, a means to an end. This, again, demonstrates that the movement is amenable to a negotiated solution to the ongoing conflict.

The 'Arab Spring' and war in Gaza

The salient role of armed resistance in Palestinian politics was further underscored following the November 2012 conflict between Hamas and Israel, during which Hamas fired rockets at Tel Aviv for the first time. A December 2012 poll by the Palestinian Centre for Policy and Survey Research found that the popularity of Gazan PM Ismail Haniyeh had risen to 48 per cent to overtake Palestinian President Mahmoud Abbas at 45 per cent – a rise of 8 per cent from the previous poll three months prior, and the highest level of support that Haniyeh had received since Hamas' election victory in 2006. Hamas' overall popularity likewise rose 7 per cent to 35 per cent, while Fatah's remained unchanged. The poll also found that positive evaluations of the Haniyeh government rose significantly, from 35 to 56 per cent over the same period. In short, armed resistance continues to be a source of domestic popular legitimacy for Hamas.

Crucial to Hamas' ethos of armed resistance, 81 per cent of respondents believed that Hamas won the war (PCPSR 2012). Indeed, according to the International Crisis Group (ICG 2012a, p. 3),

> Hamas – contrary to Israel's expectations, but consistent with past experience – would emerge the victor, not militarily certainly, but politically, having reaffirmed its staying power, attracted unprecedented international attention and yet again reduced President Abbas and the PA to passive, powerless bystanders. The public terms of the ceasefire, to an extent, confirmed this impression.

As a result of Hamas' perceived victory in the November 2012 conflict, the PCPSR (2012) found in December 2012 that 60 per cent of respondents believed that Hamas' approach based on resistance is the best way to end the occupation, whereas only 28 per cent endorsed Abbas' approach based on negotiations with Israel and international recognition. As one West Bank university student explained,

> Dealing softly with Israel produced nothing. What have we gotten after twenty years of negotiations? More settlements and more annexed Palestinian land, a Wall in the West Bank, an isolated Jerusalem and a division between the two main factions. Meanwhile missiles brought Israel to beg for a truce in a just a couple of days.
>
> (cited in ICG 2012a, p. 18)

Indicatively, the largest percentage of respondents (41%) believed that the key to ending the occupation lies in armed attacks against the Israeli army and settlements in the West Bank (PCPSR 2012).

204 *Conclusion*

In contrast to the 2008/2009 conflict, in addition, Hamas' international legitimacy was significantly boosted by the war. Not only did Hamas increase its legitimacy among the publics of the Middle East, but the Gaza Strip was visited by then Egyptian PM Hisham Kandil, Turkish Foreign Minister (now PM) Ahmet Davutoglu, the Secretary-General of the Arab League Nabil Elaraby, as well as 10 other Arab foreign ministers. These visits not only signified an increased regional acceptance of Hamas rule in the Gaza Strip, but also, at the time, they seemed to showcase a regional shift towards reformist Islamist politics as embodied by Islamist governments in Egypt, Tunisia, Turkey, Qatar and Gaza (Sherwood and Beaumont 2012). According to ICG (2012a, p. 6),

> Gaza in effect was treated as a state and Hamas officials as its statesmen.... At ceasefire talks in Cairo, Israeli officials were forced to hide their presence and President Abbas's envoy was relegated essentially to reporting, while Hamas leaders stood before the cameras with some of the most powerful regional heads of state.

Sheikh Hamad bin Khalifa al-Thani, then Emir of Qatar, also visited the Gaza Strip itself in October 2012 – the first head of state to do so (*al-Jazeera* 2012). Thus, the denouement of the November 2012 conflict further strengthens my arguments that armed resistance is a source of legitimacy for Hamas, both domestically and, in this case, internationally, as well as being perceived among the Palestinian population as instrumental in forcing Israeli concessions.

Finally, the Head of the Hamas Political Bureau, Khalid Mishal, entered the Gaza Strip for the first time in December 2012 with much fanfare to celebrate the twenty-fifth anniversary of Hamas' founding – a direct result of the November conflict and the ensuing ceasefire agreement stipulating a cessation of targeted assassinations in the Gaza Strip. Once more underscoring the saliency of armed resistance and the intertwining of politics and resistance, Mishal (cited in Erlanger 2012) told the fighters of Hamas, "to please keep your fingers on the trigger.... There is no politics without resistance."

The Arab popular uprisings from 2011 and subsequent ascension to power of Islamists in Egypt and Tunisia by electoral means were a lost opportunity to reassess attitudes towards Islamist politics in the Middle East. In many ways, Hamas election to the legislature in 2006 was an early if somewhat abortive precursor to these rebellions against the established 'secular' elite in favour of more grassroots, bottom-up movements which have existed for decades in opposition to autocratic regimes. The Arab uprisings, moreover, were a lost opportunity to bring Hamas in from the political cold. Conflict in Syria and the rise of Sunni Islamists in power, especially the Muslim Brotherhood in Egypt, had increasingly led Hamas to pull away from 'rejectionist' entities embodied by Syria and Iran and realign itself with 'moderate' Western allies such as Egypt, Turkey and Qatar. This, in turn, could have been used as a source of leverage in terms of convincing the movement to engage seriously in a realistic long-term peace deal with Israel.

Conclusion 205

The apparent success of mass popular movements and the enthusiasm with which Tunisians and then Egyptians seemed to approach democracy led a variety of commentators to all but write off al-Qa'ida-inspired jihadi entities (see e.g. Juergensmeyer 2011). With regard to the uprisings and the death of Bin Laden, Bergen (cited in Gartenstein-Ross and Vassefi 2012, p. 831) opined that it was "hard to think of anything that's more seismic in terms of undercutting al Qaeda's ideology" and these events were "the final bookends" of the war on terror. Fawaz Gerges (2012) similarly argued that

> The popular uprisings in Tunisia, Egypt, Libya, Syria, Yemen and Bahrain have not only shaken the foundation of the authoritarian order in the Middle East, but they have also hammered a deadly nail in the coffin of a terrorism narrative which has painted al Qaeda as the West's greatest threat.

It was not to be, however, as the seeming triumph of reformist political Islam was short-lived. Syria has been gripped by a civil war since 2012 which then spilled over into Iraq. By March 2015, al-Qa'ida's official affiliate, al-Nusra Front, held much of Idlib province, including the regional capital (Dearden 2015). In a similar vein, ISIS controls large swathes of both Syria and Iraq, including Iraq's second biggest city Mosul (although it should be noted that most of the territory controlled by ISIS is sparsely inhabited desert). Libya is in chaos and ruled by militias, including influential jihadis pledged to ISIS and al-Qa'ida. Al-Qa'ida in the Arabian Peninsula continued to hold territory in war-torn Yemen. ISIS and al-Qa'ida-affiliated jihadis, moreover, possess transnational intentions and advocate international political violence against Western targets. The attack on the Parisian satirical *Charlie Hebdo* in January 2015 leaving 12 media workers dead claimed by al-Qa'ida in the Arabian Peninsula, and the killing of four more civilians in a second attack on a kosher supermarket while the manhunt for the gunmen unfolded, was demonstrative of the revitalisation of transnational jihadi Islamism. Only Tunisia offers a glimmer of hope for the success of democratic governance and Islamist political participation due to the pragmatic compromises of the Islamist *al-Nahda* party.

The coup d'état against the elected Egyptian President Islamist Mohammed Morsi on 3 July 2013 was not only emblematic of the regress of reformist political Islam, but also the short-lived notion of civil rule based on free and fair elections. Counter-revolution in Egypt has led to a more repressive dictatorship than existed under Mubarak. Concomitantly, jihadi Islamism is once more on the rise with the dramatic ascendancy of ISIS, al-Qa'ida and their affiliates in Syria, Iraq, Libya, Sinai, Yemen, Somalia and Nigeria, among others. The deposal of Morsi and the kid gloves with which Western governments have treated the deprecations of coup leader Abdul Fatah al-Sisi has once again exposed the West's contingent support for democracy.

The West's hypocritical approach to the democratic process is something that the Muslim Middle East has witnessed time and time again. Is there any wonder that subversion of the democratic process has led to radicalisation? In Iran, the

206 *Conclusion*

CIA and MI-5 orchestrated coup against Mohammed Mosadegh and the reinstitution of the Shah in 1953 eventually led to the Islamic Revolution in 1979. In Algeria, the cancellation of the 1991 elections as le Front Islamique du Salut (Islamic Salvation Front) were on the cusp of victory led to the rise of radical militant Islamists and a decade of civil war. The attempted putsch against Hamas in June 2007 politically divided the West Bank and Gaza while strengthening hardliners in Hamas. Finally, the deposal of the Brotherhood led to the massacre of thousands, the imprisonment of tens of thousands and the imposition of the death penalty upon hundreds of opposition supporters, including Egypt's first freely elected President Mohammed Morsi. In this light, is there any wonder that jihadi Islam is experiencing a revival? Counter-revolution, state repression and Western intervention have all but validated the jihadi narrative espoused by ISIS and al-Qa'ida. Whither now reformist political Islam in an era of security chaos and transnational jihadists?

The fall of Morsi ushered in a dark period for the Gaza Strip as the Egyptian government not only declared the Muslim Brotherhood a terrorist organisation, but also specifically blamed Hamas and Hizbullah for fomenting unrest and violence (Malsin 2015). Palestinians, in general, were vilified by the Egyptian media. The borders with Gaza were sealed and the Egyptian military set about destroying the cross-border tunnels between Gaza and Egypt with a hitherto unseen vigour. Even under Mubarak these were generally left to provide a lifeline for the coastal enclave. The Arab uprisings which had initially seemed like a boon for Hamas, or as the ICG (2012b) put it, "a light at the end of their tunnels", led to the destruction of these tunnels. Hamas' refusal to support the regime of Bashar al-Assad not only led to the Political Bureau's relocation away from Syria to Qatar in early 2012, but also resulted in a rift with Iran. Isolated, running low on allies and cut off from the outside world by the Israeli and Egyptian enforced blockade, the situation in Gaza looked grim for Hamas following the deposal of Morsi.

Indeed, the tightening of the siege subsequent to the fall of the Muslim Brotherhood in Egypt reduced the de facto government of Gaza and Hamas to a moribund economic state. As a result, the movement agreed to sign a lopsided reconciliation deal with the PA in April 2014 that would have effectively surrendered administrative control of the Gaza Strip. The idea was that this would not only alleviate the economic suffering of Gaza, but also allow the movement to jettison the heavy responsibility of formal governance (Brown 2015). Nonetheless, at the time of writing (May 2015), in practical terms Hamas remains the security arbiter in the Gaza Strip. The alleviation of the economic situation in Gaza did not, moreover, ensue due to Israeli and US opposition to the reconciliation government. This is despite the fact that this government did not contain any Hamas officials in cabinet. Palestinian President Mahmoud Abbas insisted that the government met the conditions of political engagement, including recognition of Israel, non-violence, and adherence to previous agreements between Israel and the PLO/PA (Beaumont 2014).

Perhaps as an inevitable result of the continuation of this economically untenable status quo in Gaza and concomitant unrest in the West Bank, a 55-day war broke out between Hamas and Israel in July 2014. Following the kidnap and murder of three Israelis in the West Bank, Israel arrested hundreds of Hamas supporters in the West Bank ('Operation Brother's Keeper') under the pretext of finding the missing Israelis. According to Glenn Robinson (2015, p. 92), however, later evidence emerged that Israeli security forces already knew that the hikers were mostly likely dead, and used the event to crack down on Hamas. This, in turn, would stymie reconciliation efforts between Hamas and the Palestinian Authority in the West Bank (Youngs 2014). When a Palestinian teenager was burnt alive in East Jerusalem, Hamas had little choice but to respond to Israeli provocations in the West Bank or look weak. An Israeli official later conceded that Israel had miscalculated just how bad the economic situation was in Gaza and that "When you have somebody by the throat, you shouldn't be surprised if they kick you in the groin" (cited in ICG 2015, p. 6). To this end, Robinson (2015) argues that, while Hamas did not plan the conflict, the movement took advantage of the situation in order to boost its weak strategic position. Similarly, Berti (2014) contends that the goals of the conflict were to extract Israeli concessions, restore Hamas' resistance credentials and unify the movement. The 2014 conflict not only highlighted the inherently political nature of armed resistance, but also its instrumentality.

Over 2100 Palestinians, mostly civilian, and 72 Israelis (including 67 soldiers) were killed in the ensuing conflict. Over 18,000 homes were destroyed and over 100,000 Palestinians left homeless. UN Secretary General Ban-Ki Moon described the damage as "beyond description" (Ravid and Khoury 2014). These attacks on the Gaza Strip are now so regular that the Israeli defence establishment refers to them as "mowing the lawn" (Rabbani 2014). With regard to the conflict in 2014, moreover, one US official described the attack as not so much "mowing the lawn" as "removing the topsoil" (Perry 2014). Following a report in May 2015 by Breaking the Silence, an Israeli group which collects the testimony of soldiers who have seen combat, Alastair Dawber (2015) surmised: "The Israeli military deliberately pounded civilian areas in the Gaza Strip with incessant fire of inaccurate ordinance during last year's war against Hamas and was at best indifferent about casualties among the Palestinian population." As a result, Israel killed more Palestinians in 2014 than in any other year since 1967 (Zonszein 2015). It has been estimated that it will take more than 20 years to rebuild the damage given the present rate at which reconstruction material is allowed to enter the Gaza Strip (Associated Press 2015).

The lengthy duration of the war may be largely explained by Hamas' refusal to accept any ceasefires that did not address underlying grievances, including the payment of salaries for public servants in Gaza, the reversal of US and Israeli opposition to Palestinian reconciliation, and reconvening of the Palestinian Legislative Council to oversee the PA executive and hold it to accountability (ICG 2015, pp. 4–5). It also allowed Hamas to claim that it decided when the war was brought to a conclusion, not Israel (Berti 2014). This, in turn, validated the movement's invocations of steadfastness and burnished its resistance credentials. Hamas once more demonstrated that it was the only fighting force prepared

208 *Conclusion*

to confront Israel, whereas the PA looked on impotently from the sidelines. For Hamas, the conflict contrasted its vision of *muqawama* (resistance) versus the PA's *musawna* (talking fruitlessly) (Robinson 2015, p. 98); subsequent polls following the conflict have shown that the Palestinian public agree with Hamas.

The 2014 war in Gaza once more highlighted the role of armed resistance in accruing legitimacy and popular support within the Palestinian polity, at least in the short term. It also attracted international attention and led to increasing international calls to end the isolation of Gaza (Robinson 2015, p. 98). It has been reported that Iran and Hizbullah are seeking to renew strengthened ties with Hamas and there has been a meeting between Iranian President Hassan Rouhani and Head of the Hamas Political Bureau Khalid Mishal (Berti 2014). The brief closure of Ben-Gurion international airport due to rocket fire and Hamas' deadly commando raid penetrating Israel's border served similar propaganda purposes. Despite their largely ineffectual nature, the rockets fired by Hamas caused psychological fear in Israel (Robinson 2015, p. 97). These examples demonstrate the symbolic nature of armed resistance as propaganda within both internal and external settings.

A special Gaza war poll conducted immediately after the war by the PCPSR (2014a) found a ringing endorsement of Hamas' performance. Seventy-nine per cent of respondents believed that Hamas had won the war. Ninety-four per cent were satisfied with Hamas' military performance confronting Israeli forces. Eighty-six per cent support launching rockets into Israel if the siege of Gaza is not ended. Eighty-eight per cent support Hamas' way of confronting compared to 42 per cent before the war, with 72 per cent supporting the transfer of this method to the West Bank. Sixty per cent support a return to armed intifada, whereas 62 per cent support popular resistance. Fifty-three per cent believe that armed confrontation is the most effective way to realise a Palestinian state in contrast to 22 per cent who believe that negotiations are most effective. Khalid Mishal received 78 per cent approval for his performance. Hamas' overall performance received an 88 per cent approval rating.

This also translated into at least short-term political support. If presidential elections had been held immediately after the war, Gazan PM Ismail Haniyeh would have received 61 per cent of the vote in contrast to 32 per cent for PA President Mahmoud Abbas. Before the war, following the April reconciliation agreement between Hamas and Fatah, Abbas polled 53 per cent and Haniyeh 42 per cent (PCPSR 2014a). Haniyeh would even have beaten the popular but imprisoned resistance leader Marwan Barghouti, with the former receiving 49 per cent of the vote and the latter 45 per cent. Before the war Haniyeh would have only polled 38 per cent of the vote in a two-way contest with Barghouti on 58 per cent. In a three-way race between Haniyeh, Barghouti and Abbas, Haniyeh would receive 48 per cent, Barghouti 29 per cent and Abbas 19 per cent. Here, we can once more see the Fatah split between the Old Guard (Abbas) and the New (Barghouti) which cost Fatah so dearly in the 2006 PLC elections. Similarly, if parliamentary elections had been held immediately after the war Hamas would have won the most seats, receiving 46 per cent of the vote in

Conclusion 209

comparison to 32 per cent for Fatah. Prior to the war, Fatah was polling at 40 per cent and Hamas at 32 per cent (PCPSR 2014a). Surprisingly, optimism for reconciliation rose from 62 per cent after the April agreement to 69 per cent immediately after the war. Two-thirds of respondents believed that support from Iran, Turkey and Qatar had allowed the Gaza Strip to remain steadfast during the war.

Several months after the war and with Palestinian reconciliation at a stalemate, a December 2014 poll (PCSPR 2014a) found that Haniyeh would still easily win the presidency, polling 53 per cent to Abbas' 42 per cent. The poll also documented a surge in support for violence. Seventy-nine per cent favoured Hamas' approach of armed resistance, while 80 per cent of respondents supported individual attempts to stab or run over Israelis. This once more demonstrates that a group's exposure to violence has the propensity to lead to support for in-group militancy against the 'other'. A rising sense of threat perception amid tensions in East Jerusalem, and especially surrounding al-Haram al-Sharif, may have also contributed to this support for violence. Indeed, PCSPR poll no. 54 in December 2014 (PCSPR 2014d) found that 82 per cent of Palestinian respondents feared that they or their family members would be injured by Israelis while going about their daily business.

As time goes by and little progress is being made in terms of opening the borders, reconciliation, reconstruction and the payment of governmental salaries in Gaza, the war in 2014 has increasingly suffered from diminished returns for Hamas. According to Abu-Amer (2015), Hamas has interpreted the slow reconstruction rate to be a result of deliberate foot-dragging on the part of the PA in order to undercut Hamas' support. This has been reflected in the movement's standing in the polls. Union strikes, unpaid salaries and its ability to only provide limited social services has left the movement with limited choices; unsurprisingly this has led to renewed clashes and occasional rocket fire with Israel (Abu-Amer 2015). This once more demonstrates the need for a viable political option to avert violence. As the conflict is fundamentally political in nature, moreover, it has been repeatedly shown that there is no military solution. This was publicly recognised as early as the first intifada; yet the same deadly policies are repeated. During the first intifada, Israeli Chief of Staff Dan Shormon and other high-ranking officers publicly expressed their belief that "the IDF cannot handle the root of the matter, since the solution of the Israeli–Palestinian conflict requires a political, not a military, solution" (cited in Bar-on 1996, p. 222). In addition, Hamas is too socially embedded in the Palestinian community to be destroyed militarily (Robinson 2015, pp. 102–103).

In April 2015, nine months after the conflict, PCSPR found that PA President Mahmoud Abbas had drawn back level with Haniyeh. Similarly, Fatah had recovered to poll 39 per cent of the vote to Hamas on 32 per cent. However, these polls have been shown to be wrong in the past, not least when they failed to predict Hamas' victory in 2006. Indeed, in April 2015 the Islamic bloc won student elections at Birzeit University near Ramallah in the West Bank. The Islamists won 26 seats to Fatah's 19 in the 51-seat council (Hadid 2015). Student

210 *Conclusion*

elections are treated seriously in Palestine, as they have been used to gauge public opinion in the absence of official national polling since the 2006 election. Hamas' resistance in Gaza and corruption within the PA played key roles. As one female student opined: "Nobody believes in negotiations.... The president has abandoned us, and they take all the money that comes from abroad and distribute it among themselves" (ibid.).

Undercutting radicalisation; facilitating opportunities

Despite Israel's macabre exercises in 'mowing the lawn' in Gaza, there are still opportunities for political engagement with Hamas. Senior Hamas politician Ahmed Yousef reiterated the movement's willingness to reach a peace deal with Israel in September 2014 as long as this brings an end to the occupation (Lyons 2014). Yousef suggests that the parameters of such a deal could include a binational state, a Holy Land Federation or a two-state solution. It is more likely, however, that Israeli PM Netanyahu's last-minute election vow in March 2015 that there would be no Palestinian state on his watch will presage further conflict. Indeed, 47 per cent of Palestinians expect increased confrontations and worsening security following the re-election of Netanyahu (PCSPR 2015).

Meanwhile, as the world watched the conflict in Gaza in July and August 2014, ISIS launched a lightning offensive across Iraq, capturing one-third of Iraqi territory. These advances ridiculed the statements made by US President Barack Obama that ISIS was only a "junior varsity" or B-grade threat (McCoy 2014). In light of the revitalisation of eschatological jihad, now is an opportune time to engage with Hamas, lest a lack of progress upon lifting the siege of Gaza leads to further ISIS or al-Qa'ida-style radicalisation within the region. Although a December 2014 poll by PCSPR found that three-quarters of Palestinians believe that ISIS is a radical fringe and 74 per cent support the war against it, a concerning 12 per cent of respondents believe that it represents true Islam. Of this 12 per cent, 61 per cent support the establishment of an ISIS affiliate in Palestine. Already, a group in Gaza pledging itself to ISIS has claimed an attack on a Hamas military base (*Jerusalem Post* 2015). Rockets launched against Israel by *salafi* factions once more threaten to embroil Hamas and Israel in another conflict (Akram 2015).

A viable political outlet is imperative because Hamas sees political participation as both a form of jihad in itself and a legitimate avenue to pursue the movement's goals. Indeed, there is a dialectic between politics and resistance, whereby the former is simultaneously seen as a safeguard and a vehicle of the latter. Democratic participation, moreover, is used as a mechanism by Hamas to enhance its legitimacy, resist its enemies and further its aims. Unlike political violence aimed at liberation, political participation allows Hamas to pursue its secondary aims of reforming the Palestinian polity in order to make it more attuned to local circumstances, even if this is not in the liberal democratic sense preferred by the West. In essence, democracy is not synonymous with Westernisation. As the former Islamist Finance Minister Omar Abdul-Razeq (personal

Conclusion 211

interview 2010) points out, you cannot take the whole model of US democracy, for instance, and apply it to the specific cultural, historical and religious contexts of Palestine, *but* the idea of electoral accountability and mass political participation is adaptable to any given context. Indeed, Robert Hefner (2000) argues that there is an ongoing process of 'cross-fertilisation' between democratic ideals and Islamic values throughout the Muslim world.

Islam, accordingly, is an integral part of the political landscape within the Palestinian Territories. Thus, there is no need to demonise and exceptionalise Hamas because of its Islamic orientation; that is to say, on the basis that the movement does not necessarily conform to Western expectations that insist on a strict separation between the political and religious spheres. This strict separation of religion and politics is not as important in the Muslim Middle East as it is in the Western world. As Mundhir (survey 2010), an unaffiliated 24-year-old student studying media, observes, "Hamas is just a party. What's important is the truthfulness of what Hamas presents, sometimes it has lied and other times it has exaggerated." And yet, he continues, "Resistance is the only solution". To this end, Hamas should be judged on its political *actions* as well as its putative ideological tenets.

Hamas, moreover, has attempted to incorporate good governance into its resistance discourse. Thus, if Hamas views 'good government as resistance' then this again provides an alternative outlet to advance its goals without necessarily resorting to political violence (Sayigh 2011, p. 17). Consequently, Hamas' reframing of resistance and jihad to include electoral politics should be encouraged rather than hindered because it may help facilitate the further socialisation of the movement and thereby encourage the movement to pursue its goals in a non-violent manner. For this to be effective, however, the opportunity to advance its goals in this manner must be made available. The boycott of the legitimately elected Hamas government has resulted in the opposite. Hamas played by the 'rules' of the game when it agreed to participate in electoral politics in 2006, but it was not subsequently rewarded when it then emerged as the victorious party. This, in turn, has discredited advocates of political participation within the movement because it exposed the hypocrisy of Israel, the West and Fatah when these actors refused to deal with the democratically elected Hamas government. Hamas, in effect, is caught in a double bind. If it resorts to armed resistance, it is branded as a 'terrorist' organisation. If the movement turns to democracy and subsequently wins, the results are not recognised. In short, why bother participating if no one will recognise the results if you win? This lack of respect for the electoral process has impeded Palestinian reconciliation efforts. The split between the West Bank and Gaza has, furthermore, engendered feelings of what Palestinians call *wakseh* (humiliation or ruin) (Roy 2012, p. 75). Feelings of humiliation have been a primary factor driving resistance, armed or otherwise.

As discussed above, the West's hypocrisy and contingent support for democracy was once more underscored by the collective response to the coup d'état against the elected Islamist President Mohammed Morsi in Egypt. French President Francois Hollande described coup leader al-Sisi – 'elected' in 2014 with

212 Conclusion

96 per cent of the vote (Kingsley 2014) – as pursuing a "democratic transition process" (*Euronews* 2014). France then proceeded to sell to Egypt billions of dollars in military hardware (Eltahawy 2015). US Secretary of State John Kerry similarly spoke of al-Sisi's repression as "restoring democracy" (Ahmed 2015). By 2015 the US had restored military aid to a government which had killed thousands of protesters and sentenced hundreds of members of opposition to death, including Morsi (Ackerman 2015).

The Western boycott of the elected Hamas government and the subsequent split between the West Bank and Gaza also seems to have taken its toll on Palestinian enthusiasm for the democratic process. The boycott of the Hamas government, however, does not appear to have helped improve the image of Fatah among its constituents. The Fatah-led PA, for instance, proceeded to hold municipal elections in the West Bank in October 2012, despite the ongoing division between the West Bank and Gaza. Amid a Hamas boycott of the elections, fewer than 55 per cent of voters turned out in comparison to some 78 per cent in 2006 (this, of course, does not include the 1.5 million Palestinians in Gaza who were also unable to vote) (Abu Aker and Rudoren 2012). In some areas, such as Ramallah's sister city al-Bireh, which had been administered by Islamists since 2005, the turnout failed to reach even 27 per cent. According to Khaled Abu Aker and Judi Rudoren (ibid.), moreover, "Elections were not held in about 250 municipalities, either because no candidates registered or because those who did were running unopposed". The results were hardly impressive for Fatah: in what should have been a walkover in the absence of its main competitor, the movement won only two-fifths of the seats.

Since taking sole control of Gaza in June 2007, Hamas has proven itself to be a remarkably resilient and resourceful government entity. The movement has clearly entrenched itself as the hegemonic power in the coastal enclave to such an extent that the International Crisis Group contends that the power struggle in Gaza is no longer between Hamas and Fatah (ICG 2011a; Sayigh 2011). Rather, the main source of confrontation is between Hamas and other more hardline Islamists and *salafists*. Yezid Sayigh (2011, pp. 43–74) reports, moreover, that the movement has proven itself to be an adaptable "learning organisation" with a demonstrated ability to take local ownership of building institutional capabilities. In this regard, Hamas has been far more successful in an administrative sense than the Palestinian Authority in the West Bank, despite having access to only a fraction of the resources (ICG 2012b; Robinson 2015, p. 94).

In similar vein, perceptions of corruption continue to dog the PA. In December 2012 a poll by PCSPR, for instance, found that 74 per cent of respondents affirmed their belief that there is corruption in the PA, whereas only 53 per cent believed this to be the case vis-à-vis the de facto Hamas government in Gaza. Indeed, within the context of regional Arab uprisings in 2012, the West Bank was rocked by a series of protests and strikes against the PA, the entrenched elite, economic troubles and rising costs of living, which eventually led to the resignation of PM Salam Fayyad (Issacharoff 2012; Shiyouth and Hadid 2012; Sherwood 2013). In September 2014, a PCSPR poll found that 81 per cent of

Conclusion 213

respondents still believe the PA to be corrupt. It is important to recall that corruption was one of the main election issues during the 2004/2005 municipal and 2006 legislative elections, and Hamas was at least partially elected due to perceptions of honesty and incorruptibility. Cracking down on corruption is also a key element of Hamas' view that good governance is a form of jihad.

Hamas' programme of resistance also includes a variety of other non-violent strategies that demonstrate its pragmatism. Charity, *da'wa* (the 'call' to Islam) and institution building have long been associated with Islamic activism in the Palestinian Territories and pre-date the existence of Hamas. These non-violent acts of resistance are based on *summud* (steadfastness), *sabr* (patience), *da'wa* and *adala* (social justice) – all central messages of *The Qur'an*. Hamas views charitable works and community development not only as religious injunctions based on jihad but also as acts of resistance in themselves. Institution building and community development are predicated upon the Palestinian notion of *summud muqawim* which seeks to build alternative structures in order to facilitate autonomy and independence from an oppressive regime. This is known in civil resistance literature as constructive (as opposed to disruptive) non-violent resistance.

Islamic charity long pre-dates the existence of Hamas in the Palestinian Territories. Indeed, Hamas' mother movement, the Muslim Brotherhood, was often criticised by the nationalist *fedayeen* for its perceived passivity against the Israeli occupation. The Israeli occupation, moreover, has been characterised by policies of what Sara Roy (1995, p. 5) describes as "de-development" entailing the systematic dismantling of the indigenous Palestinian economy and rendering it totally dependent on Israel. Despite its obligations under international law as an occupying power, Israel, in addition, has only ever provided minimal services to Palestinians living in the West Bank and Gaza. This has, in turn, led to a flourishing of Palestinian civil society and grassroots actors providing for the community, chief among these being the Islamists.

The first intifada and then particularly the Oslo Accords led to the territorial fragmentation of the Palestinian Territories, not only between Gaza and the West Bank, but also the internal cantonisation of these areas by Israeli settlements. Although the Gaza Strip is today territorially contiguous (if largely cut off from the outside world due to the Israeli blockade), the West Bank has been divided into dozens of 'Bantustans'. The Israeli military retains sole control over 60 per cent of the total area, as well as East Jerusalem. The isolation of Gaza and the fragmentation of the West Bank have impeded the growth of the Palestinian economy. Israeli closures of the territories have repeatedly devastated the Palestinian economy to the extent that this process of de-development *accelerated* during the more optimistic years of the peace process (1993–2000) (Roy 1999). Palestinian GNI actually decreased throughout the 'peace' years, whereas political freedom and economic prosperity were supposed to be the results of the Oslo process (Gunning 2007, p. 249). The presence of a weak, inefficient and corrupt Palestinian Authority has only compounded these economic problems.

214 *Conclusion*

Nevertheless, amid an unfavourable political and security environment following the Oslo Accords, Hamas reframed the notion of resistance in order to equate it with community development and socio-political change. Ever sensitive to public opinion and wary of its weakness vis-à-vis both Israel and PA security forces, the movement demonstrated it adaptability by refocusing its jihad on community improvement and consolidation. During this period, Palestinian Islamists worked within the community, establishing links, building trust and accruing social capital which, in turn, tapped into latent community values pertaining to Islam's focus on social justice and charity. Personal contacts and *wasta* are highly important social, cultural and political commodities in the Palestinian Territories. When the second intifada broke out in 2000, Palestinian Islamists were at the forefront of efforts to provide for the Palestinian community. When coupled with its heightened resistance credentials emanating from the second intifada, Hamas' provision of services provided the basis for its municipal electoral successes in 2004/2005 and its eventual victory in the legislature in 2006. In other words, according to Khalid Hroub (2000, p. 35), Hamas has presented an "organic synthesis between armed struggle and social change theses".

The economic strangulation of Gaza only worsened following Hamas' 2006 electoral victory in the legislature and its subsequent armed seizure – or pre-emptive counter-coup – of the coastal enclave in June 2007. In a remarkably candid admission, Dov Weiglass (cited in Elmer 2010), an adviser to then Israeli PM Ehud Olmert, explained in 2006 that the siege is "like meeting a dietician. We need to make the Palestinians lose weight, but not starve to death." Israeli government documents disclosed by court orders reveal that the Israeli government was literally counting calories – 2279 per person per day – as to how much food was allowed to enter the Gaza Strip; that is to say, enough to avoid starvation but not enough to live in a healthy or prosperous manner (Hass 2012). As a result of the Israeli blockade, according to UNRWA Commissioner General Karen Abu Zayd (cited in Makdisi 2008), "Gaza is on the threshold of becoming the first territory to be internationally reduced to a state of abject destitution with the knowledge, acquiescence and – some would say – encouragement of the international community". And yet, paradoxically, this siege has only served to strengthen the movement and consolidate its hold as the hegemonic power within the Gaza Strip. This, in turn, has led to greater Islamisation within the coastal enclave.

Islam forms the bedrock of Hamas' resistance programme whether this be armed, political, charitable or cultural. Culture and identity are at the crux of much Islamist thought; that is to say, resistance to what is perceived to be an encroaching and secularising Western world. In essence, this is a reassertion of local identity, often defined in Islamic terms. This Islamic reference point, however, should not be viewed in essentialist, immutable and absolutist terms. Rather, it should be recognised that *The Qur'an*, like the concepts of resistance and jihad, is polysemic and may be interpreted according to time, place and culture.

Conclusion 215

Consternation over Hamas' potentially absolutist ideological agenda has often been a key point of criticism emanating from both Israel and the West because it seems to preclude peaceful coexistence with Israel. When *sharia* law is read in a superficial way, it could, potentially, lead to barbaric corporal punishments. A more nuanced investigation demonstrates that this is not strictly the case insofar as: (1) Hamas has repeatedly and publicly committed itself to a two-state solution based on pre-1967 borders, and (2) the application of the few proscribed punishments detailed in *sharia* law is far more complicated than many foreign observers are prepared to countenance. The multiple strands of resistance advocated by Hamas thus allow the movement to expand and periodically refocus its resistance agenda away from conflict with Israel to include its cultural, political, social and educational efforts, thereby preserving the movement's *raison d'être* should peaceful coexistence with Israel ensue.

In brief, Hamas sees resistance and jihad as more than merely liberation from occupation, but as holistic yet malleable principles which guide the movement's actions, not only in terms of spirituality but also in the temporal world. As Mousa Abu Marzouq (personal interview 2010), Deputy Head of the Political Bureau, elucidates,

> We, as the Hamas organisation, when we look at the political situation/ politics in the Middle East, we know exactly that we are not a liberation movement and we live in a liberation transition. But look at the other parties, Fatah, and Popular Front, all of them put 'liberation' in their names: the Palestinian National Liberation Movement – Fatah – the Popular Front for the Liberation of Palestine, the Democratic Front for the Liberation of Palestine, the Two Popular Fronts for the Liberation of Palestine, the Palestine Liberation Organisation, the Palestine Liberation Front.... All of the parties say 'liberation' except Hamas. We say that we are a resistance movement and we are in a liberation era. This, in the short term, means that we are a resistance movement working to build our state.

Resistance and jihad, moreover, are conceived of in both temporal and spiritual terms. As Robert Fisk (2011) explains with regard to the ongoing Arab uprisings, but which is also applicable to Occupied Palestinian Territories,

> Almost all of the millions of Arab demonstrators who wish to shrug off the cloak of autocracy which – with our Western help – has smothered their lives in humiliation and fear are indeed Muslims. And Muslims ... have not lost their faith.... Under the stones and coshes of ... police killers, they counter-attacked, shouting 'Allah akbar' for this was indeed from them a 'jihad' – not a religious war but a struggle for justice. 'God is Great' and a demand for justice are entirely consistent. For the struggle against injustice is the very spirit of the Koran.

Given the growing strength of eschatologically inclined jihadi Islamists throughout the Middle East and Africa, negotiations with reformist Islamists like Hamas

216 Conclusion

are imperative. The rise and fall of the Muslim Brotherhood in Egypt, as well as the civil wars in Syria and Iraq, have reduced the influence of reformist Islamist groups in favour of radical jihadi Islamists. In particular, the coup and subsequent suppression of the opposition in Egypt have strengthened the jihadi narrative that only violence can succeed in the face of dictatorial tyranny. The integration of Hamas and resolution of the Palestine/Israel conflict would highlight the benefits of compromise and negotiation in contrast to the eschatological jihadism currently embodied by ISIS and a resurgent al-Qa'ida. To do this, as the International Crisis Group (ICG 2012b, p. 21) explains,

> Hamas wants – beyond the ends of punishing attacks and, of particular importance, the stopping of targeted assassinations – life in the Gaza Strip to recover a genuine sense of normalcy. Especially if it is expected to fulfil Israel's demand that it behave as the sovereign of Gaza and ensure that attacks from the territory end, Hamas says, it must be given some of the benefits, not just the responsibilities, of sovereignty. The movement's credibility and claims to legitimacy stem largely from its resistance credentials.... If Hamas were to acquire an alternate source of legitimacy, of domestic accomplishment, its internal hand would be strengthened, and it would be in a better position to achieve an effective consensus opposing violence against Israel.

Former Head of Mossad Efraim Halevy (cited in Lynfield 2015) concurs insofar as:

> Hamas wants to achieve a sizeable benefit in terms of the quality of life in Gaza, and wants a degree of acceptance.... It would obviously be a two-way street. Hamas would have to tread a different route than it does now, but we have not given them any options but confrontation.

Ironically, given both its resistance and Islamic credentials, Hamas may be Israel's best protection against eschatologically inclined jihadists. Indeed, in an interview with CNN on 22 November 2012, Khalid Mishal (cited in Levy, E. 2012) explained: "We are ready to resort to a peaceful way, a purely peaceful way without blood and weapons, as long as we obtain our Palestinian demands. A Palestinian state and the ending of the occupation and the (West Bank security) wall." According to former United Nations Special Rapporteur on Palestinian Human Rights Richard Falk (2012), Mishal has, moreover, "indicated that once Palestinian statehood was fully realised, then the issue of the acceptance of Israeli legitimacy could be placed on the political agenda". In this light, perhaps, 'incentivisation' rather than demonisation may be the answer because, as this project has demonstrated, Hamas is not only an adaptable political actor capable of compromise, but also an indispensable one for any lasting peace between the two peoples living between the Jordan River and the Mediterranean Sea.

References

Abu Aker, K. and Rudoren, J. 2012. 'Mixed Results for Fatah Amid Low Turnout in Municipal Elections in West Bank'. *New York Times*, 20 October.

Abu-Amer, A. 2015. 'Hamas's Choices'. *Sada*. Carnegie Endowment for International Peace, 7 January.

Ackerman, S. 2015. 'Obama Restores US Military Aid to Egypt over Islamic State Concerns'. *Guardian* (UK), 1 April.

Ahmed, I. 2015. 'Mohamed Mursi Death Sentence Puts Western Democracies on Notice'. *The Age* (Melbourne), 9 June.

Akram, F. 2015. 'Gaza's Hamas Rulers Have a New Problem: ISIS-sympathetic Jihadists'. *Associated Press*, 8 June.

al-Jazeera. 2012. 'Qatari Emir in Historic Gaza Visit', 23 October.

Associated Press. 2015. "Housing Group: 20 Years to Rebuild Gaza after Fighting with Israel'. *Ha'aretz* (Israel), 30 August.

Bar-on, M. 1996. *In Pursuit of Peace: A History of the Israeli Peace Movement*. Washington, DC: United States Institute of Peace Press.

Beaumont, P. 2014. 'Palestinian Unity Government of Fatah and Hamas Sworn In'. *Guardian* (UK), 2 June.

Berti, B. 2014. 'Hamas After the Ceasefire'. *Sada*. Carnegie Endowment for International Peace, 25 September.

Brown, N. 2014. 'Netanyahu's Convenient Lies about ISIS and Hamas'. *Forward*, 30 September.

Brown, N. 2015. *Building a Better Post-Oslo Era*. Carnegie Endowment for International Peace, 4 February.

Burgat, F. 2004. 'Les courants Islamistes contemporains entre "dénominateur commun identitaire" et internationalisation de la résistance à un ordre mondialise'. *Revue Mouvements* 36: 77–88.

Cockburn, P. 2014. *The Jihadis Return: ISIS and the New Sunni Uprising*. London: Or Books.

Daraghmeh, M. 2011. 'Hamas Leader to AP: New Focus on Popular Protests'. *Houston Chronicle*, 23 December.

Dawber, A. 2015. '"Fire at Every Person': Israeli Soldiers Reveal They Were Ordered to Shoot to Kill in Gaza Combat Zones – Even If Targets May Have Been Civilians'. *Independent* (UK), 4 May.

Dearden, L. 2015. 'Jabhat al-Nusra Seizes Control of Major Syrian Government Stronghold with Rebel Coalition'. *Independent* (UK), 25 April.

Elmer, J. 2010. 'Going Organic: The Siege of Gaza'. *al-Jazeera*, 29 August.

Eltahawy, M. 2015. 'Egypt's Vanishing Youth'. *New York Times*, 15 June.

Erlanger. 2012. 'Political Leader of Hamas Visits Gaza for the First Time'. *New York Times*, 7 December.

Euronews. 2014. 'Hollande Calls On Sisi to Continue "Democratic Transition" in Egypt', 26 November.

Falk, R. 2012. 'Understanding Hamas after Khaled Meshaal's Gaza Speech'. *al-Jazeera*, 16 December.

Fisk, R. 2011. 'These Are Secular Popular Revolts – Yet Everyone is Blaming Religion'. *Independent* (UK), 20 February.

Gartenstein-Ross, D. and Vassefi, T. 2012. 'Perceptions of the "Arab Spring" Within the Salafi-Jihadi Movement'. *Studies in Conflict and Terrorism* 35(12): 831–848.

218 *Conclusion*

Gerges, F. 2012. 'The Rise and Fall of al Qaeda: Debunking the Terrorism Narrative'. *Huffington Post* (USA), 3 January.

Greenwald, G. 2015. 'Hailed as a Model for Successful Intervention, Libya Proves to be the Exact Opposite'. *The Intercept*, 17 February.

Gunning, J. 2007. *Hamas in Politics: Democracy, Religion, Violence*. London: Hurst & Co.

Hadid, D. 2015. 'In Sign of Palestinians' Mood, Hamas Wins Vote at a West Bank University'. *New York Times*, 11 May.

Hass, A. 2012. '2,279 Calories Per Person: How Israel Made Sure Gaza Didn't Starve'. *Ha'aretz* (Israel), 17 October.

Hefner, R. 2000. *Civil Islam: Muslims and Democratization in Indonesia*. Princeton, NJ: Princeton University Press.

Hroub, K. 2000. *Hamas: Political Thought and Practice*. Washington, DC: Institute of Palestine Studies.

Hroub, K. 2006. *Hamas: A Beginner's Guide*. London: Pluto Press.

International Crisis Group (ICG). 2011a. *Palestinian Reconciliation: Plus Ça Change …* Brussels: ICG.

International Crisis Group (ICG). 2011b. *Radical Islam in Gaza*. Brussels: ICG.

International Crisis Group (ICG). 2012a. *The Emperor Has No Clothes: Palestinians and the End of the Peace Process*. Brussels: ICG.

International Crisis Group (ICG). 2012b. *Israel and Hamas: Fire and Ceasefire in a New Middle East*. Brussels: ICG.

International Crisis Group (ICG). 2012c. *Light At the End of Their Tunnels? Hamas and the Arab Uprisings*. Brussels: ICG.

International Crisis Group (ICG). 2015. *Towards a Lasting Ceasefire in Gaza*. Brussels: ICG.

Issacharoff, A. 2012. 'Palestinians' Protests Against Rising Prices Turn Violent in West Bank'. *Ha'aretz* (Israel), 10 September.

Jerusalem Post. 2015. 'ISIS-linked Group Claims Responsibility for Attack on Hamas Base in Gaza', 8 May.

Juergensmeyer, M. 2011. 'The Jihadi Revolution is Dead (but Bin Laden's Death Didn't Kill It)'. *Religion Dispatches*. University of Southern California, 2 May.

Kingsley, P. 2014. 'Abdel Fatah al-Sisi Won 96.1% of Vote in Egypt Presidential Election, Say Officials'. *Guardian* (UK), 4 June.

Kirkpatrick, D. 2015. 'ISIS Video Appears to Show Executions of Ethiopian Christians in Libya'. *New York Times*, 19 April.

Levy, E. 2012. 'Meshaal: Prepared for Peace without blood, weapons'. *Y.net.news.com*, 25 November.

Levy, G. 2012. 'Israeli War Drums Ignore Hamas Move for Change'. *Ha'aretz* (Israel), 1 January.

Lynfield, B. 2015. 'It's Time for Israel to Talk to Hamas, Says Former Mossad Head'. *Independent* (UK), 10 June.

Lyons, J. 2014. 'Hamas Proposal for Israel Peace Plan'. *The Australian*, 4 September.

Makdisi, S. 2008. 'The Strangulation of Gaza'. *The Nation* (USA), February.

Malsin, J. 2015. 'Egyptian Court Sentences Ousted President Morsi to Death'. *New York Times*, 16 May.

McCoy, T. 2014. 'The Islamic State is a Formidable Tactical Fighting Force, Experts Say'. *Sydney Morning Herald*, 9 October.

Milton-Edwards, B. 1996. *Islamic Politics in Palestine*. London: I.B. Tauris.

Mishal, S. and Sela, A. 2000. *The Palestinian Hamas: Vision, Violence and Coexistence*. New York: Columbia University Press.

Orwell, G. 1945. *England, your England and other Essays*. London: Secker and Warburg.

PCSPR. 2012. *Public Opinion Poll no. 46, December 13–15*. Ramallah: PCSPR.

PCSPR. 2014a. *Public Opinion Poll no. 52, June 5–7*. Ramallah: PCSPR

PCSPR. 2014b. *Special Gaza War Poll, August 26–30*. Ramallah: PCSPR.

PCSPR. 2014c. *Public Opinion Poll no. 53, September 25–27*. Ramallah: PCSPR.

PCSPR. 2014d. *Public Opinion Poll no. 54, December 3–6*. Ramallah: PCSPR.

PCSPR. 2015. *Public Opinion Poll no. 55, April 8*. Ramallah: PCSPR.

Perry, M. 2014. 'Why Israel's Bombardment of Gaza Neighborhood Left US Officers "stunned"'. *Al-Jazeera*, 27 August.

Rabbani, M. 2014. 'Israel Mows the Lawn'. *London Review of Books*. 36(15), 31 July.

Rane, H. 2009. *Reconstructing Jihad amid Competing International Norms*. New York: Palgrave Macmillan.

Ravid, B. and Khoury, J. 2014. 'UN Chief: Gaza Destruction "Beyond Description", Worse than Last War'. *Ha'aretz* (Israel), 14 October.

Robinson, G. 2015. 'Gaza 2014: Hamas' Strategic Calculus'. *Parameters* 44(4): 91–103.

Roy, S. 1995. *The Gaza Strip: The Political Economy of De-development*. Washington, DC: Institute for Palestine Studies.

Roy, S. 1999. 'De-development Revisited: Palestinian Economy and Society Since Oslo'. *Journal of Palestine Studies* 28(3): 64–82.

Roy, S. 2012. 'Reconceptualizing the Israeli–Palestinian Conflict: Key Paradigm Shifts'. *Journal of Palestine Studies* 41(3): 71–91.

Sayigh, Y. 2011. '*We Serve the People': Hamas Policing in Gaza*. Brandeis University: Crown Centre for Middle East Studies.

Scott, J. 1990. *Domination and the Arts of Resistance: Hidden Transcripts*. London: Yale University Press.

Sherwood, H. 2013. 'US-backed Palestinian Prime Minister Salam Fayyad Resigns'. *Guardian* (UK), 14 April.

Sherwood, H. and Beaumont, P. 2012. 'Egyptian PM Arrives in Gaza as Rocket Attacks and Airstrikes Continue'. *Guardian* (UK), 16 November.

Shiyouth, N. and Hadid, D. 2012. 'Palestinian Protests Turn Violent in West Bank'. *Huffington Post* (USA), 10 September.

Wilner, M. 2014. 'US Voices Disagreement with Netanyahu's Outlook at UN on Political Islam'. *Jerusalem Post*, 9 September.

Youngs, R. 2014. *The EU and the Israeli–Palestinian Conflict: Action without a Script*. Carnegie Endowment for International Peace, 20 October.

Zonszein, M. 2015. 'Israel Killed more Palestinians in 2014 Than in Any Other Year Since 1967'. *Guardian* (UK), 28 March.

Interviews and surveys

Abdul-Razeq, O., former Islamist Finance Minister, elected MP, and Professor of Economics at an-Najah National University, Ramallah, February 2010.

Abu Marzouq, M., Deputy Head of the Hamas Political Bureau, US Specially Designated Global Terrorist Organisation and Doctor of Engineering, Damascus, May 2010.

Mundhir, an unaffiliated 24-year-old student studying media, anonymous survey, Birzeit University, Birzeit, April 2010.

Index

Abbas, Mahmoud 17, 28, 86–7, 90–1, 100, 102, 106–7, 112, 119, 122, 124, 179, 203–4, 206, 208–9
Abduh, Muhammad 168
Abdul-Razeq, Omar 97, 101, 104, 112, 114, 116, 122, 135, 143, 152, 167, 192, 210
Abdullah, King of Jordan 93n2
Abu Aisha, Sameer 13, 104, 123, 183, 191
Abu Amr *see* Arafat, Yasser
Abu Awad, Sheikh Husni 156
Abu Hein, Fadl 83
Abu Hein, Sakkar 154
Abu Jihad *see* al-Wazir, Khalil
Abu Marzouq, Mousa 7, 27, 40, 84, 100, 101, 166, 174, 178, 180, 186, 215
Abu Mazen *see* Mahmoud Abbas
Abu Shanab, Ismail 15, 85, 179
Abu Sway, Mustafa 120
Abu Zayd, Karen 214
Abu-Amer, A. 209
adala (social justice) 40, 117–18, 150, 167, 213–14
adl' (justice) 53, 166, 215
Afghanistan 21, 54, 172, 180, 202
al-Afghani, Jamal al-Din 168
al-amaliyyat al-ishtishhadiyya see self-immolation attacks
al-Aqsa intifada 25, 52, 54–7, 59–62, 65–7, 71n3, 78–82, 90, 100–2, 106–7, 111–12, 116–18, 125, 136, 138, 140, 142, 145–7, 157–8, 173–4, 214
al-Aqsa mosque 72n8, 93n2, 186
al-Aqsa TV 84
al-Assad, Bashar 89, 202, 206
al-Banna, Hassan 170, 181, 189
al-Haram al-Sharif (the Noble Sanctuary) 58, 72n2, 209
al-Ikhwan al-Muslimun see Muslim Brotherhood

al-Jamiyya al-Islamiyya (the Islamic Society) 144, 154–5
al-Jazeera 87–8
al-Malaki, Nouri 202
al-Masri, Mushir 158
al-Mujamma al-Islami (the Islamic Centre) 144, 153–5
al-Nahda (Tunisia) 194, 205
al-Nakba ('the Catastrophe') 55, 63, 135, 148, 171
al-Nusra Front 202, 205
al-Qa'ida 2–3, 21, 23, 34, 38–9, 42, 61, 72n9, 103, 126, 174, 176, 187, 202, 204–6, 210, 216
al-Qassam, Sheikh Izz al-Din 169–70
al-Quds *see* Jerusalem
al-Qutla al-Islamiyya (the Islamic Bloc) 40, 99, 209
al-Rahma 156
al-Ramahi, Mahmoud 70–1, 90, 122, 124, 172, 174–5, 177–8
al-Rantisi, Abd al-Aziz 56, 82, 84, 153
al-Shaer, Nasser ed-Din 13, 123, 182, 192
al-Sisi, Abdul-Fatah 36, 205, 211–12
al-Thani, Shiekh Hamad Bin Khalifa 204
al-Wafa Medical Rehabilitation Hospital 156–7
al-Wazir, Khalil 63, 170
Alam, S.M 22
Algeria 17n2, 39, 206
Allen, Lori 55, 84
Alshech, Eli 84, 111
Amayreh, Khalid 39, 50, 62, 178–9
American-Israeli Public Affairs Committee (AIPAC) 3, 30–1
anti-Semitism 27, 30–1, 177–9
Arab League Peace Initiative 180
Arab Revolt 1936–9, 170
Arab Spring 17, 89, 173, 202–6, 212, 215

Index   221

Arab–Israeli War 1948–9 63, 93; *see also al-Nakba*
Araj, Bader 25, 80
Arendt, Hannah 62, 64
Arsalan, Shakib 168
Asad, Talal 9, 80, 83
Ayyash, Yahiya 'the Engineer' 81

B'tselem (Israeli Information Centre for Human Rights in the OPTs) 71, 92n1
Bahrain 36, 205
Baldwin, James 160
Balfour Declaration 170
Barber, Benjamin 34
Barghouti, Iyad 103, 114–15, 120, 171, 188–9
Barghouti, Marwan 59, 85, 114, 129n5, 208
Benford, R. 8
Benthall, Jonothan 139, 150
Bergen, P. 205
Berti, B. 207
Bin Laden, Osama 3, 205
Blair, Tony 26, 42
Blau, Uri 90
Bourdieu, Pierre 9, 35, 101, 193
Bowyer-Bell, John 35
Boycott, Divestments and Sanctions movement (BDS) 30
Breaking the Silence 207
British Mandate Palestine 6, 61, 169–70, 177, 186
Brown, Nathan 53, 123, 128, 151
Brym, Robert 25, 80
Burgat, Francois 201
Bush, George, W. 3, 21–2, 105, 183
Butler, Judith 30

Cairo Agreement 2005 106
Campus Watch 30
Change and Reform 91, 101–2, 108, 115–17, 122, 126, 166, 193; relation to Hamas 12–13
Charlie Hebdo attacks 2015 205
Cheney, Dick 22
Clark, Janine 189
Clash of Civilisations 23
Clinton, Bill 92, 97
Cold War, the 22, 138
Cox, Robert 37
critical theory 37
Cronin, Audrey 25–6, 28–9, 30–2, 34

da'wa (proselytising or the 'call' to Islam) 9, 15–16, 40, 57–8, 136–7, 144, 171, 173, 187–8, 213
Dahlan, Mohammed 124
Davutoglu, Ahmet 204
Dawber, Alastair 207
de-development 149, 213
Dwiek, Aziz 7, 55, 96, 122, 151, 166, 170, 174, 183

Education 1–2, 9, 13, 15–16, 41, 83, 103, 137, 154–6, 161, 166–74, 182, 187, 199, 215; and Islamic values 136, 143, 166, 187–8, 192–3; and morals 16, 143, 155, 168, 173, 193; in Palestine 159, 190–3; international aspects 100, 103, 154, 189–91
Egypt 17–18, 32, 36, 52, 100, 138, 154, 170, 189, 204–6, 211–12, 216
el-Tagini, Mahmoud 182
Elaraby, Nabil 204
Elections 1, 15, 34, 85, 98, 101–6, 115, 125, 129, 135–43, 148, 174, 194, 205–6, 208; aftermath of PLC 2006 121–5; municipalities 1970s 108; municipalities 2004–5, 13, 84, 101, 106–12, 180; municipalities 2012 212; PLC 1996 97, 99, 107, 112; personalisation of 15, 111, 114, 119, 120–1; PLC 2006 1–2, 15, 34, 52, 65, 84, 97, 101–6, 112–21, 126–8, 142–3, 161, 174, 208, 213; professional associations 13, 15, 34, 99, 106, 190; student unions 15, 34, 99–100, 106, 209–10
End of History, the 22–3
Erlanger, Steven 121
Etzioni, Amitai 26
Euben, Roxanne 37
European Union, the (EU) 3–4, 17n4, 97, 100, 121–2, 126, 142, 159
Executive Force *see tanfithya*

Falk, Richard 216
Farrell, Stephen 55, 79, 81, 87
Fatah 2, 4, 8, 11, 15–17, 52–3, 55–6, 59–63, 67, 69, 85–7, 91, 96, 99, 102–3, 107–9, 112–13, 119–20, 124, 129, 150, 170, 173–4, 184, 191, 203, 209, 212, 215; and secularism 28, 38, 40, 171–2; and security services 65–6, 68, 98, 116–17, 122; collaboration with Israel 17, 52, 67, 90; conflict with Hamas 14, 112, 124–5, 127, 208, 211–12; corruption 17, 59, 66, 107–8, 114, 118–19, 120–1, 147–8; gangsterism 66,

222 *Index*

122; ideology 100; intra-factional divides 59, 66, 107–8, 114, 120, 208; political platform 118–19; reaction to PLC elections 2006 15, 104–5, 121–3, 126; religious roots 170–1, 189

fatwa (religious edict) 40, 111, 115, 189

Fayyad, Salam 86, 125, 212

feda'i ('he who sacrifices himself'/fighter) 8, 60, 66

fiqh (Islamic jurisprudence) 115, 175–6, 179, 181–2

Fisk, Robert 41, 119, 215

Flanigan, S. 139

Foucault, Michel 49, 101

Fourth, Article 49

Friedman, Thomas 25–6

Front Islamique de Salut, le (the Islamic Salvation Front, Algeria) 17n2, 206

Fukuyama, Francis 22–3, 26

Gaza Strip, the; conservatism 126, 191; Hamas/Fatah civil war 2007 15, 52, 65, 67–8, 104–5, 117, 123–6, 143, 151, 206, 211–12; Israeli withdrawal from 2005 14, 49, 61, 69, 70–1, 85, 91; settlements 31–2, 68; siege of 29, 31, 36, 126–7, 129, 149, 191, 206–8, 212, 214; *see also* Operation Summer Rains, Operation Cast Lead and Operation Protective Edge

Gellner, Ernest 36

Geneva Conventions 6; Fourth, Article 49, 31, 122

Gerges, Fawaz 205

Ghannouci, Rachid 194

Gold, Dore 26

Goldstein, Baruch 34, 59, 81

Goldstone Report 54, 71n4, 87, 126

Gresh, Alain 22

Guardian 87

Gulf War (Iraq/Kuwait) 1990–1 145, 172, 190

Gunning, Jeroen 12, 28, 37, 79, 109–10, 118, 121, 140–1, 147, 149, 152, 159, 188, 202

Ha'aretz 86

Hadith (Prophetic sayings) 39, 115, 155, 175

Halevy, Efraim 216

Hamas; and salafists 26–7, 61, 65, 103, 126, 174, 210, 212 (*see also* al-Qa'ida and Islamic State in Iraq and al-Sham); and the West 3–5, 17n3, 91–2, 100, 103,

152; as a localised or grassroots movement 2–5, 9, 15, 17, 27, 34, 38, 42, 58, 89, 108, 110–11, 137, 141–2, 148–9, 154, 158, 173, 184, 186–7, 201, 210; co-existence with Israel 5, 28, 34, 61, 83, 127, 177–80, 200, 202–3, 215; conflict with Fatah 14, 112, 124–5, 127, 208, 211–12; ideology 5, 12–13, 16, 22, 34, 40–2, 57–8, 88–9, 97, 99–100, 103, 105–8, 115, 118, 121, 127–8, 141, 144, 159, 166–77, 180, 183–4, 187–9, 191–4, 199–200, 211, 215; views on democracy 102–6; *see also mithaq, sharia* law, Gaza, elections, Iran, Syria, Muslim Brotherhood, Qassam Brigades

Hamdan, Usama 178

Hammoudeh, Sameer 52, 167

Hamzawy 123

Haniyeh, Ismail 85–6, 98, 117, 125, 180, 192, 203, 208–9

Hass, Amira 149

Hebron massacre 34, 59, 81

Hefner, Robert 211

Hezbollah *see* Hizbullah

hidden transcripts 38

Hizb al-Khalas al-Watani al-Islami (National Islamic Salvation Party) 99

Hizbullah (Lebanon) 3, 17, 59, 62, 68, 79, 88–9, 129n7, 138, 206, 208

Hoffman, Bruce 23–5, 27, 35, 65

Hoigilt, Jacob 190, 192

Horowitz, David 30

Hroub, Khalid 7, 40, 53, 62, 137, 146, 199, 214

hudna (long-term ceasefire) 61, 179–80

hudud (prescribed punishments) 180–2

Huntington, Samuel 23, 26

Hussein, King of Jordan 92, 93n2

Hussein, Saddam 145, 172, 182

Ibn al-Khattab, Omar 181

Ibrahimi Mosque 34, 81

ijma' (consensus) 102, 175

Ijtihad 174–6, 182

Imperialism

Intelligence and Terrorism Information Centre (ITIC) 29, 139

International Criminal Court (ICC) 31, 54–5, 122

International Crisis Group (ICG) 65, 89, 103, 157, 159, 200, 203, 212, 216

International Quartet for Peace in the Middle East 4, 91, 122, 125

Intifada 1987–1993 9, 14, 34, 48, 50, 52,

54, 56–7, 70–1, 71n3, 98, 167, 136, 146–8, 154, 156, 173, 186, 189, 208–9, 213; second intifada 2000–2005 *see* al-Aqsa intifada
Iran 26, 180, 204–5, 1979 Islamic Revolution 88, 172; support of Hamas 27, 88–9, 100, 206, 208–9
Iraq 26, 201–2, 205, 210, 216; US-led invasion of 2003 21–2, 25, 54, 71, 202; *see also* Gulf War 1990–1
Irish Republican Army 96
Irving Jensen, Michael 143, 160, 192
Islam; and behaviour 183–17; and Christianity 175, 178; and community 103, 107; and Judaism 175, 178; as an identity marker 36, 39, 166, 173, 177, 190, 214; pillars of 150, 166–7, 175; *see also Qur'an, sunnah, hadith, umma, sharia* law, *jihad, da'wa, summud, sabr, hudna, fiqh,* charity and modernity
Islamic State in Iraq and al-Sham (ISIS) 17, 23, 126, 201–2, 205–6, 210, 216
Israel; and academic integrity 29–31, 140; and the Palestinian economy 144–7, 149, 157, 213; (*see also* de-development); closures of OPTs 46, 66, 157, 157, 213–14; collective punishment 66–7, 83–4, 142, 157, 122, 159–60; creation of 6, 27, 63, 88, 93, 183 (*see also al-Nakba*); recognition of 4, 61, 177–80, 200, 216; targeted assassinations 31, 81, 83–5, 149; *see also* settlements, Operation Summer Rains, Operation Cast Lead, and Operation Protective Edge

Jad, Islah 210
Jami'yyat al-Salah al-Islamiyya (Association of Islamic Prayer) 144
Jami'yyat al-Shabbat al-Muslimat (Young Women's Muslim Association) 144, 155
Jaysh al-Murabitoun (Army of Defenders) 65
Jerusalem 69, 72, 93, 108, 144–15, 122, 178, 186, 199, 203, 207, 209, 213
Jerusalem Media and Communications Centre (JMCC) 86, 91, 116, 120–1
jihad; greater aspects of 9, 109, 193; lesser aspects of 9, 48–9, 60, 188
Jonas, Barry 138
Jordan 10, 31, 38, 58, 92, 100, 129, 170, 177, 189, 190, 216
Judaism 34, 62, 72, 178–9
Juergensmeyer, Mark 24, 41, 61

Kadayifici-Orellana, A. 177, 194
Kamikaze pilots 80
Kamil, Mustafa 168
Kandil, Hisham 204
Kaplan, Robert 23
Kassir, Samir 62, 85
Khalidi, Tarif 176
Khatib, Ghassan 81
khayr see charity
Khudabiyya, Treaty of 28, 179
Kimmerling, Baruch 8, 54
Klein, Menachem 57, 66, 106, 154, 169
Koran *see* Qur'an
Kramer, Martin 30
Kuwait 39, 100, 189–90
Kata'ib al-Shahid Izz al-Din al-Qassam; see Qassam Brigades

Lacquer, Walter 23–5, 27–9, 31, 34–5
Lebanon 10, 17, 26, 34, 38, 59, 62; Israeli withdrawal from 2005 68–70, 79–80, 129, 138, 178
Levitt, Matthew 28, 139–40
Lewis, Bernard 22
Liberalism 4, 22–3, 26, 35–6, 173, 180, 183, 210; *see also* modernity and rationality
Liberation Tigers of Tamil Elam (Sri Lanka) 55–80
Libya 26, 42, 194, 201–2, 205; and Responsibility to Protect 2002
Lundblad, L. 141

McGeough, Paul 92
McIntyre, Donald 54
Marj al-Zuhur (Lebanon) 59
Martyrdom 8–9, 14–15, 24, 59, 67, 78, 79–85, 139–40, 144, 167, 169, 173, 184; and political influence 63, 79, 84–5, 167; as a social action 80–3; symbolic aspects of 8, 83–4, 92, 120, 16–170; *see also* self-immolation attacks
Masri, Nihad 110
Mecca Accord 2007 124
Merari, Ariel 25, 80
Migdal, J. 8
Milton-Edwards, Beverley 41, 55, 79, 81, 87, 125, 199
Mishal, Khalid 49, 61, 92, 100, 180, 190, 199, 204, 208, 216
Mishal, Shaul 57, 59, 61, 107, 184
Misleh, Mahmoud 68
mithaq (Hamas charter) 9, 16, 27, 40, 115, 168, 173, 177–80, 186–7

224 *Index*

modernity 1, 4, 23, 25–7, 35–7, 41, 79, 128, 168, 173, 175, 177, 182–3, 193
Mohammed, the Prophet 9, 28, 39, 72, 103, 105, 121, 152, 155, 167, 174–5, 179, 183, 187, 194n3
Moon, Ban-Ki 207
Mosadegh, Mohammed 206
Mosques 9, 34, 40, 66, 71–2, 81, 93, 111, 115, 121, 158, 167, 173; and education 16, 154–5, 169, 187–9, 192; and networking 189; and recruitment 139, 142
Mueller, John 26
mujahid 8, 172
Munich Olympics 1972 63
Muslim Brotherhood, the 9, 174, 181, 186–7; and Islamisation 57, 72, 136, 169–71, 186; *see also da'wa*; and political violence 57–8, 171, 173, 213; in Egypt 17, 36, 138, 170, 189, 204, 206, 216; in Palestine 9, 16, 48, 57, 72n7, 136, 144–6, 153–4, 158, 187, 213

Nanji, Azim 150
Nasser, William 114, 151, 171
National Reconciliation Document 2006 90, 179–80
Netanyahu, Benjamin 62, 92, 201, 210
New York Times 25, 30, 121, 138, 179
NGOisation 146
Nietzsche, Friedrich 92
Northern Ireland 56

Obama, Barack 97, 210
Occidentalism 2
Olmert, Ehud 214
Operation Brother's Keeper 2014 207
Operation Cast Lead 2008–9, 15, 54–5, 59, 64, 70, 86–8, 189, 204
Operation Defensive Shield 2002
Operation Grapes of Wrath 1996
Operation Protective Edge 2014 54, 59, 70, 74, 206–10
Operation Summer Rains 2006 54, 59, 91, 122
Orientalism 2, 4, 14, 16, 21, 34–5, 41–2, 48, 68, 128, 168, 174–5, 187, 200–1; and the war on terror 22–8
Orwell, George 200
Oslo Accords, the; 31, 33, 51–3, 55, 59, 62, 97–100, 107–8, 112, 117, 141–2, 145–9, 157–8, 173, 213–14; *see also* settlements and de-development
Ottoman Empire, the 168, 178, 201

Palestine Papers, the 87–9
Palestinian Centre for Human Rights 173
Palestinian Centre for Policy and Survey Research (PCPSR) 61, 87, 91, 110, 158, 173, 203, 208–9
Palestinian Islamic Jihad 26, 34, 57–9, 64–5, 85, 112, 159
Palestinian Legislative Council (PLC) 13, 91, 116, 121–2, 129, 207; *see also* elections
Palestinian Liberation Organisation (PLO) 13, 52, 57–8, 87, 98, 100, 107–8, 118, 124, 145, 170–2; agreements with Israel 4, 97–8, 122, 171, 206; and armed struggle 8, 60–1, 63, 187; insider/outsider divide 107, 147–8
Palestinian prisoners 15, 89–92, 123, 167, 179–80
Pape, Robert 59, 79–80, 92
Pascovich, E. 140
Peres, Shimon 62
Perle, Richard 22
Pipes, Daniel 30
political violence; and inter-factional competition 14, 25, 49, 60, 64–8; and popular support 53, 62, 63–71, 82, 84–5, 87, 112, 116, 125, 173–4, 178, 186, 202–4, 208; as armed propaganda 14, 49, 63–4, 66; practical aspects of 14, 48, 54, 60–3, 68–71, 82–3; symbolic aspects of 8, 14, 48, 53, 59, 64, 70–1, 78, 81, 83–4, 87, 92, 170, 208; *see also* terrorism and self-immolation attacks
Popular Front for the Liberation of Palestine (PFLP) 109, 138, 215; plane hijackings 63
Post-colonial studies 14, 21, 31, 36–7
Pressman, Jeremey 65
Prisoners' Document *see* National Reconciliation Document
Putnam, Robert 9

Qaradawi, Yousef 169
Qassam Brigades, the 3, 59, 83, 140, 169
Qassam, Abdul Sattar 69, 88, 91
Qatar 88–9, 204, 206, 209
qiyas (analogy) 175, 182
Qur'an, The 1, 8, 17, 22, 24, 39, 48, 86, 115, 135, 150–2, 155, 166–8, 174, 185, 190–1, 213; interpretation of 42, 105, 156, 175–6, 181, 188, 201, 214
Qutb, Sayyid 189

Ramadan, Tariq 181

Index 225

Rane, Halim 9, 53, 202
Rationality 23, 25–6, 31, 34–6, 70, 79, 81, 128, 177
Refugees 55, 63, 67, 78, 92, 108, 118, 129n6, 148, 167, 189–90; in the Gaza Strip 32, 110–11, 154, 191; right of return 118
Rida, Rashid 168
Robinson, Glenn 207–9, 212
Rosenfeld, Maya 8, 65
Ross, Dennis 97
Rouhani, Hassan 208
Roy, Sara 29, 56, 100, 135–6, 140–1, 144, 146–7, 149–50, 156, 159, 173, 191–2, 213
Rudoren, Judi 212
Rumsfeld, Donald 22

sabr (patience) 8, 78, 89, 167–8, 213
sadaqa 150; *see also* charity
Said, Edward 4, 22–3, 140, 149
Salah, Mariam 39, 102, 122–3, 167, 175–8, 181–2, 185, 189
Sarraj, Eyad 50, 56, 78, 80–1, 83
Sarraj, Wasseem 53
Saudi Arabia 26, 36, 53, 100, 124, 145, 151, 172, 176, 180, 189, 202
Scott, James 28, 201
Secularism 1, 4, 8, 14, 28, 35, 38–41, 42n4, 80, 100, 128, 140, 154, 166, 171–2, 175, 183–4, 204, 214
Sela, Avraham 61
self-determination 6–7, 58, 63, 89, 96, 129, 199
September 11 attacks 2001 2–3, 21–2, 25–6, 41, 54, 79, 83, 103
Settlements 57, 60, 68, 169, 179, 203; in the Gaza Strip 31–2, 108; in the West Bank 51, 71, 91, 122, 213; settler violence 34, 49, 59, 71n1, 81
Shabab, Mohammed 155
Shaheen, Hafez 13, 29, 110, 126, 152, 175–6, 190
shahid (martyr) *see* martyrdom
Shalit, Gilad 87, 90–1, 122–3
Shamir, J. 56
sharia law 13, 16, 40, 42n3, 121, 171, 174, 180–3, 215
Sharon, Ariel 3, 54
Shi'ism 26–7, 88–9, 166–7, 202
Shikaki, Khali 55–6, 158, 173, 177
Shormon, Dan 209
shura (consultation) 102, 143
Sinn Fein 96
Six Day War 1967 170–2
Skocpol, Theda 26

Snow, David 8
Soviet Union; invasion of Afghanistan 172; fall of 146
Statism 28, 31, 33
steadfastness *see summud*
Student Unions *see* elections and education
Suicide bombings *see* self-immolation attacks
sulha (reconciliation) 158
Summers, Laurence 30
summud (steadfastness) 8, 15, 78, 86–8, 92, 135–6, 158, 167, 184, 202, 213
Syria 10, 38, 89, 129, 201, 205; civil war since 2012 202–5, 216; relations with Hamas 88–9, 169, 206

tadi'a' (periods of calm) 61, 83
tajdid (renewalist) 188, 193
Taliban, the (Afghanistan) 176, 180
Tamimi, Azzam 59, 121
tanfithya (Executive Force) 122–5
Terrorism; as a pejorative 41–2, 200; critical approaches to 35–8; 'new' or fourth wave 34–5, 60; state aspects of 31, 50, 70, 71n4, 202; traditional studies of 28–35, 48, 200–1; *see also* political violence and self-immolation attacks
Toros, Harmonie 37
Tuastad, Dag 84, 108, 110–11
Tunisia 31, 36, 58, 204–5
Turkey 88, 202, 204, 209

ulema (religious scholars) 168, 177, 188
umma (community of believers) 103, 167
United Arab Emirates (UAE) 31, 100
United Nations (UN) 4, 6, 72, 216; Development Programme (UNDP) 142, 147; General Assembly Resolutions 6–7, 28, 31, 118; Relief Works Agency for Palestine Refugees in the Middle East (UNRWA) 147, 151–2, 157, 190–1, 214; Security Council Resolutions 6, 18n5, 28, 122, 202
United States of America (US), the 1–4, 21–2, 25–6, 29–31, 36, 39, 52, 66, 92, 97, 100, 104, 112, 118–19, 124–6, 140, 142, 154, 179, 183, 185, 194; 2003 invasion of Iraq 21–2, 25–6, 54, 71n2, 202, 210; and democratisation 22, 36, 112, 126; attempted coup against Hamas *see* the Gaza Strip, civil war; vetos at the UN 31; *see also* Bush, George W., Obama, Barack, war on terror and September 11 attacks

226   *Index*

'urf (customary law) 145
USAID 141–2

Village Leagues Initiative 108
Volunteerism *see* charity
Von Clausewitz, Carl 60

Wahiduddin Khan, Maulana 168
Waldman, Peter 22
Walzer, Michael 26–8
waqf (Islamic endowment) 177, 186
War on Terror, the 2–3, 14, 21, 22–8, 38,
    41, 79, 142, 159, 183, 201, 205; *see also*
    September 11 attacks
wasta (contacts or 'pull') 10, 120, 151,
    153, 214
Watt, Montgomery 155
Weber, Max 64
Weiglass, Dov 214
West Bank 51; security/apartheid wall 122,

203, 216; *see also* settlements and Oslo
    Accords
Westernisation 35, 210; *see also*
    secularism
Wikileaks 87–8
Wofowitz, Paul 22
World Bank, the 145, 157

Ya'ish, Adly 109–11
Yassin, Sheikh Ahmed 24, 56, 61, 82, 85,
    92, 98, 145, 153, 179, 192
Yediot Aharonot 82
Yemen 26, 194, 205
Yousef, Ahmed 179–80, 210

Zahar, Mahmoud 99, 153
zakat (alms) 12, 16, 23, 100, 121, 141–2,
    146, 150–2, 154, 156, 166–7, 185, 191
Zedong, Mao 64
Zionism 27, 81, 107, 169–70, 178

Made in the USA
Las Vegas, NV
24 December 2023

83494631R00131